SCIENCE OF STATISTICS. PART II.

STATISTICS AND ECONOMICS

BY

RICHMOND MAYO-SMITH, PH.D.

PROFESSOR OF POLITICAL ECONOMY AND SOCIAL SCIENCE
IN COLUMBIA UNIVERSITY

New York

PUBLISHED FOR THE COLUMBIA UNIVERSITY PRESS BY

THE MACMILLAN COMPANY

LONDON: MACMILLAN & CO., LTD.

1899

CONTENTS.

INTRODUCTION.

CHAPTER I.

STATISTICS IN THE SERVICE OF ECONOMICS.

BOOK I.

CONSUMPTION AND PRODUCTION.

CHAPTER II.

STATISTICS OF CONSUMPTION.

CHAPTER III.

POPULATION AS LABOUR-FORCE.

CHAPTER IV.

Land as Factor of Production.

CHAPTER V.

Capital, Organisation, and Wealth.

Book II.

EXCHANGE.

CHAPTER VI.

PRICES.

CHAPTER VII.

MONEY AND CREDIT.

CHAPTER VIII.

Transportation and Commerce.

Book III.

DISTRIBUTION.

CHAPTER IX.

Wages.

CHAPTER X.

Rent, Interest, and Profits.

CHAPTER XI.

Competition and Association.

CHAPTER XII.

Finance Statistics.

CHAPTER XIII.

SOCIAL DISTRIBUTION.

SCIENCE OF STATISTICS

PART II

STATISTICS AND ECONOMICS

STATISTICS AND ECONOMICS.

INTRODUCTION.

CHAPTER I.

STATISTICS IN THE SERVICE OF ECONOMICS.

The Economic Organisation. Among the complicated phenomena of social life, those institutions and arrangements by which man satisfies his material wants are perhaps the most important. The economic is the foundation of all social organisation. For until man is able to supply himself with the means of subsistence, it is idle to expect any development of the higher and more refined sides of civilisation. The economic wants must be satisfied before the higher intellectual and moral wants can be. And even after the development of civilisation, the particular form of economic institutions conditions and affects the whole social organisation. An industrial population will not have the same political forms of administration and the same policy as a nation composed of agriculturalists. The influence will, indeed, often extend to the more refined manifestations of civilisation, such as the artistic, the ethical, and the religious. For all study of institutions, therefore, it is necessary to know at least the general outline of the economic organisation.

The economic phenomena, it is true, are but a part of the social. They cannot be separated from the non-economic by any fast and sharp line. Almost all social phenomena have an economic interest. Births, deaths, and marriages, physical and mental infirmity, suicide and crime, affect the economic strength and material well-being of the community as well as its social condition. But in these cases, the economic interest is a minor one. It retreats into insignificance compared with the social-ethical. Crime is an economic detriment to the community in the loss of productive labour, in the destruction of property, in the expense involved in the administration of justice and the pursuit and punishment of delinquents; but it is much more significant as an expression of imperfect socialisation, as resistance to the social will, and as suggestive of the mal-adjustment of individuals to their environment. Economic condition may be at the bottom of all this; but the predominant aspect is the social-ethical.

On the other hand, there are phenomena which are predominantly economic; that is, they have to do primarily with the satisfaction of the material wants of man. The various customs, arrangements, and institutions which serve this purpose constitute what may be called for convenience the Economic Organisation, which, to repeat, is not distinct from the social organisation but a part of it.

Description and Measurements.[1] In order to comprehend man's economic life, we must have some means of describing the economic organisation and measuring the results of economic conduct. One method of doing this may be called the historical-descriptive. In course of time man's economic activity embodies itself in systematic forms, which we variously designate as customs, laws, institutions, or principles. Such, for instance, are the use of a medium of exchange called money, the organisation of credit through banks and clearing-houses, the machinery of international exchange. On a higher plane is what may be called the organisation of industry, at an early period through slavery; later through guilds and associations; and in modern times under the

[1] *Cf.* Lexis, Theorie der Massenerscheinungen, 1877.

factory or wage-system with its accompaniments, entrepreneurs, trade unions, trusts, etc.

As a still higher manifestation of economic life come the development and recognition of the principle of economic freedom and the institution of private property. We can describe these as they have been developed and as they display themselves at the present time. We can analyse them with the purpose of discovering the motives which have controlled men in forming these institutions. We thus reach a general description of the economic organisation of society, and also an explanation of the reasons for such organisation. All this gives us simply qualitative descriptions, which are all that are necessary for understanding the ordinary phenomena of economic life.

For the purpose of further description, and especially of measuring the result of economic action, we are obliged to employ a second method, which may be called the statistical-comparative. The historical-descriptive method may give us knowledge of the general banking system of a country; the statistical-comparative method details the operations of the banking system, the amount of its loans and discounts, its issue of notes, and analyses them in connection with different periods of time, different sections of the country, city and rural districts, etc. We are thus able to watch variations in the economic conduct of man. Description may give us an account of the changing tariff policy of a country. Statistics of imports and exports may indicate the effect of tariff changes on commerce. A description of trade unions, their origin, objects and activity may be sufficient to enable us to form an opinion of the part they play in industrial organisation; but the statistics of number of members, causes of strikes, number of men involved, days and wages lost will guide us in forming a more precise opinion of their influence.

The manifestations of economic life are such as lend themselves readily to the statistical-comparative method. This is because they almost always take on a material form. The desires are psychological, and cannot be directly measured. But the satisfaction of those desires in the shape of food, clothing, shelter, and the material enjoyments of life can be described and even measured with some degree of accuracy. It is difficult to say whether the political institutions of one country secure a greater degree of liberty and happiness to the individual than those of another. It is largely a matter of opinion; and commonly each observer is prejudiced in favour of those institutions which he understands and of whose benefits he is conscious. It is difficult to say whether people are more or less religious than they used to be, for we have no means of measuring real piety. The outward observance of religious service may be kept up while it has become a hollow mockery.

In economic phenomena the measurements seem to be easier. We cannot say whether people are in reality any happier than they were three hundred years ago. But we can show that the community has a greater command over wealth *per capita*, and thus the opportunity for well-being is present at least. The artisan may be as discontented with his lot as ever; but if we can show that wages have increased and the cost of living decreased, we show that he is gaining in at least one direction. The burden of taxation is often complained of, but our only method of judging of it is by comparing the amount of the tax with the ability to pay—that is, with the economic resources of the community. Oppressive economic legislation cannot, it is true, always be clearly disclosed; but it is generally easier to follow its effect in decreased business or the paralysis of industry than it is to detect the insidious working of bad laws on the social or moral sentiments of the community.

Wealth. When we ask ourselves how we shall apply the statistical method to the facts and relations of economic life, the answer is that the first step is to describe those facts that are capable of description. And the first fact that is capable of description is, what is the sum total, at any given time, of the economic resources of a given community. For although a nation is not always happy, civilised, and prosperous in proportion to its economic resources, yet it is manifest that its power and attainments in the direction of a rich and fruitful civilisation must be, to a certain extent, controlled and conditioned by its wealth-producing power and its wealth accumulation. Wealth does not make a nation great any more than it makes an individual useful or happy; but it gives the opportunity for high civilisation in the one case, just as it gives the opportunity for usefulness and happiness in the other.

This method of describing the economic resources of the community is simply the numerical—that is, by counting units of the same kind. We give the total area of land surface, still further the portion of this area that is cultivated, and the portion that is forest or waste. We can still further subdivide the cultivated area, and enumerate the number of acres devoted to the cultivation of each particular crop. We can enumerate the head of cattle, horses, or sheep, and classify them according to the purposes for which they are used. We can count the inhabited houses, the buildings used for factories, the number of business enterprises, the miles of railroad, the tonnage of the merchant marine—in short, we can take an inventory of the wealth and the wealth-producing instrumentalities of the community.

These figures are not for the purpose merely of gratifying national vanity. They are useful in comparing the strength of one country with that of another. They explain, in some cases, peculiarities of economic life, as where the presence of free land keeps wages up by allowing an outlet for any surplus labour; or, on the other hand, conceals the dangers flowing from indiscriminate immigration. Such descriptions often serve to guide governmental action by showing in what direction economic expansion and growth are possible—as in agrarian legislation or administrative action for the purpose of reclaiming or irrigating land; or, on the other hand, they may show the failure of legislation, as when the arable land diminishes in area, notwithstanding all efforts to encourage agriculture or to establish a peasant proprietary.

Consumption. Wealth has no interest for us, except as it is brought into connection with the desires of man. Demand for wealth is the manifestation of those desires. We cannot measure the desires; but their relative strength and their variation from time to time can be measured by the statistics of consumption. By careful observation we can determine the way in which men spend their incomes, the proportionate amount devoted to food, rent, clothing, fuel, and luxuries. The variation from time to time may also be shown by the *per capita* consumption of staple articles, such as wheat, bread, meat, and sugar. We have here the foundation for a theory of consumption, showing how, in what order, and to what extent, a community demands the various forms of wealth. A complete theory of consumption, confirmed by actual experience, should be a guide to the efforts of man in the production of wealth. The statistics of consumption are at the same time the complementary side of production; that is, they measure the supply of wealth as well as the demand.

Production. A nation may have rich natural resources and not utilise them. A measure of the actual supply of wealth may be found in the annual products or producing capacity of a country. We enumerate the number of tons of coal produced from the mines; the number of bushels of grain or tons of hay, the result of the agricultural effort of the year. The output of industry may be measured by the value of the annual product. We put them all into terms of money, because that is the only common denominator which we can employ. By these estimates we again measure the relative strength of nations, or the progress of the same nation from year to year. We can also trace improvements in the methods of production, and often the effects of industrial revolutions, as in the substitution of one product for another, or of a new method of production for one less profitable.

Exchange. The modern production process is fully carried out only by what is commonly called Exchange. Men produce now, not what they need, but what they do not need, trusting through exchange to get what they do need. The community obtains thus the advantages of division of labour, of localisation of industry under the most favourable circumstances, and of production on a grand scale. Modern nations are not only pre-eminently industrial; they are also commercial. No nation now lives unto itself alone. Each is dependent upon others for the commodities which it consumes, or the raw material which it turns into manufactures, and for a market for its products. There is a worldwide division of labour, carried on by international commerce. To understand its character we enumerate the facilities for transportation and the actual work performed by means of them. We trace the mileage of railroads, the direction and character of their traffic; the movement of steamships and the course of their trade. We notice the changes from year to year, the increased facilities, the improved methods and the cheapening of the cost. It is necessary to describe the mechanism of commerce, the machinery by which trade is carried on, such as the money in circulation and in reserve, the credit institutions, such as banks, and their business as reflected in the statistics of loans, discounts, and circulation of notes. We measure actual transactions by the statistics of imports and exports, of internal commerce, of the business of stock and produce exchanges, the formation of stock companies, and the investments of capital; and we gauge the ill-success by the statistics of bankruptcies and commercial failures.

Distribution. The well-being of individual members of the community is expressed not so much by the figures of total production or of business transactions as by the share of the product enjoyed by each, and the certainty of securing it.

This is the question of the distribution of wealth. What is the income of the individual, and how far will that income go in satisfying his wants? Income, for the great mass of the community, means wages. In what way can we get statistics of wages that will give us a fair notion of the economic condition of the wage-receiving class? Mere money wages must be translated into actual income; for they are subject to the chances of irregular employment, of sickness and accident, and payment in truck. Incomes must be translated into what money will buy by elaborate statistics of prices of commodities and the proportionate part of the income devoted to the purchase of each. Income is affected also by the conditions under which the labourer earns it, the hours of labour, the condition of the workshop, and the healthfulness of the employment.

Statistics of wages are not properly statistics of the reward of labour as a factor of production, but statistics of the income of a large mass of persons, commonly called the wage-receiving or labouring class, whose income is mainly due to labour. It is impossible to measure the share of the product due to labour as labour, because it is so often associated with land, capital and entrepreneur talent, and the reward is a gross one. For a similar reason we cannot distribute (statistically) the product to land, capital and entrepreneur talent. Only, in case of capital we can measure the fluctuations of the reward in the rate of interest. And in certain cases, *e.g.* the landlord class, we can measure the total income by the statistics of the rent-roll.

There is another method by which we can measure distribution, that is by classifying the members of the community according to their wealth or income. This may be called social distribution. It distinguishes the rich and the poor. By observations at successive periods of time it tries to detect the tendency in the modern organisation of wealth towards concentration or diffusion of well-being. It tries to answer the question whether the rich are getting richer, and the poor, poorer, or the reverse. It is the most important aspect of the economic organisation.

Economic Statistics. The mass of facts expressed in figures which throw light on the economic organisation may be called Economic Statistics. We have quantities of them, overwhelming in their number (prices), and bewildering in their complexity (wages of different forms of labour). It is evident that we must have some method of arranging them so as to extract their meaning. This is the function of the Science of Statistics. Its present application does not differ from statistical method in general, or, in fact, from scientific or logical method in general. The procedure to be followed seems to be as follows:—

The first purpose is purely descriptive: figures are merely a method of expressing facts, as the amount of wheat produced, the quantity of exports and imports, the amount of the national wealth, the national income, etc.

There are technical ways of arranging the statistics even for the purpose of description—as the average—*e.g.* average wealth, average income, *per capita* wealth, *per capita* imports, average wages. These are simply for the purpose of gaining a short expression which will be descriptive and, at the same time, enable us to make comparisons.

The second step is comparison: that is, to place statistics of the same kind in juxtaposition, so as to show differences according to time, place, or circumstance. Comparisons in time are for the purpose of showing increase or decrease—as the amount of wheat produced from year to year, or imports from year to year, or prices.

Comparisons in space are to show relative importance as indicative of relative well-being or the reverse. Thus we may compare wages in Great Britain and in the United States, circulation of specie money *per capita* in France and in the United States, production of cereals in the different States of the United States.

For the same time and space we may have comparisons

according as other circumstances vary. Thus we may compare wages in different occupations, or in the same occupation for men and women, or according to the nationality of the workman. We may study the differences shown by the foreign-born and native-born in the United States in the tendency to put women and children to work in factories. All of these methods of comparison are useful in enabling us to understand the characteristics of the economic life about us.

The third step in statistical method is correlation: *i.e.* to compare different phenomena with each other, in order to establish relations of co-existence or of sequence. Thus we can compare the fluctuations in price of a commodity with its supply in order to discover the relation of demand and supply to price. Or we can study the general price-level and its variation with the quantity of specie money. Or we can attempt to study the spread of the large industry, and connect with it various phenomena as results, such as unemployment, lower wages, increased employment of women and children; or, perhaps, the reverse phenomena, lower prices, increased consumption, greater demand for labour, regular employment, and higher wages. When we establish firmly the precise relation between two phenomena, we may be said to have discovered a statistical or sociological law: *e.g.* the relation between high wages and efficient production, expansion of credit and a higher level of prices. In order to be sure that we are dealing with fixed and permanent relations, we must be sure of our technique, viz., that we have a correct method of measuring the phenomena (*e.g.* index numbers for price-level); that our observations are numerous enough to establish recurring regularities; that the deviations from the regularities are not greater nor more numerous than the law of error allows; and that other causes or disturbing influences have been eliminated or allowed for. It must be said, however, that this third stage of statistical method is seldom reached in economic statistics. Our statistics are for the most part merely descriptions or comparisons in time, space, and according to varying circumstances. They give us interesting glimpses of the interdependence of the phenomena of economic life, and often confirm common observation and experience.

Statistics and Economics. Economic statistics may be regarded thus as merely a method of describing the economic organisation which is a part of the social organisation. It is a continuation of the analysis of society which was begun in the previous volume on Statistics and Sociology. But aside from this, economic statistics may be brought into fruitful relation with the science of Economics. The theory of economics assumes to explain the action of man in the pursuit of material well-being. It shows how, under the influence of desires or wants, man proceeds to their satisfaction. How man's economic life *should* shape itself is shown by a deductive science of Economics based on psychological premises. How man *does* behave himself is shown by observation of concrete institutions, arrangements, and results; in other words, by a study of the economic organisation. Statistical observation is one method of confirming or proving the adequateness of theory as an explanation of economic life. Economic statistics are thus brought into relation with economic theory.

Still further, the actual life of any community is constantly affected by legislation, administration, and public opinion. Every community has its economic policy; and this policy is directed to the solution of so-called economic problems. But policy can have no sure basis unless it is able to analyse and understand the facts of economic life, and trace the results of economic action. Statistics furnish one method of measuring such phenomena and tracing the effects of such action. The function of economic statistics, therefore, is to verify theory, and, at the same time, to furnish data for the guidance of economic policy or practice.

With this purpose in view, we have arranged the statistics

according to the categories of economic analysis—viz., consumption and production, exchange, distribution, and the various sub-divisions. In each chapter we have in addition, under the head of "Economic Purpose," considered the topics of theory and practice upon which the statistical method seems fitted to throw light. Then, under the head of "Statistical Data," we have given the statistics themselves; criticised method under the head of "Scientific Tests"; and given what seem valid conclusions under "Reflective Analysis."[1]

[1] *Cf.* Statistics and Sociology, Chapters I. to III.

Book I.

CONSUMPTION AND PRODUCTION.

Man and Wealth. The economic activity of man takes on the form of Consumption and Production supplemented by Exchange and Distribution. The outward manifestation of such activity is found in social institutions, customs, habits of living, modes of conduct, expressions of definite purpose, which can be described and reduced to systematic form. The result of such activity embodies itself in material wealth and useful services which satisfy the desires and wants of man. We group them together and call them wealth, and say, shortly, that the object of economic activity is to produce wealth and that the science of political economy is the science of wealth. It is more and more emphasised now, that the principal thing is not wealth but man. Thus Roscher says that "the starting point as well as the objective point of our science is man." And Marshall says that "man is the centre of the problem of Production as well as that of Consumption; and also of that further problem of the relations between the two, which goes by the twofold name of Distribution and Exchange." [1]

It is necessary to bring all these things into connection with man. Instead of arranging our statistics therefore with respect to wealth, we shall arrange them with respect to man's economic activity.

Consumption. The basis of man's economic activity is his desire to satisfy his wants. Wealth is produced to

[1] Principles of Economics, p. 215.

this end. If we could describe these wants and measure their intensity, we should know how man ought to direct his economic activity. A theory of consumption (that is, a theory of wants) would seem to precede a theory of production. At least, a perfect theory of consumption would act as a guide to the most economic production. It has been pointed out by Marshall that new activities give rise to new wants, as often as new wants to new activities; and that therefore it is not true that "the Theory of Consumption is the scientific basis of Economics." Nevertheless he treats of Demand or the Theory of Consumption before taking up Supply or the Theory of Production. What little information statistical analysis can give in respect to the theory of wants is of rather fundamental importance for the whole range of economic inquiry, and can very fitly come first in order.

Production. How man shall satisfy his needs is the question of the production of wealth. The satisfaction of the primary needs is essential, of course, to mere animal existence. The economic organisation necessary is of the simplest possible kind. The earth yields food, clothing, and shelter, with simply the labour of appropriation by the individual—as among the lowest savages in the hunting and fishing stage. But man's wants are satisfied inadequately and with great uncertainty. Such men live from hand to mouth; and there is no opportunity to satisfy higher wants or to develop in social civilisation. Production must be more abundant and more certain in order to support a larger population, give them more comforts, and allow them leisure to cultivate their intellectual and social powers. Land is still the source of all wealth in the sense that it furnishes the raw material; but labour becomes more and more the active agent by which land and natural resources are manipulated in such a way that men's wants are satisfied with constantly increasing regularity, certainty, and abundance. The economic organisation becomes more and more complicated and important as the basis of all social organisation. The analysis of this economic organisation for the purpose of determining under what conditions the production of wealth shall be most abundant and certain is essential both for economic theory and as a guide to economic practice.

CHAPTER II.

STATISTICS OF CONSUMPTION.

Economic Purpose.

Economic Theory. The theory of consumption offers us three points for consideration. The first is the law of satiety. "There is an endless variety of wants, but there is a limit to each separate want."[1] If I have offered to me successive increments of the same "good," the desire becomes less and less pressing until at last the point of satiety is reached and I want no more of that "good." In fact, a further supply becomes a burden rather than a satisfaction. The one universal law is that a person's desire for a commodity diminishes, other things being equal, with every increase in his supply of that commodity. This diminution may be slow or rapid; in the former case the demand is said to be elastic, in the latter, inelastic.

The second point is comprehended under the doctrine of marginal utility. "The increment of a commodity, which a man is only just induced to acquire (whether by his direct labour or by purchase) may be called its Marginal Increment; because he is on the margin of doubt, whether it is worth his while to incur the outlay required to obtain it. And the benefit-giving power, or utility, of that increment to him may be called the marginal utility of the commodity to him."[2] This marginal utility fixes the price which the individual is willing to give for the last increment of the commodity. And as increments of the commodity are supposed to be alike, the price representing this marginal utility, multiplied by the

[1] Marshall, Principles, p. 178. [2] *Ibid.*

total number of units in the supply, will give the total price paid for the commodity. The total utility of the sum of the increments of the supply will, of course, be greater than the total price paid. Low prices increase this excess of utility over cost.

The third point relates to the rule which governs the choice of commodities for consumption. If the same commodity can be turned to several uses, I will evidently satisfy those wants which are most pressing, until some other use gives me greater satisfaction than to continue the application of the commodity to the first use. In other words, I turn to that particular use which for the time being affords the greatest marginal utility. Money is a commodity which has an infinite variety of uses, because it can be expended in any direction. I therefore distribute my income in such a way that the marginal utility of the sums devoted to different uses may be as nearly as possible the same. The economic law is that the expenditure shall flow in that direction where the highest marginal utility will be attained.

Social Consumption. When we attempt to apply these points of theory to the consumption of a whole community, we are met by two difficulties. The first is that the law of satiety and the law of marginal utility in respect to the same commodity will lead to different results according to the taste of each individual. Desires are subjective. One man may be very fond of food, a second of clothing, a third of books. The point of marginal utility will depend upon the disposition of each individual. Out of these subjective judgments we can get no law that will apply to the whole community.

The second difficulty is that we are obliged to measure the utility of any commodity in terms of money, *i.e.* in prices. But to the man with a large income, the utility of a certain pleasure will be represented by a larger price than it will be to the man with a small income. Account must be taken also of possible changes in the marginal utility of money itself, besides the fact that it is greater for the poor man than for the rich.

There are two ways in which these difficulties may be met. One is to take the consumption of a class of individuals whose tastes and whose money income are about the same, that is, about sufficient to sustain a given standard of life. For a certain range of primary wants, *e.g.* food, shelter and clothing, the desires would probably be present in about the same degree; and the marginal utility of money would be similar. We could for this class come to some conclusion, by watching their expenditure, in regard to the order of wants, and the degree to which they are satisfied, or at least determine the point where a new want comes in with a higher marginal utility. In other words, we could illustrate and confirm our theory by concrete cases.

Or we can take two communities and say that probably the average of those communities in respect to the relative number of persons with certain tastes and the relative number of incomes of different size is about the same. Then we can study the law of decreasing demand in the two communities, or the same community at different times, for the purpose of illustrating and confirming our theory. Careful statistical work in this direction might throw considerable light upon our theory of consumption (Marshall).

The Demands of Practice. The statistics of consumption are of great practical use. They show how the economic activity of the community is of necessity directed. They show what are the real primary wants of the great masses, and what proportion they bear to other desires. We can also measure how far among different classes these wants are satisfied, and what is left over for the satisfaction of other wants. Moreover, if continued from time to time they ought to show the progress that is made in the well-being of the community. They point out the connection between taxation and ability, which is the fundamental question of finance. Comparisons over space show us the characteristics of different communities, and the circumstances which determine different degrees of well-being. They should throw important light upon the power of legislation to correct certain evils (insufficient consumption), and also upon the effect of efforts to guide consumption upon the happiness of individuals (sumptuary laws).

Statistical Data.[1]

There are two ways in which we can get statistics indicating the direction at least of the consumption of the com-

[1] *Bibliographical Note. Workmen's Budgets.* By far the most important work is Engel, Die Lebenskosten belgischer Arbeiter-Familien früher und jetzt. (Bull. de l'Institut int. de Statistique, Vol. IX., 1895.) This was intended to be the beginning of a great work which should cover all countries. The author did not live to complete it. This portion is extremely valuable because it contains an introduction concerning method and the history of workmen's budgets, an application of the method to Belgian budgets, and a reprint of Engel's early essay of 1857, Die Produktions-und Consumtionsverhältnisse des Königreichs Sachsen, which became classical, and the incentive to most of the following attempts. A comparison of the Belgian budgets of 1853 and 1891 will be found in the Bulletin de la Commission Centrale de Statistique, Vol. XVII., 1897. The principal results are summarised in the Bulletin of the (U.S.) Department of Labour, No. 18, Sept. 1898, p. 708.

Next in importance is the discussion of cost of living and family budgets in the Sixth and Seventh Annual Reports of the U.S. Department of Labour, for 1890 and 1891. Other publications are: Massachusetts Bureau of Labour Statistics, Report for 1875; see also Reports of Bureaus of Labour of Illinois, Maine, Missouri, New Jersey, Ohio and Wisconsin. Returns of Expenditures of Workingmen collected by Labour Department of Board of Trade (one interesting continuous record made by same man from 1850 to 1886), [c—5861] 1889. Family Budgets: being the Income and Expenses of twenty-eight British Households, collected by the Economic Club, London, 1891-94. Higgs, Workmen's Budgets (Journal Statistical Society, June 1893), an interesting account of different methods of collecting budgets and of their meaning. For the technique of collecting budgets see Landolt, Haushalt Statistik, 1894; also Landolt, Directions sur la manière de dresser les budgets d'ouvriers industriels et d'artisans. (Bull. de l'Institut int. de Statistique, Vol. VI., 1892.) An excellent résumé of the whole subject may be found in Handwörterbüch der Staatswissenschaften, article Konsumtion by S. Bauer, with bibliography. For the Le Play method see the important essay by E. Cheysson and A. Toqué, Les budgets comparés des cent monographies de familles (Bull. de l'Institut int. de Statistique, munity. One is by taking the expenditure of typical families; the other is by taking the *per capita* consumption of the whole population.

Family Budgets. Although the range of marginal utilities for different individuals is different, yet there are classes in the community whose scale of expenditure is about the same, and there are certain commodities which necessarily enter into their consumption. The largest class in the

Vol. V., 1890), with bibliography. The great Belgian Industrial Inquiry of 1886 collected eighty-six budgets, but they are very imperfect. They are noticed by Engel (*op. cit.* p. 62), and translated into English by the English Board of Trade (Rates of Wages in Belgium [c—5269]), Lodon, 1888. An inquiry in 1891 resulted in 188 budgets, but they covered expenditures for one month only. (Engel, *op. cit.* p. 82.)

For dietaries see particularly Atwater, Foods: Nutritive Value and Cost, U.S. Department of Agriculture, Farmers' Bulletin, No. 23; see also Bulletin No. 21, Atwater, Methods and Results of Investigations on the Chemistry and Economy of Food; Engel, *op. cit.*; and article Dietetics, Ency. Britannica. Very suggestive article by Atwater, Food Consumption, in Report of the Massachusetts Bureau of Labour Statistics, 1886. Many special studies of dietaries in different parts of the United States have been made and published by the Department of Agriculture, under the title Dietary Studies in New York City (Bulletin No. 46); Nutrition Studies in Pittsburg, Pa., Tennessee, New Mexico, &c.

Per Capita Consumption. By far the most complete statistics of consumption are published in Neumann-Spallart, Uebersichten der Weltwirtschaft, especially the last edition, 1885–89, edited by Von Juraschek; Lehr, Produktion und Konsumtion, reproduces many of Neumann-Spallart's tables. The Statistisches Jahrbuch für das Deutsche Reich gives every year tables of *per capita* consumption of various commodities, and the Jahrbuch der Stadt Berlin does the same for Berlin. For Great Britain and Ireland see the Statistical Abstract each year. For the *per capita* consumption of tea, coffee and alcoholic liquors see Return, &c., with diagrams, 1894, No. 329. The Statistical Abstract of the United States contains estimates of *per capita* consumption of raw cotton, wheat, and wheat flour, corn and corn meal, sugar, coffee, tea, distilled spirits, malt liquors, wines and raw wool for each year 1868 to 1898. For a collection of the older data see Lexis, Article Konsumtion in Schönberg's Handbuch der Politischen Oekonomie, 2nd ed. Vol. I., p. 709. For Italy, see Annuario statistico Italiano, 1898, p. 190. For consumption of meat, Jahrbuch deutscher Städte, especially Vol. VI., Sec. xxiv, 1897. For consumption of wine, beer and spirits in different countries see Memorandum issued by Commercial Dept. of Board of Trade, with diagrams (408) 1897.

community is the labouring or working class. There are numerous individuals here whose income is about the same, and to whom the marginal utility of money must be about the same. Out of their incomes they have to meet necessarily the primary cost of subsistence, that is, they have to buy food, clothing, shelter, fuel, and then satisfy the desire for comforts and luxuries. It is probable, therefore, that if we could obtain an exact account of how a few typical individuals of this class spend their income, it would be indicative of how great classes in the community spend theirs. An attempt has been made in this direction in the so-called workmen's or family budgets.

We give first the original table by Engel, on account of its historic importance, and because its teachings have been confirmed by later investigations. On the basis of the Belgian inquiry of 1853 and other observations, he constructed the following table of distribution of expenditure in Saxon families:—[1]

Items of Expenditure.	Percentage of the Expenditure of a					
	Labouring Family.		Middle-Class Family.		Well-to-do Family.	
Subsistence	62·0		55·0		50·0	
Clothing	16·0	95·0	18·0	90·0	18·0	85·0
Lodging	12·0		12·0		12·0	
Firing and lighting	5·0		5·0		5·0	
Education, public worship, &c.	2·0		3·5		5·5	
Legal protection	1·0		2·0		3·0	
Care of health	1·0	5·0	2·0	10·0	3·0	15·0
Comfort, mental and bodily recreation	1·0		2·5		3·5	
Total	100·0		100·0		100·0	

Engel's Law. This table shows, in the first place, that more than half the income of the ordinary working man is necessary to meet the expenses of mere subsistence, that is, food. Comparing the families with different incomes, we reach what is commonly known as Engel's law, namely, that the poorer a family is, the greater the proportionate part of

[1] See Bibliographical note; Engel, *op. cit.*, Anlage I., p. 30.

its income which must be devoted to the purchase of food. This law has been confirmed by all later investigations.

The large number of budgets (2562) collected by the United States Department of Labour were classified according to size of income. The expenditure for food in families with an income of under $200 constituted about 50 per cent. of the total income, and then decreased with increasing income, until for families with an income of $1200 and over it constituted only 29 per cent. of the income. The table follows (Seventh Annual Report, 1891, p. 864):—

Income.	Percentage of Expenditure for Food.	Rent.	Clothing.	Fuel and Lighting.	All other Purposes.
Under $200	49·6	15·5	12·8	8·1	14·0
200— 300	44·3	14·7	14·3	7·6	19·2
300— 400	45·6	15·0	14·1	7·0	18·3
400— 500	45·1	15·3	14·4	6·6	18·6
500— 600	43·8	15·2	15·3	6·6	19·1
600— 700	41·2	15·5	15·9	5·9	21·6
700— 800	38·9	15·6	16·3	5·3	23·9
800— 900	38·1	16·1	15·1	5·3	25·5
900—1000	34·3	14·9	16·8	4·7	29·1
1000—1100	34·7	15·1	17·5	4·5	28·1
1100—1200	30·7	12·2	16·5	3·9	36·7
1200 and over	28·6	12·6	15·7	3·0	40·1
All sizes	41·1	15·1	15·3	5·9	22·7

The other items in this table are interesting. Rent takes about the same proportion of the income in all cases, except the two upper classes. Expenditure for clothing increases faster than the income. The proportionate expenditure for fuel and lighting decreases as the income increases. The most striking thing, however, is that while with the lowest income the expenditure for all other purposes is only 14 per cent., with the higher incomes these expenditures amount to 40 per cent. of the total. It cannot be said that these budgets are absolutely accurate, but it is probable that they are sufficiently so to justify Engel's second rule, namely, that the proportion which the income spent for food bears to the whole may be used as a measure of material well-being; the higher this proportion is, the less there is left for other purposes, and *vice versa*.

Engel's table for different incomes shows a somewhat different result, although the same law holds true. From the Belgian budgets of 1853 he deduced the following percentages (*op. cit.* p. 42):—

Income.	Food.	Rent.	Clothing.	Fuel and Lighting.	All other Purposes.
Under 600 francs . . .	71·5	8·5	10·9	6·6	2·5
600— 900 ,, . .	69·0	7·9	13·8	5·9	3·4
900—1200 ,, . . .	67·2	7·4	15·2	5·7	4·5
1200—2000 ,, .	63·3	6·9	16·8	5·3	7·7
Over 2000 ,, . . .	64·8	7·4	17·1	4·0	6·7
All sizes . . .	66·9	7·6	14·9	5·6	5·0

This table shows that the expenditures for rent and for fuel and lighting remain about the same proportionally as the income increases. On the other hand, the proportionate expenditure for food decreases while that for clothing increases with increasing income. That the progression is so much less marked than in the United States is due to the fact that the incomes are smaller and the holders of the incomes are nearer the verge of minimum subsistence. This is shown clearly by the comparatively small percentage set free for other purposes, which is less even in the case of the highest income than in that of the lowest in the United States. Part of this is owing to the cheapness of food in the United States, which enables the holders of different incomes to reach the point of satiety sooner than in Belgium. Some of the difference, also, is due probably to differences in classification. For instance, in Belgium spirituous liquors, money spent in taverns and money spent on garden cultivation are all placed under the head of food; this increases this item by from two to five per cent.

The Belgian budgets are much more closely analytical than those of the United States, and show some interesting minor details. For instance, they distinguish, under the head of food, between animal food and plant food. In the smallest incomes, under 600 francs, the per cent. of the whole income spent respectively for animal and plant food is 11·4 and 58·0; while in the incomes over 2000 francs, the per cent. spent for animal food is 17·3, and for plant food 40·0. That is, as the income increases the tendency is to prefer animal to plant food.

The proportionate growth of expenditure in different directions with increasing income is shown by Engel in a very elaborate table, displaying the amount devoted to each particular item. It is not necessary here to give the absolute figures, which possess but little value, but it is interesting to observe the progression in the different items. For this purpose we may represent the expenditure in the lowest income by 1·00, and the corresponding expenditures for the higher incomes by proportionate numbers. In this way we reach a table of the following sort (*op. cit.* p. 41):—

	Income				
	Under 600 fr.	600—900 fr.	900—1200 fr.	1200—2000 fr.	Over 2000 fr.
I. Food—					
Animal	1·00	1·67	3·01	4·91	6·77
Vegetable	1·00	1·37	1·57	1·98	3·08
Alcoholic liquors	1·00	3·10	5·89	12·06	27·80
Garden cultivation	1·00	2·97	3·60	6·80	2·30
Total food	1·00	1·47	1·89	2·58	4·01
II. Clothing	1·00	2·06	2·81	4·37	7·05
III. Shelter	1·00	1·42	1·73	2·30	3·88
IV. Fuel and lighting	1·00	1·35	1·74	2·28	2·73
V. Care of health	1·00	1·53	3·24	5·36	9·83
Total for physical existence	1·00	1·52	1·97	2·76	4·29
VI. Intellectual needs	1·00	2·56	6·78	20·77	17·78
VII. Moral culture	1·00	2·00	5·00	7·00	1·00
VIII. Taxes, &c.	1·00	2·75	8·50	19·10	25·00
IX. Amusement, &c.	1·00	1·97	1·75	3·83	5·36
X. Miscellaneous	1·00	14·50	8·00	17·00	21·50
Total expenditures	1·00	1·24	1·61	2·32	3·55
Total income	1·00	1·55	2·11	3·01	4·68
Deficit	1·00	1·46	1·14	1·42	1·57

It is not probable that there is any great exactness about these proportions, especially in the case of the higher incomes, where the number of budgets was comparatively small. The figures, however, reveal certain tendencies which are probably true. For instance, the amount spent in food is four times as great per unit in the highest class as in the lowest. The amount spent on animal food is 6·7 times as great, while that on vegetable is only three times as great. The amount spent on alcoholic liquors increases at a tremendous ratio. But these figures must be viewed with some suspicion on account of the small sums involved. Again, we see that the amount spent on clothing increases rapidly, much more so than that on shelter or on fuel and lighting. Altogether the amount spent for the purely physical wants is 4·3 times as great in the upper incomes as in the lower. When we come to the second class of expenditures, those for intellectual, moral and other wants, the increase is very marked and, at the same time, rather irregular. It is interesting to note, finally, that the total income increases faster than the total expenditure, but that even in the upper class there is still a deficit.

Expenditure according to Size of Family. In the United States budgets an analysis is made of the absolute expenses for various items in different families, according to the number of children. The results are shown in the following table (Department of Labour, Sixth Report, 1890, p. 679):—

	Average Expense per Family for						
	Rent.	Fuel.	Lighting.	Clothing.	Sundries.	Food.	Total.
No children	$68·75	$19·78	$4·61	$64·33	$107·73	$178·39	$443·59
1 child	64·96	21·56	4·29	77·17	110·66	189·20	467·84
2 children	76·23	22·59	4·56	83·64	94·68	211·10	492·80
3 ,,	73·79	24·42	4·77	90·15	103·89	227·56	524·58
4 ,,	70·91	24·01	4·61	100·12	92·50	233·21	525·36
5 ,,	73·95	27·03	4·80	109·14	104·94	252·72	572·59
Average	$70·87	$22·43	$4·57	$82·07	$103·13	$206·37	$489·44

It is curious to observe in this table the differences in the items. The total income increases with the number of children. But the expenditure for rent, fuel and lighting remains about the same, whatever the size of family. On the contrary, the expenditure for food increases, and in a greater ratio than the total income, and that for clothing still faster as the number of children increases. The amount left under the head of sundries varies irregularly. This would seem to show that the increased expenditure for clothing and food involved in the greater number of children compels a family to live in about the same sort of house as if there were no children. The rapid increase in the expenditure for food and clothing is shown in the following table, where the expenditure of the family with no children is placed as 100, and the other figures are made proportionate:—

	Expenditure for		Total Expenditure.
	Clothing.	Food.	
No children	100	100	100
1 child	120	106	105
2 children	130	118	111
3 ,,	140	127	118
4 ,,	155	131	118
5 ,,	170	141	129

We have thus instituted two comparisons: (1) on the basis of the expenditure of families with different income, and (2) on the basis of families of different size. By these means we have thrown some light upon the theory of consumption. It appears that food requires an expenditure among the lower classes of more than one-half of the total income. Still further that the demand for food is inelastic, the proportionate amount devoted to it decreasing with increasing income. Although inelastic, the demand for food is very pressing, increasing with the increasing number of children faster than the total income. The demand for clothing is both pressing and elastic, increasing with increasing income and with increased size of family, and very much faster than the total income. The demand for shelter is inelastic and not pressing, decreasing with increasing income, and remaining nearly stationary even with increasing family. The same is true in regard to fuel and lighting.

Cost of Food per Capita. As families increase in size, the total cost of food increases, but there is greater economy in its consumption, so that the expense *per capita* decreases. We take for comparison the consumption of the adult male, counting him as 100, the female as 90, children of age 11 to 14 years as 90, of 7 to 10 years as 75, 4 to 6 years as 40, and 1 to 3 years as 15.[1] The following table is constructed on this basis (Sixth Annual Report of Department of Labour, 1890, p. 664) :—

ESTIMATED COST OF CONSUMPTION OF FOOD OF ADULT MALE (100 UNITS) IN VARIOUS SIZED FAMILIES.

	Alabama.	Ohio.	Pennsylvania.	Great Britain.
No children . . .	$83·63	$84·68	$104·35	$86·96
1 child	74·98	77·16	90·58	80·69
2 children	70·75	71·19	84·64	66·48
3 ,, ...	59·98	68·68	72·60	66·95
4 ,, ...	52·94	53·20	61·53	57·51
5 ,, ...	58·93	53·32	54·08	51·31
Average	$68·39	$68·34	$78·84	$65·69

All these families are in the coal, iron and steel industries. Similar tables are given for other states and countries, and for particular occupations, but most of them rest on an insufficient number of families to give good results.

Comparisons. These budgets suggest other comparisons besides those involved in mere differences of income or in size of family. The first and most obvious is the comparison of the condition of the working classes in successive periods of time; the second is the comparison of budgets from different countries; the third is the comparison of the

[1] See below, Scientific Tests.

budgets of working men of different nationalities, *e.g.*, in the United States; the fourth is the comparison of budgets of working men in different occupations. It cannot be said that the material is at present sufficiently accurate and complete for altogether trustworthy conclusions upon these different points. There are, however, some interesting suggestions offered by a study of the investigations.

In regard to time, we have comparatively few budgets that represent the same country and the same class of working men. In Belgium, it is true, we have the inquiry of 1853, the later inquiry of 1886, and a still later one of 1891. The last, however, extended over only a single month and is not very complete. Comparing 1891 with 1853, it appears that the money expenditure per family of the same size had almost doubled. With this doubled income the expenditures retain almost the same proportion. In 1853 the proportion of the income devoted to food was 64·9 per cent., while in 1891 it was 65·7 per cent. One would conclude from this that in 1853 the most material wants were so inadequately satisfied that the greater portion of the increased income had gone to increase that satisfaction. The data, however, are very imperfect.[1]

The second comparison is that between countries. It is evident that in different countries the percentage of income spent for different purposes will depend upon the expense of living. Where food is cheap it will be unnecessary to spend so large a portion of the income on it. Where house rent is dear, it is probable that a large proportion will be spent under the head of shelter. It is impossible to make exact comparison, because no one can say whether the quality of the food, shelter and clothing is the same in different countries. The differences shown in the budgets may be explicable by

[1] Engel, *op. cit.*, p. 84. See also p. 97, where Engel contends that the first effect of an increased income is to indulge in material enjoyments, *e.g.* alcoholic liquors, the expenditure on which increased in this case in greater ratio even than the expenditure for food.

differences of this sort. Food is cheap in the United States, which explains the fact that the proportion is almost always less than 50 per cent. of the total income. On the other hand, house rent is high, so that the proportion spent on house rent is always in excess of that shown for European countries. In regard to clothing, very little can be said, because of the differences of custom and habits of life. The following table shows an attempt to compare the expenditure of families of the same position in Illinois, Massachusetts, Great Britain and Prussia (Department of Labour, Seventh Report, 1891, p. 862):—

	Percentage of Expenditure in			
	Illinois.	Massachusetts.	Gt. Britain.	Prussia.
Subsistence	41·4	49·3	51·4	55·0
Clothing	21·0	16·	18·1	18·0
Rent	17·4	19·7	13·5	12·0
Fuel	5·6	4·3	3·5	5·0
Sundries	14·6	10·7	13·5	10·0
Total	100·0	100·0	100·0	100·0

The American investigation of 1891 distinguished the nationality of the different individuals from whom budgets were collected. There are so many variations in respect to size of family, occupation, residence and source of income, that very little can be made out of the figures.

The expenditure of families of different occupations varies considerably. In the United States, for instance, the families in the iron ore industry have an income from all sources of $401·65, while families in the glass industry have a total income of $859·64. The expenditures for different items will show corresponding variations, but for fair comparison it would be necessary to reduce them to some common basis in order to overcome the differences in size of family.

The average expenditure for food and rent, compared with the total expenditure for families in different occupations, is shown in the following table (Dept. of Labour, Seventh Report 1891, p. 857) :—

Industry.	Expenditure for all Purposes.	For Food. Absolute.	For Food. Per cent. of Total Expenditure.	For Rent. Absolute.	For Rent. Per cent. of Total Expenditure.
Iron ore	$390·93	$183·83	47·0	$32·11	8·2
Coke	462·69	218·66	47·3	58·19	12·5
Bituminous coal	524·71	237·44	45·3	61·19	11·6
Pig iron	546·23	235·66	43·2	65·02	11·9
Steel	563·50	254·18	45·1	86·44	15·3
Woollen	594·09	262·85	44·2	90·87	15·3
Cotton	610·61	287·06	47·0	72·58	11·9
Bar iron	671·50	281·21	41·9	107·33	16·0
Glass	769·06	294·75	38·3	109·57	14·2

The method is too rough to indicate the influence of occupation on expenditure for food. As income increases, absolute expenditure for food increases and relative expenditure decreases, but the latter irregularly and with one marked exception (cotton). The proportional expenditure for rent varies irregularly, being as low as 8 per cent. in the iron ore industry and as high as 16 per cent. in the bar iron industry.

Ernst Engel[1] made an attempt on the basis of the Belgian returns for 1891 to compare the expenditure of families in different occupations. The expenditure for food varies from 69 per cent. of the total expenditure in the case of coal miners, down to 61·6 per cent. in the case of compositors and printers. It will require much more accurate data than we as yet possess to carry out these comparisons.

Nourishment of the Population. By means of family budgets we approach another problem of vital importance to the community, *i.e.* whether the earnings of the mass of the

[1] Engel also analyses the 151 family budgets of 1853, and finds the lowest expenditure among weavers and agricultural labourers, the highest among miners and petty officials. The last named spend a large proportionate part of their income on clothing and lodging in order to maintain their social position. The number of budgets is too small to give very trustworthy results (Engel, *Op. cit.* pp. 57 and 104).

people are large enough to give them food, clothing and shelter of a quantity and quality sufficient to maintain health, strength and physical well-being. This must be a grave question not only from the standpoint of the economic prosperity of the community, for underfed workmen cannot produce as efficiently as well-fed ones, but still more from the social standpoint, for low living brings great suffering in the shape of disease, mortality and suicide, besides often creating social discontent and leading to revolution. Comparisons may also be instituted in this respect between the working classes of different countries; between labourers in different occupations in the same country; and between the working class at different times.

The method of procedure is, on the face of it, comparatively simple. We ascertain from the budgets what the income of the family is, and what proportion is spent for food, clothing and shelter. The second step is by statistics of prices to learn what quantities of food, clothing and house-room the income will buy. The third step is to determine whether such food, clothing and shelter are sufficient for decent living.

Two of these last-named items, viz., clothing and shelter, are extremely difficult to handle. In the first place, because quality has so much to do with it that we cannot fix prices; and in the second place, because it is extremely difficult to say how much clothing and how much house-room is necessary for healthful and decent subsistence. In respect to food we are a little better off, because physiological chemistry enables us to say with some degree of accuracy how much and what kinds of food are necessary to maintain a man in working condition.

Necessary Nutrition. The principal classes of nutrients are described by chemists as follows[1]: (1) Proteins or nitrogenous

[1] What follows is taken almost verbatim from Atwater, Foods: Nutritive Value and Cost. U.S. Department of Agriculture, Farmers' Bulletin, No. 23.

substances, such as are contained in lean meat, white of eggs, milk, gluten of wheat, etc.; (2) Fats, such as fats of meat, fat (butter) of milk, olive oil, oil of corn, and wheat; (3) Carbohydrates, *e.g.* sugar, starch, cellulose; (4) Mineral matters, *e.g.* phosphate of lime, salt.

The chief uses of food are: (1) to form the material of the body and repair its wastes; (2) to yield heat to keep the body warm and furnish muscular and other power for the work it has to do. The principal tissue-formers are the protein compounds, especially the albuminoids. These make the flesh of the body; they build up and repair the nitrogenous materials, such as the muscles and tendons, and supply the albuminoids of the blood, milk and other fluids. The chief fuel ingredients of the food are the carbohydrates and fats. These are either consumed in the body when the food is eaten, or are stored as fat to be used as occasion demands. The different nutrients can to a greater or less extent do one another's work. If the body has not enough of one for fuel, it can use another. But while the proteins can be burned in the place of fats and carbohydrates, neither of the latter can take the place of the albuminoids in building and repairing the tissues.

We can reach a common measure of the value of different nutrients by estimating them according to their heat producing power. The unit commonly used is the *Calorie*, the amount of heat which would raise the temperature of a pound of water four degrees Fahrenheit. One pound of proteins or of carbohydrates is equal to 1,860 calories, while one pound of fats is equal to 4,220 calories.

How much food does a working man need in order to maintain his vigour? Various estimates have been made in Europe and the United States. The simplest is that of Meinert, used by Engel, viz., that a man doing ordinary work needs, daily, 100 grammes of protein, 50 grammes of fats, and 500 grammes of carbohydrates. The total is equal to about 2,920 calories.

Professor Atwater has calculated a table for America on a little more liberal scale as follows:—

	Nutrients.				Fuel Value.
	Total.	Protein.	Fats.	Carbo-hydrates.	
	Pounds.	*Pounds.*	*Pounds.*	*Pounds.*	*Calories.*
Man with light exercise	1·32	0·22	0·22	0·88	2,980
Man with moderate muscular work	1·55	0·28	0·28	0·99	3,520
Man at active muscular work	1·76	0·33	0·33	1·10	4,060

The question now is whether the ordinary diet of the working classes furnishes them with this amount of food.

There are two ways of answering this question. Perfect working men's budgets would give us the quantity of food consumed by the family, and we can calculate roughly how much of this is consumed by the adult working man. This method is necessarily very imperfect, because the quantity and quality of the food is not accurately measured.

Using the old figures for 1853 (Belgium), Engel made the following calculation (*op. cit.* p. 52):—

CONSUMPTION IN GRAMMES OF ADULT WORKING MAN IN BELGIUM.

	Proteins.	Fats.	Carbohydrates.	Salt.
Lowest class	52·6	17·30	469·1	13·0
Poor class	65·1	29·20	504·4	13·9
Comfortable class	72·7	39·30	519·2	15·4
Average	63·3	28·5	495·8	14·1
Necessary for health	100·0	50·0	500·0	

It would appear from this table that on the average the amount of proteins is less than two-thirds that which is necessary; fats are also deficient, and it is only the carbohydrates that come up to the standard.

In 1891 the nourishment of the workman in Belgium was much better. The average was: proteins, 85·9 grammes; fats, 75 grammes; carbohydrates, 521·4 grammes; salt, 11·3 grammes. The proportions for 1891 are much nearer the necessary amounts than in 1853. As the two inquiries did not cover

D

the same occupations, and the inquiry for 1891 was imperfect, too much stress must not be laid upon the comparison.

Professor Atwater has collected specimen dietaries from families and boarding houses in the United States, showing the quantity of each kind of food. Some of them are as follows (*op. cit.* p. 18):—

QUANTITIES PER MAN PER DAY.

Dietaries.		Nutrients. Protein.	Fats.	Carbohydrates.	Fuel value.
American (Massachusetts and Connecticut).		*Pounds.*	*Pounds.*	*Pounds.*	*Calories.*
Family of carpenter in Middletown, Conn.		0·25	0·28	0·76	3,055
Family of glass-blowers in East Cambridge, Mass.		0·23	0·29	1·06	3,590
Boarding house, Lowell, Mass.; boarders, operatives in cotton mills		0·29	0·44	1·21	4,650
Boarding house, Middletown, Conn.; well-paid machinists, &c., at moderate work	Food purchased	0·28	0·41	0·94	4,010
	Food eaten	0·23	0·34	0·84	3,490
Blacksmiths, Lowell, at hard work		0·44	0·67	1·75	6,905
Brickmakers, Massachusetts; 237 persons at very severe work		0·40	0·81	2·54	8,850
Mechanics, &c., in Massachusetts and Connecticut; average of 4 dietaries of mechanics at severe work		0·48	0·65	1·65	6,705
Average of 20 dietaries of wage-workers in Massachusetts and Connecticut		0·34	0·50	1·38	5,275
Average of 5 dietaries of professional men and college students in Middletown, Conn.	Food purchased	0·30	0·36	1·12	4,140
	Food eaten	0·27	0·34	1·08	3,925

These dietaries are mostly in excess of what health requires. The German army ration represents 2,800 calories upon a peace footing; 3,095 calories when on a war footing, and 3,985 calories extraordinary ration in war.[1]

Standard Dietaries. Analysing ordinary articles of food

[1] In the same manner dietaries of prisoners and of soldiers have been studied in Great Britain. (See Ency. Britannica, Art. Dietetics.)

In Hungary a great investigation was made by Keleti. Data were collected from each commune as to the ordinary food of the working class and peasants, what they customarily eat at different meals, on week-days and on Sundays, and the usual quantity. The amount of albuminoids with reference to the nutrients contained in them, the chemist is able to show what combinations of different food materials will furnish the necessary nourishment in the right proportion. Combining these quantities with retail prices, we establish standard dietaries and their cost. A large number of them have been calculated by Professor Atwater (*op. cit.* p. 29). As specimens we insert the first three:—

DAILY DIETARIES.

Food materials furnishing approximately the 0·28 pounds of protein and 3,500 calories of energy of the standard for daily dietary of a man at moderate muscular work.

Food materials.	Amount.	Cost.	Nutrients. Total.	Protein.	Fats.	Carbo-hydrates.	Fuel value.
I.	*Ounces.*	*Cents.*	*Pounds.*	*Pounds.*	*Pounds.*	*Pounds.*	*Calories.*
Beef, round steak	13	11·40	0·26	0·14	0·12	. .	695
Butter	3	5·65	0·16	. .	0·16	. .	680
Potatoes	6	1·25	0·17	0·02	. .	0·15	320
Bread	22	5·50	0·89	0·12	0·02	0·75	1,760
	44	23·80	1·48	0·28	0·30	0·90	3,455
II.							
Pork, salt	4	3	0·21	. .	0·21	. .	880
Butter	2	3·75	0·11	. .	0·11	. .	450
Beans	16	5	0·84	0·23	0·02	0·59	1,615
Bread	8	2	0·33	0·04	0·01	0·28	640
	30	13·75	1·49	0·27	0·35	0·87	3,585
III.							
Beef, liver	9	5·65	0·17	0·12	0·03	0·02	375
Butter	3	5·65	0·16	. .	0·16	. .	780
Milk, ½ pint	8	1·75	0·06	0·02	0·02	0·02	165
Corn meal	12	1·85	0·63	0·07	0·03	0·53	1,230
Bread	12	3	0·50	0·07	0·01	0·42	965
	44	17·90	1·52	0·28	0·25	0·99	3,515

in these standard dietaries was calculated, and the amount compared with the minimum necessary to sustain a man. Keleti came to the conclusion that in the major part of the communes the people had le s than was necessary to live and work. The result was recourse to alcoholic liquors, and disease, weakness and early death. Keleti, Ernährungs-statistik Ungarns, 1887.

Wages and Dietaries. It is not often that we are able to get the exact quantities of food consumed in working men's families. We have, however, statistics of wages and the cost of standard dietaries. Knowing by our budgets that from 50 to 62 per cent. of the wages can be devoted to the purchase of food, we are able to make a calculation showing whether that will suffice to give the family sufficient nourishment. Such a combination would be worked out as follows. A dietary costing say 23·8 cents daily would cost per year 23·8 times 365, which equals $86·87. Say that the consumption of a man is one-third of the consumption of a family of man, wife, two large or three small children—the expenditure for food would be 3×$86·27, equal to $260·61. If food required 62 per cent. of the income, this would mean an income of $420·00. If food represented only 50 per cent. of the expenditure, an income of $521·22 would be necessary.

The reverse process would be as follows. Taking from the table on p. 25, a family with three children, the income is $524·58, and the expenditure for food is $227·56 (equal to 43 per cent.). Counting the expenditure of the man as one-third that of the family, the result would be $75·85, which would not furnish dietary No. I., but would No. II. and No. III., or any dietary costing not more than 20 cents per day per adult, or 60 cents for the family.

Per Capita Consumption. The second way in which we can approach the problem of consumption by means of statistics is by calculating the *per capita* consumption of various commodities in different communities, or in the same community during succeeding intervals of time. The ordinary method is to take the total amount of a commodity consumed and divide it by the number of inhabitants of the country. The result is the consumption per head, or *per capita.* Where the consumption is large, it indicates well-being or prosperity on the part of the community; where it increases in successive periods it indicates increasing prosperity. While the figures do not show the condition of the individual, they do serve to indicate to some extent at least the condition of the community, and they ought to serve as indications of changing direction of national consumption. The statistics must, however, be used with considerable care on account of the difficulties connected with their attainment and their interpretation.

Some difficulties are purely technical, viz. in the way of ascertaining what is the total consumption of any commodity. These are discussed under the head of Scientific Tests. Others are in the nature of cautious use of the figures. When a commodity, for instance, is such that only a few use it, like champagne, the *per capita* consumption means nothing. Hence the rule is to take such commodities only as are in very general use. Even here, such a commodity as tobacco is used principally by males, so that its increased consumption does not indicate any increased comfort on the part of the women and children. So, too, we must not confine our attention to one article alone. Often there is a large consumption of one commodity (*e.g.* bread) because the income does not allow the purchase of a more expensive article (*e.g.* meat). In many countries there is an excessive consumption of potatoes, which is not an indication of well-being, but of poverty. One commodity is often a substitute for another. Nations that drink tea do not as a rule drink much coffee; while the great beer-drinking nations do not use much wine. The whole range of consumption must therefore be considered in making comparisons.

Consumption of Food-stuffs. The consumption of bread and meat would seem to be by far the most important subject of inquiry in this chapter. It is beset with difficulties on account of the different forms of the raw material and the different purposes to which they are put.

The consumption of grain, which is used partly for bread, partly for other cookery, for the feeding of cattle and the manufacture of liquors, varies enormously in different countries. In England, France and Italy the chief grain consumed is wheat; in other countries, like Germany and Russia, it is rye. Even in the subdivisions of the same country there are great differences; for instance, the *per capita* consumption of rye in the cities of Germany varied from 85 to 419 pounds; the consumption of wheat from 6 to 119 pounds. In France the consumption of wheat was in former times comparatively small; it is estimated that in 1400 only 33 per cent. of the inhabitants ate white bread; now it is said that the percentage is 75. (Lehr, Produktion und Konsumtion, p. 226.)

The same authority gives the estimated average annual consumption of cereals as follows (1877–82):—

PER CAPITA CONSUMPTION IN KILOGRAMS (equal 2·2 lbs.).

	Wheat.	Rye.	Barley.	Maize.	Oats.
Germany	67·5	138·5	56·5	5·0	88·6
Austria-Hungary	94·5	88·5	50·6	73·0	60·5
England	154·0	—	82·5	15·5	102·0
France	256·0	46·0	32·5	25·0	95·5
Italy	144·5	(?)	(?)	81·5	11·0
Russia	82·0	242·5	37·5	(?)	117·5
Sweden	22·5	128·5	24·0	—	111·0
Norway	8·0	82·5	30·0	—	70·5

The following table shows the *per capita* consumption of potatoes in kilograms:—

Ireland	679	Norway	329	Spain	95
Germany	500	France	292	Great Britain	93
Belgium	415	Switzerland	273	Portugal	64
Holland	358	Russia	190	Italy	25
Austria	354	Denmark	177		
Sweden	334	Hungary	165		

In the first table the great consumption of rye in Germany and in Russia is plainly seen. France and England are the great wheat consumers on account of the use of white bread. In the second table the consumption of potatoes is shown, the greater part of which is for human food, although some are used for the manufacture of brandy and starch. Ireland stands at the head, naturally; but Germany is not far behind, and the consumption is very considerable in Belgium, Austria, Holland, Sweden and Norway.

The consumption of meat is very difficult to measure exactly, because so much of it is produced at home and directly consumed without any record being made either for the purposes of taxation, or of trade, or even of prices. In some continental cities of Europe, where there is an octroi, they get exact statistics of the consumption of meat, but these cities are diminishing in number. Other statistics are, as a rule, mere estimates. Lehr says that in general the consumption of meat in rural districts, where meal, lard and potatoes form the main diet, is smaller than in the cities. Von Juraschek gives the following table, taken from De Foville, (La France Économique, 1890, p. 154):—

Years.	Millions of Kilograms of Meat produced. (France).				Kgs. per Capita.
	Beef and Veal.	Mutton and Goat.	Pork.	Total.	
1812	197	66	241	504	17
1830	306	88	270	664	21
1840	310	82	290	671	20
1852	430	106	298	834	23
1862	480	115	378	973	26
1882	685	168	387	1,240	33

Enormous progress is shown in this table, both in the total and the *per capita* consumption of all sorts of meat. The 33 kilograms *per capita* in 1882 was divided as follows:—18·2 of beef and veal; 4·5 of sheep and goat; 10·3 of pork. The consumption of beef and veal is seen to have increased more rapidly than that of mutton and pork. This probably points to an increased amount of well-being in the population of France. It is also due to the increased urban population, which is more of a meat consumer than the country For instance, in 1882 while the average consumption of meat was estimated at 33 kilograms, among the urban population it was 64·6 kgs. (compared with 53·6 in 1862 and 49 in 1840); for the country population it ran as low as 22 kgs. (compared with 18·5 in 1862 and 15 in 1840). The urban population considered here was that of towns of not less than 10,000 inhabitants. For Paris the consumption of meat is still greater and is increasing faster, as is seen in the following table:—

CONSUMPTION PER CAPITA OF MEAT.

		In 1862. Kgs.	In 1882. Kgs.	Increase. Kgs.
Urban	Paris	66·6	79·3	12·7
population	Other cities	50·0	58·9	8·9
	Total urban	53·6	64·6	11·0
Rural population		18·6	21·9	3·3
All France		25·9	33·0	7·3

The curious thing in this table is not only the superior consumption of Paris compared with that of the other towns, and the superior consumption of the towns compared with the rural population, but the greater rapidity of increase in the case of Paris. The explanation of this superior consumption is the greater wealth of towns and also the more strenuous exertions of city livers and the greater hurry and worry of city life compared with rural. The statistics are not all exact, as is seen by the extraordinary fluctuations in the consumption of different cities, and of the same city in different years. In 1884, for instance, the *per capita* consumption of meat was 111 kgs. at Vannes, and only 34 kgs. at Brest; the inhabitants of Chaumont suddenly increased their consumption of meat from 80 kgs. in 1882 to 125 kgs. in 1884.[1]

We have similar figures of the consumption of meat in the cities of Germany. They are founded upon the official

[1] De Foville, La France Économique, p. 155.

statistics of the city slaughter-houses, and the inspection of meat. They are not altogether trustworthy, because the weight of the slaughtered beasts is estimated and because some of the meat slaughtered in the city is exported. They vary widely from city to city. Among the higher were (1895) Wiesbaden, 102 kgs. *per capita*; Lübeck, 97 kgs.; Munich, 73 kgs. Among the lower were Altona, 39 kgs.; Halle, 42 kgs.; Königsberg, 45 kgs. Berlin with suburbs was estimated at 69 kgs. in 1891; 71 kgs. in 1892; 71 kgs. in 1893; 75 kgs. in 1894; and 73·5 kgs. in 1895.[1]

The consumption of meat shows great fluctuations. This is due partly to variations in economic well-being, that is, to good and bad times, partly to fluctuations in the crops of hay, oats and so forth, which determine whether it is profitable to keep cattle or to slaughter them, and partly to cattle diseases, which decrease the supply of cattle. In modern times the local supply is often increased by the importation of meat, salted, smoked, canned or frozen. This business is subject to the fluctuations of the supply, to changes in freight rates, in tariffs, and in the severity of inspection. The increasing dependence of such a country as England on the foreign supply is shown in the following table (Lehr, *Op. cit.*, p. 227):—

ENGLAND. CONSUMPTION OF MEAT PER CAPITA.

	Home product. Kgs.	Import. Kgs.	Total. Kgs.
1868	93·2	7·3	100·5
1890	83·5	41·0	124·5

The Comforts of Life. There is a range of articles which, although not strictly necessaries of life, enter into the ordinary consumption of the mass of the people. The quantity and increase in the consumption of these commodities is an important index of well-being. They are sugar, tea, coffee, tobacco, wine, and beer. The consumption of sugar at two

[1] Jahrbuch Deutscher Städte, 1896, Vol. VI. p. 264.

different periods is shown in the following table (Neumann-Spallart, Uebersichten, p. 275):—

CONSUMPTION OF SUGAR PER CAPITA, KILOGRAMS.

	1870–74.	1885–89.
Great Britain and Ireland	22·6	32·6
United States of North America	17·6	24·5
Switzerland	6·7	16·2
Denmark	12·0	16·2
France	7·8	10·7
Holland	8·6	9·8
Sweden	6·1	9·4
Germany	6·7	7·8
Norway	4·5	6·2
Finland	3·4	4·7
Belgium	8·3	4·2[1]
Italy	2·9	3·1

The interesting things in this table are the enormous consumption of Great Britain and the United States, and the increased consumption of almost every nation during the period. The consumption in Great Britain is due partly to the use of sugar in manufacturing, but principally to the enormous consumption of tea. There is no doubt, however, that it represents a high material condition of the great mass of the people. The same is probably true of the United States. In Europe, Switzerland and Denmark occupy a high position, while Italy stands very low on account of its poverty and possibly on account of its climate.

The consumption of tea and coffee for 1885–89 is shown in the following table (Neumann-Spallart, Uebersichten der Weltwirtschaft, pp. 293 and 303):—

	Tea. Kgs.	Coffee. Kgs.
Australia	3·35	0·54
Gt. Britain and Ireland	2·24	0·37
Canada	1·76	0·08
United States	0·63	3·79
Holland	0·52	4·85
Russia	0·28	0·06
Denmark	0·17	2·26
Norway	0·04	3·48
Sweden	0·02	3·12
France	0·014	1·76
Austria-Hungary	0·012	0·87
Belgium	0·01	4·02
Italy	0·001	0·52

[1] Probably too small.

Aside from China and the other countries of Asia whose tea consumption is unknown, it will be seen that the Anglo-Saxons are the great tea consumers of the world. Besides Australia, Great Britain, Canada, and the United States, there remain only Holland and Russia whose tea consumption is considerable. In the other countries of Europe its use is confined to the upper classes or for special occasions. In the consumption of coffee, Holland and Belgium take the lead, but the other countries of northern Europe all use considerable quantities. A marked exception is Great Britain, where the consumption is only 0·37 kgs. *per capita.* The United States is a large consumer of coffee, although it is also a very considerable consumer of tea. The use of coffee does not seem to be increasing of late years. In 1875–81 the consumption in Germany was 2·29 kgs., and in Great Britain it was 0·44 kgs. This may be the effect of higher prices and taxes; but it may mean that the desire for coffee is pretty well satisfied, or that it is being replaced by tea. The consumption of the latter commodity is rapidly increasing, especially in Great Britain (1·7 kgs. in 1868–70; 2·24 kgs. in 1889–90).

The statistics of the consumption of tobacco are very uncertain, because of the fact that tobacco is everywhere heavily taxed, so that there is great inducement to smuggle it; and tobacco takes on a variety of forms, so that it is difficult to express the consumption simply by weight. Neumann-Spallart (p. 324) gives the following estimates in kilograms (1885–89):—Holland, 3·3; Belgium, 2·1; Switzerland, 2·1; Denmark, 1·7; Germany, 1·5; France, 1·07; Great Britain and Ireland, 0·67; United States, 1·8. Consumption depends a great deal, of course, on the cheapness of the tobacco, as is shown by the figures for Switzerland and Belgium. The figure for the United States is a very loose estimate.

The consumption of alcoholic liquors is a subject of very great interest but one upon which it is difficult to get exact information. They take on a great variety of forms, which it is impossible to reduce to a common denominator. The following table gives some estimates of the consumption of beer and wine (Neumann-Spallart, pp. 358 and 375):—

CONSUMPTION OF WINE AND BEER.

	Wine (1886–90). Liters.	Beer (1890). Liters.		Wine (1886–90). Liters.	Beer (1890). Liters.
Belgium	3·2	177·5	Russia	3·3	4·6
Great Britain	1·7	136·2	Servia	0·4	4·1
Germany	5·7	103·8	Greece	109·5	3·3
Denmark	1·2	102·9	Spain	115·0	1·3
Switzerland	60·7	40·0	Italy	95·2	0·9
Norway	0·9	37·5	Bulgaria	104·2	1·0
Holland	2·2	34·6	United States	—	58·0
Austria-Hungary	22·1	32·0	Australia	—	53·5
Sweden	0·5	27·2	Canada	—	14·8
France	94·4	22·5			

It will be seen from this table that where beer is largely consumed there is less consumption of wine, and *vice versâ*. In Germany the consumption of beer runs up to 227·3 liters *per capita* in Bavaria; 184·2 liters in Wurtemberg; 103 liters in Baden. In France the consumption of beer in the large cities showed extraordinary variations, from 376 liters in Lille to 12 liters in Paris, 10 liters in Marseilles, 9 liters in Lyons, 6 liters in Bordeaux, 5 liters in Havre. The consumption of wine is greatest in Spain, Greece, and Bulgaria; but is also very great in Italy and France. In Germany it is much less, and in Great Britain still less.[1]

An attempt is sometimes made to reduce the various

[1] A "Memorandum" (408) 1897, prepared by the Board of Trade (England) gives the following estimates of the consumption of wine, beer and spirits *per capita* for 1896:—

	Wine (gallons).	Beer (gallons).	Spirits (gallons).*
United Kingdom	0·40	30·7	1·01
France	29·50	5·2	1·85
Germany	1·05	25·5	1·94
United States	0·22	12·7	0·83

* Proof gallons containing 50 per cent. of alcohol.

kinds of spirituous liquors to one common measurement of pure alcohol, estimating that they are one-third pure alcohol. On this basis the consumption of pure alcohol was in Germany, 1892–93, equal to 4·5 liters; in France, 4·32; in Austria-Hungary, 4·37; in Switzerland, 3·16; in Denmark, 4·4; in Norway, 1·84; in Sweden, 3·25; in Holland, 4·46; in Belgium, 4·45; in Italy, 1·4 liters. In some of the cities of France the consumption ran as high as 18·3 liters.[1]

Fuel and Clothing. The consumption of coal per head of the population has been reckoned (1893) as follows:—United Kingdom, 3·30 tons *per capita;* Germany, 1·33; Belgium, 2·48; the United States, 2·41; France, 0·92; Italy, 0·14; Sweden, 0·38. The differences in coal consumption are due principally to the extent of the use of steam power and to the presence or absence of other fuels.[2]

The consumption of clothing would be a very interesting item by which to measure the economic well-being of different communities. It is an item, however, which it is impossible to reduce to statistical units. We can measure the consumption of raw cotton and of raw wool, but this is an indication rather of the industrial activity of a country than of its economic well-being. An example is given below in the consumption of raw cotton in Germany.

The way in which a population is housed is a matter of great interest, and may be termed the consumption of house-room. Here, however, we are again without statistical measurements, except those of overcrowding already treated of in "Statistics and Sociology."

Increased Consumption. It would be a matter of considerable interest to follow up from year to year the *per capita* consumption as an indication of the increased consuming power of a community or of changes in its productive activity. Examples of what may be done are shown in the

[1] Lehr, *Op. cit.*, p. 230. [2] Coal Tables. Printed, 1894.

following table, giving the *per capita* consumption in kilograms for Germany of coffee, tea, cotton, and petroleum for a period of nearly sixty years. The first two articles show the increased consuming power of the community; the two latter articles show changes in economic consumption. The *per capita* consumption of coffee, which was 1·01 in the years 1836–40, rose to 2·41 in the years 1891–95. The consumption of tea has also increased, but is still insignificant. The consumption of raw cotton has increased very largely, showing the growing industrial character of Germany. The consumption of petroleum has increased tenfold in thirty years, showing the introduction of a new commodity. The table follows (Stat. Jahrbuch für das Deutsche Reich):—

ESTIMATED CONSUMPTION OF COTTON, COFFEE, TEA, AND PETROLEUM. GERMANY.

Years.	Cotton.		Coffee.		Tea.		Petroleum.	
	Total. Tons.	Per cap. Kgs.	Total. Tons.	Per cap. Kgs.	Total. Tons.	Per cap. Kgs.	Total. Tons.	Per cap. Kgs.
1836–40	8,917	0·34	26,600	1·01	122	0·004		
1841–45	13,246	0·47	35,373	1·25	137	0·004		
1846–50	15,782	0·53	39,810	1·34	172	0·01		
1851–55	26,441	0·85	49,054	1·57	621	0·02		
1856–60	46,529	1·39	59,770	1·79	646	0·02		
1861–65	46,831	1·33	65,924	1·87	637	0·02		
1866–70	68,281	1·81	82,827	2·20	748	0·02	70,436	1·87
1871–75	116,390	2·84	93,249	2·27	1,018	0·02	154,504	3·75
1876–80	124,549	2·86	101,366	2·33	1,381	0·03	235,280	5·40
1881–85	152,329	3·34	110,907	2·44	1,564	0·03	389,335	8·54
1886–90	201,046	4·19	114,263	2·38	1,912	0·04	556,697	11·61
1891–95	252,381	4·95	122,897	2·41	2,614	0·05	755,915	14·82

The Statistical Abstract for the United Kingdom gives the quantities of certain imported articles retained for home consumption per head of the total population for each year. The general course of consumption for twenty-five years is seen in the following table. We have taken articles not produced in Great Britain, where the imports less the re-exports may reasonably be taken as the home consumption :—

	Cocoa. lbs.	Coffee. lbs.	Tea. lbs.	Wine. gall.	Sugar raw.[1] lbs.	Sugar refined. lbs.	Tobacco. lbs	Spirits imported & excisable. gall.
1871 . .	0·23	0·97	3·91	0·51	41·45	5·28	1·35	1·06
1876 . .	0·31	0·99	4·49	0·56	50·00	8·77	1·46	1·27
1881 . .	0·31	0·89	4·58	0·44	58·89	8·44	1·41	1·08
1886 . .	0·42	0·87	4·92	0·36	47·73	18·96	1·44	0·94
1891 . .	0·57	0·76	5·36	0·39	47·23	32·94	1·61	1·04
1896 . .	0·62	0·69	5·77	0·40	43·76	41·53	1·73	1·02

The striking thing about this table is the very great increase in the consumption of tea and sugar, and the tendency of coffee, wine and spirits to remain stationary. Other imported articles also produced at home showed the following increase *per capita* from 1871 to 1896 (twenty-five years):—Bacon and ham, 3·4 lbs. to 15·9 lbs.; butter and margarine, 4·7 lbs. to 11·1 lbs.; cheese, 4·2 lbs. to 6·2 lbs.; wheat and wheat flour, 150 lbs. to 257 lbs.; eggs, 12·6 to 40. These figures show that the whole population must be extending its consuming power.

Scientific Tests.

All statistics of consumption labour under very great technical difficulties. In regard to family budgets, a word may be said as to the method of attaining the facts. There are three methods in use: the first is the so-called extensive method, and consists in sending out circulars to a large number of families, and asking that they be filled out and returned. This is altogether inadequate, for it is found by experience that very few circulars are returned, and that these are generally very imperfectly filled out. A modification of this method is that pursued by the United States Department of Labour, namely, to collect a large number of returns, made, however, under the super-

[1] Includes the proportionate amount of raw sugar refined and re-exported.

vision of expert agents. The advantage of this, of course, is that the returns are controlled, more or less, by the agent. They must, however, remain for the most part mere estimates of expenditure of incomes. The second method is that of Le Play, namely, a detailed study of the whole life of the working man's family by some one who will live with them or near them, and acquaint himself thoroughly with their circumstances. This is the intensive method, and gives us the most vivid and detailed picture of family life. It requires, however, great skill and tact on the part of the investigator, as well as great expenditure of time and energy. The third method is the family account system, that is, to persuade some intelligent working man or his wife to keep an exact account in a book provided for that purpose of all the expenditures as well as the sources of income for the family, for a period of at least a year. According to Engel and Landolt, this third method is the most desirable, and at the same time the most practical. It does not give us the number of cases that the extensive method does, but it gives more exact information, and if the families are chosen with care, they will be typical of large numbers of others.

A second technical difficulty is in regard to the size of family. It makes a great difference whether it consists of a man and his wife, or of a man and his wife and several children, and in the latter case, whether the children are young or old. To select purely typical families is a matter of considerable difficulty, because the typical family in regard to numbers may not be the typical family in regard to social condition, or the family from which it is possible to get accurate returns. Various statistical devices have been employed to overcome this difficulty. The most obvious is, of course, to seek some unit which can be employed instead of the family of a varying number. The simplest case is to count two children as equal in their demands to one adult, and thus to reduce all families to the unit of the single adult. This, however, is a very crude method, because much depends upon the age of the children. The second method is to assign a different consuming power to different members of the family, according to sex and age. The units adopted in the United States investigation of 1890-91 were as follows :—

To husbands	100
To wives	90
To children from 11 to 14 years, inclusive .	90
To children from 7 to 10 years, inclusive .	75
To children from 4 to 6 years, inclusive . .	40
To children from 1 to 3 years, inclusive . .	15

These assigned quantities are merely arbitrary and rest upon no scientific basis as to the relative consuming power of women and children compared with that of the working husband.

A more elaborate system is that proposed by Ernst Engel, who starts with infancy, represented by unity, and adds one-tenth for each advancing year up to the age of 20 for women and of 25 for men. This results in a table of the following sort (*op. cit.* p. 5):—

Years.	Units.	Years.	Units.	Years.	Units.
0 . . .	1·0	9 . . .	1·9	18 . . .	2·8
1 . . .	1·1	10 . . .	2·0	19 . . .	2·9
2 . . .	1·2	11 . . .	2·1	20 . . .	3·0
3 . . .	1·3	12 . . .	2·2	21 . . .	3·1
4 . . .	1·4	13 . . .	2·3	22 . . .	3·2
5 . . .	1·5	14 . . .	2·4	23 . . .	3·3
6 . . .	1·6	15 . . .	2·5	24 . . .	3·4
7 . . .	1·7	16 . . .	2·6	25 . . .	3·5
8 . . .	1·8	17 . . .	2·7		

In this table a woman of the age 20 and over is credited with 3 units; a man of the age 25 and over is credited with 3·5 units; a child is credited with the number of units opposite its age. Take, for instance, a household consisting of father and mother and four children of the ages 10, 8, 6, and 4 years: these together compose 13·3 units, of which 3·5 belong to the father, 3·0 to the mother, 2·0 to the first, 1·8 to the second, 1·6 to the third, and 1·4 to the fourth child;

a second family, also with four children, but of the ages 18, 16, 14, and 12 years, would count as 3·5, plus 3·0, plus 2·8, plus 2·6, plus 2·4, plus 2·2 units, making in all 16·5 units. The same income would evidently amount to less for the second family than for the first. In order to reach a basis for comparison, we should divide the income of the second family by 16·5, and of the first family by 13·3, and thus get the income per unit.

This table of Engel's is also very conventional. He attempts to support it by a parallel table showing the increased weight of the human body with increasing years. The object of such a table, however, is not to measure the exact consumption of individuals of different ages, but to furnish an apparatus by which the expenditures of families of different composition may be reduced to some unit for comparison. Engel desired to give this unit the name of Quet, after the famous Belgian statistician Quetelet.

In respect to *per capita* consumption, there are various technical difficulties in ascertaining the full amount. Where the whole supply of a commodity is imported, as tea in the United States or England, and there is no great inducement for smuggling, the figures of imports probably represent fairly well the total consumption. Where the same commodity is exported, of course the exports must be deducted from the imports. Even here we have some technical difficulties, as, for instance, the importations of one calendar year do not represent the consumption of that year, for part of the importation may be stored for a considerable time before it is consumed. The second difficulty is that there are different qualities of the same article, and the prosperity of the community may take on the form of consuming a better quality. This would not appear in the statistics; and would not probably be a matter of very great importance. A more serious difficulty is that the same article may take on a variety of forms, as sugar may be imported in the form of raw sugar, refined sugar, molasses or confectionery; breadstuffs may be imported either as wheat or as flour, or even as biscuits; meat may be imported either as live stock, as frozen meat, as salted meat, or as canned meat. The difficulty is to reduce these different forms to one common expression. We can only do this in a rough way by estimating, for instance, how many bushels of wheat are represented by one barrel of flour, or the relation between the saccharine strength of sugar and molasses. In some other commodities this difficulty is insuperable. *Per capita* consumption of steel, for instance, includes the use of steel for railroad iron and for cutlery—two purposes so entirely different that it is absurd to class them together.

Again, the same commodity may be used for entirely different purposes, as, for instance, sugar is used as food and in certain industries. An increase in the use of sugar simply for chemical purposes would not indicate the prosperity which is supposed to be shown by its increasing consumption as food.

When a commodity is both imported and produced at home, it is very difficult to get at the total consumption. The technical method is to add together home production and importation, and deduct the export. If the article is heavily taxed, we have statistics of home production, but they are imperfect because the tax itself leads to illicit manufacturing. If the commodity is not taxed, the home production is generally a matter of mere estimate, because there is no occasion for it to be officially measured. In the case of a great crop like cotton, the statistics of receipts at the principal cities and of exports give us some basis for estimating the total product, but in the case of a commodity like oats or hay, largely consumed where it is produced, it is almost impossible to keep track of the total consumption. Where a commodity is exported in a different form from the raw product, as in the case of manufactured tobacco, it is difficult to get at the net consumption.

Reflective Analysis.

We started out with the notion that a theory of consumption might act as a guide to production. Our statistics give us approximate facts in regard to actual consumption. They do not show us what men might desire to consume, but what they are obliged to consume owing to the limited resources at their command. Workmen's budgets with the large proportion of income devoted to food are evidence of poverty rather than of wealth. They do show, however, the direction which consumption necessarily takes in the actual world about us and under present conditions, and thus throw light on the necessary economic activity of the community. They give us also guidance in certain questions of economic policy. These things have been so well summarised by Engel in his classical essay that I cannot do better than repeat his points.

Corollaries from Engel's Law.[1] In the first place, it is evident that a great part of the economic activity of the community must be directed to the production of food. It must gain this food, either by direct production or by the production of things which can be exchanged for food. It is evidently the true policy of a country not to hinder or discourage such production. So large a proportion of the income of the mass of the community being spent for food, any discouragement there is a very great burden. It is evident that we have here also some guidance for taxation. A tax on food must rest more heavily on the lower classes than on the higher, inasmuch as a greater proportion of the income is spent for food. The next most important item is clothing, which is of especial interest, because expenditure for clothing increases so fast with increasing size of family. Anything that will make clothing cheaper will be a great

[1] See Engel's original essay, Die Produktions- und Consumtionsverhältnisse des Königreichs Sachsen, reprinted in Bulletin de l'Institut international de Statistique, Vol. IX., Liv. I., Appendix I., p. 28.

economic gain for all sizes of income, especially in large families. The inelasticity of the demand for shelter, even in such a country as the United States, reveals a lack of appreciation of what should be a prime condition of comfortable existence, namely, plentiful house-room. It is probable that the community needs education in this direction.

Engel has pointed out that we can use the single figure, namely, per cent. of income devoted to food as an index of material prosperity. The larger this figure, the poorer the population or the family; the smaller this figure, the greater the command which such a family or community has over the comforts and luxuries of life.

The individual family also can gauge its expenditure according to these average budgets. A Belgian labourer, for instance, of the lowest class, who spends more than 21 per cent. of his income for rent, will encroach upon his food supply, that is, he must run into debt. In the United States, for ordinary families, rent requires about 15 per cent. of the total income. So in the same way in regard to clothing, the normal expenditure is about 15 per cent. of the total income. When a family spends more upon luxuries and comforts than the normal budget allows, we may call that extravagance; where it spends less on clothing and house-room than the normal budget allows, we may call that parsimony or miserliness. We have some indication also of the difficulty which the poorer classes have in satisfying the higher wants. Where so large a proportion of the income is demanded for bare food, it is extremely difficult to provide decent habitation, respectable clothing, and even more difficult to secure satisfaction for the moral and intellectual needs. It requires a tremendous effort and the greatest care to provide for even a small expenditure in these directions. Moreover, the slight margin that does exist may be entirely wiped out by some unexpected loss or misfortune, such as lack of employment, accident, or sickness. While we inculcate, therefore, upon the lower classes the necessity o thrift and the desirability of moral and intellectual self-culture, we must not forget the tremendous effort required to attain these objects. As Engel points out again, we learn to estimate the sacrifice involved where a family of the poorer classes does succeed in raising itself above the level of bare subsistence, and of making a step upward. How much sacrifice is involved in sending a son to college or in educating children for a better position than they would have had if simply placed in the factory at the earliest possible age? What constant sacrifice it means when a common labourer, after years of toil, has been able to provide for himself a small annuity or pension for his old age.

Increasing Consumption. While family budgets show us the enormous struggle of the community to supply itself with the means of existence, the statistics of *per capita* consumption show increasing success in this struggle. General averages, it is true, do not show the fate of individuals. With increasing wealth there may be, and doubtless are, many individuals lacking the necessaries, not to speak of the comforts of life. But in the case of the necessaries and common comforts of life the demands of the rich are soon satisfied. Increased consumption sufficient to raise the *per capita* rate means the participation of numerous individuals in such consumption. The whole mass of the community must be progressing. Our statistics serve, therefore, as a measure of the increasing well-being of the community. The subject will be further considered in the chapter on Social Distribution.

CHAPTER III.

POPULATION AS LABOUR-FORCE.

Economic Purpose.

The Factors of Production.[1] Production depends upon the co-operation of land and labour. Land is the passive instrument, labour the active agent. Land is commonly called the first factor of production, and labour the second. As, however, labour is seldom applied as mere muscular force, but always through some instrument, tool or machine, a third factor is introduced which is called capital. The distinction between land and capital is that the latter is the result of previous labour. Again, as the productivity of labour, when applied to land and aided by capital, depends very much (overwhelmingly in fact) upon the *way* in which it is applied, a fourth factor is sometimes introduced and called "organisation."

Population as Labour-Force. Economic theory has various remarks of a rather commonplace kind in regard to labour as a factor of production. Production will depend upon the quantity and quality of labour and the way it is applied. The quantity of labour is simply the question of population; and, physiologically speaking, there is no reason to fear that there will not be enough people in the world. The number of the population is of more importance in questions of distribution and consumption than in production. Nevertheless, the mere number is sometimes of interest, as in the

[1] See Marshall, Economics, Book IV., The Agents of Production, Land, Labour, Capital and Organisation.

settling of new countries—*vide* the importance of immigration in the economic growth of the United States.

Of greater importance is the question of the quality of the labour-force. A man is a man; but he may be of very different value as a producer of wealth, just as he may be of very different quality as a citizen. He has varying efficiency, owing to varying physical, mental, and moral character. Some men, and the men of some nations, have greater physical strength than others. The better-fed, better-housed, and healthier, longer-lived workman is more efficient as labour-force than the physically weak and half-starved. Skill, intelligence, and energy are equally important—the foundation of the doctrine of the economic justification of free education and specialised training. Innumerable contrasts may be drawn between the labour-force of a highly-civilised, competitive nation and one half-civilised, uneducated, and bound down by superstition and tradition. So also honesty, truthfulness, and trustworthiness are moral qualities increasing the efficiency of the individual labourer.

The method of application is the third thing to which economists have directed attention, especially under the heads of co-operation and division of labour, the use of machinery, and production on a large scale. Men may co-operate by bringing their united forces to bear where the force of a single one would be ineffective; or they may co-operate by doing different parts of the same work, gaining in dexterity, saving the use of tools, economising time and skill, &c. By machinery, they bring to their aid natural forces, or substitute automatic motions for the less perfect ones directed by human eye and muscle; and in the factory system, or production on a large scale, they reach the highest degree of division of labour and specialisation of skill.

Economic theory lays down the above postulates as conditions for the abundant production of wealth. The object of statistics is to furnish confirmatory evidence; to compare the increase of population and the increase of wealth;

to note the quality of the labourer in respect to physical strength, skill, intelligence, energy, trustworthiness, and to measure the product accordingly; to show how much more productive the factory system, with its division of labour and use of machinery, is than hand-labour. Doubtless all of these things are matters of common observation and experience. No one will dispute that the cotton-mill turns out more cloth with less labour than the old spinner and weaver; but statistics confirm the facts of common observation by quantitative measurements. We try to show just how much more productive one system is than another.

The Demands of Practice. Economic theory contents itself with the general demonstration of the increased production of wealth as the quantity of labour grows, its quality improves, and its application is made in better fashion. The details of this general process are innumerable, and constitute the course of economic and industrial evolution. The details, however, are of immediate interest to economic practice. What is the quantity and quality of labour at the command of a certain nation at a certain time? How far has the division of labour gone? Is industry conducted on a large or on a small scale? What are the consequences of the introduction of the factory system? Does it give rise to increased employment of women and children, or the reverse? What are the facts about unemployment? At what period of life do men seek particular occupations, and at what age are they retired? All these are questions of economic practice which are of immediate interest. The object of statistics is to answer them, or to assist in answering them, or to show by what methods they may be answered.

Statistical Data.[1]

Quantity of Labour. The labour-force of the community consists, roughly speaking, of the whole population. Men,

[1] *Bibliographical Note.* The general statistics of population in regard to sex, age and conjugal condition, are to be found for the United States in

women, and even children, the last often at an early age, are engaged in the work of satisfying their economic needs.

the U.S. Census, 1890: Population, Part I. For other countries see the current Censuses. For the statistics of occupations, we have three important sources, U.S. Census, 1890: Population, Part II., Statistics of Occupations, with elaborate introductory analysis, pp. lxxv–clxxi. Many of these analyses are faulty in method: see The Federal Census (Amer. Econ. Assocn. Publications, New Series, No. 2, the Statistics of Occupations, pp. 78–107).

For England we have the Census of 1891, particularly Vol. IV. General Report, pp. 35–60. Also the Blue book: Occupations of the People (468), 1895.

For Germany we have the great Berufszählung of June 14th, 1895, the results of which may be found in Vierteljahrshefte zur Statistik des Deutschen Reichs; 1896, III. Ergänzungsheft; 1897, II. Ergänzungsheft. The chief figures are published also in the Statistisches Jahrbuch für das Deutsche Reich, 1897 and 1898. They are reproduced also in the Bulletin of the U.S. Department of Labour, No. 12, Sept. 1897, p. 624.

The Massachusetts Census of 1895, and that of 1885, give a very careful analysis of occupations, and are worth examination.

The statistics for other countries will be found in their respective Censuses.

The Annual Reports of the Labour Department of the British Board of Trade give the summaries of the occupation statistics from the Census of 1891. The same Board has published a Report on the Employment of Women and Girls by Miss Collet [c.—7564] 1894. This Report has been continued by Report on Changes in the Employment of Women and Girls in Industrial Centres, Part I. Flax and Jute Centres [c.—8794] 1898, which was noticed in the Bulletin of the U.S. Department of Labour, No. 17, July, 1898, p. 621. The previous Report was noticed in Bulletin No. 1.

In regard to the classification of occupations, see the Reports of M. Bertillon to the International Statistical Institute, particularly the Report made at Chicago (Bulletin, Vol. VIII., Part I., 1895, p. 226), and also in the same volume, the articles by Körösi, p. 148, and Davis R. Dewey, p. 183. A translation of M. Bertillon's scheme may be found in the Publications of the American Statistical Association, Vol. III., 1892–93, p. 379. It was published originally in the Bulletin de l'Institut International de Statistique, Vol. VI., Part I., 1892, p. 263.

Reference should be made, also, to Charles Booth, Life and Labour of the People of London, 9 vols., 1892–97, and to his article, Occupations of the People of the United Kingdom, 1801–81. (Journal of the Statistical Society, Vol. XLIX., June, 1886, p. 314–435.)

For the number of persons in particular industries, and the changes from year to year, see Massachusetts Annual Statistics of Manufactures.

The quality of labour is so different that comparisons in space between different nations are useless and misleading.

For general treatment of the subject, particularly in respect to the employment of women and children, see Hobson, The Evolution of Modern Capitalism, 1894; and Wright, The Industrial Evolution of the United States, 1895. Both authors treat also the questions of the substitution of machinery for labour and the irregularity of employment.

Unemployment. See U.S. Census, 1890: Population, Part II., pp. cxxxvi–cxlii. (of very little value). Massachusetts Bureau of Labour Statistics, Reports for 1887 and 1893. For England, see Annual Reports of the Labour Department on Trade Unions. Monthly returns are also published in the Labour Gazette. See also General Report on the Wages of the Manual Labour Class in the United Kingdom [c.—6889] 1893, and Tabulation of the Statements of Men living in certain Districts of London [c.—5228] 1887. Also, Report of the Select Committee on Distress from Want of Employment (321), 1896. For the lack of employment in the United States in 1893, see especially the Report of the Massachusetts Commission on the Unemployed, 1895.

For Germany we have the very important inquiry in regard to unemployment, covering the two dates June 14th and Dec. 2nd, 1895. The results are published in Vierteljahrshefte zur Statistik des Deutschen Reichs, 1896, IV. Ergänzungsheft. This is probably the most exact census of any that we have.

Miscellaneous. Die Berufsstatistik von Oesterreich und Ungarn. Bespr. von H. von Scheel. (Jahrbücher für Nationalökonomie und Statistik, Band LXIV., 1895, p. 426.) Engel, Die gewerbliche Dichtigkeit (Zeitschrift des Königl. Preuss. Stat. Bureaus, 1878, p. 330). Schulze-Gaevernitz, The Cotton Trade, 1895. Report of the U.S. Department of Labour on Industrial Depressions, 1886; Reports for 1891 and 1892 on Cost of Production; and the Report for 1899 on Machinery and Labour. D. A. Wells, Recent Economic Changes, 1890. U.S. Census, 1890: Manufactures, Part III., p. 174 (showing number of spindles per employee and labour cost per spindle). Massachusetts Bureau of Labour Statistics, Bulletin, July, 1898 (Fallacies of Occupation Statistics). American Journal of Sociology, Vol. III., 1897–8, pp. 139–144, Women and Child Labour, bibliography of the subject. J. A. Hobson, Influence of Machinery on Employment (Political Science Quarterly, Vol. VIII., 1893, pp. 97–123). Carroll D. Wright, the Unemployed (The Social Economist, Vol. II., 1891–2, pp. 71–79). Special Study of Peddlers in Germany (Vierteljahrshefte, 1897, I., p. 67). C. C. Closson, The Unemployed in American Cities (Quarterly Journal of Economics, Vol. VIII., 1893–94). Schoenhof, Economy of High Wages, 1892. Reports of the British Chief Inspector of Factories and Workshops (containing accounts of the enforcement of the factory laws). Denis, La Dépression Économique, 1895, gives general figures of the number of persons employed in agriculture, industry, &c.

The most populous nation is not always the best off economically. In fact, the reverse seems to be true, as compare China and India with the countries of Europe. It is only where we have about the same conditions that we can use the total population as an index of economic strength. Possibly the increasing population of Germany compared with the stationary population of France may suggest that for future economic development, the growth of industry, the planting of colonies, and the increase of foreign trade, Germany may find itself in a more favourable position as regards labour-force than France. Another interesting contrast is that between England and Ireland. In 1841, England had 55 per cent. of the total population of the United Kingdom, and Ireland, 30. In 1891, the percentages were 72 and 12½. Doubtless the change in proportionate population has followed economic conditions, rather than produced them; but it is interesting to note that even gross population may sometimes serve as an index of change in relative economic strength. Some interesting contrasts may be found in the United States, as, for instance, from 1880 to 1890, the population of Maine and Vermont was nearly stationary, while that of Nevada actually decreased (by 26 per cent.); on the other hand, Massachusetts and Connecticut increased 25 per cent., and California 40 per cent.[1]

Comparisons in time show that in almost all civilised countries, population is increasing.[2] Mere labour-force grows more abundant. There seems to be room for this increase. As will be shown later, *per capita* wealth and *per capita* production have increased faster than population. With increasing labour-force, we have had a law of increasing rather than of decreasing returns. The fears of the Malthusians seem thus to have been met by improvements in methods of production. How this has been done constitutes the history of the

[1] U. S. Census, 1890: Population, I., p. xiii.

[2] Statistics and Sociology, pp. 364, 368, and 378.

economic evolution of the nineteenth century. How long the same process will continue, viz., increasing population with proportionately still greater efficiency, is the difficult problem of the future. In new countries, we have had the additional advantage of abundant land.

Persons in Gainful Occupations. Another expression for population as labour-force is given by the statistics of persons engaged directly in productive occupations.

In 1890, out of a population of 62,622,250 in the United States, 22,735,661 were returned as engaged in gainful occupations. This was 36·3 per cent. of the total population, or 48 per cent. of the population ten years of age and over. This would show that a little over one-third of the population support themselves and the remainder; and that nearly one-half of the population ten years of age and over are obliged to work.[1]

Comparisons of different sections of the United States are not very useful, because circumstances vary so much. In a Western State like Montana, where the population is composed largely of adult males, the proportion engaged in gainful occupations is very large—67 per cent. In a manufacturing State, where there is opportunity for the employment of women and children, like Rhode Island, the proportion is also large—56 per cent. West Virginia (41 per cent.) shows the agricultural state with large numbers of women and children. Comparisons in space are dependent upon the age, sex, and industrial constitution of the population.

Comparisons in time are not much better. In 1880 the proportion of persons engaged in productive occupations was 34·7 per cent., compared with 36·3 per cent. in 1890. The difference is probably due to the smaller proportion of children in 1890. The proportion above the age of ten years was 47·3 per cent., which was nearly the same as in 1890, viz., 47·9 per cent.

In England, according to the census of 1891, 45 per cent.

[1] U.S. Census, 1890: Population, II., p. lxxx.

of the total population were returned as occupied. In Germany, according to the industrial census of 1895, 40 per cent. of the population were directly engaged in gainful occupations, besides 2·6 per cent. of servants.

Sex and Age of Persons in Gainful Occupations. As everywhere in population statistics, careful attention must be paid to sex and age. Under the ordinary definition of gainful occupations, the women and children who are engaged simply in household duties at home are excluded, although domestic servants hired to do the same work are included. The result is that the number of women enumerated under this head is always much less than that of men, and the number of girls is much less than that of boys. The distribution according to sex and age in the United States in 1890 is shown in the following table (U. S. Census, 1890: Population, Part II., p. cxxi.):—

Age period.	Males in occupations.		Females in occupations.	
	Number.	Per cent. of males of corresponding age.	Number.	Per cent. of females of corresponding age.
10—14 years	400,586	11·2	202,427	5·8
15—19 ,,	1,904,865	58·6	906,240	27·3
20—24 ,,	2,856,993	92·0	947,220	30·6
25—34 ,,	4,989,814	97·4	807,670	17·3
35—44 ,,	3,626,356	97·9	441,067	13·2
45—54 ,,	2,538,459	96·6	313,363	12·9
55—64 ,,	1,514,615	92·9	180,387	12·0
65 years and over	910,895	73·8	98,158	8·3
Age unknown	78,507	—	18,039	—
Aggregate	18,821,090	77·3	3,914,571	17·0

Of all persons engaged in gainful occupations, females constitute only one-sixth; and, moreover, of all females ten years of age and over, only one-sixth are engaged in gainful occupations. What these particular occupations are we shall consider later on. For the purpose of studying the direction in which the labour-force of the community is exerted, the statistics of males are sufficient.

The number engaged in gainful occupations at each age-period, is instructive. About 11 per cent. of the boys of the age 10 to 14 are already employed; and at the age 15 to 19 nearly 59 per cent. are engaged in gainful occupations. From 20 to 65, more than nine-tenths of the male population are employed; and even after the age of 65 nearly three-fourths of the males are at work. For females, the maximum is reached at the age 20 to 24 years; and thereafter both the absolute and relative numbers decrease.

An interesting analysis of the constitution of the population at different ages is shown by the German statistics (1895) which distinguish four classes, viz., those actively engaged in some occupation (Erwerbsthätige); servants (für häusliche Dienste im Haushalt ihrer Herrschaft lebenden); dependents (Angehörigen ohne Hauptberuf); and persons without occupation (Personen ohne Hauptberuf). One hundred persons of each age class are distributed as follows (Vierteljahrshefte zur Statistik des Deutschen Reichs, 1897, II., Ergänzungsheft, p. 3):—

	Workers.	Domestic servants.	Dependents.	Without occupation.	Total.
Under 20 years	18	2	78	2	100
20—30 years	65	6	28	1	100
30—40 „	59	2	38	2	100
40—50 „	59	1	37	3	100
50—60 „	58	1	34	7	100
60—70 „	49	1	31	19	100
70 years and over	29	1	31	40	100
All ages	40	3	53	4	100

Under the age of 20, four-fifths of the population are dependent or without occupation. Between 20 and 30 the number of workers and servants increases, and the number of dependents is smaller. From 30 to 60 about three-fifths are workers, and two-fifths dependents, or without occupation. Above 60, those without occupation, either because they have acquired a competence or a pension, or because they have failed in life and are paupers, prisoners, or inmates of asylums and benevolent institutions, become numerous. This is a vivid picture of the course of human life worthy to be compared with mortality tables, dissolution of marriage, and crime at different ages.[1]

How and by whom the work of the world is actually carried on is indicated by tables complementary to the above, showing the distribution by ages of 100 males or females engaged in gainful occupations (U. S. Census, 1890: Population, Part II., p. cxxiii):—

Age.	Males.	Females.
10—14 years	2·1	5·2
15—19 ,,	10·1	23·2
20—24 ,,	15·2	24·2
25—34 ,,	26·5	20·6
35—44 ,,	19·3	11·3
45—54 ,,	13·5	8·0
55—64 ,,	8·0	4·6
65 years and over	5·3	3·0
	100·0	100·0

The large number of women in the lower age classes is owing to their employment as domestic servants. About one-half of the men doing the work of the world are between 15 and 35 years of age.

The more interesting complementary table from Germany is as follows (distribution of 100 of each category):—

Age.	Workers.	Servants.	Dependents.	Without occupation.
Under 14 years	0·9	2·5	59·5	12·1
14—20 years	19·2	41·8	5·9	6·8
20—30 ,,	26·6	38·8	8·7	5·3
30—40 ,,	19·0	7·9	9·3	5·0
40—50 ,,	14·9	3·8	7·1	8·1
50—60 ,,	11·4	2·8	5·0	14·2
60—70 ,,	6·1	1·7	2·9	22·2
70 years and over	2·0	0·7	1·6	26·3
	100·0	100·00	100·00	100·00

[1] Statistics and Sociology, pp. 117, 146, 169, and 278.

This brings out clearly the concentration of domestic servants in the lower ages, the comparative youth of the workers, and the advanced age of those without occupation.

The Grand Occupational Groups. A great deal is made in economic and sociological writings of the terms agricultural, commercial, industrial, and professional classes. We speak of one community as agricultural, of a second as largely commercial, of a third as changing from the agricultural to the industrial stage. Common observation is sufficient to characterise most cases; as no one would hesitate to say that England is industrial and Ireland, agricultural; the New England States, manufacturing, and the South, agricultural. That the South is becoming more industrial is also a matter of common observation. It is desirable to gain a more precise measurement of these facts for comparisons both in space and time. For although the terms agricultural, industrial, professional, &c., are somewhat indefinite and elastic, yet they connote important social and economic characteristics which it is interesting to follow both in space and time. The method of doing this is to group our persons engaged in gainful occupations into certain great classes. This has already been done in "Statistics and Sociology," page 119, where the figures for the principal countries are given. For convenience we repeat those for the United States, adding the figures for 1880 brought to the same basis as those of 1890 (U.S. Census, 1890: Population, Part II., p. lxxxviii.):—

	1890.		1880.	
	Number.	Per cent.	Number.	Per cent.
Agriculture, fisheries, and mining	9,013,336	39·6	8,004,624	46·0
Professional service	944,333	4·2	603,202	3·5
Domestic and personal service	4,360,577	19·2	3,503,443	20·1
Trade and transportation	3,326,122	14·6	1,866,481	10·7
Manufacturing and mechan. industries	5,091,293	22·4	3,414,349	19·6
All occupations	22,735,661	100·0	17,392,099	100·0

Comparisons in Space. The statistics of occupations may be used to make what may be called an occupational chart or map of any given country, showing in what portions of the country agriculture or industry is more prevalent. The simplest way to do this is by a table, showing the number of each class per 100 persons of the age of ten years and over, engaged in gainful occupations. The statistics of the United States, arranged according to grand sections, but separated according to sex, may be found in the Census, 1890, volume on Population, Part II, p. lxxxix. The proportions for males are as follows:—

PER CENT. OF MALES IN EACH CLASS OF OCCUPATIONS OF TOTAL MALES TEN YEARS OF AGE AND OVER ENGAGED IN GAINFUL OCCUPATIONS.

	The United States.	North Atlan. Div.	South Atlan. Div.	North Cen. Div.	South Cen. Div.	West Div.
Agriculture, fisheries, and mining	44	22	60	47	68	36
Professional service	3	3	3	4	3	4
Domestic and personal service	14	17	12	14	10	22
Trade and transportation	16	22	12	16	10	19
Manufacturing and mechan. industries	22	35	13	19	9	19
Total	100	100	100	100	100	100

It is seen from this table that a very small fraction of the population is engaged in professional service, and the proportion does not vary materially from section to section. Variations in domestic and personal service are greater; but the statistics are rather uncertain. What is manifest beyond a doubt is the prevalence of agriculture in the South, and the corresponding dominance of manufactures and trade and transportation in the North.

The full table in the Census volume gives the particulars for the States, showing the following characteristics:—

"In Massachusetts, Rhode Island, and Connecticut, the males engaged in manufacturing and mechanical industries in 1890 constituted very nearly one-half of all males in gainful occupations, the exact percentages being 47·1 for Massachusetts, 48·5 for Rhode Island, and 45 for Connecticut. In New Hampshire the males in manufacturing and mechanical industries constituted 38·5 per cent., and in New Jersey 38·7 per cent., New York 33 per cent., and in Pennsylvania 31 per cent. In twenty-four States and territories the males engaged in agriculture, fisheries, and mining constituted more than one-half of all males in gainful occupations. . . . These States and territories comprise all in the South Central division, all but Delaware, Maryland, and the District of Columbia in the South Atlantic division, and all but Ohio, Illinois, Michigan, Wisconsin, and Minnesota in the North Central division."

The English Census gives a similar occupational table for the different counties, the basis of the distribution, however, being 1,000 persons in the population of the age of ten years and over. The table, therefore, must not be compared with the above table for the United States. Specimens of the table, showing the distribution for all England and Wales, for the City of London, for three agricultural counties, and for two industrial counties, are given below. (Census, England, 1891, Vol. IV., p. 121.):—

NUMBER OF PERSONS, PER 1,000 PERSONS TEN YEARS OF AGE AND OVER, ENGAGED IN VARIOUS OCCUPATIONS.

	Professional.	Domestic.	Commercial.	Agricultural.	Industrial.	Unoccupied
England and Wales . .	42	86	63	61	333	415
London	58	120	105	5	311	401
Huntingdonshire . . .	35	88	30	232	181	434
Herefordshire	39	108	35	186	188	444
Lincolnshire	33	88	44	181	205	449
Lancashire	29	60	74	20	454	363
West Riding	51	47	31	31	456	389

The characteristic feature in such a table as the above is the presence or absence of industry. In England as a whole the industrial class is much more prominent than the agricultural. But in such a county as Huntingdon the agricultural class numbers 232, while the industrial class numbers only 181 out of 1,000 persons of the age of ten years and over. In the industrial counties, on the other hand, such as

Lancashire, industry employs 454 persons, and in the West Riding, 456 persons out of 1,000 of the age of ten years and over. London shows a very large number in the commercial class. It is to be noticed also that in the agricultural counties, the number of the unoccupied class is greater than the average for England and Wales; while in the industrial counties the number is less. This points to the employment of women and children in industry.

A similar distribution of persons employed in agriculture and industry for Germany shows the following result:—Out of 1,000 persons in the population, there were employed in 1895 in agriculture 163·8, and in industry, 195·7. In 1882 the figures were: 188·8 for agriculture, and 161·2 for industry, showing the industrial change that has come over Germany during recent years.[1]

Engel's Industrial Density. A second method for attaining the same end is to calculate the number of the agricultural or industrial class living on each square mile or each square kilometre of territory. In Germany, for instance (in 1875), the number of persons engaged in industry to the square kilometre was 12; the number of persons engaged in agriculture to the square kilometre was 10·3. In Prussia the figures were 10·4, and 8·6; for Bavaria, 9·4, and 16·0; for Saxony, 42·1, and 16·6; for Württemberg, 14·7, and 11·5. One sees that Saxony is industrial and Bavaria agricultural.

A further refinement is attained by analysing the number of persons employed in each particular industry per 100 square kilometres in each province or district. This is what may be called the industrial density of population, and shows us what is the chief seat of each industry. For instance, in Prussia the chief seat of the textile industry outside of Berlin is found in Düsseldorf, Aachen and Erfurt. It has

[1] For details of the German census of occupations see Vierteljahrshefte zur Statistik des Deutschen Reichs, 1896 and 1898.

For figures and cartograms showing distribution of the agricultural and industrial population of Germany, see Stat. Jahrbuch für das Deutsche Reich, 1898.

been suggested that such occupational density of population might be used for social comparisons; as, for instance, the connection between certain industries and the consumption of alcoholic liquors, or the prevalence of certain diseases, or even the dominance of political parties. It is probably true that with the further perfection of our occupational and vital statistics, such correlation may be established between many of these facts, so that the true way for the correction of certain evils will at least be indicated.[1]

Comparisons in Time. Statistics of occupations carried on from decade to decade show us that the relative number of persons engaged in different employments is constantly changing. If the classification remains the same and the figures are trustworthy, this should show us the course of industrial evolution, and in what direction the productive power of the community is turning. Two factors, however, affect the number of persons engaged in any particular industry at different times. One is the relative importance of the industry itself; if it is growing, it will employ a greater number; if it is decaying, it will employ a less number. The second factor is changes in the method of production in the industry, brought about by the introduction of machinery. The effect of this may be to decrease the number of workmen necessary for producing the same product, or to increase the amount of product produced by the same number of workmen. In either case the industry may be flourishing, although the census returns show the same, or even a smaller number of persons engaged in it. The introduction of machinery also often allows the employment of women and children instead of men, so that the full significance of a change can only be ascertained by an analysis of the number of employees by sex and age. It is somewhat difficult, therefore, to interpret the real meaning of changes in the number of persons in the same occupation from decade to decade. By careful analysis, however, much instruction can be gained

[1] Zeitschrift des Preuss. Stat. Bureaus, 1878, p. 330.

in respect to characteristic features of the industrial development of modern communities.

In the United States we have, in the first place, the increase in grand groups of occupations. While population from 1880 to 1890 increased 24·6 per cent., the number of persons ten years of age and over engaged in gainful occupations increased 30·7 per cent. The increase in agriculture, fisheries, and mining was, however, only 12·6 per cent., and in domestic and personal services, 24·5 per cent. On the other hand, the number of persons engaged in professional services increased 56·6 per cent.; in manufacturing and mechanical industries, 49·1 per cent.; and in trade and transportation, 78·2 per cent. These general figures show clearly the tendency of the modern community to apply less of its labour-force in agriculture and the extractive industries, and a larger proportion to the work of manufacturing, of transportation, and of trade.

In Germany, from 1882 to 1895, notwithstanding increasing population, the agricultural class decreased in absolute numbers by 724,148, while the number of persons (with dependents) engaged in industry, mining, and building increased by more than four millions. This led to a great shifting of the population dependent upon each occupation, as shown in the following table :—

	1882.	1895.
Dependent on agriculture, fisheries, &c.	42·5	35·7
,, ,, industry, mining and building	35·5	39·1
,, ,, trade and transportation	10·0	11·5
,, ,, domestic service	2·1	1·7
,, ,, professions, including army and navy	4·9	5·5
Without occupation	5·0	6·4
	100·0	100·0

This same process of evolution may be traced in England. The most marked change is shown in the decrease in the number of persons employed in agriculture. The total number of persons who were returned as farmers in 1881 was 223,943; in 1891 the number was 223,610. "This decline is very small, but is accompanied by a decline in the number of sons or other close male relatives of farmers living with them in the farm-house, and who may be regarded as practically engaged in agriculture. The number of these persons fell from 75,197 in 1881 to 67,287 in 1891. This is a decline of over 10 per cent., and appears to indicate unmistakably that the younger generation are not nearly so disposed to adopt agricultural life as was the case at even so recent a date as 1881."[1]

A similar decline occurred among those employed on farms as shepherds, carters, or agricultural labourers. In 1881 the number of males employed was 830,452; in 1891 it had fallen to 756,557; while the female agricultural labourers fell in the same period from 40,346 to 24,150. The figures together show a fall of 10·3 per cent. The reasons for this decline are stated as follows:—

"The causes, or main causes, to which this falling off in the number of agricultural labourers is due, appear to be three. Firstly, there is the attraction of towns, where the labourer sees not only a prospect of higher wages, but the certainty of a more varied and interesting life; the comparative monotony of rural existence becoming more and more distasteful with the advance of education, as is indicated by the migration into the towns being, as is stated, highest from districts in which the labourers are the best educated. Secondly, there is the natural effort of the farmer to meet the continuous fall of prices of his produce by cutting down his labour bill to the utmost in his power; and thirdly, there is the diminished demand for labour due to the conversion of arable land into permanent pasture. A comparison of the Agricultural Returns for 1891 with those for 1881 shows that at the later date there were 1,074,077 fewer acres of arable land in England and Wales than had been the case ten years earlier. Moreover, of the arable land that still remained, an increased proportion was under clover and rotation grasses, and a correspondingly smaller proportion under corn and green crops, a change which also implies diminished demand for labour."

We have not space to follow out in detail the rest of this interesting study, which will be found in Vol. IV. of the

[1] Census, England, 1891, Vol. IV., p. 43.

English Census for 1891. Some of the facts commented on by the chief of the Census Department are as follows:—Remembering that the population increased during the decade by 11·7 per cent., we have a point of comparison for the increase during the decade in various occupations. The industrial class, for instance, increased by 15 per cent.; and the increase would have been much greater had it not been for the exceptionally small growth of two large groups, namely, the building trades and the textile industries. The former increased only about 2 per cent., and among masons, slaters and tilers, carpenters and joiners, there was an actual decrease. No explanation is given for this decrease or slow growth of the number of men engaged in building trades.

In the textile industries the number of persons employed increased only 6 per cent., while there was an actual falling off in the lace, linen, and silk industries. The workers in hemp, jute, and other coarse fibrous materials were almost exactly the same as in 1881. This apparent stationariness has given rise to considerable anxiety lest England should be losing her supremacy in this branch of industry.

The most important branch, the cotton industry, however, shows a gain of 12 per cent., while the imports of raw cotton increased 19 per cent. during the decade.

In the other particular trades, there have been various changes due to various causes. Since 1881, the makers of machines, tools, and other instruments, have increased 27·7 per cent. in number; the number of miners has increased 26·9 per cent., among whom the coal miners have increased 35·5 per cent., while the copper, tin, and lead miners show an absolute decrease; the workers in metal remain about the same, except that the blacksmiths and whitesmiths show an increase of 16 per cent., while the nailmakers show a decrease of 47 per cent., owing to the substitution of machinery for hand work, and the increased use of wire and other foreign-made nails. These figures are an interesting comment on the changes which occur in the large industries.

While the agricultural class shows marked decrease, and even in the industrial class there are cases of decrease, the number of persons engaged in the general work of distribution has increased. The shopkeeping class, such as booksellers, grocers, butchers, coal dealers, &c., has increased 28 per cent. The commercial class proper, such as bankers, insurers, brokers, and others engaged in commercial transactions, increased 31·4 per cent., commercial clerks alone increasing 36·2 per cent., and commercial travellers 24·2 per cent. "The increased diffusion of education has apparently flooded the country with candidates for clerkships."

The number of persons engaged in transportation has increased 26 per cent., those on railways 34 per cent., those engaged in road traffic 30 per cent., and those engaged in water traffic 12 per cent. The railway does not do away with carters and road carriers, but it competes actively with water transportation.

A second method of comparison in time is to show the distribution of 10,000 persons of the age of ten years and over in different occupations at different dates. In England, for example, out of 10,000 males of and above ten years of age, 8,314 were occupied in 1891, and 8,324 in 1881, showing a slight decrease. Of 10,000 females of the of age ten years and over, 3,442 were occupied in 1891, and 3,405 in 1881, showing a slight increase. The number of males in particular employments where there were considerable changes is shown in the following table :—

Occupation.	Per 10,000 Males of and above 10 years. 1891.	1881.	Increase.	Decrease
Agricultural labourers	694	867	—	173
Housebuilding trades	641	714	—	73
Coal miners	485	407	78	—
Machine makers	197	173	24	—
Railway employees	176	149	27	—
Grocers, &c.	128	111	17	—
Commercial clerks	217	188	29	—

The above is the really scientific method of watching changes in occupations from decade to decade. It shows how the labour-force of the community is shifting about, seeking probably the most favourable opportunity. The sample given above is sufficient to confirm the conclusions just reached, that agriculture and the building trades are absorbing less of the labour-force; while trade and transportation, together with coal mining and machine-making, are absorbing a greater portion. The details of this analysis may be found in the Annual Reports of the Labour Department of the Board of Trade, beginning with 1893-4.

Particular Occupation Groups. The basis of all occupation statistics is the return of the individual as to his particular employment. The number of particular employments is very large, running up into the thousands. Those of a similar character are, therefore, thrown into groups; and these minor groups are then classified under the grand designations, Agriculture, Professional Service, &c., as above. The number of minor occupation groups is not fixed by any common agreement, and varies widely from country to country. In the United States Census of 1890 there were 218; while in the English Census there were 349. International comparison, therefore, is impossible, except in certain great groups, such as agricultural labourers, railway employees, &c. Even from decade to decade in the same country, the number is apt to vary. In the United States, for instance, the number of occupation designations in 1860 was 584, in 1870 it was 338, in 1880, 265, and in 1890 it was reduced to 218, and, for some tables, to a still smaller number. It is impossible to reproduce the figures here. They may be found in the volume on Population, Part II. p. cxviii., and in the Abstract of the Eleventh Census, p. 78.[1]

[1] A comparison of the number of persons engaged in the various classes of gainful occupations in the United States at the Censuses of 1870, 1880 and 1890, by William C. Hunt, will be found in the Bulletin of the U.S. Department of Labour, No. 11, July, 1897, p. 393.

Employment of Women. As we have already seen, the number of females in gainful occupations in the United States is only about one-sixth of the total number. It is a matter of considerable social interest to know in what branches of industry women are employed, whether the number is increasing or decreasing, and whether they are single or married—that is, seeking to support themselves, or to supplement the wages of the husband. We have here two currents of opinion which do not exactly run counter to each other, but which proceed from different standpoints. The one desires that the woman, especially the married woman, shall be withdrawn from the factory; while the second seeks enlarged opportunities for women to earn their own living, especially if they are not married.

In the United States, the women engaged in gainful occupations were distributed as follows :—

	Number.	Per cent. of total of each group.
Agriculture, fisheries, and mining	679,059	7·5
Professional service	311,682	33·0
Domestic and personal service	1,667,686	38·3
Trade and transportation	228,309	6·9
Manufacturing and mechanical industries	1,027,525	20·2

These figures need explanation. The apparently large number of women under Agriculture is due to the fact that in the South wives and daughters of farmers were often returned as farmers. This is particularly true of the coloured women, who constitute no less than 427,000 of the above number.

Of the women engaged in Professional Services, the great mass are either professors and teachers, or musicians and teachers of music.

Under the head of Domestic and Personal Service were 1,216,639 domestic servants; 216,631 laundresses; 86,089 housekeepers and stewardesses; 32,593 boarding and lodging-house keepers; and 41,396 nurses and midwives.

All these occupations are connected with woman's traditional sphere as housewife.

Under Trade and Transportation, we have the opening of new opportunities for women, as bookkeepers, clerks, stenographers and typewriters (113,261), and also their employment as saleswomen (58,451).

It is concerning the last head, women employed in Manufacturing and Mechanical Industries, that most question will arise. But of these women, no less than 288,328 were dressmakers, 60,087 milliners, and 168,040 seamstresses. These are employments not demanding great physical strength, and which do not unfit women for household duties in case of marriage. There remain 223,658 women employed in textile mills, 63,809 tailoresses, 27,991 tobacco and cigar factory operatives, and smaller numbers employed in various manufactures. From these figures it would not appear that the employment of women in factories has reached any great dimensions in the United States.

In England, the number of women engaged in gainful occupations is greater proportionally than in the United States. As we have already seen, about 35 per cent. of all females ten years of age and over are in gainful occupations. Here again the principal categories are domestic servants, school teachers, nurses and midwives, charwomen, washing and bathing service, lodging and boarding-house keepers, confectioners and pastry cooks. There are, however, over 400,000 females in textile factories.[1]

Increased Employment of Women. The statistics of the United States show that from 1880 to 1890 the number of males engaged in gainful occupations increased from 14,744,942 to 18,820,950, or 27·6 per cent.; while the number of females increased from 2,647,157 to 3,914,711, or 47·4 per cent. The employment of women, therefore, seems to have increased faster than the employment of men. If we analyse the grand groups of occupations, we get the following

[1] Census of England, 1891, Vol. IV., p. 58.

results: In agriculture, fisheries, and mining, males have increased 12·5 per cent., females 14·3 per cent.; in professional service, males 48·5 per cent., females 75·8 per cent.; in domestic and personal service, males 16 per cent., females 41·2 per cent.; in trade and transportation, males 71·8 per cent., females 63·3 per cent.; in manufacturing and mechanical industries, males 43 per cent., females 62·9 per cent.

A closer analysis of these figures will show that the increase is not so alarming as would appear at first sight. The increase in agriculture is probably due to the large number of women in the South whom the Census of 1890 included under the term farmers, planters, and overseers. The increase under the head of professional service is due to an increased number of female teachers. Under the head of domestic and personal service the increase is found among domestic servants, laundresses, and nurses and midwives, and very likely is due to a more complete enumeration.

Under trade and transportation there has been a very great increase in bookkeepers, clerks, stenographers, and typewriters, undoubtedly due to the increased employment of females in those capacities. Under manufacturing and mechanical industries there has been an enormous increase in dressmakers, milliners, and seamstresses (from 282,544 to 494,458). There has also been an increase of females employed in boot and shoe factories, as paper-box makers, as carpet makers, as hosiery and knitting-mill operatives, in printing works, in silk mills, and under the general heading of mill and factory operatives not specified. On the other hand, the number of females employed in cotton and woollen mills has remained almost stationary. On the whole, therefore, it does not appear that there has been any very great tendency to increased employment of women in factories.[1]

In England the employment of women has been very care-

[1] The Eleventh Annual Report of the Commissioner of Labour, 1895–96, is devoted to an investigation of work and wages of men, women and children. The facts were obtained from 931 establishments situated in

fully studied by Miss Collet. From 1881 to 1891 there was a slight increase; but with many variations in different occupations. Some have decreased: *e.g.*, domestic indoor servants, cotton and cotton-goods manufacturers, shirt makers, seamstresses, agricultural labourers, and farm servants. Among those that have increased are tailoresses, nurses, hotel servants, milliners, lodging and boarding-house keepers, and grocers—including tea, coffee, and chocolate makers, and dealers. Miss Collet ascribes these changes to the introduction of machinery in some industries, and to the movement of population to the cities.[1]

Substitution of Women for Men. It is an interesting question to determine whether women are taking the places of men, or whether they are a simple addition to the labour-force in various occupations. Figures for Massachusetts, comparing the proportionate number of females to males in manufacturing industries in 1885 and 1895, show that at the former period the number of females was 33 per cent., and at

27 different States. From these establishments information was asked covering two periods, by the "present period" being meant some week in the years 1895–96, and by the "former period" some week antedating, by at least ten years, the week selected in 1895 or 1896. The following figures show the number of males and females employed, and the percentage of increase:—

	Former period.	Present period.	Increase per cent.
Males, 18 years or over . .	26,479	43,195	63·1
,, under 18 years . . .	4,175	7,540	80·6
Females 18 years or over . .	27,163	45,162	66·3
,, under 18 years . . .	6,743	12,751	89·1

This table seems to show that the proportion of females employed in these industries has increased a little faster than the proportion of males. Taking these facts in connection with the Census returns, Commissioner Wright is of the opinion that the proportion of females, taking all the occupations in the country into consideration is gradually increasing. (The Census statistics have been severely criticised by H. L. Bliss in three articles, Eccentric Official Statistics, in the American Journal of Sociology, Vol. III.)

[1] Report on the Statistics of Employment of Women and Girls [c.—7564], 1894.

the latter period 34·6 per cent. of the total number of employees. The change, therefore, has been insignificant.[1]

The English Census has selected some particular occupations showing changes in both directions. The proportionate number of women to men increased from 1881 to 1891 among commercial clerks, bookbinders, and in the flax, linen, hosiery, and tobacco manufactures. On the other hand, the proportion of women to men has decreased in the worsted, cotton, silk, lace, and glove manufactures.[2] Mr. John A. Hobson calculates that in certain leading groups of manufactures in England the number of females employed increased from 463,600 in 1841 to 1,447,500 in 1891; while the number of males increased only from 1,030,600 in 1841 to 1,576,100 in 1891. An examination of his table shows a rapid increase in the proportionate number of women employed down to 1861; since that time, although the absolute number has increased, the relative number has remained about the same.[3]

Married Women in Factories. In regard to the conjugal condition of women engaged in occupations in the United States, we have the following figures (U.S. Census, 1890: Population, Part II., p. cxxvi.):—

Whole number of women in occupations . 3,914,571, or 17 per cent. of the women ten years of age and over.
Single women in occupations . . . . . 2,733,825, or 28 per cent. of all single women ten years of age and over.
Married women in occupations . . . . 515,260, or 4·6 per cent. of all married women.
Widowed women in occupations . . . . 630,268, or 29·3 per cent. of all widowed women.
Divorced women in occupations . . . . 35,218, or 49·0 per cent. of all divorced women.

It appears from this table that less than 5 per cent. of the married women in the country are employed in gainful occupations. More than one-half of these married

[1] For details in regard to the different industries, see Massachusetts Statistics of Manufactures, 1895, p. 203.

[2] Census of England, 1891, Vol. IV., p. 59.

[3] Hobson, The Evolution of Capitalism, p. 290, 1894.

females (269,258) are coloured women, and are chiefly employed in agriculture. In fact, 22·7 per cent. of the coloured married women were reported as in gainful occupations; while among the native white married women, only 2·2 per cent.; and of the foreign white married women, only about 3 per cent. were returned as in gainful occupations. There were only 109,712 married women reported as engaged in manufacturing and mechanical industries, being about 10·7 per cent. of the total number of women engaged in those industries. The larger number of these married women were employed as dressmakers, milliners, and seamstresses, although there were 23,018 engaged in textile factories, and 4,627 engaged as tobacco and cigar factory operatives. The number of married women, therefore, in factories appears to be comparatively small.[1]

The proportionate number of widows, as will be seen from the above table, is very much larger. But here also the coloured number nearly one-third of the whole. Of the widows, more than one-third are employed in agriculture, and more than one-third in domestic and personal service.

The English Census of 1891 did not tabulate the returns of married women in factories. The office, however, extracted from the enumeration books fair samples of the women

[1] Of all the women engaged in gainful occupations in 1890, 13·2 per cent. were married, and 16·1 per cent. were widows. The proportions for the different occupations were as follows:—

	Married.	Widowed.
Agriculture, fishing and mining . . .	22·5 per cent.	33·2 per cent.
Professional service	6·9 ,,	4·6
Domestic and personal service . . .	12·8 ,,	16·3 ,,
Trade and transportation	7·4 ,,	9·7 ,,
Manufacturing and mech. industries	10·7 ,,	9·4 ,,
All occupations	13·2 ,,	16·1 ,,

This result was confirmed by the special investigation of the Department of Labour on Work and Wages of Men, Women and Children, which showed that out of 79,987 females employed in 931 industrial establishments, only 6,775, or 8·5 per cent., were married. (Report, 1895–96, p. 18.)

over twenty years of age employed in several industries, with their condition as regards marriage. The results were as shown in the following table, which gives the proportion of single, married, and widowed women in 1,000 women over twenty years of age employed in the specified industry (Census, England, 1891, Vol. IV., p. 59):—

	Single.	Married.	Widows.
Cotton (Lancashire)	528	411	61
Lace (Nottingham)	473	411	116
Carpet (Kidderminster) . . .	587	319	94
Woollen cloth (Huddersfield) .	634	273	93
Worsted (Bradford)	698	244	58
Boots (Northampton)	512	427	61
Glass (Prescot, &c.)	708	165	127
Pottery (Staffordshire)	371	531	98

The number of cases upon which these estimates are based is too small to be entirely trustworthy. The Labour Department of the Board of Trade made, in 1894, a special investigation in the cotton, woollen, and worsted mills of Lancashire, Cheshire, and Yorkshire. The investigation was a very elaborate and complicated one; the general result was as follows (Report, Employment of Women [c.—7564], p. 31):—

"In the cotton mills in Lancashire and Cheshire 67·2 per cent. of the women and girls employed were women over 18 years of age, and of these adult women 32·9 were either married or widowed.

"In the woollen mills in Yorkshire 83 per cent. of the women and girls employed were women over 18 years of age, and of these adult women 29·8 per cent. were either married or widowed.

"In the mixed woollen and worsted mills in Yorkshire 76·9 per cent. of the women and girls employed were women over 18 years of age, and of these adult women 23·6 per cent. were either married or widowed.

"In the worsted mills in Yorkshire 62·9 per cent. of the women and girls employed were women above 18 years of age, and of these adult women 21·2 per cent. were either married or widowed.

"Of the married or widowed women in cotton mills, about 12 per cent. were widowed, and in the woollen and worsted mills about 17 per cent. were widowed."

In regard to the employment of women in general, Miss Collet's report comes to the following conclusion (*Ibid*, p. 72):—

"Briefly, then, the employment of married women has decreased, casual employment has diminished, and the slight increase in the employment of women and girls generally is due to the increased number of young women and girls under 25 with definite occupations, and to the increased employment of middle-class women."[1]

In Germany, in 1895, there were 5,246,303 women engaged in gainful occupations, besides 1,313,957 engaged in domestic service. Their distribution by industry and conjugal condition is shown in the following table (Vierteljahrshefte, 1897, II. Ergänzung, p. 3):—

	Single.	Married.	Widowed.	Total.
Agriculture	1,651,524	615,301	486,329	2,753,154
Industry	1,048,818	250,666	221,634	1,521,118
Commerce	323,966	129,176	126,466	579,608
Day labourers	122,266	28,595	83,004	233,865
Others	135,815	22,643	18,190	176,648
	3,282,389	1,046,381	935,623	5,264,393

The total number of females in Germany in 1895 was 26,361,123, so that women in gainful occupations constituted about 20 per cent. of all females. There were 17,935,019 women above the age of fourteen, and of these 5,212,377, or nearly 30 per cent., were returned as engaged in gainful occupations. The number of women employed in factories in 1895 was 260,303 of age sixteen to twenty-one, and 403,813 over twenty-one years of age, making a total of 664,116.[2]

Employment of Children. It is a question of interest to know how many children are actively engaged in the work of production, in what occupations they are engaged, and whether the number is increasing or decreasing. Public opinion now demands that very young children shall not be employed, that the employment of children shall not interfere with their education, and that they shall not be employed in

[1] Miss Collet's method has been criticised by Ludwig Sinzheimer, in Braun's Archiv für soziale Gesetzgebung und Statistik, Vol. VIII., p. 682, 1895.

[2] Stat. Jahrbuch, 1898, p. 8. Vierteljahrshefte, 1896, IV., p. 70.

occupations injurious to their health or morals, or beyond their strength. When these requirements are fulfilled, it does not seem desirable to interfere with the efforts of children of the working classes to add to the family income, and to learn an occupation which will be useful for them in later years. There is only the danger that the employment of children on a large scale in machine industries may bring in an unusual competition with the labour of adults.

Our best statistics in regard to child labour are from England. The following table shows the number of boys and girls of ten and under fifteen years of age engaged in the undermentioned groups of occupations, arranged in descending order of magnitude (including all groups where more than 10,000 children were engaged), in England and Wales in 1891. (Annual Report of Labour Department): —

	Boys.	Girls.	Total.
Textile trades :—			
Cotton	39,956	52,451	92,407
Wool and worsted	16,681	19,567	36,248
Mixed or unspecified materials	3,372	3,896	7,268
Flax and linen	206	484	690
Hemp and other fibrous materials	1,731	514	2,245
Silk	1,926	3,685	5,611
Textile trades	63,872	80,597	144,469
Domestic and personal service	8,667	110,198	118,865
Conveyance of goods and messages, &c.	96,576	2,576	99,152
Agriculture	71,519	1,517	73,036
Clothing trades	16,619	35,020	51,639
Mining. Coal	31,318	249	31,567
Other minerals	1,208	175	1,383
Provision of food and lodging	18,393	3,246	21,639
Building and furnishing trades	14,005	1,183	15,188
General labourers	13,081	95	13,176
Iron and steel manufacture	10,501	472	10,973
Commercial and other clerks	9,732	523	10,255
Total *occupied* children of 10 and under 15 years of age	419,209	262,194	681,403
Total *unoccupied* children of 10 and under 15 years of age	1,191,649	1,350,515	2,542,164
Grand total number of children of 10 and under 15 years of age	1,610,858	1,612,709	3,223,567

Of the boys ten and under fifteen years of age, 26 per cent. are occupied; of the girls, 16·2 per cent.; of all children, 21·1 per cent.

If we take all the textile trades together, they show the largest number of children employed; next to these trades comes domestic and personal service, which employs young girls; and then the conveyance of goods and messages, employing young boys. Agriculture employs over 70,000 boys, and there are 31,000 boys employed in coal mines. In the clothing trades we have 35,000 girls, but the number of girls in the other trades (aside from the textiles) is insignificant. On the whole, while the table shows a total of 681,000 children under fifteen years of age who are occupied, a large proportion of these are engaged in services which are not injurious to their health or morals.

The English Census of 1891 [1] gives a comparison of the number of children in certain specified industries in 1871 compared with 1891. "Formerly," the Report says, "a large number of children under ten years of age were employed both in factories and in field labour; but compulsory attendance at school has practically put an end to this." In regard to children of the age from ten to fifteen, a comparative table shows that in almost every industry the proportionate number employed has decreased.

The number of children under thirteen years of age (half-timers) in textile factories was 80,844 in 1870; 125,886 in 1874; 110,585 in 1878; 91,651 in 1885; and 86,468 in 1890.[2]

A second method of comparison is to take the number of persons in each age-group and show the percentage engaged in gainful occupations. For the United States, the distribution of males and females by age periods is shown in the table on p. 62. In reference to children, it is there shown that there were 400,586 boys of the age ten to fourteen years engaged in gainful occupations. This constituted 11·2 per

[1] Vol. IV., p. 60.

[2] Rept. Labour Dept., 1895-96 [c.—8230], p. 183.

cent. of the total number of boys of that age, *i.e.* about one in nine. There were also 202,427 girls of the age ten to fourteen years engaged in gainful occupations, constituting 5·8 per cent. (about one in sixteen) of the total number of girls of that age. If we ask what are the occupations in which these children are engaged, the answer is that 64 per cent. of the boys, and 41·4 per cent. of the girls are in agriculture; 12·6 of the boys, and 38·3 per cent of the girls are in domestic and personal service. These certainly are not very harmful occupations even for young children. A small percentage, 9·8 per cent. for males, and 2·6 per cent. for females, are in trade and transportation; while 13·6 per cent. of the males, and 17·5 per cent. of the females are engaged in manufacturing and mechanical industry. The different distribution of the boys and girls shows that the boys are engaged largely on farms and as messenger boys, while the girls are in domestic service or in factories.

If we ask what element of the population is most inclined to put its children at work, the answer is that coloured children show the greatest proportionate number employed, namely, 30 per cent. of the boys, and 20 per cent. of the girls; next are the foreign-born, 16 per cent. of the boys and 10 per cent. of the girls; of the native whites of native parentage only about 7·5 per cent. of the boys, and 2·5 per cent. of the girls, are in gainful occupations.[1]

In regard to the increase of child employment in the United States, it is impossible to obtain an exact comparison, because the age classification was different at the last two censuses. At the census of 1880, there were 825,187 males of the age ten to fifteen, or 24·4 per cent., and 293,169 females of the age ten to fifteen years, or 9 per cent. of the whole number of that age, engaged in gainful occupations. These figures are much larger than the figures for 1890, both absolutely and relatively. It is true that the age period in 1880 covers one additional year, but allowing for that, it is

[1] U.S. Census, 1890: Population, Part II., p. cxxii.

calculated that the percentage of children of the age ten to fifteen in gainful occupation was 16·8 per cent. in 1880, and only 10·3 per cent. in 1890.[1]

In regard to employment of children, therefore, the conclusion seems to be that both in the United States and in England it has decreased during the last ten years. It must be noted, of course, that the figures are probably below the truth, because of the reluctance of parents to acknowledge that their children are at work when it is contrary to the factory laws. It is probable, however, that the influence of factory legislation and of public opinion is inducing employers to dispense with child labour as much as possible. Commissioner Wright thinks that women are being substituted for children, especially in the factories of New England.[2] In New England cotton factories the number of adult employees increased from 1880 to 1890, while the number of children decreased. In the South, on the other hand, the number of children in cotton factories more than doubled.[3]

For Germany the number of children under fourteen returned as engaged in gainful occupations in 1895 was only 181,453, of whom 129,437 were boys, and 52,016 were girls. There were also 33,501 children engaged in domestic service.[4] The number under age sixteen employed in factories (1895) was 146,110 boys and 75,639 girls, or a total of 221,749, by far the largest number being between fourteen and sixteen years.[5]

Labour-Force according to Race and Nationality. In the United States, all analysis of population is extremely interesting on account of the peculiar constitution of the population, consisting as it does of four elements: the native-born whites of native parents, the native-born whites of foreign parents, the foreign-born whites, and the coloured.

[1] U.S. Census, 1890: p. lxxxvi; Eleventh Ann. Rept. U.S. Dept. Labour, 1895–96, p. 26.

[2] Industrial Evolution of the United States, p. 206.

[3] U.S. Census, 1890: Manufactures, III., p. 173.

[4] Vierteljahrshefte, 1897, II., Ergänzung., p. 14.

[5] *Ibid.*, 1896, IV., p. 70.

These may be called the native Americans, the second generation of immigrants, the immigrants, and the coloured.[1]

The practical questions that suggest themselves are:—(1) how much does each of these elements contribute to the labour-force of the country? (2) how much does each element contribute to the labour-force engaged in particular occupations, as agriculture, mining, the building trades, &c.? (3) where may we expect to find the labourers of each element of the population? The first two of these questions are interesting as an indication of the influence of immigration on the economic development of the United States. The third may be used as a guide to future immigration policy—for it enables us to say what immigration means so far as labour-force is concerned.

The total number of persons ten years of age and over engaged in gainful occupations may be distributed as follows (U.S. Census, 1890: Pop., Part II., p. cxvii.):—

	Both Sexes. Number.	Both Sexes. Per cent.	Males. Per cent.	Females. Per cent.
Native white—native parents	10,895,023	47·9	50·7	34·7
Native white—foreign parents	3,542,408	15·6	14·6	20·6
Foreign white	5,104,757	22·5	23·0	19·8
Coloured	3,193,473	14·0	11·8	24·9
Total	22,735,661	100·0	100·0	100·0

It appears from this table that, at the present time, the so-called native Americans, that is, the native whites of native parents, contribute less than one-half of the total labour-force of the community. The two elements of the foreign population, namely, the immigrants and their children born on this soil, contribute together no less than 38 per cent. of the total labour-force. It must be remembered also that the distinction between the two is carried back only two generations; and there must be many immigrants of the third generation represented among the native Americans. It is probably within reason, therefore, to say

[1] See Statistics and Sociology, p. 302.

that one-half of the white labour-force in the United States is due to immigration. This shows us what an enormous factor immigration has been in the economic development of this country.

Race and Nationality according to Particular Occupations. It is interesting to follow out the grand groups of occupations in order to see how the different elements of the population contribute to them. We have the following comparison showing the number of each element in each of the grand groups of occupations (U.S. Census, 1890: Pop., Part II., p. cxvii.):—

	Agriculture, Fisheries & Mining.	Professional service.	Domestic & personal service.	Trade & Transportation.	Manufacturing & Mechan. Industries.
Native white—native parents	56·8	67·9	30·8	51·8	40·6
Native white—foreign parents	8·8	16·3	14·2	22·1	24·4
Foreign white	14·5	12·1	31·5	21·4	31·4
Total coloured	19·9	3·7	23·5	4·7	3·6
	100·0	100·0	100·0	100·0	100·0

The distribution of the different elements in the different occupations is extremely interesting. In agriculture the native Americans more than hold their own. The coloured are also heavily represented, partly, perhaps, on account of the employment of their women and children in the fields. In professional service the native element is still more strongly represented, and next to it the native whites of foreign parents. In domestic and personal service the foreign whites and the coloured are both strongly represented. It is in manufacturing and mechanical industries that the foreign whites and the native whites of foreign parents come out most strongly. Interesting details in respect to minor occupations may be found in the Census volume.

Occupations of the Foreign-born. We turn now to our third analysis, namely, to show what becomes of the immigrants after they reach this country. Our statistics of immigration show that for many years about four-fifths of the immigrants have been unskilled labourers, together with some skilled mechanics, farmers, and merchants. It is impossible to arrange the statistics of immigration under exactly the same categories as the statistics of occupations in the Census. This is because more than one-half of the immigrants put themselves down simply as labourers. If we take the immigrants as represented by the foreign-born now in this country, we find that 25·5 per cent. are in agriculture; 2·2 per cent. in professional service; 27·5 per cent. in domestic and personal service; 14 per cent. in trade and transportation; and 31 per cent. in manufacturing and mechanical industries.[1] It appears probable, therefore, that the large number who put themselves down as labourers go largely into the factories and simpler mechanical trades after their arrival in this country. This is an interesting illustration of the mobility of labour both in regard to place and to occupation under the modern industrial system.

We can, in like manner, follow the particular nationalities in the grand groups of occupations. For instance, there are 1,501,063 Germans in gainful occupations, distributed as follows per 100: Agriculture, 27·5; professional service, 2·1; domestic and personal service, 22·4; trade and transportation, 13·9; manufacturing and mechanical industries, 34·1 These figures show the liking of the Germans for agriculture and the handicrafts. There are 1,065,651 Irish, who are distributed as follows per 100: 15·5 in agriculture; 1·6 in professional service; 42·4 in domestic and personal service; 15·2 in trade and transportation; 25·3 in manufacturing and mechanical industries. These figures show the large number of the Irish who are domestic servants and common labourers. Similar figures might be given for the other nationalities. The Scandinavians are largely represented in agriculture (38 per cent.); the French Canadians in manufactures (58 per cent.); the Italians in domestic and personal service, &c.[2]

[1] U.S. Census, 1890: Pop. Part II., p. cxlviii.

[2] U.S. Census, 1890: Pop., Part II., pp. cxlix. and clviii.

Workers and Dependents. **Many censuses attempt to estimate what proportion exists between the actual workers and those dependent upon them. This varies widely in different countries and in different industries, largely according to the number of women and children employed, and also according to the attractiveness of the industry for single men. Both of these causes would diminish the proportionate number of dependents to workers.**

The United States census, unfortunately, did not carry out this analysis, nor did the English. For Germany we have a very elaborate presentation of the relations for different industries (Vierteljahrshefte, 1897, IV., Ergänzung., p. 23).

It appears that for every hundred workers (Erwerbsthätige) there are:—

In trade and commerce	143	dependents.
In industry	140·7	,,
In agriculture	118·6	,,
In casual labour	85·4	,,
In public service	85·4	,,
Without occupation	47·4	,,
Together	120·1	

The small proportion in the category, "without occupation," is owing to the fact that these persons are largely inmates of public institutions; in the public service and as casual labourers (Lohn-Arbeit wechselnder Art) they are largely single men. The relatively small number in agriculture is due, probably, to the employment of women. The analysis is not without sociological interest, and is carried out in many directions in the reference above.

Principal and Minor Occupation. A minor inquiry is as to whether a man devotes himself entirely to one occupation or earns part of his living from a second. The latter is a sign of undeveloped industry. It includes also cases where dependents and persons without a chief occupation exercise a secondary one. For Germany we have the following figures (Vierteljahrshefte, 1896, III., Ergänzung., p. 5):—

OF PERSONS ENGAGED IN AGRICULTURE, &C., AS PRINCIPAL OCCUPATION, SO AND SO MANY EXERCISE ALSO A SECONDARY OCCUPATION, VIZ.:—

	Absolute Numbers.	Percentage of number in principal occupation.
Agriculture	1,049,542	12·66 per cent.
Industry	1,491,865	18·00 ,,
Trade	384,104	16·43 ,,
Domestics	31,333	7·24 ,,
Professional	115,277	8·60 ,,
Without occupation	201,335	6·15 ,,

Agriculture was the favourite secondary occupation, it covering 73·73 per cent. of all cases of secondary occupation. Industry covered 12·5 per cent. and trade 11·5 per cent. The consequence was that while agriculture was the principal occupation in 8,292,692 cases, it was a secondary occupation in 3,649,445 other cases, so that there were 11,942,137 cases where agriculture was an occupation. In the same way there were 8,281,230 persons whose chief occupation was industry, and 618,411 persons to whom industry was a secondary occupation, making 8,899,641 persons engaged directly or indirectly in industry. The corresponding figures for trade and transportation were 2,338,508, 569,643, and 2,908,151.

Employment and Unemployment. Whatever may be the quantity and quality of the labour-force at the command of the community, it is necessary that it should be regularly employed in order to produce the maximum result. It is an important question how much time is lost during the year by lack of employment. Part of this time is lost because certain occupations can be carried on only during certain seasons, owing to conditions of temperature and climate; part is lost because of the seasonal character of the demand for certain goods; part owing to commercial disturbances; and part owing either to the misfortune of the workman as sickness, or to his fault, drunkenness or neglect of duties, or owing to labour disturbances, strikes and lockouts. The question of employment may be viewed from two standpoints: (1) as loss of productive power or failure of the community to reap the full advantage of its productive capabilities; or (2) from the standpoint of distribution as loss of income to the working man and as entailing suffering, uncertainty, and perhaps permanent injury to his productive power. The second question is of much greater social interest than the first. The statistics can, however, be arranged under the first point of view and will be given here.

We can approach this question statistically in several ways: (1) We might inquire of each individual how many days he had lost during the year and the reasons for the loss of employment. This would be the ideal way, and if we had full and truthful answers it would give us a complete picture of the conditions of employment. This method is practically impossible of realisation, owing to the ignorance and untruthfulness of men. (2) We might ascertain on a given census day how many men were unemployed. This is easier but gives less information. (3) We might ascertain from employers in particular trades how the number of men actually employed fluctuates from month to month or from year to year. This would give us some notion of the irregularity of employment in particular trades. (4) Similar information might be obtained from well-organised trade-unions in regard to the number of members out of employment at a particular time. (5) Special investigation might be made in seasons of particular distress through public or private charitable relief agencies, in order to ascertain how widespread is the lack of employment causing the distress. All of these methods have been used. They serve different purposes. The following review is an attempt to balance their relative usefulness and to gauge their scientific validity.

Total Amount of Unemployment. The crudest attempt to

answer the question of unemployment was that made by the Eleventh Census of the United States. On the population schedule was placed the inquiry: (17) Months unemployed during census year? The answers to this question were tabulated as follows (U.S. Census, 1890, Pop., Part II., p. cxxxviii.):—

NUMBER UNEMPLOYED.

In	Males. No.	Males. Per cent.[1]	Females. No.	Females. Per cent.[1]
All occupations	3,013,117	16·0	510,613	13·0
Agriculture	1,120,827	13·5	108,973	16·0
Professional service	54,654	8·6	87,920	28·2
Domestic and personal service	689,307	25·6	130,774	7·8
Trade and transportation	247,757	8·0	15,114	6·6
Manufacturing and mechanical industry	900,572	22·2	167,832	16·3

The above table would seem to show that 16 per cent. of the males and 13 per cent. of the females are out of work during a portion of the year. These results, or at least their interpretation, are extremely doubtful for the following reasons: (1) They refer only to the principal occupation. Men may, however, be working at some secondary occupation and thus not really be out of work. (2) It is doubtful how far "vacation time" was returned as unemployment. The large percentage of females under professional service returned as unemployed is explained as due to school teachers, who are normally unemployed during a portion of the year. But the number of female school teachers was 246,066, besides 34,519 female musicians and teachers of music, and 10,815 artists and teachers of art who are normally out of employment during a portion of the year. The question was not answered uniformly. A person paid by the year is not out of employment during his vacation. Nor is a farmer out of employment during a portion of the year, although a farm labourer hired by the month might return himself as unemployed

[1] The percentages are percentages of the total number, ten years of age and over, engaged in gainful occupations.

during a portion of the year. This ambiguity vitiates the whole table. (3) It is a general rule of statistics that the answer to a question which requires deliberation, *i.e.* deliberate memory and calculation, will be more or less uncertain. When we consider that many of the schedules are filled out by wives for their husbands, children for their parents, neighbours or house-keepers for occupants of the house, the answers would naturally be in many cases inaccurate and uncertain.

This last consideration applies especially to the return of number of months out of employment, and vitiates the following table (U.S. Census, 1890: Pop., Part II., p. cxxxvii):—

UNEMPLOYED DURING CENSUS YEAR.

Time.	Males.		Females.	
1— 3 months . .	1,553,759	51·6 per cent.	265,106	51·9 per cent.
4— 6 „ . .	1,179,426	39·1 „	188,992	37·0 „
7—12 „ . .	279,932	9·3 „	56,515	11·1 „
		100·0 „		100·0 „

The Massachusetts Bureau of Statistics of Labour (Report for 1887) attempted from the State census returns of 1885 to calculate the average amount of time lost during the year by all persons employed in gainful occupations. The returns showed that 29·6 per cent. of all persons engaged in gainful occupations were unemployed during some portion of the year. They were unemployed at their principal occupation on an average 4·11 months. If this amount of unemployment had been uniformly distributed among all persons engaged in gainful occupations, each one would have been unemployed an average of 1·22 months. In other words, in Massachusetts, one-third of all workers were unemployed one-third of their time; or on the average, persons in gainful occupations work a little less than eleven months during the year. There are some variations in different localities and in different occupations. In Boston, 81·6 per cent. were continuously employed, as against 70·4 per cent. in the Commonwealth. The same criticisms apply to this attempt as to that of the Federal census.

Number Unemployed at a given Date. The German officials took advantage of the Census of Occupations, June 14th, 1895, and of the regular census, December 2nd, 1895, to find out the number of persons actually idle so far as their principal occupation was concerned at two dates, one in summer and the other in winter. The result was as follows (Vierteljahrshefte zur Statistik des Deutschen Reichs, 1896, IV. Ergänzungsheft, p. 2):—

NUMBER OF PERSONS OUT OF EMPLOYMENT, GERMANY.

	On June 14th, 1895.	On December 2nd, 1895.
Men	218,603	553,578
Women	80,749	217,427
Total	299,352	771,005

The number in summer was only 0·6 per cent. of the total population, or 1·4 per cent. of the population in gainful occupations. In winter the number was 1·5 per cent. of the entire population, or 3·5 per cent. of the population in gainful occupations. This last percentage would seem to indicate the usual amount of unemployment at the worst season of the year.

The number in winter is 157 per cent. greater than in summer. This is due to the fact that winter interrupts agriculture and building, and much work of a casual nature. The relation of the trades to each other is shown in the following table:—

PERCENTAGE OF UNEMPLOYED TO TOTAL NUMBER IN EACH INDUSTRY.

	Summer.	Winter.
Agriculture	0·7	3·6
Industry	2·8	6·0
Trade	2·5	3·9
Casual labourers	2·8	5·8

Unemployment is greatest in industry and among casual labourers. The greatest increase in unemployment owing to winter weather is found in agriculture, where unemployment in winter was five times as great as in summer.[1]

The duration of unemployment could only be ascertained by asking how long unemployment had lasted up to the day of the census. The returns were classified as follows:—

Time.	June Census.	December Census.
1 day	1·1 per cent.	2·5 per cent.
2— 7 days	9·9 ,,	12·3 ,,
8—14 ,, ...	20·6 ,,	25·9 ,,
15—28 ,, ...	11·7 ,,	17·1 ,,
29—90 ,, ...	23·8 ,,	24·6 ,,
Over 90 ,, ...	16·5 ,,	10·6 ,,
Unknown	16·4 ,,	7·0 ,,
	100·0 ,,	100·0 ,,

Other facts brought out by this investigation were:—that in summer 40 per cent. of the unemployment was said to be due to sickness; in winter only 28 per cent. The number unemployed of the age of twenty to thirty was greater than their relative number in the total population would justify, and was probably due to the fact that single men have less stability in work than married men. The number of unemployed was greater in large cities than in medium sized and small cities and the country, relatively to the number of the population.

The German census seems to be correct in method and to give instructive results. It cannot give the total amount of unemployment, but it asks a simple question which can be answered definitely.

Fluctuation in Employment. The number of persons employed varies from month to month owing to seasons, and from year to year owing to commercial causes. The Massachusetts Statistics of Manufactures attempt to gauge annually the amount of variation by giving (from employers'

[1] Some particular occupations showed very high percentages of unemployment in winter, not due to sickness: sea and coast shipping, 27·5 per cent.; day labourers, 20·8 per cent.; stone masons, 18·7 per cent.; bricklayers, 18 per cent. These are all seasonal employments.

returns) the average, lowest and highest number employed during the year in the principal industries. For instance, for 1897 we have:—

Number of establishments	4,695
Average number of persons employed	313,816
Number employed, at period of smallest employment	260,970
Ditto, at period of greatest employment	363,774
Excess of greatest over smallest number	102,804

This would seem to show that there were 100,000 persons who find employment when the factories are most active, but who do not find employment when the factories are least active. Of course, some may be transferred from one industry to another, and others seek work only in the active period, but the fluctuation is very extraordinary—30 per cent. of the maximum number employed at the busiest season.[1]

The cause of these great fluctuations in many industries is the seasons. Some industries can be pursued in summer,

[1] The annual returns apply only to large factories. For all wage-earners in manufacturing industries, the Massachusetts census of 1895 showed that the average number of persons employed was 432,272, ranging from 357,249, the number employed at the periods of employment of the smallest number, to 518,744, the number employed at the periods of employment of the greatest number, the excess of greatest over smallest number being 161,495. If we take the number of persons employed at the period of greatest employment as 100, then it would appear that 31 persons out of every 100 are unemployed at some time during the year. The percentages for different cities were as follows: in Boston, 34·2; in Fall River, 14·4; in Worcester, 30·9; in Lowell, 19; in New Bedford, 16; in Lawrence, 21·7; in Lynn, 43; in Haverhill, 52; in Brockton, 28. It is clear from these figures that the range of unemployment was much narrower in Fall River, New Bedford, Lowell and Lawrence, which are leading textile cities, than in Lynn, Haverhill, or Brockton, which are leading boot and shoe cities, or than it was in Boston or Worcester, which are cities of diversified industry. (Census of Massachusetts, 1895, Vol. V., p. 263.)

The method is of doubtful value, because it is evident that the same person might be employed at one time in one industry and at another time in another industry, thus increasing the maximum number and depressing the minimum number employed.

The limited value of the method was pointed out in the General Report on the Wages of the Manual Labour Class in the United Kingdom, 1893.

but not in winter. In other industries the demand comes at certain seasons, and just before the demand there is plenty of employment, while after it there is less. For example, in Massachusetts, in 1897, the brick, tile and sewer pipe industry employed 2,398 persons in July, and only 588 in February. In the manufacture of earthen, plaster and stoneware the maximum employment was in September; in glue, isinglass, and starch it was in February; in straw and palm leaf goods there were 4,014 employees in March, and only 786 in July; that was on account of the season. In the case of large manufactures these monthly fluctuations are often insignificant in comparison with the general condition of business. That is strikingly shown in the statistics of unemployment in the nine principal industries during the year 1893. In the boot and shoe industry, the greatest amount of employment is usually in August and September, while in 1893 it was in March; by November of that year the number employed was 20 per cent. less than the maximum employment. In the cotton goods manufacture the maximum employment is usually in November and December, while in 1893 it was in May, and by September the number employed was 22 per cent. less than the maximum. In the worsted goods manufacture the maximum employment is usually in December, but in 1893 it was in May, and by September the number employed was 28 per cent. less than the maximum. The seasonal fluctuations and the effect of the year 1893 in the case of all industries in Massachusetts is shown in the following table :—[1]

PERCENTAGES OF UNEMPLOYMENT (Massachusetts).

	1889.	1890.	1891.	1892.	1893.
January . . .	3·42	5·10	1·57	4·45	2·61
February . . .	2·13	3·71	1·11	2·98	1·98
March	1·61	2·71	0·72	2·07	0·91

[1] Mass. Bureau Labour Statistics, Rept., 1893, p. 124. The maximum number employed during each year is taken as the normal number, and indicated by (—). The percentage of unemployment is calculated from this as base.

PERCENTAGES OF UNEMPLOYMENT (Massachusetts)—*continued.*

	1889.	1890.	1891.	1892.	1893.
April	1·52	2·77	0·30	1·01	—
May	1·38	2·50	—	1·10	0·37
June	1·37	2·04	0·66	1·74	2·92
July	2·35	3·13	1·89	2·85	8·32
August	1·69	2·45	1·73	2·38	17·49
September . . .	0·53	1·05	0·83	0·95	22·33
October	—	—	0·30	0·07	15·27
November . . .	0·30	0·76	1·02	—	15·14
December . . .	0·96	1·42	0·76	0·24	14·78

In ordinary years the lack of employment in different industries is spread over the year, giving quite uniform results. The exceptional character of the year 1893 is shown by the fact that while usually the percentage of unemployment in September is less than one per cent., in that year it ran over 22 per cent.

The Board of Trade in England receives returns every month from the principal trade unions, giving the number unemployed at the end of each month. For the building trades the greatest amount of unemployment is in January and February; while for the printing and kindred trades it falls in October, and in the engineering, metal and shipbuilding trades, in October and November. The fluctuations from year to year are shown in the following table (Annual Reports, Labour Dept. Board of Trade):—

CYCLICAL FLUCTUATIONS IN EMPLOYMENT. ENGLAND. MEAN PERCENTAGE UNEMPLOYED.

	Engineering, Metal and Shipbuilding Trades.	Building Trades.	Printing and Kindred Trades.	All Unions making returns.
1887	9·4	5·9	2·9	8·2
1888	6·0	5·5	2·4	4·9
1889	2·3	3·3	2·5	2·1
1890	2·2	2·2	2·2	2·1
1891	4·1	2·5	4·0	3·5
1892	7·7	3·0	4·3	6·3
1893	11·4	3·8	4·1	7·5
1894	11·3	4·1	5·7	6·9
1895	8·2	3·8	4·9	5·8
1896	4·2	1·8	4·3	3·4

These averages are supposed to represent the number out of employment at any one time. The different years are not strictly comparable, because the number of trade unions making returns from year to year is not the same. But the returns represent the chance of employment, so to speak, during the different years. Of course they apply to a comparatively small body of skilled men, and the percentage of unemployment among unskilled labour would probably be greater.

Amount of Time Lost through Unemployment. General statistics of the amount of time unemployed during the year, as we have seen above, are worthless. For particular industries we may have more accurate returns. An example is given by the Department of Labour in England, which gives the returns from the Manchester and Leeds branch of the Amalgamated Society of Engineers, based on the entries in the vacant books. Some of the facts are as follows (Report, 1896–97, p. 72):—

	1887.	1888.	1889.	1890.	1891.	1892.
Percentage of members unemployed for *some time* during the year	42·2	34·5	19·8	24·6	43·7	42·2
Percentage of members unemployed at *same time* during year	8·1	6·4	2·2	2·1	4·6	10·2
Number of working days lost per member	24·7	19·6	6·5	6·5	14·0	31·2
Average number of working days lost by unemployed members	58·3	56·9	33·0	26·4	32·1	73·8

This table is interesting as showing the fluctuations from year to year in a highly skilled and prosperous trade. In the best years one-fourth of the members may expect to lose some time, and in bad years this proportion mounts to 44 per cent. Taking the mean of the five years, it appears that 67 per cent. of the members lost no time; 7·1 per cent. lost one day and under one week; 12 per cent. lost one week and under one month; 7·7 per cent. lost one month and under three months; 6·3 per cent. lost over three months.

Another method of tracing fluctuations of employment in particular industries is by giving the number of days during which factories are run or mines worked. Thus the Massachusetts Statistics of Manufactures gives every year the average number of days that the enterprises included in the returns were in actual operation. In 1897, for instance, the number of working days exclusive of Sundays and seven legal holidays was 307. The average number of days in operation for all industries was 283·3; in worsted goods it ran as high as 294·4; in carpetings as low as 243·7. It is to be noticed that this is a weighted average, each establishment being weighted according to the average number of employees.

The Department of Labour, Board of Trade, gives the average number of days per week that coal mines are in operation in Great Britain.

Unemployment during Special Times of Distress. It is very important for the community to know how many men are out of employment during a temporary commercial depression, in order to adopt adequate measures of relief. The machinery for securing such data is utterly inadequate, as was shown in the United States during the winter of 1893–94. Various estimates were made at the time by private individuals, city officials, officers of charity organisations, &c., but they differed widely from each other. Mr. C. C. Closson, on the basis of replies to 300 circular letters, estimated that in 38 American cities there were 491,000 persons out of employment; Bradstreet's estimate for the same cities was 581,950. Closson's estimate for New York City was 85,000, Bradstreet's 80,000, while the police census showed only 67,280. It would seem as if some more efficient machinery might be devised for ascertaining promptly and accurately the facts of unemployment.[1]

[1] Quarterly Journal of Economics, Vol. VIII., 1893–94.

In England we find similar loose estimates. In 1887 a tabulation of the statements of men living in certain districts of London covered 29,451 men in 35 industries.[1] Of these 27 per cent. were out of work, and 53 per cent. reported that they had been out of work during the last five months.

The Select Committee on Distress from Want of Employment[2] was unable to form any estimate of the usual amount of unemployment. "On the one hand, Mr. Keir-Hardie has stated his opinion that, excluding paupers and persons idle through frost, the number of the unemployed in the United Kingdom may be put down at 1,750,000, and he estimated that the number of unemployed and the dependent upon them would amount to 6,000,000." On the other hand, the Rev. W. Tozer estimates the number at 280,000 in normal times. He takes the number of the labouring class at 13,000,000 and deducts 2½ million agricultural labourers and 2½ million domestic servants, leaving 8,000,000 manual labourers. Applying the trade union percentage (3½) of unemployment to this number would give 280,000. He considers that one half of these consists of "the old, the infirm, the physically and mentally incapable," so that the number of "capable, willing, sober and industrious unemployed" does not exceed 140,000. This, of course, is a minimum number, for the percentage of unemployment would be apt to be greater outside the trade union than within it. These extravagant estimates either way show us how far we are from accurate information in regard to what is one of the most important questions of society, viz., how far is labour-force actually at work?

Scientific Tests.

No analysis of the population according to productive power can, from the nature of things, be very precise. We

[1] Parl. Bluebook, 1887 [c.—5228].

[2] Parl. Bluebook (321), 1896.

can, of course, classify the people according to age and sex, but that gives us no information in regard to the strength and intelligence of the individual workman. Still further, the productive power of labour depends very much upon the machinery by which it is applied. The question of employment or non-employment is another one which it is difficult to treat statistically, because a great deal of unemployment escapes observation. We can only get a general notion of what is normal unemployment and of the effect of commercial crises and hard times upon the number of men at work.

Among the technical difficulties of the subject the greatest is connected with the classification of occupations. It would seem to be a very easy matter for each person to fill out a schedule showing what his occupation is. But when it comes to actual classification the difficulties are very considerable. The first is that many persons pursue two or more occupations, as, for instance, a man may be a storekeeper and a postmaster; a farmer during the summer, a fisherman during the winter; a clergyman and a school-teacher. The rule laid down in the English Census was: firstly, that a mechanical handicraft or constructive occupation should invariably be preferred to a shopkeeping occupation; secondly, that if one of the diverse occupations seemed of more importance than the others, it should be selected; and thirdly, that in default of such apparent difference the occupation first mentioned should be taken, on the ground that a person will be likely to mention his main business first.

The second difficulty is to determine whether we shall choose to classify persons or occupations. If a man is employed as a carpenter in a cotton mill, shall he be classified as a carpenter or as a cotton mill operative? Does a bank clerk come under the head of commercial clerks, or under that of banking? Should railroad labourers be classified under the general heading labourer, or under the head railroad employees? The difficulty is that there are really two systems of classification, one of individual occupation and the other of trades and industries. Either one is perfectly logical and each is desirable. It is important to know how many cabinet makers there are in the United States, and also whether those cabinet makers are employed in making furniture, in finishing houses, railway cars or pianofortes. So a painter is a painter, whether he is employed in painting houses, or agricultural machines or ships. On the other hand, it is interesting, for the purpose of tracing the progress of industry, to know how many men are actually engaged in cotton mills from decade to decade, whether they are machine tenders, common labourers or artisans employed in making repairs. The industry as a whole gives employment to that total number of men. What we really want, therefore, is a census both of occupations and of men employed in industries. At first sight, it would seem comparatively easy to classify the figures in both ways. This, however, is rendered difficult by the inconsistencies of the returns, a railroad labourer sometimes being returned as a labourer, sometimes as a railroad employee. The result is that our actual classification confuses the two things. This confusion is shown in the classification of occupations in the United States Census. Under the head of Manufacturing and Mechanical Industries we have makers of agricultural implements (not otherwise classified), but a note explains that these persons are generally returned as blacksmiths, carpenters, iron and steel workers, machinists, painters, woodworkers, &c. We have under one head blacksmiths, and under another head apprentices to blacksmiths. We have under one head printers, lithographers and pressmen, but in addition we have under other heads compositors, electrotypers, and stereotypers. All of these, evidently, belong to the printing trade. On the other hand, the cotton mill operatives, the silk mill operatives, and the woollen mill operatives seem to be generally returned in one body. Under the head of domestic and personal service there are returned nearly two million labourers. It is probable that most of these should have been either under agricultural labourers or connected with specific trades. Under the head of Trade and Transportation we have the heading, clerks and copyists, irrespective of where they may be employed. But in addition to this heading, we have stenographers and typewriters, bookkeepers and accountants.

How uncertain the classification is may be seen by the changes which were made from 1880 to 1890. These changes are summarised as follows:—First: Fishermen and oystermen, lumbermen and raftsmen, miners, quarrymen and woodchoppers, were transferred from "Manufacturing and Mechanical Industries" to "Agriculture, Fisheries, and Mining." Second: saloon-keepers, bar-tenders, stewards and stewardesses, and employees in warehouses were transferred from "Trade and Transportation," and engineers and firemen (not locomotive) from "Manufacturing and Mechanical Industries" to "Domestic and Personal Service." Third: collectors and claim agents, auctioneers, livery-stable keepers, clerks and copyists not otherwise described, clerks in government offices, clerks in hotels and restaurants, hostlers and messengers, were transferred from "Domestic and Personal Services," and clerks and bookkeepers in manufacturing establishments and rag-pickers were transferred from "Manufacturing and Mechanical Industries" to "Trade and Transportation." Fourth: whitewashers were transferred from "Domestic and Personal Service" to "Manufacturing and Mechanical Industries."

These changes made a difference in the summing up of occupations in 1880 of 334,131 in "Agriculture, Fisheries and Mining"; of 32,407 in "Domestic and Personal Service"; of 56,225 in "Trade and Transportation"; and of 422,763 in "Manufacturing and Mechanical Industries." These examples are sufficient to show that the classification is a confused one, sometimes following out the line of occupations, sometimes that of trades. The result, of course, is that it is difficult to use the figures for the purpose of comparing the increase or decrease of persons employed in particular occupations from decade to decade.

In England, we have precisely the same difficulties, and very large numbers of the labouring class were vaguely and indefinitely returned as labourer, artisan, mechanic, apprentice, factory-hand, &c. The changes that were made from 1871 to 1891 are described in the Bluebook, Occupations of the People (468), 1895.

In the actual classification of occupations an approach to a scientific system is made in the English Census. For instance, under Industrial Class is put, first, Books, Prints and Maps. Under this head are arranged (under the subdivision Books) publisher, bookseller, librarian, bookbinder, printer, newspaper agent, newsroom keeper; and (under Prints and Maps) lithographer, copper and steel plate printer, map and print colourer and seller. This is an attempt to classify persons according to the nature of their industry.

In this uncertainty of classification in the particular countries, it is evident that international comparison is extremely hazardous. The International Statistical Institute, under the leadership of Dr. Jacques Bertillon, has proposed a general system of classification under which all national classifications might easily be brought. He proposes a series of three nomenclatures, the first having 61 rubrics, the second being expanded into 206 rubrics, and the third into 499. Each statistician would be at liberty to have as many subdivisions as he liked, 61, 206, or 499, but in grouping them he should follow the above system. In that way uniformity in the composition of the grand groups would be attained.[1]

[1] Bulletin de l'Institut international de Statistique, Vol. VIII., Part I., 1895, p. 226.

Reflective Analysis.

There is evidently no exact connection between the number of the population and the productive power of a nation. More depends upon the quality of the labourer and the way in which labour is applied than upon the mere number of people or the quantity of crude muscular force. Ireland contains one-eighth of the population of the United Kingdom, but has only one-twentieth of the wealth, and probably less than one-twentieth of the annual income. In Ireland, too, we have had a most astonishing fluctuation in population from four millions in 1801, to eight millions in 1841, and back to four millions in 1891. Wealth does not seem to have fluctuated in the same proportion, for the population of 1841 was certainly worse off than that of 1801, and the population of 1891 is probably better off than that of 1841.

In a progressive country, wealth increases faster than population. From 1875 to 1885, the population of the United Kingdom increased 11 per cent., but wealth probably increased at a much greater ratio. *Per capita* wealth is greater at each succeeding decade. This means that the quality of labour and its method of application is more important than mere numbers. England's industrial supremacy depends upon her trained and disciplined force of labourers and the capital which supplies them with the best means of production. As long as quality of labour and capital remain intact, an increasing population may be employed and add more than proportionally to wealth ; while if skill and energy decay and capital is lacking, increased quantity of labour would only be a burden. The question of population has been too much emphasised in political economy, while in socialistic schemes the question of quality of labour and the growth of capital has not received sufficient attention. The fundamental questions of political economy are: What will inspire the labour-force of a community with skill, energy, intelligence, and trustworthiness, and what will enable this labour-force to be applied with the greatest effectiveness. Modern orthodox political economy answers the latter question by the glorification of the entrepreneur, the captain of industry,—but that is only half an answer. The socialists pretend to answer the first by their schemes of equality or at least distributive justice, but that is less than half an answer. The modern community must find an answer to both questions if it is to continue to progress.

The question of quality being so important in labour-force, it would seem that any analysis of quantity, such as number of adult males, the number in particular occupations, &c., would be altogether useless. For short periods of time and restricted areas, we may assume quality and method of application to remain unchanged, and thus our quantitative measurements have some significance. The rapidity of the growth of the United States has been due not only to the virgin soil and the abundance of its natural resources, but also to the effectiveness of the labour-force supplied by immigration. This labour-force was composed most largely of adult males in the period of greatest physical strength. It was the kind of labour most needed for the development of a new country. It was under the direction of men of skill and energy, with capital supplied from older communities or accumulated out of current profits. It is not surprising that the country made enormous progress in the accumulation of wealth. No such effective labour-force has ever been at the service of a community before, and it is not probable that it will ever be again. For the future of the United States a significant change will take place. With increasing population, the proportionate importance of immigration will be apt to diminish, and the relative number of women and children in the community will increase. The relation of productive to unproductive population will approach that of older countries. The man will be obliged to support a larger number of dependents. The relative quantity of labour-force will be less. Another consideration is that with the development of the country, mere crude labour-force will be less needed. Two lines of thought are suggested by these facts. The first is the same as that mentioned above, viz. that quality of labour and means of applying it are the vital issues of the future. The second is that we have here a test for estimating the value of immigration and for guiding immigration policy. Crude manual labour is less needed; skill, intelligence, and trustworthiness are of increasing value. Any restriction or control of immigration should take account of this. Our statistics of the favourite occupations of particular nationalities are a partial guide to an estimate of the influence and value of that particular immigration.

A complete analysis of the labour-force of a community according to occupations would enable us to detect and appreciate the changes in industrial organisation which are constantly occurring. It is these changes which give rise to economic and social problems, and which result in those dislocations of the social organisation, manifesting themselves in hardship and suffering of particular classes, in vain struggles to retain economic position, in discontent, protest, and sometimes revolution. If we could discern exactly what changes were going on, we could often adapt ourselves to them, or at least submit to the inevitable. The general statistics seem to show a decreased labour-force applied to agriculture and an increased amount utilised in trade and transportation and in manufacturing and mechanical industries. This means concentration of population in cities, production on a large scale, dependence of workmen upon employers, a numerous industrial class,—in short, an industrial democracy. We must adjust our political and social institutions to this kind of population.

Increase or decrease of the number of persons in particular occupations, as in the cotton industry in England, should serve as a guide to practical questions of national policy as well as to the conduct of business and the policy of trade unions and labour organisations. Our statistics of the employment of women and children from time to time, in various occupations and among different classes of the population, enable us to form an idea of the practicability and success of that policy which demands that married women shall be kept at home and that children shall receive an opportunity for physical and mental development. The statistics are reassuring on this point.

The great hardships of the modern industrial system fall upon the workmen in the shape of uncertainty of employment and loss of employment by the introduction of machinery, and the substitution of women, children, and labour with low standard of living. Our statistics of unemployment seem to show that the first evil has been exaggerated. The other question awaits more refined statistics of occupations.

CHAPTER IV.

LAND AS FACTOR OF PRODUCTION.

Economic Purpose.

Economic Theory.[1] Land is the second factor of production. It is the passive instrument upon which labour is expended, or (if we include natural forces under land) the blind force which man directs toward the accomplishment of certain ends as a substitute for his own labour. The analysis of land as a so-called factor of production resolves itself into mere description of the instrument and the way it responds to the action of the other factors. We observe, for instance, that land is of different kinds, fitted for different purposes, *e. g.* arable, pasture, and forest land; that it is of different degrees of fertility owing to different physical and chemical composition, exposure, situation, &c.; and that there is an elastic limit to its productive power. Hence is formulated the law of diminishing return from land with increased application of labour and capital. All of these things are important, for they mark the ultimate limit of population and of wealth; and, under the régime of private property, they affect the distribution of wealth by creating rent. It is therefore not without profit that political economy dwells upon these characteristics of land as a factor of production.

In practical economic life, the character of the land and the use made of it by any particular community is a fact of very great interest. Land becomes then limited in quantity and quality. It determines the total amount of the product.

[1] Marshall, Principles of Economics, B. IV. Ch. 2.

Its character determines the occupations of masses of men. Changes in the use to which it is put affect the whole social organisation. The question of its control and cultivation becomes of prime importance. Legislation, or the action of the community, can often modify the form of its control or the method of cultivation. Politics needs here the guidance of practical political economy in order to learn what has been and will be the effect of political and social action.

The Office of Statistics. Can we get quantitative measurements which will be useful to us as indicating the importance of land as a factor of production and enable us to watch the effect of changes in its use? There are several directions in which statistics may be of service. They may be classified as follows:—

Territorial Statistics: or the area considered as *area.*

Agricultural Statistics: or the way in which the area is used for agricultural purposes.

Production Statistics: or the results of the use of the land.

Methods of Cultivation: or the relation of capital to land.

Tenure of Land: or the relation of labour to land.

The substitution of cultivation of land in one place or the cultivation of one kind of crop for another place or crop; *i. e.* the most general manifestion of the action of the law of diminishing returns.

When we ask what can statistics do in this connection, the answer is that they are mainly descriptive. We can enumerate the number of acres under cultivation or the number devoted to particular crops, the amount produced, the average per acre, &c. We can note the productive power of the land in respect to food-stuffs, live stock, mineral products, material for textiles, and other commodities. We can classify farms according to size and tenure. We can note differences in place as characterising agriculture and the use of land in different countries. We can note differences in time as indicative of changes in production.

Statistical Data.[1]

The quantity of wealth produced depends, in the first place, upon the amount and kind of land at the service of man, and secondly upon the purposes to which land is applied.

Territorial Statistics. Only about one-fourth of the surface of the earth is inhabitable land—the rest is water and wilderness. In civilised countries even, a portion of the surface is uninhabited or allowed to remain uncultivated. Thus, in the United States, the gross territory is calculated at 3,025,600 square miles, exclusive of Alaska, and the net land surface at 2,970,000 square miles, leaving about 55,600 square miles of water. Of this territory, not more than two-thirds is populated (more than two inhabitants to a square mile), *i.e.* 1,947,280 square miles. The amount of land under cultivation at particular periods has been influenced by the public

[1] *Bibliographical Note.* For territorial statistics of the United States see U.S. Census, 1890, Population, Part I. ; popular presentation of the same in Gannett, Building of a Nation: for acute criticism of United States census methods in calculating areas, see Willcox, Area and Population of United States at Eleventh Census (Amer. Econ. Assocn. : Econ. Studies, Vol. II., No. 4., 1898).

Agriculture: For area devoted to particular crops and yield of crops: For United States: U.S. Census, 1890, Vol. on Agriculture; Criticism of same by N. I. Stone, Statistics of Agriculture in the Federal Census (Amer. Econ. Assocn. Publications, New Series, No. 2, 1899). Annual Reports of the U.S. Department of Agriculture; Statistical Abstract of the United States. For England: Agricultural Returns for Great Britain, 1898; Statistical Abstract for the United Kingdom. For Germany: the Statistisches Jahrbuch; for complete harvest statistics for Germany: Vierteljahrshefte, Part III., p. 99, 1897. For Italy: Annuario Statistico. For France: Annuaire Statistique. For all countries: The British Statistical Abstract for Foreign Countries; the Statistical Abstract for India; and the Statistical Abstract for the Colonies. For international comparison of the production of cereals, see Beerbohm's Corn List.

Products from Land: Besides the statistical year books or abstracts mentioned above, see especially for international comparison: Neumann-Spallart, Übersichten der Weltwirtschaft, 1885–89, edited by Von Juraschek. For consumption of meat in cities see Statistisches Jahrbuch Deutscher Städte.

The reports of the Royal Commission on Agriculture, 1895–98, contain numerous valuable tables showing the production of wheat and other land policy. The gross territory has been greatly increased from time to time—by the Louisiana purchase, 1803 (1,171,931 square miles); by Florida, 1821 (59,268 square miles); by the annexation of Texas, 1845 (375,239 square miles); by the Mexican cession, 1848 (545,783 square miles); by the Gadsden purchase, 1853 (45,535 square miles); and finally by the purchase of Alaska, 1867 (570,000 square miles), not included in the above 3,025,600 square miles.

All the above additions increased the public land of the government, except Texas, which retained its public land, with the exception of certain areas in the North and West, which it sold to the United States for $16,000,000. These now form part of New Mexico, Colorado, and Kansas. The total area of public land, excluding Alaska, was approximately 1,440,000,000 acres. Of this area, the United States had, on June 30th, 1892, alienated 873,000,000 acres, leaving 567,000,000 acres. The principal purposes had been for:—

Homesteads	130,000,000	acres.
Cash sales	224,000,000	,,
R. R. grants patented	79,000,000	,,
Swamp lands to states	70,000,000	,,
Land bounties for military purposes . .	61,000,000	,,

---

cereals, acreage, price, number of live stock, price of meat, &c. For testimony of how agricultural statistics are gathered see evidence of Mr. T. H. Elliott, Vol. III., (c—7,400—III.) p. 101. See also testimony of Major Craigie in regard to consumption of meat, *Ibid.*, p. 221.

Size and Tenure of Farms: For United States see U.S. Census, 1890, Vol. on Agriculture; also Vol. on Home and Farm Proprietorship. For England: Returns as to Number and Size of Agricultural Holdings in Great Britain in 1895 (c.—8,243), 1896. For France: Statistique Agricole, Résultats généraux de l'Enquête décennale de 1892, 1897, quoted in Conrad's Jahrbücher, Jan. 1899, p. 87; for earlier figures, see De Foville, La France Économique, 1890; also the same author's Le Morcellement, 1885. For Germany, see Vierteljahrshefte. II. Ergänz. 1897, for the Agricultural Census of 1895. An elaborate study of the whole question of small farms with international comparisons has been made by Major P. G. Craigie in the Journal of the Royal Statistical Society, for March 1887, Vol. L., p. 86. For the question of tenancy in the United States, see N. I. Stone, Farm Tenures in the United States (Amer. Statistical Assocn. Publications, 1899).

Of the remainder left in the hands of the government, a large part, say 100,000,000 acres, consists of Indian reservations. Another part, 103,000,000 acres, has been granted to railroads, but not yet patented. Another part has been granted to settlers, but title not yet passed. With trifling exceptions, the agricultural land has passed from the hands of the government to private individuals.[1]

The result of this policy has been the rapid settlement of the territory of the United States. In 1790, only 29 per cent of the area was settled; in 1890, 54 per cent. The settled area has increased eight fold since 1790; the population, sixteen fold. On the whole, the increase of population has been twice that of land.

Agricultural Statistics: The Cultivated Area. Of the whole area of land in a country, only a portion is used directly for the purposes of production; this is the cultivated area, or the total area included in farms. Of the area included in farms, only a portion again (especially in the United States) is actually improved or really under cultivation. We have, therefore, two approximations: (1) The area of farms; (2) The improved land in farms. It is not pretended, of course, that these figures are exact. They do not rest upon any survey, but simply upon the statements of farmers. They are of interest as showing the process of taking up land in the United States and the changes going on from decade to decade.

Farm Land in the United States. In 1890, of the total land surface of the United States only 623,218,619 acres, or 32·8 per cent., were included in farms, and of this farm area only 357,616,755 acres, or 57·4 per cent. were returned as improved. The rest was forest or unimproved land. The result is that, of the total area of the United States, less than one-fifth is improved farming land. "Improved" has a wide meaning, including all land once cultivated unless afterwards actually abandoned, and all permanent meadow and pasture land.

[1] U. S. Census, 1890, Pop., Part I., p. xxxiv.; Gannett, The Building of a Nation, pp. 46, 49, and 66.

The statistics for 1880 and 1890 are as follows (U. S. Census, 1890, Agriculture, p. 3):—

	1880.	1890.	Increase.
Number of farms . .	4,008,907	4,564,641	13·86 per cent.
Area (acres) ,, . .	536,081,000	623,218,619	16·25 ,, ,,
Improved land . . .	284,771,042	357,616,755	25·58 ,, ,,
Unimproved land . .	251,310,793	265,601,864	5·69 ,, ,,

There are two influences determining the proportionate amount of improved land—one is the character of the territory, and the other is the newness of settlement. The interaction of these two influences is seen by an examination of the proportion of improved land to total area in different parts of the country. In the North Atlantic States, only two-fifths of the total area is improved; and in Maine, the proportion sinks to one-sixth. The land is settled but not very fertile. In the prairie states, Illinois and Iowa, nearly three-fourths, in Ohio more than two-thirds, and in Indiana nearly three-fifths of the area is improved. Here we have fertility and population combined. In Arizona, Washington and Colorado, only one acre in twenty is cultivated. Here we have sparse population and much waste land.

Unimproved Land in Farms. An enormous amount of the land included in farms is not improved. It only nominally belongs to the cultivated area. For the different sections the proportion varies, seeming to show great differences in methods of cultivation. The following table shows the proportion of land in farms still unimproved for the different sections, the corresponding figures for 1850 being added to show that agriculture is now becoming more intensive in the United States:—

PERCENTAGE OF UNIMPROVED LAND IN FARMS.

	1890.	1850.
The United States	42·6	61·5
North Atlantic Division	32·5	38·4
South ,, ,, ...	58·4	67·9
North Central ,, ...	28·2	57·4
South ,, ,, ...	57·6	71·6
Western ,, ...	51·3	92·5

The movement in the North Central and the Western States is very marked, showing how large areas are taken possession of and then gradually improved. The several states show some striking contrasts. In the prairie states, very little land in farms is left unimproved (*e.g.* Illinois, 15·8 per cent.; Iowa, 16·6 per cent.). Where there are forests or swamps, a great deal is left unimproved (*e.g.*, Maine and New Hampshire, 50 per cent.; North Carolina, 65·4 per cent.; Florida, 68·8 per cent.). Rather curious is the amount in some southern states (Alabama and Mississippi, 61·1 per cent.).[1]

Arable, Pasture, and Forest Land. If we try to make an international comparison of the proportion of cultivated land, we shall find that it depends mainly upon the topographical character of the country. But still further the character of the country determines the particular purpose for which the cultivated land is used. We can therefore proceed a step further in our classification and distinguish between arable land, meadow and pasture land, vineyards, forest land, and uncultivated or waste land. There are some difficulties in the classification, for the same land may be used one year as arable and the second year as meadow land. But the broad lines of classification are sufficiently distinct and show us in a general way the use which each country makes of its soil.

De Foville gives the following figures (percentages) for the different countries of Europe:—[2]

	Arable.	Meadow and pasture.	Vineyard.	Forest.	Uncultivated.
Belgium	59·5	13·8	—	16·8	9·4
France	53·7	15·0	5·3	17·0	9·0
Germany	51·2	11·5	—	27·2	9·9
Great Britain	39·0	27·9	—	4·7	28·4
Hungary	35·9	25·4	1·4	27·1	10·2
Holland	32·8	37·0	—	7·2	23·0
Austria	31·4	28·3	0·8	32·6	6·9
Italy	29·2	25·8	6·6	18·1	19·3
Ireland	28·6	56·3	—	1·7	13·4

[1] For details, see U. S. Census, 1890: Agriculture, p. 84. Abstract of the U. S. Census, 1890, p. 93.

[2] La France économique, 1890, p. 93.

Very marked differences are observable in this table. In Belgium, France and Germany, more than one-half of the land is under the plough. In Ireland more than one-half of the land is meadow and pasture. In Austria, nearly one-third of the land is forest. In Great Britain, 28·4 per cent. of the land is still uncultivated, being probably the mountainous country of Wales and Scotland. And even in Holland, 23 per cent. of the land is reported as uncultivated.

In Germany a distinction is made between meadow and pasture land. In 1893 out of one hundred acres of land, 48·8 were arable, garden, or vineyard; 11 were meadow land; 5·3 were pasture land; 25·8 were forest and timber land; 9·1 were house and court room. This shows that Germany on the whole has nearly one-half of her whole territory under the plough. The proportions differ, naturally, in different parts of the kingdom. In Posen 62·4 per cent., in the province of Saxony 60·9 per cent., and in the Kingdom of Saxony 57 per cent. was ploughed land.[1]

In a new country the uncultivated and forest lands are of special interest. In the United States the greater portion of the territory was once covered with forest, and it is estimated that nearly one-third of the land is still forest land. The Tenth Census of the United States made an elaborate investigation of the forests and published maps showing the territory covered by them, the kind of trees and their density. The last item was rather an interesting statistical experiment. The forests were classified as yielding one cord of wood to the acre, one to two cords, and from three to five cords. Special maps were also made with reference to the lumber industry, and cartograms showing for different sections whether wood or coal was used most for fuel.[2]

Acreage devoted to particular Crops. The analysis of the purpose for which land is used may be carried one step further by estimating from year to year the amount of land devoted

[1] Stat. Jahrbuch für das Deutsche Reich, 1895, p. 14.

[2] U.S. Census, 1880: Volume on Forests.

to each kind of crop. These estimates change frequently, but they are interesting in themselves and taken from period to period they show the direction of changes in agriculture. The following table shows the acreage of the principal crops of the United States for 1880 and 1890 (U.S. Census, 1890: Agriculture, p. 86):—

	1890.	1880.
Cereals.	Acres.	Acres.
Indian corn	72,087,752	62,368,504
Wheat	33,579,514	35,430,333
Oats	28,320,677	16,144,593
Barley	3,220,834	1,997,727
Rye	2,171,604	1,842,233
Fibres.		
Cotton	20,175,270	14,480,019
Flax	1,318,698	—
Hay (acres mown)	52,948,797	30,631,054
Rice	161,312	174,173
Tobacco	695,301	638,841

It will be seen from this table that the acreage of almost every important crop increased from 1880 to 1890, with the exception of wheat. That crop seems to be stationary or going backward. The most important centre of the corn culture is the North Central States which contained more than 44 million out of the 72 million acres devoted to corn in 1890. The North Central States also had 22 million out of the 33 million acres which were devoted to wheat; and 32 million out of 53 million acres devoted to hay. The South Central States, naturally, have the greater portion of the land devoted to cotton.[1]

The countries of Europe have statistics similar to those of the United States of the area of land under different kinds of cultivation. The agricultural returns for Great Britain and Ireland give the following figures for the year

[1] The estimated acreage for 1897 was as follows:—Wheat, 39,465,066; Indian corn, 80,005,051; oats, 25,730,375; barley, 2,719,116; rye, 1,703,561. (Agricultural Returns for Great Britain, &c. [c-9304], 1899, p. 240.)

1898 (Journal Royal Statistical Society, December, 1898, p. 726):—

	Eng. & Wales.	Scotland.	Ireland.	United Kingdom including Isle of Man & Channel Islands.
Total area, acres . . .	37,315,735	19,455,788	20,706,258	77,671,114
Total acreage under crops	27,584,264	4,892,767	15,191,152	47,792,474
Corn crops	6,128,911	1,271,424	1,390,941	8,816,756
Green ,, ...	2,513,878	619,643	1,105,026	4,261,492
Clover and grasses under rotation . . .	3,303,256	1,607,933	1,252,889	6,210,851
Permanent pastures and grass not broken up .	15,178,288	1,381,214	11,390,950	27,978,809

In this distribution of land, the large amount under permanent pasture and grass in both England and Ireland, is significant. In Scotland, the small amount under crops is noticeable. In Ireland, more than two-thirds of the acreage under crops is pasture and grass land.

The total area in the United Kingdom devoted to the cultivation of corn crops is diminishing. In 1875 it was 11,399,030 acres; in 1885, 10,015,355 acres; in 1895, 8,865,338 acres.

The area of wheat in 1875 was 3,514,088 acres; in 1895, it was 1,456,042 acres, showing a diminution of two million acres in twenty years. In 1898, however, it had recovered to 2,158,465 acres.

The process of diminution went on rapidly from 1871 to 1891, and the relations in Great Britain alone are shown in the following table (Journal Royal Stat. Soc. March, 1892, p. 122):—

Out of 1000 Acres of Arable Land.

	1871.	1881.	1891.
Total corn crops	526	504	481
Wheat	194	160	140
Barley	130	139	128
Oats	148	165	176
Clover and rotation grasses	237	247	286

Another method of showing the change is as follows (Commission on Agriculture, Vol. III, p. 620):—

WHEAT AREA, ENGLAND.

10 years,	1872-1881	equal	100
5 ,,	1881-1886	,,	82·1 per cent.
5 ,,	1887-1891	,,	75·9 ,,
3 ,,	1892-1894	,,	63·5 ,,
Decrease whole period			36·5 ,,

This constant abandonment of wheat cultivation reveals the difficulty with which the English farmer has had to contend in low-prices, and explains the enormous falling in rents which has crippled the English landlord.

The statistics of Germany show remarkable stability in the area devoted to the principal crops. Compare the following figures (1 hectare = 2·47 acres) (Stat. Jahrbuch, 1898, p. 22):—

Area devoted to	1896.	1886.
Rye	5,982,180 hectares.	5,838,902 hectares.
Wheat	1,926,885 ,,	1,916,633 ,,
Barley	1,676,329 ,,	1,731,480 ,,
Potatoes	3,052,790 ,,	2,915,747 ,,
Oats	3,979,643 ,,	3,806,535 ,,
Hay-land	5,909,693 ,,	5,909,701 ,,

Production Statistics: The Yield of Land. The preceding tables showed the number of acres devoted to the various kinds of crops. Another method of estimating the agricultural productivity is by giving the gross yield of each kind of crop. An analysis of this sort is undertaken by the Eleventh Census in the volume on agriculture and is interesting and instructive both as informing us concerning the agricultural resources of the United States and as an example of statistical method in trying to make comprehensible the main facts in regard to production of land.

Cereals. Taking, for example, the production of cereals in the United States, statistical analysis may be extended on the following lines:

(1) Total cereal production.

(2) Production of different sorts of cereals, absolute figures and percentages.

(3) Changes in production at successive periods, *i.e.*, comparison in time.

(4) Production of different sections, *i.e.*, comparison in space.

Numbers 3 and 4 can be displayed in a variety of ways:—absolute production; yield per square mile of territory; number of bushels to the acre; number of bushels per acre of improved land; and *per capita* production.

An analysis carried out on the above lines for the total cereal crop and then for each kind of crop gives us the best possible picture of the main features of agricultural production in the United States. The total cereal production at different decades is shown in the following table. (U.S. Census, 1890, Agriculture, p. 6):—

Years.	Total cereal production. (bushels.)	Percentage of increase by decades.	Number of bushels per capita of total population.
1889	3,518,816,904	30·4	56·2
1879	2,697,580,229	94·4	53·8
1869	1,387,299,153	12·0	36·0
1859	1,239,039,947	42·8	39·4
1849	867,453,967	40·9	37·4
1839	615,525,302	—	36

The last two columns of this table show an astonishing increase in cereal production from 1869 to 1879. The increase during the last decade was not so great, but it more than kept pace with the growth of the population, the total production *per capita* being 56 bushels in 1889, as compared with 53 bushels in 1879. The Census continues:—

"In regard to distribution by locality, the centre of cereal production appears to have been gradually moving Westward since the first settlement of the country, and in advance of the centre of population. The Eleventh Census discloses the fact that while the centre of population has advanced only as far as South Eastern Indiana, that of cereal production has crossed the Mississippi River."

At present the great cereal producing regions are the North Central and Western States. Nearly one-fifth of the total area is found in the States of Illinois and Iowa; the addition of Kansas and Missouri raises the proportion to over one-third; while the further addition of Nebraska, Indiana and Ohio, making seven States in all, accounts for practically one-half of the total cereal acreage of the country. If we take the total production, the figures for the States will be somewhat different, owing to the different yield per acre of different kinds of crops. The centre of cereal production will still remain in the Northern half of the Mississippi valley, more than one-half of the total product being contributed by the five States of Iowa, Illinois, Kansas, Nebraska, and Missouri.[1]

As the cultivation of cereals is concentrated in a small group of States, so there is a concentration of production within the limits of many individual States. In Michigan, twenty-five out of eighty-four counties produced 82 per cent. of the corn, 74 per cent. of the oats, and 79 per cent. of the wheat. In Wisconsin, sixteen out of sixty-eight counties produced 89 per cent. of the barley, 66 per cent. of the corn, 53 per cent. of the oats, and 59 per cent. of the wheat of the State. In California, eight out of fifty-three counties contained over three-fifths of the cereal acreage of the State.[2]

The Census carries out an elaborate analysis of the distribution of wheat, oats, and corn, according to altitude, mean annual temperature, and mean annual rainfall. The figures are not particularly instructive. The greatest production is found at an altitude of 500 to 1,000 feet, which includes, of course, the great prairie States of the West; 44 per cent. of the wheat, 52 per cent. of the oats, and 45 per cent. of the corn are produced at that altitude. In regard to temperature, corn is produced most freely in the regions where the mean annual temperature is from 50 to 55 degrees; oats, where the mean annual temperature is 45 to 50 degrees; while wheat is more scattered and more inclined to lower temperatures. A mean annual rainfall of

[1] U.S. Census, 1890: Agriculture, p. 7.

[2] *Ibid.* p. 10.

from 30 to 40 inches is found in the regions producing the greatest quantity of oats and corn; while wheat is more evenly scattered above and below this limit.

The varying production of three of the principal crops in the United States is shown in the following estimates of the Department of Agriculture:—[1]

CROPS OF WHEAT, CORN, AND OATS SINCE 1878.

Year.	Wheat. Bushels.	Corn. Bushels.	Oats. Bushels.
1879 (Census) . .	459,483,137	1,754,591,676	407,858,999
1880	498,549,868	1,717,434,543	417,885,380
1881	383,280,090	1,194,916,000	416,481,000
1882	504,185,470	1,617,025,100	488,250,610
1883	421,086,160	1,551,066,895	571,302,400
1884	512,765,000	1,795,528,000	583,628,000
1885	357,112,000	1,936,176,000	629,409,000
1886	457,218,000	1,665,441,000	624,134,000
1887	456,329,000	1,456,161,000	659,618,000
1888	415,868,000	1,987,790,000	701,735,000
1889	490,560,000	2,112,892,000	751,515,000
1890	399,262,000	1,489,970,000	523,621,000
1891	611,780,000	2,060,154,000	738,394,000
1892	515,949,000	1,628,464,000	661,035,000
1893	396,131,725	1,619,496,131	638,854,850
1894	460,267,416	1,212,770,052	662,086,928
1895	467,102,947	2,151,138,580	824,443,537
1896	427,684,347	2,283,875,165	707,346,404
1897	530,149,168	1,902,967,933	698,767,809
1898	675,148,705	1,924,184,660	730,905,643

Other Countries. The agricultural statistics of other countries are published from year to year and are easily accessible in the various statistical abstracts[2] and trade journals, so that it is not necessary to repeat them here. An attempt is often made to estimate the total world production of different crops from year to year as indicative of the increasing food supply and also of variation in available supply as affecting prices. These estimates often

[1] As quoted by the "Financial Chronicle," February 4, 1899. For latest estimates and many interesting details consult the files of that journal.

[2] Particularly the Statistical Abstract for Foreign Countries, London, annually. See also, Agricultural Returns for Great Britain, 1898.

differ widely from each other. In fact, accuracy in this matter is not to be expected. As an example of such estimates the following is given (Bureau of Statistics, Treasury Department, "Monthly Summary of Finance and Commerce," March 1898):—

WHEAT PRODUCTION OF THE WORLD.

Countries.	Average five years, 1893–1897. Bushels.	Countries.	Average five years, 1893–1897. Bushels.
United States	456,267,034	British East Indies	228,539,800
Dominion of Canada	49,136,400	Cyprus	2,150,000
Mexico	13,750,000	Japan	17,414,500
		Persia	20,800,000
Argentina	61,000,000	Russia, Asiatic	80,776,000
Chili and Uruguay	22,923,600	Turkey in Asia	48,600,000
Austria-Hungary	188,562,000	Australasia	36,237,000
Belgium	18,263,200		
Bulgaria	34,837,400	Algeria	21,514,800
Denmark	4,550,800	Cape Colony	3,390,200
France	309,999,600	Egypt	10,800,000
Germany	107,004,000	Tunis	6,760,000
Greece	4,760,000		
Italy	116,600,600	Total	2,471,220,834
Netherlands	4,943,400		
Montenegro	235,000		
Portugal	7,420,000	*Recapitulation.*	
Roumania	54,081,000		
Russia in Europe	376,823,800	North America	516,367,434
Servia	8,370,200	South America	83,923,600
Spain	94,816,800	Europe	1,414,015,600
Sweden and Norway	4,467,800	Asia	378,212,200
Switzerland	4,320,000	Australasia	36,237,000
Turkey in Europe	20,300,000	Africa	42,465,000
United Kingdom	53,707,000		

NOTE.—Per cent. of five-year average, 1893 to 1897.

North America	*20·89
South America	3·40
Europe	57·22
Asia	15·30
Australasia	1·47
Africa	1·72
	100·00

* Of this, 18·46 per cent. is from the United States.

Average Yield per Acre. In the production of crops as much depends upon the average yield per acre as upon the amount of land devoted to the crop. In the same country we have the greatest variety of land, some yielding small crops with little labour, and some yielding large crops with great labour. From year to year, also, the yield depends upon the climate and the favourable season. For instance, the yield per acre of wheat in England was 33·6 bushels in 1896, and only 26·2 bushels in 1895. An average for a single year is not, therefore, very trustworthy. Between countries we can distinguish, however, by the yield, whether the method of cultivation is extensive or intensive. The following table shows the contrast between an old and a new country. (Statistical Abstracts for the United Kingdom and for the United States):—

AVERAGE YIELD PER ACRE (BUSHELS), 1897.

	United States.	United Kingdom.
Wheat	13·4	29·1
Barley	24·5	32·9
Oats	27·2	38·8
Corn	23·8	—
Rye	16·1	—

The average yield of wheat per acre in Great Britain, and the proportional yield on the basis of 28 bushels = 100 or normal crop is shown in the following table (Commission on Agriculture, Vol. I., p. 447):—

	Yield, bushels per acre.	Compared with standard 28 bushels = 100.
Average, 1857–8 to 1862–3	28·4	102
,, 1863–4 to 1868–9	30·8	110
,, 1869–70 to 1874–5	27·2	97
,, 1875–6 to 1880–81	22·6	81
,, 1881–2 to 1886–7	27·8	99
,, 1887–8 to 1892–3	29·7	106
,, 1893 to 1897[1]	29·1	104

This table shows how fluctuating the yield of wheat is even when we group six years together. The average yield

[1] From Stat. Abstract.

has not materially increased during a period of forty years.

Production Statistics: Meat Supply of the World. Next to the cereals, the most important food product is meat. We are met here by the difficulty that the meat supply is not an annual product like wheat, but only that portion of the live stock that is slaughtered for food. We have very few statistics showing the amount thus slaughtered, and are therefore obliged to approach the question indirectly by giving first the statistics of live stock actually present at any period, often including animals which are not used for food purposes as well as those that are.

The meat supply is an interesting question for the modern economic world. Increasing density of population and the growth of cities and factory towns in Europe and parts of the United States make the demand for meat greater, while they diminish the facilities for producing the supply. This is only partly offset by the fact that wheat land has become less rentable, and has been turned, to a certain extent, into pasture and meadow land. In general, therefore, the capacity of the older countries for producing meat has decreased, while the demand has increased. The deficit has been met by the supply from new countries, so that we have this very interesting transformation, namely, that the Old World is seeking its meat supply, as well as its wheat, from the New World. The principal use of the statistics is to display this transformation, and to measure the rapidity with which it is going on. Turning our attention first to Europe, we have the following figures (Neumann-Spallart, Übersichten, p. 186):—

TOTAL NUMBER OF CATTLE, SHEEP, AND SWINE IN EUROPE.

	Cattle.	Sheep.	Swine.
1880–85	94,832,000	180,148,000	44,236,000
1887–88	97,372,166	165,758,378	44,041,276

If we bring these figures into relation with population, the movement is brought out even more clearly:—

NUMBER OF CATTLE, SHEEP, AND SWINE PER 1,000 OF THE POPULATION.

Europe.	Cattle.	Sheep.	Swine.
1865–1874	331	700	152
1880–1889	300	549	137

This table shows a marked decrease in the supply of cattle, sheep, and swine, and especially of sheep, and shows that, so far as mere numbers are concerned, Europe is no longer keeping up its supply of live stock.

The particular countries of Europe show this movement in different degrees. For Great Britain and Ireland, we have the following figures (Statistical Abstract for the United Kingdom):—

	Cattle.		Sheep.		Swine.	
	Number.	Per 1000 of Pop.	Number.	Per 1000 of Pop.	Number.	Per 1000 of Pop.
1868 . .	9,083,416	293	35,067,812	1,150	3,189,167	103
1890 . .	10,789,858	269	31,667,195	772	4,362,040	101
1897 . .	11,004,034	265	30,567,061	760	3,682,819	91

These figures show a decrease in every category, if we take account of the increase of population. The decrease in the number of sheep, both absolute and relative, is especially marked. It is to be remembered that during this same period the amount of arable land decreased in Great Britain and Ireland. One would have supposed that this would have led to an increase in the number of sheep rather than the reverse. This table throws an interesting side light upon the ordinary thesis of political economy—that if the British farmer cannot raise wheat, he can turn his hand to the raising of live stock.

In France, from 1850 to 1872, the number of live stock diminished. Since that time it has increased and, with the exception of sheep, faster than the population.

In Germany,[1] from 1873 to 1897, the number of cattle increased from 15,776,702 to 18,490,772; the number of swine from 7,124,088 to 14,274,557; while the number of sheep diminished from 24,999,406 to 10,886,772. We have

[1] Stat. Jahrbuch, 1898, p. 26.

here a very remarkable movement, showing, perhaps, the increased demand for beef and pork owing to increased population, while the diminution in the number of sheep indicates, perhaps, the influence of external competition in the wool market.

Other countries of Europe show varying relations.[1] In general, the number of live stock decreased down to 1872–3, then increased, reaching a maximum in 1886–7, since which time it has again decreased. Almost everywhere there has been a notable decrease in the number of sheep.

Comparisons between different Countries. An effort is sometimes made to compare the live stock resources, so to speak, of different countries with each other. For this purpose the absolute numbers are of no avail, because countries differ so widely in population and in area. European statisticians are accustomed to reduce the absolute figures to a per mille relation for population, or to some common unit (square kilometre) for area. Such comparisons are very rough and only indicate in a general way the power of each country in this direction. The question of quality—that is, difference in weight, size, and breed of the animals—has to be entirely disregarded. The number of cattle, sheep, and swine per 1,000 of the population is shown in the

[1] Absolute numbers for other countries are as follows. (Vierteljahrshefte zur Statistik des Deutschen Reichs, 1898, II., p. 147) :—

	Cattle.	Sheep.	Swine.
France (1892)	13,364,434	21,504,956	6,337,100
Russia (1888)	27,662,656	48,220,119	10,742,074
Austria (1890)	8,643,936	3,186,787	3,549,700
Denmark (1888) . . .	1,463,440	1,303,880	770,793
Holland (1891)	1,532,100	810,600	547,400
Sweden (1891)	1,920,110	1,345,337	655,073
Norway (1890)	1,004,191	1,412,295	120,737
Switzerland (1886) . .	1,212,538	341,804	394,917
Australia (1891) . . .	11,818,540	124,286,491	1,068,441

Similar comparative figures for different countries may be found in Agricultural Returns for Great Britain, 1898, p. 254.

following table (Vierteljahrshefte zur Statistik des Deutschen Reichs, 1898, II., p. 147):—

	Cattle.	Sheep.	Swine.
Denmark (1888)	670	597	353
Norway (1890)	505	710	61
Sweden (1891)	400	280	136
Servia (1882)	446	1954	576
Switzerland (1886)	428	121	140
Austria-Hungary (1890)	362	133	149
France (1892)	349	561	165
Germany (1892)	355	275	246
Great Britain and Ireland (1893)	296	839	87
Belgium (1880)	251	66	117
Russia (1888)	306	529	118
Holland (1891)	340	180	121
United States (1894)	848	719	722
Australia	3,109	32,693	281

It is not necessary to comment on this table. It brings out clearly the characteristics of different countries in regard to raising cattle, sheep, and swine.

A second method of comparing the number of live stock in different countries is to take the number per one square kilometre (equal ·386 sq. miles), as in the following table[1]:—

	Cattle.	Sheep.	Swine.
Germany (1883)	29·2	35·5	17·0
,, (1892)	32·4	25·5	22·3
France (1892)	25·3	40·7	12·0
Great Britain and Ireland (1893)	35·6	101·0	10·4
Austria (1890)	28·7	10·6	11·7
Hungary (1884)	15·1	32·9	14·9
Denmark (1888)	38·1	32·0	20·1
Holland	47·1	24·9	16·8
Sweden	4·3	3·0	1·5
Norway	3·1	4·4	0·4
Russia	5·6	9·7	2·2
United States (1894)	7·0	5·9	5·9
Australia (1891)	1·4	15·2	0·1

The mere number of live stock does not show us very much in regard to the actual meat supply. That depends on the weight of the beasts and how many are slaughtered each year. Common observation shows that the weight of animals

[1] Same authority. See also Conrad's Handwörterbuch der Staatswissenschaften, Art. Viehstatistik.

has increased with the progress of agriculture. In France, for instance, the living weight of an ox was estimated in 1840 at 413 kilograms on an average, while in 1873 the average was taken at 500 kilograms. In Germany the weight of an ox in 1883 was estimated at 466 kilograms, and of a cow at 380 kilograms;[1] in 1893, the figures were 497 kilograms and 416 kilograms respectively. On the other hand the "Fleischgewicht" of an ox varied in German cities from 510 kilograms in Aachen down to 250 kilograms in Altona.[2]

In some countries we have statistics of the number slaughtered each year. In Holland, for instance, from 1871 to 1880 the number of swine slaughtered each year was 79 per cent. of those living at the end of the year. In 1888 it was 92 per cent. The number slaughtered can be greater than the number living at the end of the year. With better breeds and improved methods of fattening, the tendency is to slaughter the beasts younger, so that the actual meat supply becomes a larger percentage of the number of animals in existence at any one time. In France, for instance, it is said that formerly sheep were allowed to live until they were three or four years old for the sake of their wool. Since the price of wool has gone down, lambs are slaughtered at the age of twenty-one or twenty-two months. While the absolute number of sheep may therefore decrease, the meat supply may increase. These facts are adduced in order to show the difficulties in the way of measuring the actual meat supply of any country.[3]

[1] Neumann-Spallart, p. 192.

[2] Statistisches Jahrbuch Deutscher Städte, VI., p. 257 (1897). It gives full statistics of the meat supply in 35 cities.

[3] Neumann-Spallart, p. 192. An estimate by Mr. R. E. Turnbull (Commission on Agriculture, Vol. IV., p. 547) of the home supply of meat in England, average for fifteen years, 1879–94, is as follows :—

	Cwts.		
Beef and veal	11,025,785	= 48	per cent.
Mutton and lamb	6,089,215	= 26½	,,
Bacon and pork	5,855,545	= 25½	,,
	22,970,545	100	

Live Stock in New Countries. That the tendency of Europe is to depend less and less upon itself for its meat supply is confirmed by the statistics of live stock in new countries. The deficit of Europe is made up from America and Australia. The great quantity of pasture land, the reproductive power of free herds, the comparatively small consumption of the home population, the cheapness of feeding, and the improved methods of transportation enable these countries not only to supply themselves but also to send quantities of meat to Europe. We have two sets of statistics showing this movement. First, we have the number of live stock at successive periods; and secondly, we have the statistics of the exportation of live stock and meat. For the United States we have the following figures or estimates for successive periods (Stat. Abstract, 1895 and 1898):—

	Milch Cows.	Oxen and other cattle.	Sheep.	Swine.
1870 . . .	10,095,600	15,388,500	40,853,000	26,751,400
1895 . . .	16,504,629	34,364,216	42,294,064	44,165,716
1898 . . .	15,840,886	29,264,197	37,656,960	39,759,993

These figures show the enormous wealth of the United States in live stock, and also the increase during twenty-five years. The figures include only live stock on farms. Of late years there seems to have been a decrease, due, perhaps, to more conservative estimates or improved quality.

The export movement is shown in the Statistical Abstract of the United States, and will be commented on in the chapter on "Commerce." It is sufficient to say here that the United States exports annually nearly half a million head of live stock, and over a million pounds of fresh, canned, salt, or pickled meat.

Of other new countries, the Argentine Republic reported in 1892, 22,000,000 cattle and 75,000,000 sheep. The export of meat has increased enormously during the last few years. Australasia is noted for its enormous number of sheep, returned in 1897 at more than 103,551,108.[1]

[1] Agricultural Returns for Great Britain, 1898.

Production Statistics: Minerals. Important natural resources are found beneath the surface of the land and constitute the mineral wealth of the country. We have no means of measuring this except by the annual product. The total extent of the mines and how long they will last is simply a matter of estimate; and their real productivity for the future will depend upon the expense of working them. About the only use of our statistics is to compare the annual product of different countries and to watch the variations from year to year. This gives us some notion of the industrial power of different nations and of the changes from year to year. The most important mineral in all respects is coal, which forms the basis of industry by its use for traction purposes, for factory power, for smelting iron, for gas works and for heating. Next to coal comes iron, associated closely with it and really the fundamental metal for all industrial purposes. The statistics of gold and silver are of so much importance in the theory of money that they will be treated of in the chapter on "Money". As indicative of the use of statistics in this connection, we shall give some of the recent statistics of coal and iron. (Statistical Abstract for Foreign Countries, 1885—1895, p. 315):—

PRODUCTION OF COAL IN DIFFERENT COUNTRIES. TONS (000's OMITTED.)

	1870.	1880.	1890.	1895.
United Kingdom . . .	110,431	146,969	181,614	189,661
United States	—	63,823	140,883	172,426
Germany [1]	34,003	59,118	89,291	103,958
France [1]	13,180	19,362	26,083	28,020
Austria (proper)[1] . . .	6,444	14,310	24,260	28,112
Belgium [1]	13,697	16,887	20,366	20,451

A glance at this table shows the importance of the United Kingdom in the production of coal; it reveals the enormous increase during the last twenty-five years in all countries and especially in Germany and the United States. The explanation of this increase is, of course, the growth of railroads, of steamships, and of the use of iron.

[1] Metric tons of 2,204 lbs.

The statistics of iron show the same great movement as those of coal. The production of pig-iron in the four countries of the world where the production is the greatest has been as follows (*Ibid.*, p. 316) :—

	1870. Tons.	1880. Tons.	1890. Tons.	1895. Tons.
United Kingdom . . .	5,963,515	7,749,233	7,904,214	7,703,459
United States	1,665,178	3,835,191	9,202,704	9,446,308
Germany [1]	1,391,000	2,729,000	4,658,000	5,464,000
France [1]	1,178,000	1,725,000	1,962,000	2,004,000

This table shows the importance of the iron industry in the United Kingdom and also the enormous strides that have been made in the production of iron in Germany and especially in the United States.[2]

Production Statistics: The Textiles. Land is the source of the materials with which man clothes himself; *i.e.*, either the direct source, as for vegetable fibres, such as cotton, flax, or hemp, or the indirect, as for animal fibres such as wool and silk. It is only necessary to say a word in characterisation of each.

Cotton. The United States is by far the most important source for this product. The Census of 1890 returned an area of 20,175,270 acres, or 31,523 square miles, devoted to the production of cotton during the preceding year. The total crop gathered from this area was 7,472,511 bales of an average weight of 477 pounds, amounting to 3,564,387,747 pounds,

[1] Metric tons of 2,204 lbs.

[2] The production of other minerals in the United States, Great Britain, and Germany, is shown in the following table (year 1896):—

	United States.* (Short Tons.)	United Kingdom.† (Tons.)	Germany.‡ (Metric Tons.)
Copper	230,030	556	717,300
Lead	188,000	30,818	157,500
Zinc	81,499	7,110	729,900
White tin . . .	—	4,838	—
Petroleum . . .	60,960,361 bls.	—	—

* Statistical Abstract of the United States, 1897, p. 321.

† Statistical Abstract of the United Kingdom, 1897, p. 214.

‡ Statistisches Jahrbuch für das Deutsche Reich, 1898, p. 36.

an average of 177 pounds to the acre. The Census volume on Agriculture (page 42) gives a short sketch of the history of cotton in the United States. In 1791, the total production was 2,000,000 lbs.; in 1801 it was 40,000,000 lbs.; and in 1821 it had risen to 180,000,000 lbs. The Census of 1840 was the first to include agricultural products in its inquiries, and it reported the crop of cotton for the preceding year at 790,000,000 lbs. It rose continuously until 1860, when it was 2,397,000,000 lbs. The war interrupted the progress so that the crop reported in 1870 was only 54 per cent. of that of ten years previous. In 1880 the South had recovered and raised a larger crop than before the war, namely, 2,607,000,000 lbs. The cotton cultivation is concentrated in the Gulf States, Texas raising 19·5 per cent., Georgia 16·5 per cent., Mississippi 14·3 per cent., and Alabama 13·7 per cent.; that is together 64 per cent. of the total crop. The cotton crop of 1897 was estimated at 11,180,960 bales.

Cotton is also produced in India, China, and Egypt.

Wool. Wool is extensively produced both in Europe and in the countries of the New World. The annual production is subject to great fluctuations on account of mortality among sheep, and especially because the price of wool determines whether the sheep shall be raised for their wool or as a meat product. The figures, therefore, are of comparatively little permanent value. The gross product is estimated by Neumann-Spallart at 374 million kilograms for Europe and 605 million kilograms for other countries. The production of wool was returned in Great Britain and Ireland at 153,000,000 lbs. for 1892; in the United States at 111,661,581 lbs. (scoured) in 1898; for Australasia (net exports) 644,865,162 lbs. in 1895.

Production Statistics: Sugar, Coffee, Tea, and Tobacco. These are articles of comfort or luxury of such universal use that statistics of their production, export and import, and of their consumption throw important light on the resources of nations and on the question of well-being. So far as consumption is concerned, we have already treated them in Chapter II. The ordinary statistics may be found in the handbooks and statistical abstracts. Reference may be made especially to Neumann-Spallart, Uebersichten der Weltwirtschaft. We shall mention here simply one or two characteristic facts showing the tendency of modern development.

Sugar. Sugar was formerly a tropical product, and Europe was dependent upon the West and East Indies for its supply. During the last thirty years the beet-sugar industry has sprung up, greatly changing the whole course of the industry and altering the relations of supply. In 1896-7, the production of beet-sugar was reckoned at 4,822,000 metric tons,[1] while that of cane-sugar was only 2,432,000 metric tons.

Coffee. This came formerly from the East Indies, thence it was transplanted to the West Indies and to South America, which latter country is now the principal producer. In the Dutch East Indies the production is still large, but is declining. Neumann-Spallart (p. 290) gives the following figures which apply to the year 1888-9 :—

Brazil	3,840,600	metric centners (220·4 lbs.).
Dutch East Indies	708,710	,, ,,
Venezuela	390,381	,, ,,
Guatemala	322,000	,, ,,
Haiti	270,264	,, ,,
Porto Rico	162,273	,, ,,
British East Indies	121,816	,, ,,
San Salvador	103,170	,, ,,
Colombia	100,000	,, ,,
World	6,490,247	,, ,,

[1] Grandeau, La Question sucrière (Journal des Economistes, Vol. 34, 1898, p. 192). The principal countries producing beet-sugar were :—Germany, 1,835,000 tons ; Austria-Hungary, 956,000 tons ; Russia, 736,000 tons ; France, 700,000 tons ; Belgium, 275,000 tons ; Holland, 162,000 tons ; Sweden, 100,000 tons ; Denmark, 30,000 tons.

Tea. Down to the beginning of the seventies China was almost the only source of supply for the Western World; then Japan came in as a competitor, and more recently British India, especially Ceylon, has exported large quantities to Europe. The total production of China is entirely unknown. Only the smallest part is exported. This export reached the maximum of 144·3 million kilograms in 1886, but declined to 109 million kilograms in 1891. Japan exports about 61 million lbs., and the British East Indies about 107 million lbs. per annum.[1]

Tobacco. This is a very important crop on account of its great value. It is difficult to estimate the total production, because, wherever it is produced, great quantities are consumed at home; and as it is everywhere heavily taxed, the tendency is to underestimate the production. In the United States, the area devoted to tobacco culture in 1889 was 695,301 acres, and the crop was estimated at 488,256,646 lbs. Over one-half of the area devoted to the cultivation of tobacco was in the states of Kentucky and Virginia. Kentucky alone produced 45 per cent. of the total crop. Cuba is a most important producer, owing to the quality of its tobacco, but large quantities are raised also in the British East Indies, in Turkey, in the Dutch East Indies, and on the continent of Europe. Neumann-Spallart estimates the total annual product of the world at 1,636 million lbs.

Statistics of Land Holding: Size of Farms. Political economy has busied itself considerably with the question of cultivation on a large and on a small scale. This is commonly called the question of large and small farms. The two systems have different consequences, both economic and social, and it is of interest to determine for any given community which system prevails. It is of still further interest to determine whether the tendency is towards an increase or decrease in the size of farms. The basis for all such study is of course the statistical, or the

[1] Neumann-Spallart, p. 302.

enumeration of farms according to their size. For the purpose of comparison we can either calculate the average size of the farms, or—the better method—classify the farms according to size. In this classification it is interesting to observe not only the relative number of farms in each class, but also the relative proportion of the area comprised in the farms of each class. It is necessary to consider both of these facts in arriving at any conclusion as to the social significance of the distribution of farms.

International comparison of the size of farms is of comparatively little value, because the conditions of agriculture vary so much in different countries. Where there is rich soil, as in Belgium, the small farm is able to exist. Where the land is poor, as in Eastern Prussia, it is necessary to have larger spaces. Where land is plenty, as in Australia or the United States, it is more profitable to cover a large area extensively than to apply labour to a small space intensively. The size of farms gives us some interesting indication of the possibilities of various kinds of agriculture in different countries, but any close comparison is futile. It is necessary, therefore, to study each country by itself.

Farms in France. The classical country of small farms is France. It has been noted for many years for its system of peasant proprietorship, which means that the cultivator is almost always the owner of the soil that he cultivates. De Foville declares that there are nearly six million farmers in France, and that there are eight million land-owners in all. This system has been lauded, especially by the English economists, as offering the greatest inducement to the careful and intensive cultivation of the soil. It has been criticised by others as leading to the breaking up of the soil into small parcels separated from each other, which can only be cultivated with great difficulty and at great expense. The number of "parcels" was said to be 135 million in 1882. The classification according to size of farms—that is, farming establishments—in 1892, was as follows (Statistique Agricole, 1897, p. 357–8):—

	Number of farms.	Area in hectares.	Per cent. of no.	Per cent. of area.	Average size, hect.
Under 1 hectare (2½ acres) .	2,235,405	1,327,300	39·2	2·7	0·59
1 hectare to 10 hectares (2½—25 acres)	2,617,558	11,244,700	45·9	22·8	4·29
10 to 40 hectares (25—100 acres)	711,118	14,313,400	12·5	29·0	20·13
Over 40 hectares (over 100 acres)	138,671	22,493,400	2·4	45·6	162·21
	5,702,752	49,378,800	100·0	100·0	8·65

It will be seen from this table that nearly two-fifths of all the farms are below one hectare—that is, below two and one-half acres in extent; but these farms together cover only a little more than two and one-half per cent. of the farm surface. They have an average size of only one and one-half acres. On the other hand, the large farms of over 100 acres, while they constitute only 2·5 per cent of the total number, cover 45 per cent. of the total surface. The most influential category seems to be the farms of from 1 to 10 hectares, which make up nearly one-half of the total number and cover more than one-fifth of the total surface. The average size of all farms is 8·6 hectares, or about 22 acres. Size varies greatly from one region to another. In the mountainous districts, such as the Hautes-Alpes, it runs as high as 17 hectares, while in the valley of the Seine it runs as low as 2 hectares.

If we compare the figures of 1892 with the similar figures for 1882, it appears that no very great change has occurred. What movement there has been, has been in the direction of diminishing the number, or rather size, of the medium farm while the small parcels and the large farms have gained. But conditions seem to be very nearly stationary.[1]

[1] For latest figures see Statistique Agricole, 1897, as above, quoted in Conrad's Jahrbücher, Jan. 1899, p. 87. For figures for 1882 and comment, see De Foville, La France Economique, and Le Morcellement, by the same author.

Farms in Germany. The most recent statistics are for the year 1895. The classification of farms is as follows (Stat. Jahrbuch, 1898):—

	Number.	Area in hectares.	Per cent. of number.	Per cent. of area.
Under 2 hectares (5 acres) . .	3,236,367	1,808,444	58·2	5·6
From 2 to 5 hectares (5—12½ acres)	1,016,318	3,285,984	18·3	10·1
From 5 to 20 hectares (12½—50 acres)	998,804	9,721,875	18·0	29·9
From 20 to 100 hectares (50—250 acres)	281,757	9,869,837	5·1	30·3
Over 100 hectares (over 250 acres)	25,061	7,831,801	0·4	24·1
	5,558,317	32,517,941	100·0	100·0

The classification is not exactly the same as in France. The first category under 2 hectares, that is 5 acres, corresponds to what may be called "parcel" farms. The remaining categories represent the small peasant farms, the medium-sized peasant farms, the large peasant farms (Grossbauer) and finally the large estates. It will be seen that the "parcel" farms are the most numerous, but that they cover only 5·6 per cent. of the cultivated area. The real cultivators in Germany are the medium-sized and large peasant proprietors who represent 23 per cent. of the number and 60 per cent. of the total area of farms. It is said, that since 1882 these medium possessions have gained somewhat in proportionate area and the "parcel" and large farms have lost slightly.

The following table is interesting as showing the way in which farms of different sizes are cultivated (Vierteljahrshefte, 1897, II., Ergänz. p. 60):—

PERCENTAGE OF AREA DEVOTED TO

	Farming.	Gardens.	Vineyards.	Forest.	Waste.	Remaining.
Under 5 acres . .	69·3	4·1	1·5	17·1	3·5	4·5
5 to 12½ ,, . .	77·1	1·2	1·0	13·2	4·9	2·5
12½ to 50 ,, . .	76·6	0·6	0·3	14·8	6·1	1·6
50 to 250 ,, . .	74·5	0·4	0·07	16·7	6·9	1·4
250 acres and over	70·5	0·4	0·02	23·3	2·6	3·0
All farms . .	74·0	0·77	0·29	17·5	5·2	2·14

Size of Farms in Great Britain. In contrast to France and Germany, the number of small farms is comparatively small in Great Britain. The last inquiry in the year 1895 gave the following results (Return, &c., [c—8243], 1896):—

	Number.	Per cent.	Acres.	Per cent.
Above 1 acre and not exceeding 5 acres	117,968	22·7	366,792	1·1
,, 5 acres ,, ,, 20 ,,	149,818	28·8	1,667,647	5·1
,, 20 ,, ,, 50 ,,	85,663	16·5	2,864,976	8·8
,, 50 ,, ,, 100 ,,	66,625	12·8	4,885,203	15·0
,, 100 ,, ,, 300 ,,	81,245	15·6	13,875,914	42·6
,, 300 ,, ,, 500 ,,	13,568	2·6	5,113,945	15·7
,, 500 ,, ,, 1000 ,,	4,616	0·9	3,001,184	9·2
,, 1000	603	0·1	801,852	2·5
	520,106	100·0	32,577,513	100·0

It appears from this table that, disregarding all the holdings of a single acre or less, the total number of agricultural holdings was 520,000. Of these, more than one-fifth were of the smallest class not exceeding five acres in extent; but the land occupied by this class was not much more than 1 per cent. of the cultivated surface. The most important class of farms is that between 100 and 300 acres, constituting 15 per cent. of the number, and 42·6 per cent. of the cultivated area.

The average size of farms in Great Britain is 63 acres, in England 65 acres, in Wales 47 acres and in Scotland 61 acres. It varies largely from county to county, *e.g.* from 122 acres in Northumberland down to 40 acres in Lancashire. In Scotland the variations are still greater, the average size in Sutherland running down to 12 acres.

Contrary to common opinion, it is not the large farms that are most devoted to pasture. Many of the smallest type of holdings practically consist of plots or paddocks of permanent grass. In the next two classes, from 5 to 50 acres, there are nearly 2 acres of grass for every single acre of arable land. In the holdings over 100 acres, the arable area is greater than the pasture. In the holdings running from 500 to 1,000 acres in extent, 58 per cent. of their cultivated surface is returned as arable land. This is, however, the mean of very widely different local ratios. There are counties like Cheshire or Derbyshire where the arable area is small. On the other hand, among the large farms of Suffolk only one acre in four and in Cambridgeshire only one acre in five is returned as permanent grass.

Besides the holdings enumerated above, there is a total of 579,133 smaller holdings, distinguished into 37,143 acre plots and 541,990 smaller units of cultivation. These smaller plots are held by various tenures and are used for a great variety of purposes. They are commonly called allotments, and are detached pieces of land used as gardens by artisans and others. The number varies greatly in different parts of England.[1]

The subject of small farms in England has received very careful treatment from Major Craigie, of the Board of Agriculture, in an article in the Journal of the Statistical Society, for March 1887. Some of the points that he raises are as follows:

In the first place the small cultivator is not extinct even in England. Major Craigie instances a parish in the Isle of Ely, where 47 per cent. of the occupations are between one-fourth and one acre, and another parish in Warwickshire where nearly one-half of the holdings are under one acre. Such small farms exist, mainly, in the neighbourhood of large cities where there is a demand for vegetables and other garden produce. Their cultivator, too, commonly plies some other trade besides that of farmer. There results from this fact the curious phenomenon that the small farm flourishes least in the counties which are the most rural.

On the other hand, the small farm does not seem to be

[1] Return as to Number and Size of Agricultural Holdings in Great Britain in 1895, [c—8243], 1896.

effective in preventing the depopulation of the rural districts. As a matter of fact the county with fewest small holdings has retained most labourers. The mere creation of small farms does not seem to be effective in retaining the population, unless there is a market for the produce. In regard to the possibility of the small farmer continuing to exist in England, opinions differ. Major Craigie believes that he still has a chance, although his existence is somewhat precarious. Mr. Druce (quoted by Major Craigie) believes that the small men living from hand to mouth, and depending solely on the crops of the present year, are less able to stand the pressure of bad times than the large ones. On the other hand, there was evidence given before the Royal Commission on Agriculture tending to show that the large farmers had suffered the most from bad times on account of the amount of capital required to keep up their farms and because of the wages they were obliged to pay, notwithstanding the decreased prices.[1]

Major Craigie also shows that the proportionate amount of labour required on the large farms was much less than on the small farms. It appeared that one man was employed for every two and a half acres in case of holdings under 5 acres in size, while on the large farms above 300 acres, one man was employed for every 40 acres. In respect to this smaller number of men engaged on large farms, we may look at it from two points of view. If we consider simply the economy of labour, it would seem desirable to get our agricultural products with the smallest expenditure of human force possible. If we consider it a misfortune to diminish the number of persons directly connected with the land, then we should deplore the movement.

The United States. This is a country of large farms compared with the countries of Europe. The following table shows that while the average size of farm was 137 acres, over 50 per cent. were under 100 acres. The land is well distributed

[1] Commission on Agriculture, Vol. I. p. 14. Also questions, 5901 ff.

according to American notions of agriculture (U.S. Census, 1890: Agriculture, p. 118):—

SIZE OF FARMS IN THE UNITED STATES.

	Cultivated by owners.	Rented for money.	Rented on shares.	Total.
Under 10 acres	98,990	26,181	25,023	150,194
10 and under 20 acres	132,970	46,921	85,659	265,550
20 ,, ,, 50 ,,	505,313	137,709	259,755	902,777
50 ,, ,, 100 ,,	840,178	100,613	180,694	1,121,485
100 ,, ,, 500 ,,	1,594,641	135,748	278,305	2,008,694
500 ,, ,, 1000 ,,	70,911	5,216	8,268	84,395
1000 acres and over	26,725	2,271	2,550	31,546
	3,269,728	454,659	840,254	4,564,641

PERCENTAGE.

Under 10 acres	2·8	5·8	3·0	3·3
10 and under 20 acres	4·1	10·3	10·2	5·8
20 ,, ,, 50 ,,	15·5	30·3	30·9	19·8
50 ,, ,, 100 ,,	25·7	22·1	21·5	24·6
100 ,, ,, 500 ,,	48·8	29·8	33·1	44·0
500 ,, ,, 1000 ,,	2·2	1·1	1·0	1·9
1000 acres and over	0·8	0·5	0·3	0·7
	100·0	100·0	100·0	100·0

Tenancy of Farms. Political Economy has always laid great stress on the question of the ownership of farms, *i.e.*, whether the actual cultivator was the owner or not. The preceding table gives the facts for the United States. Of all farms in 1890, 71·6 per cent. were cultivated by the owners; 10 per cent. were cultivated on money rent; 18·4 per cent. were cultivated on shares. The corresponding figures for 1880 were 74·5; 8; and 17·5 per cent. During the decade there was an increase of 9·56 per cent. in farms cultivated by owners; of 41·04 per cent. in farms cultivated by payment of a money rent; and of 19·65 per cent. in farms cultivated on shares. This would seem to indicate a slight increase in tenancy. According to the preceding table the farms rented for money and cultivated on shares show a lower percentage of small farms than those cultivated by the owner.

Distribution of Tenancy. If we examine the proportion of farms cultivated by owners, on money rental, or on shares, in different states of the United States, we find very great differences due to population and methods of agriculture. Tenancy is very prevalent in the South among the negroes. The farms were classified as follows in 1890 (U. S. Census, 1890: Agriculture, p. 118):—

South Atlantic Division:			
Cultivated by owner	461,057	61·5	per cent.
,, on money rent . .	96,098	12·8	,,
,, ,, shares	192,445	25·7	,,
South Central Division:			
Cultivated by owner	668,972	61·5	,,
,, on money rent . .	151,901	14·0	,,
,, ,, shares	265,899	24·5	,,

The last two classes of farms together are here 38·5 per cent., while in the North Atlantic Division they constitute only 18·4 per cent., in the North Central 23·4 per cent., and in the Western only 12·1 per cent. of the total number.

A somewhat different result is found in the statistics of farm and home ownership. Here the figures apply to families, not to farms. The percentage of farm-occupying families owning and hiring was as follows:—[1]

	Owning.	Hiring.
United States	65·9	34·1
North Atlantic Division . . .	78·6	21·5
South ,, ,, . . .	54·2	45·8
North Central ,, . . .	73·5	26·5
South ,, ,, . . .	51·7	48·3
Western ,, . . .	81·1	18·9

In some of the States, the proportion of farm tenant families runs still higher, *e.g.*, Mississippi 62·3; South Carolina, 61·5; Georgia, 58·1; Alabama, 56·8.

How these statistics are to be interpreted is not quite clear. It has been asserted that the growth of tenancy is a

[1] U. S. Census, 1890: Farms and Homes, pp. 19, 25 and 286. The volume on Agriculture, p. 5, attempts to explain the difference between these two sets of figures, but not very satisfactorily.

symptom of the concentration of wealth and of the inability of members of the community to buy or retain farms. The independent farmer cultivating his own acres, his own master, and with every inducement to exercise energy, skill and intelligence, is (it is said) disappearing and being replaced by the tenant, listless, unattached to the soil, and dependent upon the owner.

Tenancy, however, may arise in various ways. It may be a step from the position of mere labourer to that of farm owner. In the South it is a system which enables the negro to obtain some interest in the land. It may mean simply the gradual breaking up of large farms, owing to improved methods of production. It may mean the movement of old farmers to town, and the leaving of the farm in the hands of a son or a successor.

The general statistics of the number of tenants and of the size of farms are not sufficient to answer these questions. It is necessary to study the facts of farm tenancy as explained by local circumstances. For instance, Mr. Holmes describes the general distribution of farm tenancy throughout the United States as follows:—

"It is noticeable that farm tenancy is higher where the average values of farm acres are high than where they are low, and *vice versâ*. . . . The general fact is that farm tenancy is low throughout the Appalachian Mountain regions and also in the country close to the coasts of the Atlantic Ocean and Gulf of Mexico; while farm tenancy is high in the cotton belt and elsewhere in the regions where the negroes are a large portion of the population. There is some apparent relationship between high farm tenancy and high farm acre values, but this apparent relationship may often only be a coincidence. As will subsequently be shown, there is an apparent relationship between the two in the neighbourhood of cities.[1]

There seems to be no relation between farm tenancy and density of population.

It does not appear that there is any direct relation between tenancy and the size of farms or the value of individual

[1] *Ibid.*, p. 24.

farms. For instance, the average value of farms in California is $12,533, while farm tenancy is represented by 23·9 per cent.; in Illinois, farm tenancy is represented by 36·7 per cent., and the average value of farms there is $4,933.[1]

In every division of the United States the tenancy is lower in the counties that have no cities and towns of at least 8,000 population. For the whole of the United States the proportion is different (U.S. Census, 1890: Farms and Homes, p. 41):—

PROPORTION OF FARM-OCCUPYING FAMILIES HIRING THEIR FARMS.

	For counties containing cities and towns of 8,000 pop. and over.	For all other counties.
The United States	29·71	35·10
North Atlantic Division .	22·46	20·34
South ,, ,, .	47·03	45·75
North Central ,, .	28·24	26·06
South ,, ,, .	56·72	47·59
Western ,, .	23·71	17·96

It is claimed, especially in some parts of the West, that the foreclosure of mortgages accounts for the increase of farm tenancy; but this has not been established statistically. It is true that farms are somewhat heavily mortgaged in the United States, but they are less so than homes. Under the assumption that a farm may be encumbered to two-thirds of its value, farms are burdened to the extent of twelve to sixteen per cent. of possible incumbrance. It is shown also, in the volume on Real Estate Mortgages, that the mortgage indebtedness is heaviest in the richest parts of the country. It is also shown that the principal object of mortgage indebtedness is real estate purchase and improvement. It does not seem probable that the pressure of mortgage indebtedness has had much influence in turning farm owners into tenants. It is true that farms have been bought, especially in the West, for speculative purposes, and in such cases the nominal owners have, perhaps, been obliged to give way to the mortgagee and to continue on the farm as tenant.

[1] *Ibid.*, p. 41.

But such persons never really owned the farm—they were simply speculating on a rise in value.

The statistics for the United States, therefore, show that farm ownership is still the prevailing system. The tendency towards the increase of the tenant system is not very great. Much of it, especially in the South, may be interpreted in a favourable sense as a step towards ownership. The rest is due to a variety of circumstances which make it expedient to cultivate land by a system of lease rather than of individual ownership.

Tenancy in France. The latest figures (1892) for France in regard to ownership and tenancy are as follows:—

	Number.	Surface.
Cultivated by owners . . .	70·7 per cent.	52·8 per cent.
Lease	22·1 ,,	36·3 ,,
Métayage	7·2 ,,	10·9 ,,

The average size of farm cultivated by owners was 5·41 hectares; of leased farm, 11·89 hectares; of métayage, 10·95 hectares. The number of land-owning cultivators has decreased. The number of tenants has increased from 1,302,904 in 1882 to 1,405,569, or from 27·09 per cent. to 29·33 per cent. of the number of occupiers.[1]

For Germany we have a very elaborate classification. Out of 5,556,900 agricultural enterprises (landwirthschaftliche Betriebe), the cultivators were divided as follows:—

	Number.	Per cent.
Cultivating their own land exclusively . .	2,260,669	40·7
,, leased land exclusively	912,747	16·4
,, leased land (more than half) . .	532,870	9·6
,, ,, ,, (less than half) . .	1,160,703	20·9
,, by other forms of tenancy . .	983,581	17·7

But of the total area, 86·1 per cent. is owned land and 12·4 per cent. is leased land, showing that in Germany the cultivator is still the owner.[2]

[1] Statistique agricole, 1897, p. 369; quoted in Conrad's Jahrbücher, January, 1899, p. 87.

[2] Vierteljahrshefte, 1897, II., Ergänzungsheft, p. 58.

In Germany they have studied the question how far the farms are worked by people with whom agriculture is not the chief employment. They found that out of 100 farms the principal occupation of the proprietor was as follows:—

Agriculture	57·8
Gardening and fishery	1·8
Industry	26·9
Trade	2·6
Transportation	2·4
Other occupations	8·4

It thus appears that the farm is a help to other persons, especially to those engaged in industry. It is also shown that out of the 57·8 occupiers of farms whose chief occupation was agriculture, 13 were farm labourers, that is, men who, while working for wages on one farm were cultivating land on their own account. So, too, out of the 27 whose chief occupation was industry, 14 were dependents, that is, manual labourers who added to their income or resources by cultivating a piece of land. It is thus shown that one very favourite scheme of economic reformers, namely, that artisans should at the same time have their piece of land, is actually in operation in Germany.[1]

Scientific Tests.

There is very little to be said under this head except that the statistics of land, of agriculture, and of production are very imperfect, and it is doubtful if they can be made much more than estimates. This should be understood by all who use them. It arises from the very necessities of the case. It is impossible to measure exactly every piece of land in the United States according as it is devoted to crops, pasture, forest land, etc. It would take years to do it, and, when it was done, conditions would have changed so that the facts would be of no value. In the same way we cannot pass the

[1] *Ibid.*, p. 62.

crop of wheat or corn or cotton through a Government scale and know exactly how much is produced.

Respecting land, the census enumerator inquires of each farmer, the size of his farm, the number of acres of improved and unimproved land, the number of acres devoted to certain crops, to pasture, etc. These data are necessarily imperfect. In an old country like England, where the land is carefully cultivated, and the farmer is more or less a man of business, the extent of each field may be known. But under conditions such as prevail in the United States, it is impossible.

The amount of error in such statistics cannot be determined. For general purposes great accuracy is not needed. If there is a general tendency towards increasing the amount of improved land in farms, it will appear in the aggregate of returns even if particular farmers make mistakes about the exact acreage. It is not so much that the mistakes balance each other, *i.e.* the over-estimates balance the under-estimates, although this doubtless occurs, as that men under the same circumstances will probably act in the same way. For example, when wheat no longer pays to cultivate, there will be a tendency among farmers to let the land less well-fitted for wheat go into something else. The statistics would confirm general observation and give us a rough measure of changes in time and differences in space: *e.g.* the constantly decreasing area devoted to wheat in England; the predominance of pasture and meadow in Ireland.

The more detailed the inquiries the more cautious must we be in using the results. The statistics often carry the inquiries down to such minor crops as hops, vetches, beans, etc. Area means little in such crops, because the yield varies according to the character of the soil.

The statistics of production are also mere estimates, made by farmers, of what they have produced during the census year. These are inaccurate, especially among small farmers who consume what they produce, *e.g.* hay for feeding stock. It may be doubted if farmers know accurately even what they sell. It is wise to confine the statistics to the principal crops.

Besides the census, yearly estimates are made of the crops by Agricultural Departments or by trade papers. These are extremely rough. An observer in each neighbourhood makes an estimate of about the number of acres devoted to each crop and the probable yield per acre. The result gives the total product. These figures can be more or less controlled later by the receipts of grain at elevators, exports, etc. Here again the figures are fit only for comparative purposes.

The figures for mineral products are obtained from the mining companies, and as these are comparatively few in number and are conducted on business principles the statistics are probably trustworthy, or adapted at least for general purposes of comparison.

Statistics of live stock are the most difficult of all, because of the differences in weight and quality of the animals. We can help ourselves out by rough averages from market experts.

The most interesting question of technique is connected with the statistics of tenancy and size of farms. Movements in these two phenomena are of the highest importance. If statistics could show us that tenants are taking the place of owners as cultivators, or that the large farm is absorbing the small one, they would furnish most valuable material for economic reasoning. The interpretation of such a movement would still remain as the problem of Economics, but we should have at least the facts.

Such a task does not seem to be beyond the power of statistical analysis. But the following suggestions may be made:—(1) It is advisable to make particular studies of small districts, rather than to collate the statistics for whole countries. Owing to the character of the soil and the methods of cultivation, what is a large farm in one district would be a small one in another. Especially in the United States it is profitable to study sections rather than the whole country. That the average size of a farm is 137 acres does not mean very much. For the East it would be large; for the West it would be small. The same remarks would apply to any classification of farms according to size. (2) For the same reason international comparison is futile. That the average size of a farm in France is 12½ acres, while in the United States it is 137, shows simply that the two systems of agriculture are entirely different—nothing more. (3) Statistics of ownership and tenancy must be brought into connection with the particular conditions of the district and the time, or they will be misinterpreted. Analysis by tenancy and size of farm gives us a little more accurate information, for it shows us where tenancy, for instance, is more profitable. Analysis by location, *e.g.* near a great city, or by kind of cultivation, *e.g.* garden culture, sheep-raising, cotton-growing, etc., gives us further indications of the possibilities of various systems of tenancy. We must consider also the character of the population, for instance, the negroes in the South, to whom tenancy may mean an advance in economic and social position. In short, we have here a case where the big figures mean nothing, the detailed study everything.

Reflective Analysis.

Statistics show that land as a factor of production contributes more and more to the wealth of civilised man. It does this by constant addition to the cultivated area, owing to the settlement of new territory. How far this process can continue is open to doubt. The public lands of the United States are not exhausted, but the better part of them have been sold or alienated. What Africa has still to offer seems problematical. But even when land is taken nominally into the farm area, there seems room for enormous progress still by turning unimproved into improved land. This opens the way for the application of capital. Still further, the land may be used for different purposes, and thus the advantage gained of adaptability to particular uses. The great factor in this advance is the improved methods of transportation, which enable us to raise our bread where it can be raised to greatest advantage. The land of England can thus be turned from wheat growing to cattle raising or sheep breeding. Improved transportation brings in the law of diminishing returns on a large scale, for it creates a new margin of cultivation which no application of capital and labour can overcome. This undoubtedly brings about dislocation in the productive process, and hardships to particular classes. It is of advantage to the general community because it makes bread cheaper, and hence all sorts of labour more productive as commanding more real wealth. The general thesis of political economy in respect to the advantages of free trade and division of labour is illustrated on a grand scale by the statistics of agriculture.

The grand movement indicated by the statistics of agriculture and of agricultural production is that Europe is depending more and more upon new countries for its bread, meat, and the raw material of manufactures. The process of production as thus developing, interests numerous classes, the agriculturists of the old countries and those of the new, the manufacturers who depend upon cheap food and raw material, the importers and exporters of bread-stuffs and manufactures. In short, almost the whole community finds itself involved in this complicated network of transactions, the fundamental thing being the production of food in the cheapest way. The future prosperity of nations depends upon this question: Will the new countries be able to continue to produce cheaply; or, after exhausting the virgin soil, will conditions resemble those of the old countries? Such is the hope of those who advocate protection to agriculture in Germany and France. But such hope is bound to be defeated. The margin for improvements is so great that wheat will be produced for many years to come almost as cheaply as now. A second question is equally important. If both food and raw material are produced side by side and cheaply in the new countries, will not manufactures themselves seek the same spot? In other words, will the countries of the old world be able to maintain even their industries, or at least that part of their industries which depend upon a foreign market? The primary indication of this movement is found in the statistics of agriculture, but they must be supplemented by those of exports and imports and of manufactures. The signs are that industry on a large scale is about to seek new countries.

The statistics of methods of cultivation, ownership and size of farms have lost some of their significance under the new conditions of production. The demand for cheapness is so overwhelming that methods of agriculture must adapt themselves to it. The small cultivator on the small farm must content himself with catering to special needs, as in vineyards or kitchen gardening or dairy producing, where skill and painstaking care are necessary. The staple crops must be cultivated on a large scale with the aid of machinery. Attempts to preserve or create peasant proprietors can have only a limited success, unless surrounding conditions are very carefully studied. At the same time, with increased cheapness of bread and meat, there should be a greater demand for other agricultural products. It is here that the small farmer will find his opportunity.

CHAPTER V.

CAPITAL, ORGANISATION, AND WEALTH.

Economic Purpose.

NAKED labour can rarely be applied to land with very great results. It must be armed with tools, implements, and reserve subsistence funds. These constitute capital; and capital is so important that it is called the third factor of production. Moreover, in the modern industrial process very much depends upon the way labour is applied, *i.e.* upon organisation, which is sometimes called the fourth factor of production.

The Demands of Theory. Theory maintains that labour armed with capital is more productive than labour without capital. This is a self-evident proposition, and it can be illustrated in a great variety of ways from observation of individual cases of production and from the history of industry in general. Theory does more than maintain this bald proposition. It endeavours to show that capital is directly productive; that increased production of wealth is dependent upon increased capital; and that in the modern world, capital is becoming a more and more important factor. It deduces also a law of increasing returns, viz. that, so far as capital and organisation are concerned, production on a large scale is relatively more fruitful than production on a small scale. It explains this as due to the division of labour, to economies in the use of raw material, to more complete exploitation of machinery and buildings, and to market and other distributive advantages. Theory analyses also the different forms which capital takes on, the way in which it is applied, the extent to which it is a substitute for labour, the laws and the consequences of such substitution. It finds illustration of its theses in the evolution of the industrial organisation, the growth of the factory system, the concentration of industry, and the resulting increase of wealth by this co-operation of labour and land, furnished with abundant capital and scientific organisation.

The Demands of Practice. While theory indicates the importance of capital as a factor of production and shows its relation to increasing wealth, practice finds abundant opportunity for watching the details of the movement. It is of interest to a community to know how fast its concrete capital is growing, in what industries it is being invested, its concentration in various forms, railroads, mines, textile works, etc. Particularly important for actual economic life and conduct is the relation of machinery to labour, the transition from the small industry to the large. Every such transition causes a greater or less dislocation. It throws some men out of employment; it destroys the value of some investments and increases that of others. What is the gain that outweighs the loss? It is important to know also in what stage of industrial evolution we are standing. It is impossible to stop such movements; and it is absurd to attempt to restore the old forms when they have lost their vitality. We must adapt our economic policy to the new forms.

Office of Statistics. Our object here must be to get quantitative measurements indicating the importance of capital and the changes that are going on from time to time and place to place in different industries. So far as we can, we must measure the different forms of capital, that is, the amount devoted to particular uses, *e.g.*, raw material, machinery, buildings, and their relative importance in different industries. Methods of industrial organisation escape statistical measurement except in very general figures, showing the concentration of business under particular forms, in particular localities, and in large establishments. By the skilful use of different figures we can, however, make a picture of the process of change from one form of industrial organisation to another, and may even measure the rate of change. Finally, we can measure the total wealth of the community,—the result of the modern productive processes, —compare the wealth of different communities, watch the progress in time, and use our statistics for various other purposes, such as measuring the burden of taxation, relative well-being, social tendencies, etc.

Statistical Data.[1]

Statistics of Capital. It would seem to be a matter of practical interest to know the amount of capital employed in any community with a view of determining whether it is increasing or decreasing, and how it is employed. There are various difficulties in the way. The first is that of definition: What do we mean by capital? There is great dispute among economists on this point, especially as to whether food and consumption goods are to be considered as capital.

[1] *Bibliographical Note.* The volumes on Manufactures of the Eleventh Census of the United States constitute the most elaborate attempt made anywhere to collect and present the facts of industrial life. Part I. contains the general statistics of manufacturing establishments, capital, number of employees, wages, cost of raw material, value of products and miscellaneous expenses; Part II. contains the statistics of manufactures in cities; Part III. contains special statistics of certain important industries. All three parts contain elaborate analyses of the figures. Part III. is the most important. See, also, the Manufacturing Statistics of the Ninth and Tenth Censuses, especially the introductions by Francis A. Walker. Equally important are the Censuses of Massachusetts for 1885 and 1895. That State publishes, also, the Annual Statistics of Manufactures, covering the large establishments in the principal industries of the State. Both the Federal and the Massachusetts methods have been subjected to severe criticism by S. N. D. North in the essay, Statistics of Manufactures in The Federal Census (Amer. Econ. Assocn. Publications, New Series, No. 2, 1899). See in the same volume, W. C. Ford, Statistics of Manufactures in Cities, and William A. Steuart, Statistics of Manufactures in the Eleventh Census. The last is a defence of the census methods. The Michigan census of 1894 gives statistics of manufactures, capital invested, value of products, etc. For capital invested in railroads, see the Reports of the Statistician

It is not necessary for us to decide the question, for our statistics at best are so rough that it makes little difference whether we include these things or not. If we use capital in its broadest sense as all wealth which aids in the further production of wealth, then it is very difficult to differentiate the capital of a country from its wealth. For almost every portion of wealth contributes directly or indirectly to the maintenance of that state of efficiency and of civilisation which is necessary for economic prosperity. On the other hand, if we think of the active producer bringing together land, labour and capital for the purpose of producing wealth, we get down to the conception of trade capital, that is, the amount and form of wealth necessary to equip labour for the process of production. We have therefore two conceptions of capital, each valuable in its way and furnishing opportunity for statistical analysis.

There are two ways of approaching statistics of capital corresponding to these two conceptions. The first is to

of the Interstate Commerce Commission. For capital in agriculture see the Eleventh Census, 1890, Agriculture.

For the general facts in regard to the growth of capital and the modern organisation of industry, see John A. Hobson, Evolution of Modern Capitalism, 1894, and Carroll D. Wright, Industrial Evolution of the United States, 1895. Hobson gives numerous references. For description of the modern industrial organisation, see Schulze-Gaevernitz, the Cotton Trade, 1895; David A. Wells's Recent Economic Changes, 1890, is also very valuable. Lehr, Produktion und Konsumtion gives a full description of the different forms of capitalistic enterprise, and contains an elaborate bibliography.

For the size of industrial establishments, see the German Industrial census of 1895, Vierteljahrshefte zur Statistik des Deutschen Reichs, 1898, I-II. See also Massachusetts Annual Statistics of Manufactures.

For estimates of national wealth, see the U.S. Census, 1890: Wealth, Debt and Taxation, Part II. Giffen, The Growth of Capital, 1890. This is the most valuable work that we have. De Foville, article Richesse, in the Dictionnaire des Finances, a translation of which appeared in the Journal of the Royal Statistical Society for December, 1893, p. 597. For criticism of the United States valuation see Plehn, Valuation and Taxation, in The Federal Census (Amer. Econ. Assocn. Publications, New Series No. 2, pp. 369-414).

estimate the total amount of National Capital. We can do this by making estimates of the national wealth either by a census of the principal forms of wealth, such as lands, railroads, farms, ships, stock of goods, etc., or by estimates on the basis of property or income taxes. In these estimates we can make a rough distinction between capital and wealth by restricting the former term to that form of wealth which yields an income. But such division can have no great degree of accuracy. National capital and national wealth fall together. For this reason they will be treated of in the third portion of this chapter dealing with the results of production, which in fact become the means of further production.

The second method is to take leading branches of industry and try to ascertain the amount of trade capital actually employed at any given time. The addition of all the sums would give us the trade capital of a country. Such a sum total is scarcely possible on account of the difficulty of enumerating all the petty enterprises in which capital is employed. We therefore generally confine ourselves to the large industries and to enterprises of some size. For getting the sum total of capital in a community, this method is not so good as the first. For the purpose of analysing the functions of capital, and its relation to land and labour, it is more useful. We take up this problem first.

Statistics of Manufactures. The most elaborate attempt to obtain statistics of manufactures has been made in the United States. In the Eleventh Census, enumerators were charged with the duty of visiting every establishment of productive industry, embracing not only mills and factories, but also the operations of small establishments and the mechanical trades. But the collection of statistics of productive industry in 1,042 cities was assigned to special agents. The items concerning which information was demanded were:—number of establishments, capital, miscellaneous expenses, employees and wages, cost of raw material, and value of products. It is important to notice these items, for by combination and comparison it is supposed that the operations of industries on a large scale can be revealed. The most difficult of all to determine is the amount of capital.

The Eleventh Census uses the term capital in a broad, realistic sense, viz., as the amount of wealth actually employed in the particular business. This means the value of land, buildings, machinery, tools and implements, of raw material on hand, stock in process of manufacture, and finished product. It also includes cash on hand, bills and accounts receivable. The notion seems to be to take all the investment, so to speak, at a given moment, the amount which the manufacturer has at stake—his trade capital in the business sense of the term.

Leaving further consideration of this conception to the critical part, let us consider the chief results of the inquiry itself. The figures for the United States were as follows (U. S. Census, 1890: Manufactures, Part I., p. 8):—

Number of establishments reporting	355,415
Capital	$6,525,156,486
Miscellaneous expenses	631,225,035
Average number of employees	4,712,622
Total wages	$2,283,216,529
Cost of material used	5,162,044,076
Value of products	9,372,437,283

We have here some very important figures, which would seem to be capable of throwing light on the development and characteristics of industry in the United States. The first of the questions we naturally ask is:—How fast have manufactures increased during the decade? Unfortunately, the methods used in the Eleventh Census were not the same as in the Tenth, so that the results are not comparable. The increase is said to have been (U. S. Census, 1890: Manufactures, Part I., p. 4):—

In capital	121	per cent.
Number of employees	66	,,
Total wages	131	,,
Cost of materials used	48	,,
Value of product	69	,,

If the figures were trustworthy, it would be an interesting deduction that the total amount paid in wages, and the amount of capital employed, had increased nearly twice as much as the value of the products.

Such comparisons are impossible, however, in the existing state of the data. It will be better to confine ourselves to the figures of 1890.

Distribution of Manufactures. Taking the figures for 1890, we can distribute them either according to space or according to industry. The one method shows us the localisation of industry, the other, the importance of different industries.

The localisation of industries is by States and cities. We can use as a measure, either the number of establishments, or the amount of capital, or the number of employees, or the value of the total product. The first is worthless, because the establishments vary in size, from the blacksmith producing $500 per annum, to the mill turning out millions of dollars worth of product a year. "Number of employees" is interesting, especially in questions of social relations. "Value of total products" is a good test, but is largely influenced by the importance of the raw material that enters into the product. Perhaps "capital employed" is as good a test as any, because it will vary in general with the product, the number of employees, the amount of raw material used, etc.

Taking capital employed and gross product, the States showing the largest amounts are as follows (U. S. Census, 1890: Manufactures, Part I., p. 8):—

	Capital.	Value of Product.
New York	$1,130,161,195	$1,711,577,671
Pennsylvania	991,243,115	1,331,794,901
Massachusetts	630,032,341	888,160,403
Illinois	502,004,512	908,640,280
Ohio	402,793,019	641,688,064

Michigan ($262 million), New Jersey ($250 million), Wisconsin ($246 million), come next in amount of capital.

It will be seen that the order remains about the same in

the two columns. The table brings out well which are the manufacturing States.

The concentration in cities is, of course, marked, and is shown by the amount of capital and total product (U. S. Census, 1890: Manufactures, Part II., pp. 13, 14, and 30):—

	Capital.	Gross Value of Product.
New York	$426,118,272	$777,222,721
Philadelphia	375,249,715	577,234,446
Chicago	359,739,598	664,567,923
Brooklyn	161,730,500	269,244,147
St. Louis	141,872,386	229,157,343
Boston	118,198,539	210,936,616
Pittsburg	108,368,838	126,859,657
Cincinnati	104,483,032	196,063,983

The capital and the total product follow about the same order.

The total amount of capital (direct investment) in 165 cities having 20,000 inhabitants and over, was $3,996,705,734, or more than one-half (61 per cent.) of the entire capital of the country. This proportion is partly due to the more perfect statistics in the cities. Including the value of hired property, the total amount was $4,829,878,742.

The localisation of particular industries, cotton goods, woollen goods, etc., by States and great cities, may be followed in the volumes on Manufactures, especially Part III.[1]

[1] In 1890 New England and the Middle States produced nearly 90 per cent. of the total value of textile products in the United States; New England alone 50·6 per cent., Massachusetts alone, 25·6 per cent. "It is to be noted that the States in which any single branch of the textile industry is successful, are those in which each of the others chiefly flourishes. The development of the cotton manufacture in the South is the only conspicuous exception to this rule. The rule may be tested by observing that the limited number of States in which the silk manufacture has a large development are States in which the cotton and wool manufactures are increasingly and successfully carried on" (U. S. Census, 1890, Manufactures, Part III., p. 7). The woollen industry was at first widely distributed, following the production of wool and the location of water power; now it is increasingly concentrated. In 1870 New England possessed 40 per cent. of the machinery capacity; in 1880, 47·5 per cent.; and in 1890 50 per cent. Eight leading States contained in 1870, 67·8 per cent.; in 1890, 83·8 per cent. of the machinery capacity (*Ibid.*, p. 15).

The Importance of Industries. This may be measured either by capital or total product. Some of the more important industries are as follows (U. S. Census, 1890: Manufactures, Part I., p. 36):—

	Capital.	Product.
Lumber and other mill products from logs and bolts	$496 million	$403 million
Foundry and machine shop	382 ,,	412 ,,
Iron and steel	372 ,,	430 ,,
Cotton goods	354 ,,	267 ,,
Gas	258 ,,	56 ,,
Liquors, malt	232 ,,	182 ,,
Flour and grist mill	208 ,,	513 ,,
Printing and publishing	195 ,,	275 ,,
Woollen goods	130 ,,	133 ,,
Lumber, planing mill, sash and door, etc.	120 ,,	183 ,,
Slaughtering and meat product (excepting retail butchers)	118 ,,	564 ,,

These eleven industries (all having a capital above $100,000,000), are the great fundamental ones, dealing principally with raw materials.

Internal Relations of Manufactures. The above figures of distribution of manufactures by locality and the relative importance of particular industries in the United States have but a temporary and local interest. The statistics are purely descriptive. The question, however, arises whether on the basis of the elaborate analysis (the seven items given on page 160), we cannot establish the relation of these things to each other, and to industry in general. Questions that suggest themselves are:—What sized capital is employed in different industries? What is the relation of amount of capital to number of workmen and total wages paid? to gross product? to net product? to miscellaneous expenses? We cannot expect minute accuracy in the answer to these questions, because the statistics are only rough. Can we expect any answer at all, or are the answers untrustworthy and misleading?

Average Amount of Capital. The character of an industry,

whether it is on a large or small scale, whether it employs machinery or hand labour, whether it requires a large or small investment, would seem to be indicated by the average amount of capital per establishment. We have some interesting figures of the following sort (U. S. Census, 1890: Manufactures, Part I., p. 36):—

	Number Establishments.	Capital.	Average per Establishment.
All Industries	355,415	$6,525,156,486	$18,359
Agricultural implements	910	145,313,997	159,686
Awning, tents, and sails	581	3,063,009	5,272
Bicycle and tricycle repairing	83	172,070	2,073
Bicycles and tricycles	27	2,058,072	76,225
Blacksmithing & wheelwrighting	28,000	34,500,139	1,232
Iron and steel	645	372,678,018	577,795
Boots and shoes, custom work and repairing	20,803	14,230,081	684
Boots and shoes, factory product	2,082	95,282,311	45,765
Boots and shoes, rubber	11	17,790,970	1,617,361
Carpets and rugs, other than rag	173	38,208,842	220,860
Carpets, rag	854	975,381	1,142
Clothing, men's, custom work and repairing	13,591	54,109,273	3,981
Clothing, men's, factory product	4,867	128,253,547	26,352
Clothing, women's, dressmaking	19,587	12,883,089	658
Clothing, women's, factory product	1,124	21,259,528	17,369
Flouring and grist mill products	18,470	208,473,500	11,287
Gas, illuminating and heating	742	258,771,795	348,749
Petroleum, refining	94	77,416,296	823,578

The above are but specimens of the 364 industries included in this table. They are grouped together in order to bring out the following facts: In many industries there are really two branches, first the manufacture, conducted on a large scale; and second the custom work and repairing, conducted on a small scale. Compare bicycles and bicycle repairing; boot and shoe factory product and boot and shoe repairing, etc. With all the progress of the large industry, there is always room for the supplementary industry on a small scale. Again, some industries seem by their nature to remain small —*e.g.* blacksmithing and wheelwrighting; awning, tents and sails; flouring and grist mills. Some industries by their nature are large—as iron and steel, gas, and petroleum. Many other interesting examples throwing light on the constitution of industry will be found in the full table.

Relation of Capital to Gross Product. It is apparent from the table on page 163 that the gross product does not depend closely upon the amount of capital employed. This is owing to the fact that in some industries very expensive machinery is required, and the process of production demands considerable time. In others, the principal expense is the raw material, and the return comes in quickly. What capital seeks is profit; and this does not depend upon gross product, but upon the excess of gross product over all expenses. The conditions are so different in different industries that no rule can be laid down. The following proportions will illustrate this. For each $100 of product (gross) there is employed an amount of capital as follows (U. S. Census, 1890: Manufactures, Part I., p. 49):—

	Capital.
In agricultural implements	$178·80
In awnings, tents, and sails	39·12
In blacksmithing and wheelwrighting	63·53
In iron and steel	86·48
In boots and shoes, custom work and repairing	40·82
In boots and shoes, factory product	43·18
In boots and shoes, rubber	95·49
In flouring and grist mill product	40·56
In gas, illuminating	454·09
In petroleum	91·08

The results in this table are somewhat surprising. The difference between the large and small industry does not seem to be very great, *e.g.* boots and shoes. Generally, the large industry seems to employ a large amount of capital for $100 of product; but there are many instances of the reverse, as sugar and molasses refining, $19·50; distilled liquors, $29·76; slaughtering and meat packing $20·90. There is no such thing as measuring the efficiency of capital from the relation between capital and the gross product.[1]

Relative Importance of Capital and Labour. Which is the more important factor in production? We cannot decide this. All we can say is that capital plays an increasingly important rôle in many industries. Sometimes the total amount of capital employed is contrasted with the amount of wages paid during the year, but evidently the two figures are not comparable, for under capital is comprised much fixed capital, only the wear and tear on which must be replaced in the total product. The total capital reported at the Eleventh Census was $6,139 million, while the wage-bill was $2,171 million, or about one-third. In the Massachusetts Statistics of Manufactures for 1897(pp. 15 and 68) capital was represented by $394 million and the wage-bill by $132 million, or about one-third again. (In 1894 the figures were 417 and 111, or 26·6 per cent.) But if we examine the particular industries

[1] In the textile industries "the relationship between capital and the value of the product varies in accordance with the material used. The silk manufacture, utilising the most costly and delicate of the fibres, produces much the largest value of product relatively with the amount of capital, and, after silk, the wool manufacture. The product of the latter is valued at $24,640,768 in excess of the capital utilised, while the capital in the cotton manufacture is $86,039,119 in excess of the value of the product." (U. S. Census, 1890: Manufactures, Part III., p. 9.)

In the glass industry $100 of capital was necessary to produce $100 gross product; but in plate glass the amount necessary was $210; in window glass, $90; in green and black glass, only $84. The large amount in the plate-glass branch was owing to the costly machinery and the necessity of carrying a large amount of stock. (*Ibid.*, p. 314.)

there are wide fluctuations, as follows (Mass. Stat. Manufactures, 1897, p. 188 ; 1894, p. 241):—

	Capital invested.	Total Wages paid.	Proportion of Wages to Capital, 1894. 1897.
Boots and shoes	$23·0 million	$22·5 million	(78) 98 per cent.
Carpetings	6·7 ,,	1·6 ,,	(18) 24 ,,
Cotton goods	110·6 ,,	26·4 ,,	(19) 24 ,,
Leather	7·6 ,,	3·0 ,,	(32) 40 ,,
Machines and machinery	27·6 ,,	9·1 ,,	(24) 33 ,,
Metals and metallic goods	18·3 ,,	6·7 ,,	(34) 36 ,,
Paper	21·0 ,,	3·8 ,,	(16) 18 ,,
Woollen goods	25·4 ,,	6·3 ,,	(20) 25 ,,
Worsted goods	16·4 ,,	4·5 ,,	(19) 27 ,,

The above table is interesting as showing the variety of combinations between capital and labour. The differences are due to the investment in some industries of large sums in expensive machinery, or in purchasing and holding large stocks of raw material. In boots and shoes the value of stock used was $61 million to a capital of $23 million ; while in cotton goods it was only $49 million to a capital of $110 million.

The figures in parentheses show the relation of wage-bill to capital in 1894. The numerous and important changes show how worthless this method of comparison is. The amount of capital invested and the amount paid in wages fluctuate according to the exigencies of the business and the judgment of the entrepreneur as to the most profitable combination of capital and labour for the purpose of making a profit. There is no rule of relative importance of labour and capital applicable to two industries, or even to the same industry at two periods of time.

Efficiency of Capital and Labour. The Massachusetts Bureau of Labour Statistics has attempted to penetrate still further into the mysteries of manufacturing industry and express in figures the relation of added wealth to the two factors, capital and labour, which produce it. For this purpose it takes what it calls "industry product," that is, the gross product less the raw material employed. This "industry product" represents the additional wealth produced by the united efforts of capital and labour. How efficient is each in producing it? To bring this out the Bureau calculates the relation of this "industry product" to $1,000 of capital on the one hand, and to each employee on the other, and reaches a table of the following sort (Mass. Stat. Manufactures, 1897, p. 189):—

	Industry Product. Per $1,000 capital invested.	Industry Product. Per employee.
Boots and shoes	$1,684·21	$811·11
Carpetings	363·50	533·60
Cotton goods	329·19	460·26
Leather	746·36	879·78
Machines and machinery	586·81	1,039·76
Metals and metallic goods	667·35	897·88
Paper	407·15	931·21
Woollen goods	416·02	626·29
Worsted goods	575·38	742·61

This table makes a brave showing. The Bureau even goes so far as to say: "These figures afford an indication of the efficiency of the capital invested in these industries during 1897, and those which present the average industry product per employee may be considered as indicating the efficiency of labour." But is it not absurd to say that capital is four times as efficient in the boot and shoe industry as in carpetings; or that labour is 50 per cent. more efficient? The word "efficiency" is out of place. What the figures really show is that the form of capital invested and the kind of labour employed are different in the contrasted industries. In one industry capital may take on the form of very expensive machinery (fixed capital), and the industry product need not be large in order to pay profit and wear and tear. In another industry (boots and shoes?), capital may take on the form of carrying a large stock of raw material, cash for paying wages, great wear and tear, and the industry product must be large in order to replace these things. But these relations can be brought out more clearly simply by giving the items of which "capital" is made up in each industry.

The case is still more obvious in "efficiency" of labour. Where skilled labour is employed, the proportion of "industry product" to each labourer would be large; where unskilled labour is employed, the proportion would probably be small; or even where the labour is of the same grade, if "industry product" in one case included a large amount as return for circulating capital, the proportion to each labourer would be large without regard to efficiency. It seems impossible by crude statistics to measure the efficiency of either capital or labour.

Further Analysis of Capital. One of the prominent items in all the above analyses is the total amount of capital. The question arises what is included under the term "capital." The Eleventh Census used the term in a very broad sense as meaning the amount of resources at the command of the business man for the purpose of carrying on production. Its inquiries were arranged under the following heads:—[1]

Capital invested (both owned and borrowed):—

(1) Value of plant (the value should be estimated at what the works would cost in 1890, if then to be erected, with such allowance for depreciation as may be suitable in the individual case):

Land	$775 million
Buildings	878 ,,
Machinery, tools and implements	1,584 ,,
Total	$3,238 ,,

(2) Live capital (or live assets):

Raw materials on hand	—
Stock in process and finished product on hand	—
Cash on hand, bills receivable, unsettled ledger accounts and sundries not included in any of the foregoing items	—
Total	$3,286 million
Grand total	$6,525 ,,

[1] The schedule is found in U. S. Census, 1890: Manufactures, Part I, p. 10, and the figures on p. 86. The totals for the items under live assets

The above schedule shows plainly the conception of capital employed by the Census office. It is not probable that the absolute figures are of any great value, because the terms themselves are vague, and many estimates would probably be carelessly made. The classification is interesting as showing that the "live assets" are about equal in value to the "plant" or direct investment. For the other items we turn to the statistics of investment in manufactures in 165 cities where we find the following particulars (U.S. Census, 1890: Manufactures, Part II., p. 13):—

Hired property	$833 million	17 per cent.
Land	444 ,,	9·2 ,,
Buildings	506 ,,	10·5 ,,
Machinery, tools and implements	912 ,,	18·8 ,,
Raw materials	464 ,,	9·6 ,,
Stock on hand and finished products	641 ,,	13·3 ,,
Cash, bills receivable and sundries	1,028 ,,	21·3 ,,
	$4,829	100·0 ,,

Counting the hired property as fixed capital, its proportion of the whole would be 55·6 per cent., while that of circulating capital would be 44·3 per cent. The hired property would probably be principally land and buildings, so that it should be divided between the two, but in what proportion is indeterminate. Machinery, tools, and implements would seem to have about the same value as lands and buildings owned, together; while cash and bills receivable amount to about the same as raw materials, stock in hand, and finished product.

Without laying much stress on these figures, they show the function of the capitalist entrepreneur, not only in furnishing the land, buildings, and implements, but also and almost equally in providing the live assets necessary for carrying on

are not given except for selected industries (Table 8, p. 654), for industries in 165 cities (Part II), and for selected industries in Part III. For 165 cities we have also the value of property hired ($833 million), and estimating it for the country at $323 million, we have a total of $1,156 million to be added to the above capital, making a grand total of $7,681 million, as the capital invested in manufacturing industry in the United States in 1890.

the business. There is no method of testing the accuracy of these figures except by comparing the returns in selected industries in order to determine whether there are wide fluctuations in the proportions found in the different industries which are not explicable by the nature of the business. A few attempts of this sort show the following results (Percentages):—[1]

	Agricultural implements.	Boots and shoes.	Carriages and wagons.	Cheese, butter, condensed milk.	Flouring and grist mills.	Leather.	Paper.	Slaughtering and meat packing.
Value of Plant . . .	21·8	22·5	36·0	72·6	65·5	27·7	68·3	37·3
Land	4·3	2·2	12·2	6·0	11·4	7·8	10·9	10·7
Buildings	9·4	5·7	15·8	34·8	20·0	12·5	22·1	17·4
Machinery, etc . .	8·2	14·5	8·0	31·7	34·0	7·4	35·2	9·1
Live Assets	78·1	77·4	63·9	27·3	34·0	72·2	31·6	62·6
Raw materials . .	7·5	15·3	14·4	2·3	11·3	12·0	6·8	8·8
Stock and finished product	12·4	17·2	20·5	12·9	5·4	40·2	7·8	34·6
Cash, bills receivable, etc.	58·2	44·8	28·9	12·0	17·7	19·6	17·0	19·2

It seems from this table that the relation of fixed to circulating capital differs in an extraordinary way in different industries. In the manufacture of agricultural implements only 22 per cent. of the capital is embodied in land, buildings, and machinery; in the cheese, butter, and condensed milk industry nearly three-fourths of the capital is thus employed. Again, the amount of cash, bills receivable and sundries, for which capital is needed, appears extraordinarily large in the manufacture of agricultural implements and in the boot and shoe factory. It is undoubtedly true that the employment of capital varies greatly in its nature in different industries, but the extraordinary variations seen in this table probably point to carelessness and inaccuracy in the returns.

Part III of the Statistics of Manufactures gives detailed statistics of capital and miscellaneous expenses in certain

[1] Calculated from Table 8, U. S. Census, 1890: Manufactures, Part I., p. 654.

specified industries. How widely the forms of capital differ is shown in the following table giving the figures for three prominent industries, cotton goods, chemicals, and glass (U.S. Census, 1890: Manufactures, Part III., pp. 194, 286 and 324):—

	Cotton Goods.	Chemicals.	Glass.
Value hired property . . .	$8,301,464	$12,098,037	$ not given.
Aggregate direct investment .	354,020,843	168,462,044	40,966,850
Plant	230,993,567	72,640,007	25,437,450
Land	23,225,097	17,100,441	5,097,726
Buildings	69,742,664	26,228,463	11,401,021
Machinery	138,025,806	29,311,103	8,938,703
Live assets	123,027,276	95,822,037	15,529,400
Raw material . . .	37,796,009	19,299,270	2,159,860
Stock on hand, etc. .	41,388,280	27,241,216	6,339,196
Cash, bills receivable, etc.	43,842,987	49,281,551	7,030,344
Miscellaneous expenses . .	16,716,524	13,640,343	2,267,696
Rent	488,735	941,660	70,265
Taxes	2,689,632	715,188	177,578
Insurance	1,213,322	874,606	287,850
Repairs	3,987,748	1,756,900	350,810
Interest	4,098,435	1,359,920	412,321
Sundries	4,238,652	7,967,369	968,872

Plant represents 65 per cent. of the direct investment in the cotton industry, 43 per cent. in chemicals, and 63 per cent. in glass. The complementary figures show the importance of "live assets." The insufficiency of the returns of miscellaneous expenses is well illustrated in the coke industry, where out of 218 establishments reporting, only 112 reported taxes, 45 insurance, 69 repairs, 22 interest paid on cash in business, and 46 sundries. It is impossible to report such items where other industries are carried on by the same establishment or firm.[1]

Method of Industrial Organisation. The way in which labour is applied through capital and capital through labour constitutes what may be called industrial organisation. In modern life, through the application of steam to machinery,

[1] U. S. Census, 1890: Manufactures, Part III., pp. 350 and 389.

it is taking on the form of the large factory system, with its great plant, its division of labour, and its extended market. The fact itself is obvious to common sight. We can use statistics only to indicate the process of change and the rate at which it is going on. We have statistics of the concentration of industry in large establishments, and of the increased use of machinery and steam power. As showing the first, we have the fact that in many industries, while the number of establishments is decreasing, the output is increasing. In England the number of cotton mills increased (during twenty years, 1870–1890) from 2,453 to 2,538, while the number of spindles increased from 33,995,221 to 40,511,934, and the number of power-looms from 440,676 to 615,714.[1] The average number of spindles in a cotton mill in 1850 was 10,858, while in 1885 it was 15,227. Mr. Wells finds that the average product from a manufacturing establishment in the United States was 60 per cent. greater in 1880 than in 1860.

The process of concentration is shown still further by the following figures, 1880 to 1890.[2] In the manufacture of agricultural implements the number of establishments decreased 1,033 or 53 per cent., while the number of employees increased 2,964 or 7·5 per cent., and the value of products $12 million or 18·4 per cent. In boot and shoe factories, the number of establishments increased 6 per cent., the number of employees 25 per cent., and the value of product 33 per cent. The number of pairs of shoes increased 43 per cent. In 1880 each establishment had on an average 57 employees and a product valued at $84,763. In 1890 the figures were 67 and $105,980. The number of flouring and grist mills decreased by 5,868 or 32 per cent., while the product increased slightly. The number of paper factories decreased 18 per cent., while the number of employees increased 22 per cent., and the value of the product 35 per cent. The number of establishments engaged in manufacturing cotton is smaller

[1] Hobson, Evolution of Modern Capitalism, pp. 90 and 92.

[2] U. S. Census, 1890: Manufactures, Part I, p. 56.

than in 1850-60, although their spindle capacity is now nearly four times as great as in 1850.[1]

The tendency of the woollen industry is towards larger mills. The majority of the establishments in the earlier days of the industry were one and two set mills, and this is still the case in the Southern and Western States. But in the Eastern States the larger mills now predominate. In 1840 the census reported 2,585 fulling mills, and the value of the woollen goods made in the household with the assistance of these auxiliary mills probably exceeded the value of the factory product. The reverse process sometimes takes place. In old times all the processes in the woollen industry were carried on in the same factory, owing to its isolation. Now, there is a tendency to subdivide, the scouring being done in one establishment, the carding and combing by another, the spinning by another, the weaving by another, the dyeing and finishing by still another.[2]

Another method of representing the growth of the large industry is by classifying establishments according to the number of workmen employed. For Germany we have the following figures showing the change from 1882 to 1895 (Vierteljahrshefte zur Statistik des Deutschen Reichs, 1898, I., Ergänz., p. 10*):—

	No. of establishments. 1895.	1882.	Persons employed. 1895.	1882.	Per cent. increase in Establishments.	Persons.
Small establishments, 5 persons and under	2,934,723	2,882,768	4,770,669	4,335,822	1·8	10·0
Medium size . .	191,299	112,715	2,454,257	1,391,720	69·7	76·3
6—10 persons .	113,547	68,763	833,409	500,097	65·1	66·6
11—50 persons .	77,752	43,952	1,620,848	891,623	76·9	81·8
Large establishments	18,955	9,974	3,044,343	1,613,247	90·0	88·7
51—200 persons	15,624	8,095	1,439,776	742,688	93·0	93·9
201—1000 persons	3,076	1,752	1,155,836	657,399	75·6	75·8
1000 and over .	255	127	448,731	213,160	100·8	110·5
Totals	3,144,977	3,005,457	10,269,269	7,340,789	4·6	39·9

[1] *Ibid.*, Part III, p. 8.

[2] *Ibid.*, Part III, pp. 13—18.

This table shows that the large establishments increased in number more rapidly than the small, and that the number of workmen increased faster than the number of establishments.

Motive Power in Manufactures. The total power used in manufactures in the United States in 1890 was 5,954,655 horse power, of which 4,662,029 or 78·3 per cent. was steam, and 1,263,343 or 21·2 per cent. was water power. During the decade steam power had increased from 2,185,458 horse power or 113 per cent., while water power had increased from 1,225,379 or only 3·1 per cent.[1]

National Wealth. In the first part of this chapter we considered what may be called trade capital, or the sum of wealth used to carry on business. Information concerning such trade capital can be obtained only for large industries and for them only incompletely. The numerous small enterprises, and the capital used by individuals, such as merchants and tradesmen, escape enumeration. The second method of estimating capital is to calculate the total national wealth, and then to estimate the proportionate amount of this wealth used as capital.

A direct census of national wealth is impossible. There are two ways of estimating it. One is to take the chief modes of investment, such as manufactures, agriculture, &c., get at the amount of each, and add these amounts together. The second is to take an income or other tax as a basis, and estimate the probable value of the capital producing the income, or yielding the tax. The method to be used depends upon the circumstances of the particular country.

United States Census Method. In the United States, owing to the absence of an income tax, it is necessary to use the first of the above methods. The Census Office is accustomed to make an estimate of the national wealth, arranged according to items. The true valuation for 1890 was given as

[1] U.S. Census, 1890: Manufactures, Part I., p. 745.

follows (U.S. Census, 1890: Wealth, Debt, and Taxation. Part II., p. 7):—

Total	$65,037,091,197
Real estate, with improvements thereon	39,544,544,333
Live stock on farms, farm implements and machinery	2,703,015,040
Mines and quarries, including product on hand	1,291,291,579
Gold and silver coin and bullion	1,158,774,948
Machinery of mills and product on hand, raw and manufactured	3,058,593,441
Railroads and equipments, including $389,357,289 for street railroads	8,685,407,323
Telegraphs, telephones, shipping, canals and equipment	701,755,712
Miscellaneous	7,893,708,821

The information necessary for these items is gathered from different sources. The amount of real estate, with improvements thereon, is based on assessed values raised to a true value according to the judgment of the Census Office. For the purpose of ascertaining the relation of true value to assessed value, 25,000 inquiries were sent throughout the country to persons believed to be familiar with the value of real estate, and the replies received were carefully considered in connection with the reports of the assessors. The value of live stock on farms, and of farm implements and machinery was taken from the Census on Agriculture, that is, from the returns of farmers. The value of mines and quarries was taken from the Census report on Mineral Industries; that of gold and silver from the estimate of the Director of the Mint; that of railroads, mill machinery, and shipping from the Census returns. The value of telegraphs and telephones was based upon the net earnings therefrom, capitalised at 5 per cent. The miscellaneous items were arrived at in various ways.

No great confidence is to be placed in this estimate of the national wealth of the United States. The assessed valuation of the real estate and personal property taxed was only $25,473 million, and there is no assurance that the assessed value and the true value have any such relation as that indicated (about 40 per cent). There are in fact very wide variations, as for instance the assessed valuation in New York is 44 per cent., in Pennsylvania 43 per cent., in Illinois 16 per cent., in Ohio 45 per cent., in Massachusetts 77 per cent. of the supposed true valuation. With such uncertainty in regard to the total figures the attempted distribution of wealth among the different States and the accompanying maps are valueless. Still more useless are the figures of growth of national wealth during successive decades, since these estimates were made on different plans.[1]

Giffen's Method. Another method of ascertaining national wealth is on the basis of an income tax. The best example is the well-known estimate by Sir Robert Giffen of the income and wealth of the United Kingdom, made at the successive periods 1865, 1875, and 1885. The method is to take the income tax returns for each kind of property and capitalise them at a certain rate. Land, for instance, is supposed to be worth 26 times its annual value, houses 15 times, quarries, mines, and iron works 4 times, gasworks 25 times, railroads 28 times, etc. By this method the capitalised value in 1885, of the incomes returned was £7,619,751,000. To this is added certain other sums which escape taxation, making the total income-bearing capital £8,577,436,000. An estimate of moveable property not bearing income, and of government and local property, brings the grand total of national wealth up to £10,037,436,000. The details of the estimate for 1885 are shown in the following table (Giffen, Growth of Capital, p. 11):—

Income and Wealth of the United Kingdom, 1885.

	Income. £	Year's purchase.	Capital. £
Under Schedule A—			
Lands	65,039,000	26	1,691,313,000
Houses	128,459,000	15	1,926,885,000
Other profits	877,000	30	26,310,000
Under Schedule B—			
(Farmers' profits)	65,233,000	8	521,864,000
Under Schedule C—			
(Public funds, less home funds)	21,096,000	25	527,400,000
Carried forward	280,704,000	...	4,693,772,000

[1] For criticism of the method and figures see Plehn, in The Federal Census (Amer. Econ. Assocn. Publications, New Series, No. 2, p. 369 ff.)

INCOME AND WEALTH OF THE UNITED KINGDOM, 1885—*continued.*

	Income. £	Year's purchase.	Capital. £
Brought forward	280,704,000	...	4,693,772,000
Under Schedule D—			
Quarries	933,000	4	3,732,000
Mines	7,603,000	4	30,412,000
Ironworks	2,265,000	4	9,060,000
Gasworks	5,026,000	25	125,650,000
Waterworks	3,260,000	20	65,200,000
Canals, &c.	3,546,000	20	70,920,000
Fishings	618,000	20	12,360,000
Market tolls, &c.	590,000	20	11,800,000
Other public companies	34,789,000	20	695,780,000
Foreign and colonial securities, &c.	9,859,000	20	197,180,000
Railways in United Kingdom	33,270,000	28	931,560,000
Railways out of United Kingdom	3,808,000	20	76,160,000
Interest paid out of rates, &c.	5,041,000	25	126,025,000
Other profits	1,435,000	20	28,700,000
Trades and professions, one-fifth of total income of £180,000,000	36,096,000	15	541,440,000
Total under income-tax	428,843,000	...	7,619,751,000
Trades and professions omitted, 20 per cent. of amount assessed, or £36,000,000, of which one-fifth	7,219,000	15	108,285,000
is	960,000[1]	15	14,400,000
Income of non-income-tax paying classes derived from capital	67,000,000	5	335,000,000
Foreign investments, not in schedules C and D	50,000,000	10	500,000,000
Movable property not yielding income, *e.g.*, furniture of houses, &c., works of art, &c.	...	...	960,000,000
Government and local property, say	...	...	500,000,000
	554,022,000	...	10,037,436,000

There are, of course, elements of uncertainty in such an estimate of the national capital and wealth. One is the question whether the income returned is the true income; the error here is in defect rather than in excess. The second is in regard to the number of years purchase assigned to each item of income. That must be a matter of expert opinion,

[1] Estimate of income escaping assessment by raising limit of exemption in 1876.

and Sir Robert Giffen fully explains the reasons for each figure. The third element of uncertainty lies in the estimates contained in the latter part of the table. This also is a matter of expert opinion. It must be conceded that there is room for considerable error in giving the exact figures. But with a carefully administered income tax, and with the estimates subject to the criticism of experienced men, this is probably the best method we have of arriving at a judgment in regard to total national wealth.

Growth of Capital. Even if these estimates of national wealth are not exact, they are useful for comparative purposes. If the same method is pursued at successive periods, say ten years apart, we can reach an opinion in regard to the increase of national wealth, the rate of that increase, and also as to the changing importance of different forms of investment.

These points are brought out in the following table, showing the amount of capital at three different periods, viz., 1865, 1875, and 1885, and the absolute and per cent. increase or decrease during the two decades (Giffen, Growth of Capital, p. 43):—

	1865.	1875.	1885.	Increase in 1865–75. Amount.		Increase or decrease in 1875–85. Amount.	
	Mlns.	Mlns.	Mlns.	Mlns.		Mlns.	
	£	£	£	£	per cent.	£	per cent.
Lands	1,864	2,007	1,691	143	8	-316	-15·7
Houses	1,031	1,420	1,927	389	38	507	35·7
Farmers' profits	620	668	522	48	8	-146	-21·9
Public funds less home funds	211	519	527	308	146	8	1·5
Mines	19	56	31	37	195	-25	-45·0
Ironworks	7	29	9	22	314	20	-69·0
Railways	414	655	932	241	58	277	42·0
Canals	18	20	71	2	11	51	255·0
Gasworks	37	53	126	16	43	73	138·0
Quarries	2	4	4	2	100	...	...
Other profits	55	84	116	29	53	32	38·0
Other income-tax income, principally trades and professions and public companies	660	1,128	1,664	468	71	536	47·5
	4,938	6,643	7,620	1,705	35	977	14·7

	1865. Mlns. £	1875. Mlns. £	1885. Mlns. £	Increase in 1865–75. Amount. Mlns. £	per cent.	Increase or decrease in 1875–85. Amount. Mlns. £	per cent.
Brought forward . .	4,938	6,643	7,620	1,705	35	977	14·7
Trades and professions omitted	75	105	108	30	40	3	3·0
Income from capital of non-income-tax paying classes	200	300	349	100	50	49	16·0
Foreign investments not in Schedule C and D .	100	400	500	300	300	100	25·0
Movable property not yielding income . .	500	700	960	200	40	260	37·0
Government and local property, say . . .	300	400	500	100	33	100	25·0
	6,113	8,548	10,037	2,435	40	1,489	17·4

It seems from this table that the national wealth of Great Britain increased from 1865 to 1875 by 40 per cent., and from 1875 to 1885 by 17·4 per cent. We must notice, however, that during the latter period there was a considerable fall of prices. Sir Robert Giffen estimates this at about 15 per cent. If now we decrease the valuation of 1875 by 15 per cent. we have a total of 7½ instead of 8½ thousand millions, upon which an increase to 10 thousand millions is very nearly 40 per cent. Applying the correction to the 1885 figures and adding 15 per cent. to them, the total would be 11½ thousand millions, which again is an increase of nearly 40 per cent.

For more distant periods the author has utilised some older estimates and arrives at a comparative table of the following sort (Growth of Capital, p. 110):—

Growth of Capital and Population in the United Kingdom since 1812.

Year.	Population (millions).	Property (mllns. stgl.)	Property per head, £.
1812 (Colquhoun)	17	2,700	160
1822 (Colquhoun-Lowe)	21	2,500	120
1833 (Colquhoun-Pablo de Pabrer.)	25	3,600	144
1845 (income-tax)	28	4,000	143
1865	30	6,000	200
1875	33	8,500	260
Present time	37	10,000	270

Different Kinds of Capital. The table on page 177 shows that land and houses are the most important form of investment. During the twenty years, however, land has lost the first place and has been superseded by houses. This is owing to the decrease in the rental value of agricultural land. Farmers' profits have also diminished. The decrease in mines and iron-works Sir R. Giffen thinks due to inflated values in 1875. Other items have increased, but at varying rates. The increase in railways and in trades and professions is especially noticeable.

Other uses to which such estimates of national wealth may be put are enumerated (page 136) as follows:—

To compare the income of a community where estimates of income exist with its property.

To measure the burden of national debts upon different communities.

To measure, in conjunction with other factors such as aggregate income, revenue and population, the relative strength and resources of different communities.

To compare the aggregate accumulation in a community with that proportion of the accumulation which can be described as free savings, and which is gradually invested through the agency of the Stock Exchange.

To throw light on the question of the changes in the value of money.

De Foville's Method. A careful estimate of national wealth in France has been made on the basis of inheritance taxes. It appears that the amount of property passing annually by successions or donation *inter vivos* is about 6¼ million francs. M. de Foville calculates that the mean interval between generations, or rather between the occasions when property passes to the succeeding generation is about 36 years. This would mean that $\frac{1}{36}$ of the total wealth of France passes by succession or donation each year. Multiplying therefore 6¼ million francs by 36 we get the sum of 225,000 million francs as the total private wealth in France.[1]

[1] Dictionnaire des Finances. Art. Richesse.

This estimate is supported by another method of valuing the wealth of France by separate items as follows:—

	Milliards of frs.
Lands	75
House property (including factories)	50
Specie	5
Convertible securities	70
Agricultural implements, live stock	10
Other personal property, exclusive of that of which the value has already been reckoned under real property	15
	225

Scientific Tests.

The principal question under this head is whether it is possible by the statistical method to measure the amount of capital invested in industry. We have here some evident fallacies.

Capital Stock. In the case of corporations there is the so-called capital stock. This capital stock bears no necessary relation either to the amount of money originally invested, or to the present value of the plant or to the total amount of money necessary to carry on the business. In many cases the amount is too small, as when profits have been turned into capital without increasing the amount of stock. In other cases the amount is too large, as where the stock has been watered, or new stock issued to represent the value of a franchise, or the earning capacity of a business. In the case of consolidation of several businesses it is often the practice to issue new stock which has no basis except the increased earning capacity of the old plant under the new administration. Finally, in the case of many enterprises, especially railroads, the bonded indebtedness represents in whole or in part the cost of the enterprise, while the stock is more or less fictitious and represents only the expectation of profits. For instance, the railroads of the United States are said to represent the following sums invested, in 1896:—

Capital stock	$5,290,730,567
Bonds	5,416,074,969
Floating debt	339,502,302
Total	$11,046,307,838

There is no assurance that the railroads cost this amount originally; and there is still less assurance that it would cost this amount to replace them at the present time. The same remarks would hold true in regard to the nominal capital stock of banks and banking companies, of insurance companies, of mines and mining companies, and of those manufacturing companies which are carried on under the corporate form.

Credit Capital. Owing to the above fallacies connected with nominal capital stock, the efforts of statisticians have been directed towards estimating the amount of capital actually used at a given time in the principal industries. The earliest of these efforts was made by Carroll D. Wright in the Massachusetts Census of 1885. It is true that in previous United States censuses, and also in Massachusetts, manufacturers had been asked to return the amount of capital invested, but the Federal returns were so manifestly inadequate that they were expressly repudiated by General Walker, who advised the abandonment of the whole inquiry. In Massachusetts Mr. Wright found occasion to believe that the nominal amount of capital of certain corporations was fully one-third short of the actual amount in use. He accordingly adopted a new classification, with the following results, for 1885 (Mass. Census, 1885, Manufactures, p. 76)[1]:—

Land	$34,412,516	6·87	per cent.
Buildings and fixtures	84,474,127	16·87	,,
Machinery	100,955,619	20·17	,,
Implements and tools	14,298,711	2·86	,,
Cash	173,440,947	34·65	,,
Credit capital supplied by partners and stockholders	19,481,405	3·89	,,
Credit capital (bills payable, accounts on long time)	73,531,052	14·69	,,
	$500,594,377	100·00	,,

[1] See U. S. Census, 1870, Industry and Wealth, p. 381; U. S. Census, 1880, Manufactures, p. 39; North, Statistics of Capital in The Federal Census (Amer. Econ. Assocn. Publications, New Series, No. 2, 1899).

The peculiar thing about this classification is the introduction of credit capital in addition to the fixed capital invested and the circulating capital represented by cash. The Bureau recommended the following method of estimating this credit capital, viz., to take the interest account and the average rate of discount for the year, and calculate the average amount of loans such interest account would represent. For example, if the interest account of a firm was $6,000 and the rate of discount were 6 per cent., that would represent the use of $100,000.

There is something very specious in this effort to include credit capital with fixed capital in the statistics of manufactures. It rests upon the feeling that the power of a manufacturer to turn out products depends not only upon his money actually invested in buildings, machinery, &c., but also upon his credit. So much of his credit as he chooses to exercise at any particular time (say on the average during the year), either by advances from partners and stockholders, by loans or by credit given to customers, is so much added to the producing power at his command in the form of capital.

This conception of capital seems unrealisable by statistics. The amount of credit capital added to the total by the Census of 1885 in Massachusetts seems very large ($93,000,000), yet it appears that only 2 per cent. of the returns gave credit capital supplied by partners, and only 12·5 per cent., returns of other credit capital. It is doubtful if manufacturers are willing or able to answer such a question.

In the second place, there is danger lest credit capital be duplicated in the return of machinery, raw material, and cash. Suppose the money borrowed from the bank has been spent in machinery, in purchasing supplies or raw material, why should it be counted a second time?

Assets as Capital. The United States Census of 1890 modified this idea somewhat, but still continued to treat capital as the gross assets of a business at a specified time. It therefore included not only land, buildings, machinery, raw material, and cash, but also finished products on hand, bills receivable, and unsettled ledger accounts. These represent the total assets of a business, and the total assets represent the productive power used in the shape of capital. This may be called the broadly concrete conception of capital, and it was maintained that any manufacturer could furnish these items from his books. But here again, although only part of the credit power of the manufacturer is included in his capital, there is danger of duplication, as shown by Mr. North in the following illustration:—

Suppose one mill sells to another $100,000 worth of cloth, and receives a note in payment. The note enters into the credit capital of one mill, and the cloth into the raw material of the second.

Concrete Capital. The Massachusetts Census of 1895 narrowed the definition still further, and tried to cover only the actual instruments of production, raw material, and what may be called accessories, such as cash, stock in process of manufacture, and articles to be used in the industry. This definition rejects finished goods, bills receivable, and current accounts. It may be called the narrowly concrete definition of capital.

The Massachusetts schedule is as follows (Stat. Manufactures, 1897, p. 160):—

A. Value of land occupied by the establishment (if owned).
B. Value of buildings and fixtures (if owned).
C. Value of machinery and motive power (if owned).
D. Value of implements and tools (not included under C).
E. Value of patent rights, patterns, &c. (if owned).
F. Cash on hand and in bank at the date of making the return.
G. Value, at cost, of raw materials and articles to be used in the industry, on hand at the date of making the return, including goods in process of manufacture.

Clearly, items A to F in the list of inquiries above given include forms of capital necessary to carry on the establishment. They are all items of capital devoted to production. As to the item G, the case is not so plain. It includes items of "stock" and also items of "product," although as yet incomplete. At all events, they are forms of capital invested antecedent to the completion of the productive processes, and necessary for, indeed actually employed in, those processes. The inquiries as they stand at least have the merit of being distinct, susceptible of definite replies without duplications, and seem to omit none of the capital devoted to production.

We need not enter into the merits of this classification compared with that of the United States Census. The latter attempts to arrive at the sum necessary to carry on business whether that sum is invested in machinery, or in cash on hand, or consists of finished product, or of credit given to purchasers. The Massachusetts report attempts to single out that portion of the above items actually used in the work of production. It is doubtful if either system will reach satisfactory results, for the following reasons:—

(1) However perfect the classification, there is a fundamental difficulty in the inability or unwillingness of business men to answer such questions. What is the true value of land, buildings, machinery, patent rights, patterns, &c.? Is it what these things cost originally? or is it the cost with an allowance for depreciation? or is it what they would bring in the market? These estimates might be widely different from each other, and yet all be honestly made. But, still further, there is absolutely no assurance that business men will take the trouble to make such estimates, and there is no means of controlling them after they have been made.

(2) One great difficulty always felt in statistics of capital is in respect to the value of land occupied but hired. A manufacturer occupying hired premises will not return such premises as capital. The rent that he pays becomes simply one of the expenses of business. It is true that we can ask him as to the value of buildings hired, but there is always danger, either of deficient returns, or of duplications where several manufacturers occupy the same building. The same

thing is true of motive power that is hired, and in some cases of machinery.[1]

(3) So too the relation of capital to gross and net product, to wages paid, &c., can never be fully displayed by statistics, because the conditions and circumstances under which production is carried on vary so enormously from industry to industry, and from time to time. All attempts to calculate profits by a combination of these figures shatter upon the uncertainty of the figures themselves, and upon the presence of unknown and unascertainable elements and influences which make up the life of business enterprise, but which cannot in any way be measured.

It seems best, therefore, to abandon the attempt to get statistics of capital. They are entirely uncertain and unreliable, and can be utilised only for the roughest generalisations, which are sufficiently obvious to all having any knowledge of business. On the other hand, they may give rise to very misleading inferences in regard to questions of the relative importance and the relative reward of capital and labour.

Gross and Net Product. The United States Census purports to give the gross product of all the manufacturing industries of the United States during the census year, and for each previous census back to 1850. These industries are brought under 369 classes, and the gross product given for each. A further analysis shows the gross product of the manufacturing industry for each state, and comparison is made for each census since 1850. Not content even with this, a further table attempts to specify the total product for particular industries in each state, and even for the counties in each state. If these figures were correct, we should have

[1] If of two mills producing the same amount of goods, one owns a building worth $100,000, and the other hires a similar building, there is a difference of that amount in the capital necessary to produce the same amount of product. The Eleventh Census estimated the value of hired property at $1,156 million, but it makes but little use of the figure. The Massachusetts Census omits it altogether.

a very detailed picture of the manufacturing industry of the United States, and comparisons could be made both in space and time.[1]

The material is far too imperfect for any such comparisons, and for the following reasons:—

(1) The term gross product is itself incapable of precise use, and is misleading. It includes the value of the raw material. But often the raw material of one factory is the finished product of another, and thus the gross product includes many duplications. Not only this, but the more industry is carried on in separate establishments, the greater this duplication; while the more the different processes are concentrated in one establishment, the less the duplication. The gross product would vary from one time to another, or from one industry to another, according to simple changes in the process of manufacturing or organisation of industry. The numerical results, therefore, have no significance.[2]

(2) The returns themselves are imperfect, and vary from census to census, from industry to industry, and from place to place in the degree of imperfection. The returns of 1890 were more perfect than those of 1880; the returns for cities were more complete than those for rural districts; and in some cases, it was found necessary to close the canvass without obtaining returns from large establishments. Industries are also classified according to the product of chief value. The totals given in the special reports will not agree with the totals in the general report. For instance, many of the establishments which appear under the title Iron and Steel in the special report on that industry, appear in the general report under the head of some specialised product, as nails, wire, and cotton ties. The result is very confusing, but apparently unavoidable. Comparisons of totals built up on

[1] U.S. Census, 1890: Manufactures, Part I., pp. 4 and 5; tables 4 and 6.

[2] North, *op. cit.*

such different bases must be misleading. But if it cannot be used for comparative purposes, "gross product" seems to lose all significance.

(3) By deducting from the value of gross product the cost of the raw material, we have "net product." This is supposed to represent the value added to the raw material by the manufacturing process. If, however, the figures, both for gross product and value of raw material, are uncertain (as they are), the result must be equally uncertain. Nor can it be used to indicate the profitableness of the industry, for miscellaneous expenses have still to be taken out, and the value of the gross product is its estimated value at the factory. Proportions established between this net product and capital, or total amount of wages, or cost of raw material, are sure to be misleading.[1]

(4) For comparisons in time, we have a further difficulty, viz., that the standard of value may have changed. In 1870, values were measured in a paper currency. An attempt was made to allow for this by reducing values 20 per cent. In 1890, prices were lower than in 1880, and hence the same product might have been turned out, but its value would have been much less. An index number of prices might, perhaps, be used to indicate the changes due to falling prices, but it simply introduces another uncertainty.[2]

It is sometimes recommended that we take not the value of the product, but the quantity of certain units, as yards of cloth, tons of iron, &c. But the units vary in quality from one census to another, and it would, of course, be impossible to sum up the total amount of industrial product in such heterogeneous terms. It seems obvious, therefore, that in reality we must confine our study of the productivity of industry

[1] U. S. Census, 1890: Manufactures, Part II., p. xxx.

[2] In the iron and steel industry the increase of products from 1880 to 1890 was from $296,000,000 to $498,000,000, or 61·4 per cent.; while the increase in tons was from 7,265,140 to 18,216,215 or 150·7 per cent. (U. S. Census, 1890, Manufactures, Part III., p. 385).

to particular branches where we can make some estimate of changes in units and in values.[1]

Reflective Analysis.

Statistics confirm the theories of political economy in regard to the importance of capital, as a factor of production. Wealth increases faster than population, that is, capital increases faster than labour-force. The great producing nations are the ones that are increasing in wealth at the most rapid rate. The community not only supports itself, but devotes a part of its wealth to further production. When one thinks of the enormous sums of money invested in railroads during the last forty years, the question arises: Whence did this wealth come? The answer is, that it produced itself to a large extent. The new methods were so productive, that they afforded a large excess as profit, and these profits were turned again into capital. The same thing occurs in single industries. The capital employed in the cotton industry in 1850, was estimated at $74,509,931; in 1890 it was $354,020,843. This capital has been largely acquired in the industry itself and re-invested. New industries spring up also, and are furnished with capital, *e.g.* the petroleum industry, which reported a capital of $77,416,296, in 1890, in the United States. Another process is going on, which can be vaguely traced in the statistics, viz.: the turning of hand industries into machine industries. For instance, bread and bakery products employed a capital of 19 million dollars in 1880, and over 45 million dollars in 1890. The same thing is seen in the size of establishments. There were, *e.g.*, 5,531 brick and tile establishments in 1880, and the number had but slightly increased in 1890 (5,828), but the capital had increased from 27 to 82 million dollars, and the product from 32 to 67 million dollars. This concentration of capital seems

[1] Some slight attempts in this direction are made in the volume on Manufactures, Part I., p. 57 ff.

to be the irresistible tendency of the times. It is the counterpart of the localisation of industry in large cities due to urban growth, which in turn is due to railroads and improved means of transportation. The whole system hangs together, and it is impossible to escape it. The flexibility of the modern industrial organisation is such, however, that there is decentralisation in two ways—first, certain industries are very widespread, owing to their nature—such as those connected with building, or local repairs, or in the manufacture of articles too heavy to transport. The second thing is the localisation of industries in small cities rather than in large, in order to escape some of the burdens of large cities—rent, taxes, &c. Concentration of capital and production on a large scale will be the system of the future. This means increased employment of capital to produce the same product, that is, the increase of fixed capital, the choosing of more elaborate and round-about methods. This can be illustrated statistically by the increase of capital compared with product, and if our statistics were more perfect, might be illustrated by the increased proportion of capital devoted to machinery and implements.

In regard to the relative importance of capital and labour, our statistics undoubtedly show the growing importance of capital.[1] That is, labour must be applied through the aid of more and more complicated and expensive machinery and implements. This points the moral that capital must be encouraged, not discouraged; and, also, that it is very easily reached by legislation and popular movements. Increase of capital still means, on the whole, increased employment for labour, although, temporarily, it may mean displacement of labour in particular industries. The figures for increase of wages in the Eleventh Census are, probably, exaggerated; but, taken with other wages statistics (Ch. IX.), they show that the compensation of labour is increasing

[1] "The characteristic of pre-machinery industry is the small proportion which capital bears to labour," Hobson, *op. cit.*, p. 40.

rather than decreasing. This confirms the well-worn commonplace of political economy, that the interests of capital and labour are one; that an abundance of capital is the prerequisite for high reward of labour. There are two facts in the modern organisation which prevent capital from tyrannising over labour. One is the abundance of capital, which still keeps alive competition; the second is the mobility of labour, which enables labour to go from one employment to another. Capital, taking on the form of machinery, encourages both of these movements, for often capital invested in the newest machinery can compete successfully with capital in the older machinery; and, the simpler and more automatic the machinery, the easier for labour to turn from one employment to another. It is probable that capital will become more and more dependent upon labour, while increasing enormously in amount. Labour-force will still remain the active agent in the production of wealth, only it will be not simple labour, but labour armed with the most perfect tools, and commanding the forces of nature.

Book II.

EXCHANGE.

Exchange in its Relation to Consumption and Production. In early forms of economic life, man satisfies his wants directly, that is, each one produces what he consumes. As the processes of production become more complicated, especially as the division of labour is introduced, each one produces that for which he is best fitted, trusting to be able to exchange his own product for that of some other individual. He now satisfies his wants indirectly. The baker gains shoes by producing bread; the shoemaker gains bread by producing shoes. Many persons produce that which they themselves never consume, as the chemist may never use the chloroform which he manufactures, or the silk weaver never wear a silk gown. As Karl Marx says, in modern life a man produces that which he does *not* need. This process may extend itself to nations, and is then called international trade.

Two consequences follow. The first is that the productive process becomes very complicated and elongates itself, so to speak, into a constant trading or exchange. Production is not complete until the article produced has been parted with and the object desired by each individual has been gained. Exchange is really only a branch of production.[1] In fact, as

[1] *Cf.* J. B. Clark, "Production, indeed, as it is carried on in a social state, is a process that includes both Exchange and Distribution." (Quarterly Journal Economics, Vol. XIII., Oct. 1898, p. 3.)

we have already seen, a considerable section of the community devotes its energy entirely to the business of trading, transportation and exchange. Any treatment of Production without Exchange is necessarily incomplete, while any treatment of Exchange, as a phenomenon separate from Production, is artificial and can be excused only on grounds of convenience.

A second consequence is that the economic happiness of each individual depends not only upon his ability and willingness to produce in the narrow sense of the term, but also, and perhaps to an even greater degree, upon his power of exchanging that which he has produced for that which he needs. The so-called process of Distribution by which each one has determined *for* him the degree to which his wants shall be satisfied, takes place through Exchange. Exchange is in itself the process of Distribution, which is thus inextricably interwoven with the process of Production. We are thus led from Production through Exchange to Distribution, which in its turn brings us back to Consumption, thus completing the cycle. In fact, all together they constitute simply the economic activity of the community—the economic conduct of man.

But, just as in Production we find it convenient to distinguish land, labour, and capital as particular factors of production (although in actual life they are never separated, for it is the capital-using man working with natural objects who produces wealth), so it is convenient to study separately the phenomena of Exchange and Distribution. In Exchange we find the explanation of how the processes of Production have come to be so intricate and complex, while in Distribution we study the effect on the individual of this complicated Production-Exchange process.

In Exchange our inquiries will be turned in three directions: (1) The terms of the Exchange, *i.e.*, the question of value and prices; (2) the mechanism of exchange, *i.e.*, money and credit; (3) the concrete phenomena of exchange

—the physical act—*i.e.*, trade, commerce and transportation. In regard to the order of treatment there seems to be little choice; in fact, any order of treatment that seems to imply sequence is bad. The phenomena, volume of trade, money, and price, are simultaneous and co-existent. Our order is the one we have pursued in the previous book, namely, from processes up to their manifestation in economic organisation. As in the previous book we worked from labour, land and capital up to national wealth, so here we shall work through prices, money and credit up to internal and foreign trade.

CHAPTER VI.

PRICES.

Economic Purpose.

The Law of Prices. The terms (expressed in money) on which commodities or services are exchanged constitute their price. The office of economic theory is to explain the way in which this price is fixed. On the one hand, we have one or more buyers having a greater or less desire to possess the commodity or acquire the service and willing to pay a greater or less price for it. On the other hand, we have one or more sellers willing to give up the commodity or render the service for a greater or less compensation. The price at any particular time and place will be fixed at that point where the amount ready to be disposed of at that price will be just carried off by the demand at that price. At such a point demand and supply are said to be in equilibrium.

If we wish to explain the price of any commodity we must, therefore, investigate the conditions of demand and supply. Generally speaking, when the demand is great and the supply small, prices will be high, and *vice versâ*. If we wish to explain fluctuations in prices we must examine again the conditions of demand and supply. This is not an easy matter; for on the one hand demand is affected by a great variety of things, and, on the other, supply is not readily determinable.

Demand is controlled first of all by the law of satiety; that is, as desires are satisfied they lose their strength, and the demand falls off. The demand for a particular commodity is often affected by the power of substituting some other commodity for it in case it becomes dear, as tea for coffee, mutton for beef, etc. Demand is affected also by the power of postponing the gratification of a want until a supply comes in from some other place or from a new source.

The supply of commodities varies greatly. In some cases it is absolutely limited and cannot be increased, whatever price may be offered. In the case of perishable goods, the whole amount must be taken off at once; while where the goods are durable, a portion of the stock may be withheld for future demands. Where time is allowed, new quantities of the goods may be supplied. But this increased quantity may be produced at the same cost as before, or it may be produced at an increased cost (law of diminishing return); or at a diminished cost (law of increasing return). When one considers the combinations possible under these circumstances, it is easily seen what a complicated matter it is to explain variations in prices or to predict future prices.

Effects of Changing Prices. Variations in prices affect all individuals in the community. The price which he gets for his product determines for the producer whether his labour and business ability are rewarded or not. On the other hand, for the consumer prices determine how far his income will go. A general change in price-level may affect whole classes. Rising prices may stimulate business and make the fortune of the entrepreneur or the bold speculator; falling prices may depress trade and discourage speculation. When prices and wages change simultaneously and in exact proportion, the condition of the labouring class may remain the same. But if one lags behind the other, great temporary inconvenience may be felt by the labourer in enhanced cost of living, or by the employer in a disproportionate cost of production represented by wages. Finally, when we have contracts to be fullfilled at a distant date and expressed in terms of money, a change in price-level may make it easier or more difficult for the debtor to pay; or it may make the return to the creditor of greater or less purchasing power than the sum which he lent.

The Statistical Problem. In view of these circumstances it is not surprising that the course of prices is an object of constant interest to the business man and the consumer. But still further, the course of prices is an object of solicitude whenever we consider the condition of different classes in the community. We have, therefore, enormous records of prices, which are collected merely as matters of interest to people engaged in trade; while in addition we have attempts to manipulate these records in such a way as to explain the causes of the variations and their effect upon different classes. We have here a field peculiarly adapted to the exercise of the statistical method. The single individual price is in itself of little interest. What is needed is a combination of prices to show a general price-level, a succession of combinations to show general movements, and the correlation of these movements with other phenomena which shall explain them.

The statistics of prices must therefore be arranged and manipulated in the following directions:—

(1) Determine the prices of single commodities in such a way as to show a representative price for a given period, such as a day, week, month or year.

(2) Arrange these average prices so as to show changes from period to period, as for instance from year to year.

(3) Combine the prices of many commodities so as to get a general price-level for the purpose of detecting movements of prices as a whole.

(4) Compare changes in prices with other phenomena connected with commodities such as demand and supply, cost of production, legislation, etc., so as to understand the cause of the change.

On the basis of such statistics we may then:—

(5) Analyse the effect of changes in particular groups of commodities or in the whole price-level on various classes in

the community and on the prosperity of the community as a whole.

(6) Seek the connection between the general level of prices and the supply of the precious metals, the quantity of money, the use of credit, and the methods of business in a given community and the world at large.

(7) Consider the use of price statistics for the purpose of supporting propositions for changes in the monetary system, such as bimetallism; for reform of the banking system; and for the establishment of other standards for deferred payments such as the tabular standard.

Statistical Data.[1]

The first step in the statistics of prices is to establish price quotations for certain specified articles from day to day. This is now done for a great variety of commodities on the

[1] *Bibliographical Note.* The most complete and exhaustive treatment of the subject of index numbers is to be found in the memoranda prepared by Prof. Edgeworth for the Report of the Committee appointed to Investigate the best Methods of ascertaining and measuring Variations in the Value of the Monetary Standard. These are published in the reports of the British Association for the Advancement of Science, 1887, 1888, 1889 and 1890. See, also, the short article by Edgeworth on Index Numbers in Palgrave's Dictionary of Political Economy, containing valuable bibliography. For an account of the different index numbers and also his own American number, see Falkner's Introduction to the Report of the Senate Committee on Wholesale Prices, 1891. Sauerbeck's Index Number is published every year in the Journal of the Royal Statistical Society; for an elaborate explanation see his papers in that Journal for 1886 and 1893. The London *Economist* publishes the *Economist* Index Number every year. For Soetbeer's Hamburg Index Number, see his "Materialien." It has been translated into English and published as an appendix to the Report of the Royal Commission on Gold and Silver, 1887-88. Another translation was published as an appendix to the Report of Mr. Edward Atkinson on Bimetallism, by the U.S. State Department (Consular Reports, 1887). The whole subject of index numbers is discussed in the Report of the Royal Commission on Gold and Silver, 1887-88. See also the testimony of Professors Marshall and Nicholson before that Commission on the relation between money and prices. See, also, the valuable

various exchanges, through price lists published by dealers, and through market reports published in trade journals. It is necessary of course to have the same standard or grade of article, as well as the same weight or measure, and to have the price for the same market. This can be done for certain standard articles whose quality or grade is well established, and the quotations are those of the wholesale market. The price for the week or the month is commonly simply the average of the daily prices, and the price for the year is the average of the monthly prices.

Taking these prices for a given commodity for a succession of years we have a history of prices for that commodity. Such price lists show numerous fluctuations because of temporary causes, as for instance:—(a) in case of agricultural products, variations in the harvest from year to year coupled with variations in the demand due to the success or failure of the crops of other countries; (b) changes in temporary demand,

memorandum by Mr. Palgrave published in Vol. III. of the Royal Commission on the Depression of Trade, 1896. Index Numbers have been severely criticised by Mr. G. Pierson in the British Economic Journal, Vol. V. p. 109, 1895. He was answered by Mr. Sauerbeck in the same volume of that Journal. In Volume VI., 1896, Mr. Pierson rejected the whole theory of index numbers, and was answered by Professor Edgeworth. An excellent *résumé* of the history and theory of index numbers may be found in the Article by Robert Zuckerkandl on Preis (Handwörterbuch der Staatswissenschaften); see also Mayo-Smith, Movements of Prices (Political Science Quarterly, Sept. 1898).

Jevons has a classical article, On the Fall in Prices due to the Increased Supply of Gold, republished in the volume, Investigations in Currency and Finance, 1884. See, also, Giffen, Essays in Finance, 2 vols. 1880 and 1886; and, The Case against Bimetallism, 1892. Nicholson, Money and Monetary Problems, 1895.

Prices of standard articles are found in the various Trade Journals. They are also published in the [monthly] Summary of Commerce and Finance by the United States Bureau of Statistics of the Treasury Department. They are published quarterly for Germany in the Vierteljahrshefte zur Statistik des Deutschen Reichs. Prices may also be found in the Statistical Abstract for the United Kingdom and the Statistical Abstract for the United States. Prices of principal commodities in Italy in 1871-96 are given in the Annuario Statistico Italiano, 1898.

as for instance, military supplies in case of war, changes in fashion, variations in the seasons, *e.g.* clothing, boots and shoes, rubber goods, straw hats; (c) changes in legislation affecting particular commodities, as a tariff tax or bounty; (d) increased use of some other commodity as a substitute for the given commodity, as bicycles for horses; (e) improvements in method of production or in cost of transportation or in handling, introduced with greater or less rapidity.

Index Numbers. For the business man these changes in single commodities from year to year are of very great interest and importance. For the community, the question is whether the prices of important commodities like wheat, or sugar, or iron, have on the whole increased or decreased. This can be shown by the ordinary method of graphic representation by means of a line which rises or falls according as the price goes up or down. Or it may be shown by taking a certain year, or an average of a number of years, as 100, and representing the price of succeeding years as proportionately above or below 100. This constitutes what is called an index number.

An illustration of this is the price of English wheat as given by Sauerbeck:—

		s.	d.		
Average,	1867–77 . .	54	6	=	100, average point.
,,	1855 . . .	74	8	=	137, or 37 per cent. above the average point.
,,	1898 . . .	34	0	=	62, or 38 per cent. below the average point.

The index number represents a simple percentage of the average point. A single important article like wheat, with prices arranged in this way, or depicted graphically by a falling and rising line, gives us interesting information in regard to the course of prices over long periods. It is evident that we can extend our system to other important articles and gain similar information in regard to each. The results, however, may then be more or less contradictory. We may find that some articles have risen in price, while others have fallen, or even if they have moved in the same direction, that they have not moved in the same degree. In order to gain a notion of the whole movement, we add together the proportionate numbers for each year and take the average. It is convenient, too, to group together articles which appear to have something in common. An example of this method is Sauerbeck's table of index numbers for the year 1898, based on the average 1867–77 as 100[1]:—

		Total Numbers.	Average.
1. Vegetable food, corn, etc., (wheat, flour, barley, oats, maize, potatoes, and rice)	With 8 Index Nos.	538	67
2. Animal food, (beef, mutton, pork, bacon, and butter)	,, 7 ,,	542	77
3. Sugar, coffee, and tea	,, 4 ,,	205	51
1—3 food	,, 19 ,,	1,285	68
4. Minerals, (iron, copper, tin, lead, and coals)	,, 7 ,,	493	70
5. Textiles, (cotton, flax, hemp, jute, wool, and silks)	,, 8 ,,	405	51
6. Sundry materials, (hides, leather, tallow, oils, soda, nitrate, indigo, and timber)	,, 11 ,,	698	63
4—6 materials	,, 26 ,,	1,596	61
General average	,, 45 ,,	2,881	64

Such a table means simply this—that a certain aggregate of commodities, 1 bushel of wheat, 1 barrel of flour, 1 ton of iron, etc., in the years 1867–77 and in the year 1898, cost sums that were related to each other as 100 to 64. Similarly, index numbers are calculated for each commodity and each group of commodities, and for each year,

[1] Journal of Royal Stat. Soc., Vol. LXII., 1899, p. 187.

resulting in a continuous table of index numbers as follows:—

SUMMARY OF INDEX NUMBERS (SAUERBECK). GROUPS OF ARTICLES, 1867–77 = 100.

	Vegetable food (corn, &c.)	Animal food (meat, &c.)	Sugar, coffee, and tea.	Total food.	Minerals.	Textiles.	Sundry materials.	Total materials.	Grand Total.
1879 . .	87	94	87	90	73	74	85	78	83
1880 . .	89	101	88	94	79	81	89	84	88
1881 . .	84	101	84	91	77	77	86	80	85
1882 . .	84	104	76	89	79	73	85	80	84
1883 . .	82	103	77	89	76	70	84	77	82
1884 . .	71	97	63	79	68	68	81	73	76
1885 . .	68	88	63	74	66	65	76	70	72
1886 . .	65	87	60	72	67	63	69	67	69
1887 . .	64	79	67	70	69	65	67	67	68
1888 . .	67	82	65	72	78	64	67	69	70
1889 . .	65	86	75	75	75	70	68	70	72
1890 . .	65	82	70	73	80	66	69	71	72
1891 . .	75	81	71	77	76	59	69	68	72
1892 . .	65	84	69	73	71	57	67	65	68
1893 . .	59	85	75	72	68	59	68	65	68
1894 . .	55	80	65	66	64	53	64	60	63
1895 . .	54	78	62	64	62	52	65	60	62
1896 . .	53	73	59	62	63	54	63	60	61
1897 . .	60	79	52	65	66	51	62	59	62
1898 . .	67	77	51	68	70	51	63	61	64
Average									
1888-97 .	62	81	66	70	70	59	66	65	67
1878-87 .	79	95	76	84	73	71	81	76	79

It will be observed that this table is based entirely upon the wholesale prices of foods and raw materials. The total index number shows that since the period 1866–77 there has been a fall of 36 per cent. in average prices. The fall has been greatest in the textiles. In fact, the index number for cotton has fallen to 37, and of silk to 46. The next heaviest fall has been in sugar, coffee and tea, the index number for sugar being as low as 40. The least fall has been in animal food. In most cases the fall seems to have reached its lowest point about 1896.

As an example of a second index number which is based

on the prices of manufactured articles, as well as of food and of raw material, we give the index number calculated by Professor Falkner, and published in the Senate Report on Wholesale Prices, 1891, Part I., p. 99. The base that is used is the year 1860, and the prices from 1862 to 1878 have been reduced to a gold basis:—

FALKNER'S INDEX NUMBERS (GOLD PRICES), BY GROUPS OF ARTICLES, 1860 = 100.

Year.	Food.	Cloths and clothing.	Fuel and lighting.	Metals and implements.	Lumber and building materials.	Drugs and chemicals.	House furnishing goods.	Miscellaneous.	All articles.
1860	100·0	100·0	100·0	100·0	100·0	100·0	100·0	100·0	100·0
1861	95·8	94·9	103·5	102·5	108·9	101·3	96·8	100·7	100·6
1862	107·7	121·1	94·8	114·3	145·6	113·6	87·3	101·2	114·9
1863	91·7	132·0	73·8	96·5	122·1	101·0	84·8	89·0	102·4
1864	106·6	167·7	115·9	115·6	142·3	109·5	105·9	99·3	122·5
1865	100·1	138·4	110·0	88·5	84·2	125·6	83·8	93·8	100·3
1866	124·1	161·7	200·2	122·1	133·4	164·3	132·3	122·1	136·3
1867	121·8	133·7	145·8	119·8	132·8	156·9	118·2	119·9	127·9
1868	118·6	106·0	157·9	108·7	125·8	128·4	97·4	118·5	115·9
1869	120·1	108·8	152·5	104·2	122·3	118·7	89·0	119·7	113·2
1870	126·8	114·9	162·0	105·4	122·3	123·3	100·2	122·6	117·3
1871	152·9	120·4	130·2	110·4	136·8	125·9	116·1	134·4	122·9
1872	122·2	131·1	136·8	117·3	153·0	122·8	112·9	121·6	127·2
1873	115·2	121·5	119·4	115·2	152·5	125·6	96·8	117·5	122·0
1874	118·0	114·8	134·3	108·7	139·0	131·8	98·3	116·5	119·4
1875	116·0	106·8	139·1	104·4	127·7	128·2	84·4	109·2	113·4
1876	109·1	95·3	128·2	96·1	121·7	108·0	77·3	101·2	104·8
1877	113·3	95·9	101·7	94·2	118·5	115·2	74·4	111·3	104·4
1878	105·5	91·9	91·7	90·8	115·2	112·6	73·3	110·2	99·9
1879	97·6	91·1	95·3	88·4	115·1	110·9	68·6	102·1	96·6
1880	107·6	104·5	100·2	96·3	130·9	113·1	85·2	109·8	106·9
1881	110·9	99·9	113·7	91·1	131·3	110·4	77·6	108·8	105·7
1882	118·8	98·7	110·1	91·2	137·5	107·6	78·1	114·6	108·5
1883	118·8	94·8	114·2	87·5	134·3	98·1	77·5	117·3	106·0
1884	108·9	88·9	102·4	81·0	129·5	95·7	76·3	111·9	99·4
1885	98·7	84·8	89·6	77·4	126·6	86·9	70·1	97·5	93·0
1886	99·5	85·1	86·2	75·8	128·5	83·9	68·4	91·3	91·9
1887	104·2	84·7	88·6	74·9	126·5	83·6	66·4	88·6	92·6
1888	109·4	84·7	94·9	74·9	124·8	86·0	66·9	89·3	94·2
1889	111·9	83·6	95·3	72·9	124·0	88·8	70·0	88·8	94·2
1890	104·6	82·4	92·5	73·2	123·7	87·9	69·5	89·7	92·3
1891	103·9	81·1	91·0	74·9	122·3	86·3	70·1	95·1	92·2

This table shows, also, the general fall in prices, especially since about 1872. But the different groups behave in a very extraordinary way. Food is at about the same level as in 1860, while lumber and building materials have actually increased 22 per cent. The manufactured articles, such as cloths and clothing and house-furnishing goods, show a very great decrease.

We seem to have here a most fascinating instrument of investigation. The phenomenon price in all its bewildering variety is here made objective, reduced to a measurable expression, so that we can manipulate it at will. We can say prices are higher or lower, prices are rising or falling, certain things are becoming cheaper or dearer; it is but a step then to say that certain persons or classes are better or worse off, the workman or the capitalist, the debtor or creditor, the producer or consumer, the active business man or the idle annuitant; it is but a step further to correlate the rise or fall of prices with other phenomena, such as the decreased production of gold, improvements in transportation, discovery of the precious metals, monopolistic control of industry, increased speculative activity.

It is evident, however, that a scientific proceeding sufficiently accurate to accomplish the first of these objects in a satisfactory way might be altogether too imperfect and rude to carry us far on our way in attempting the second and third. And this is, in effect, the exact position of index numbers. They are sufficient to establish the general course of prices, but they are too imperfect to establish facts of the second and third class.

We have first of all the technical difficulties of establishing the index number itself. These are:— (1) of getting prices; (2) of detecting changes in the quality of articles; (3) of determining how many articles shall enter into the number; (4) of measuring the relative importance of articles; (5) of providing for changes in the relative importance of articles; (6) of providing for the entrance of new commodities.

Prices and Qualities.[1] The first question is a simple technical one, but in itself of sufficient difficulty, viz., how to fix the price of each commodity that enters into the index number, and to be sure that the article known under a particular name, such as iron or tea, continues to be always of the same quality. For it is evident that if under tea we have at one time one quality, and at a later period another, a change in price means nothing.

Prices may be either the prices of actual mercantile transactions taken from the books of business firms (Falkner's method); or the published prices of local markets or of Exchanges (Gazette prices of English wheat); or the published prices of recognised authorities (Pixley and Abel's quotations of the price of silver). Another expedient is to take the declared values of certain important articles of import or export, and divide the total values by the total quantities for a year. This is supposed to give an average price. A third method is to take the prices of certain standard commodities as found in the purchases of public institutions like hospitals, poor-houses, army and navy commissariat, &c. (Soetbeer).

All of these methods evidently give us wholesale prices of important commodities. They are of value from the very fact of their publicity, of their being fixed by strenuous competition, and on account of the magnitude of the transactions involved. Even in wholesale prices there are difficulties owing to changes in grading and quotation from time to time. The quality of wheat is not the same from harvest to harvest, and an additional price may be paid for a bushel of English standard wheat because it is heavier, or mills somewhat better, although the difference may not be sufficient to change its grade. American cotton may be freer from dirt and better packed as time goes on. Sir R.

[1] See Sauerbeck (Journal Royal Stat. Soc., Vol. XLIX. 1886, p. 590). Falkner, Theory and Practice of Price Statistics (Pub. Amer. Stat. Assocn. Vol. III., p. 119).

Giffen testified that they had great difficulties at the Board of Trade in fixing the standard grade of steel.[1] The custom of dealing with these commodities by warehouse receipts calling not for the identical goods but for quantities of a certain grade, tends, however, to establish the qualities so that they change little from year to year.

Choice of Commodities. Index numbers vary greatly in the number of commodities. The *Economist* has 22, Sauerbeck 45, Soetbeer 114, and Falkner 223. It is an interesting question how many articles it is desirable or necessary to have, and how they are to be chosen. The smaller the number, the less the labour; and it is easier, as a rule, to get trustworthy prices from year to year of a few standard articles than of a long list of commodities. On the other hand, if the object of an index number is to establish changes in price-level from year to year, and especially to study the effects of such changes and to analyse their causes, it would seem at first blush that we ought to have as many articles as possible; and it might even be contended that the ideal number would be based upon the prices of all commodities which are bought and sold.

But aside from the difficulty of getting trustworthy prices of the less important articles, the risk of change of quality, and the labour of manipulating so many quotations, it does not appear either desirable or necessary to multiply the number of articles, especially when we are using index numbers as merely a rough indication of the direction of changes in price. For this purpose a few very important articles may suffice, while in extending the number (unless we can reach the ideal noted above) we run the risk of distorting the general index by undue emphasis upon certain kinds of commodities. When, for instance, we follow the same raw material, such as iron ore, through all its subsequent stages as pig iron, bar iron, steel, wire, and all the numberless forms of manufactured iron, such as cutlery, implements, and utensils, the question is whether we are not

[1] Gold and Silver Commission, 1887-8, Questions 818, 917.

giving undue weight to this one commodity by numerous repetitions. Professor Falkner,[1] for instance, has 25 quotations for pocket knives out of a total of 54 for metals and implements, and a grand total of 223 articles. On the other hand he has but 15 quotations for house-furnishing goods, of which seven are for wooden pails and tubs. He has but two quotations for vegetables (both potatoes) and four for fish, of which three are for salted mackerel. Undue prominence seems to be given to articles of no very great importance. If the system could be carried out for all commodities, probably extremes might balance each other, and no harm be done. But it is impossible to carry it out for all articles, and it seems to be purely accidental that a few commodities are so numerously represented.

Nor does it seem to be necessary to multiply quotations of articles of minor importance. If those articles follow the general direction of change of the more important commodities, then their presence is unnecessary. If they show the opposite tendency, then their numerous representation gives them the power to drag the index number in their direction, so that it no longer is representative of the real change in prices. A striking example of this is given by Professor Falkner on page 92 of the first volume of his report. He there gives the index number of metals and implements, omitting pocket-knives. From 1860 to 1891 the index number, after omitting pocket-knives, is higher than the general number in every year except two. As specimen years take the following:—

INDEX NUMBERS OF METALS AND IMPLEMENTS.

Year.	With pocket-knives.	Without pocket-knives.
1860	100·0	100·0
1865	191·4	218·7
1870	127·8	128·8
1875	117·5	131·0
1880	96·3	105·1
1885	77·4	79·6
1890	73·2	77·7
1891	74·9	78·1

[1] Senate Report on Wholesale Prices, 1891, Part I., p. 92.

The general impression of rising and falling prices remains the same in the two series of numbers; either series might therefore answer the general question of the change of price-level. But if the welfare of any class in the community were dependent on the prices of metals and implements, it would be a grave question whether or not we should include 25 quotations of pocket-knives, or which index we should select. It becomes a matter then not only of direction but of degree of change. A case of more human interest is the following[1]:—

Among the articles which go to form the important index number for food are four kinds of fish. All of them show a rising price since 1860, and the single quotation of cod-fish gives an index number of 312 for 1891, on the basis of 100 for 1860. The whole index number for food shows a rise from 100 in 1860 to 103·9 in 1891. This is a very interesting fact, because food is a most important article of consumption, and this rise is in marked contrast with the fall of the great mass of commodities. If, however, we exclude the single item cod-fish, the number for 1891 becomes 99·9, and if we exclude all four quotations of fish, which cover simply cod-fish and mackerel, the number becomes 94·9. That is the rise of $3\frac{1}{8}$ per cent. is turned into the very considerable fall of 5 per cent. In other words, by giving four quotations out of 53 to cod-fish and mackerel, a change of eight points is made in the index number for food.

The objection to numerous quotations of one article and scant representation of others, is brought out still more clearly in a second table, in which Mr. Falkner has arranged his articles according as prices have risen, or fallen, or remained stationary. In this table we find that in the case of nine articles prices have remained stationary, in the case of 153 they have fallen, and in the case of 61 they have risen. This shows, of course, a decided tendency

[1] *Ibid.*, p. 59.

to fall; but of the 153 no less than 25 are pocket-knives again.[1]

It is evident from the above examples that the mere addition of quotations does not in itself strengthen our confidence in an index number. Many other experiments have been made with somewhat contradictory results. For instance, Mr. Sauerbeck, in order to test his index number based on the wholesale prices of 45 commodities, has added thereto the wholesale prices of 61 other commodities, principally food and raw material, and those of 51 manufactured, or partly manufactured articles. On this plan, using the period 1867–77 as 100, the index number for 1885 would be (Gold and Silver Commission, First Report, 1887, p. 321):—

For 45 principal articles	71·9
,, 61 sundry articles, food and raw materials	84·8
,, 51 manufactured and partly manufactured articles . .	73·6
For 157 articles	77·5

The result of this experiment seems to show that the addition of minor articles and of manufactured articles to the forty-five principal articles of food and raw material has a decided tendency to raise the index number. The same thing has been noticed by Mr. Falkner in the comparison of the four principal index numbers when they are reduced to the same base. If we take 1860 as equal to 100, then the index number for 1891 would be[2]:—

According to the *Economist*	(22 articles) . .	81·0
,, ,, Sauerbeck	(45 ,,) . .	75·4
,, ,, Soetbeer	(114 ,,) . .	90·3
,, ,, Falkner	(223 ,,) . .	92·2

Here again the introduction of a large number of articles seems to raise the index number.

[1] *Ibid.*, p. 59.

[2] Senate Report on Wholesale Prices, 1891, Part I., pp. 226, 255 and 295.

In a similar way Professor Pierson[1] finds that, taking 1861–70 as a base, Soetbeer's and Kral's prices (114 and 265 articles respectively), for the period 1881–3 showed scarcely any change; while Sauerbeck's showed a very considerable fall. Still further comparing the prices of 1885 to 1891 with those of 1861 to 1870, according to Soetbeer we find a rise in the purchasing power of gold of 16 per cent., while according to Sauerbeck it is much greater than that. According to Pierson, Soetbeer's number is to be preferred simply because it includes a larger number of commodities. But Sauerbeck has answered that these additional commodities are as a rule of small importance and very eccentric in their variations. Hops, for instance, rose from 255 in 1881 to 413 in 1882, and to as much as 517 in 1883, to decline to 243 in 1885 and 213 in 1886. That Soetbeer's index number did not fall in 1882 and 1883 can be ascribed to this single article, as its rise affected the two years to the extent of 1·4 and 2·3 per cent. respectively. Another example is resin, which jumped from 110 in 1860 to 480 in 1862, to 542 in 1863, and 605 in 1864. Had it not been included Soetbeer's price-level in 1864 would have been 125·07 instead of 129·8 or 3·3 per cent. lower.

All these examples tend to show that the eccentricity of a single article may have great effect on index numbers. Even in regard to the *Economist* number, it has been often remarked that its high level for the years 1863 to 1866 was partly due to the great rise in the price of cotton, exaggerated by the fact that cotton comprises four out of the twenty-two commodities for which prices are quoted. The remedy for these difficulties lies partly at any rate in the so-called weighted index number.[2]

[1] British Economic Journal, Vol. V., 1895, p. 109. Sauerbeck's Answer, *Ibid.*, p. 161.

[2] The following comparison of three index numbers reduced to the same year as base (1873) is taken from the Final Report of the Com-

Articles according to their Importance. In an ordinary index number each commodity has equal influence on the final average. The consequence is that a fall of 25 per cent. in wheat, for instance, would be offset by a rise in price of 25 per cent. in indigo. In such a case the index number would not change, although of course it would be absurd to say that no change in price-level had occurred. This defect in index numbers has always been recognised. An attempt is sometimes made to offset it by introducing the same commodity more than once. As already mentioned, the *Economist* gives to cotton four numbers out of twenty-two. So among the forty-five commodities in the Sauerbeck number wheat is represented twice and flour once; beef, mutton, sugar, iron, coal, cotton, wool, and oil, each twice. This evidently is a very rough way of equalising the importance of commodities. It seems better to seek a system of weights which shall adjust the relative share of each commodity in determining the final index number. The system of weights ordinarily used is that of the total production or consumption of each article. The most famous example of such a calculation is that of

mission on Gold and Silver, 1888, p. 154. It is difficult to explain the variations :—

	Economist. 22 Art.	Sauerbeck. 45 Art.	Soetbeer. 114 Art.
1873	100·0	100·0	100·0
1874	97·7	91·9	98·5
1875	94·0	86·5	94·2
1876	91·7	85·6	92·7
1877	92·5	84·6	92.7
1878	85·8	78·4	87·6
1879	74·6	74·8	84·7
1880	85·8	79·3	88·4
1881	80·5	76·6	87·6
1882	82·8	75·7	88·4
1883	79·8	73·9	88·4
1884	74·6	68·5	82·6
1885	70·8	64·9	78·9
1886	68·6	62·2	...
1887	70·1	61·3	...
1888	75·3	...	...

Mr. Palgrave, who weighted the *Economist* number according to the relative value of each article in the consumption of the United Kingdom. Taking indigo, for instance, the value imported in 1885 was £2,130,000 sterling, and deducting therefrom the value of the re-exports, £1,530,000 sterling, there remained, roughly £600,000 as the value of the indigo consumed in this country. Then taking wheat, the amount imported in 1885 less the re-exports was valued at £33,360,000 sterling. Beyond this, there was the home growth of wheat given at a total value of close upon £16,000,000 sterling. The net import and home production of wheat in 1885, may, therefore, with a sufficient approach to accuracy, be stated at £49,360,000 sterling. It therefore would appear that in 1885 wheat was 82 times as important as indigo, and a rise or fall of 1 per cent. in the former would in a truly adjusted index number have the same relative importance as one of 82 per cent. in the latter. The importance of other articles is estimated in the same way. Peculiar difficulties are found in some cases as, for instance, the production of meat, which is based on the total number of cattle, sheep, and pigs in the country, and an estimate of the average life and of average price. In the case of cotton it is necessary to deduct the value of cotton goods exported. On the basis of such estimates the *Economist* total index number, 2,200, is divided each year among nineteen commodities according to their relative importance. Out of the 2,200 in 1885, raw cotton was assigned 263; wool, 142; meat, 524; iron, 150; and the other articles similarly. The index number for 1885 is then multiplied in the case of each article by the figure denoting its importance and divided by 100. This series of numbers added up gives a new index number into which commodities enter according to their importance. In other words we have a weighted instead of a simple arithmetic mean.[1]

[1] Commission on Depression of Trade, 1886, 3rd Report, Appendix B., p. 351.

The chief question of interest is how far this system of weighting changes the index number. This is answered by the following table, the first column of which gives the simple and the second the weighted index number[1]:—

Year.	Simple.	Weighted.
1865–69	100	100
1870	91	90
1871	90	93
1872	97	100
1873	102	104
1874	100	108
1875	95	97
1876	93	99
1877	94	100
1878	87	95
1879	76	82
1880	87	89
1881	81	93
1882	83	87
1883	80	88
1884	75	80
1885	70	76

The weighted number follows the same general direction as the simple number, although it seems to have a tendency to remain a little higher.

When we have a larger number of articles this system of weighting seems to have but little influence upon the index number. Mr. Sauerbeck, for instance, is accustomed to test his number each year in two ways:—

"Firstly, by using the same index numbers of the separate articles, but calculating each article according to its importance in the United Kingdom on the average of the three years 1894–96, when the mean for 1897 is 62·5, against 60·5 in 1896; or on the average of the five years 1871–75, when the mean for 1897 is 62·6, against 60·2 in 1896. The unweighted number was 62 in 1897 against 61 in 1896. Measured according to quantities the rise was therefore greater than shown by the index numbers, and this was principally due to the

[1] *Ibid.*, p. 328.

advance in such important articles as wheat, meat, and potatoes, which was greater than the decline for sugar, cotton and wool.

"Secondly, by calculating the quantities in the United Kingdom at their actual values (the production on the basis of my price tables, the imports at Board of Trade values, and consequently a considerable portion according to a different set of prices) and at the nominal values on the basis of the average prices from 1867–77. In this case the mean is 63·5, against 62·0 in 1896, and the rise is also greater than according to the ordinary index numbers." (Journal Stat. Soc., Vol. LXI., 1898, p. 154).

The first method is identical with that of Palgrave already described. The second is a modification and may be explained as follows:—

We take the quantities produced of each commodity during the year 1897, and multiplying by the price we obtain the total value for the year 1897. Now taking the same quantities we estimate what would have been the values at the prices of the standard period 1867-77. The difference between the two (the quantities having remained the same) must be due to a change in prices. For instance, the total value of the 45 commodities in 1897 was 464·2 million pounds sterling. Their value at the prices of 1867-77 would have been 731·5 million. The proportion between the two is as 63·5 to 100. The index number for 1897 is therefore 63·5.

The weighted index number is an improvement upon the simple average. Much has been made of the fact that it does not ordinarily differ a great deal from the simple, as an argument in favour of the trustworthiness of the latter. It has even been shown that one does not need to calculate the relative importance of the commodities for each year, but that a single year will suffice. In general, *relative* production of standard articles does not differ much from year to year, and where it does differ, the resultant error will not be very great, the individual errors tending to offset each other. Edgeworth has calculated index numbers according to seven different methods applied to the same data and found the numbers for 1885 to be 70, 70·6, 73, 69, 72, 72, 69·5.[1]

[1] British Association, Report, 1888, p. 211.

There remains the question of new commodities coming extensively into use after the system of numbers has been constructed. The change from year to year will not probably be great, but eventually it will be considerable, *e.g.* introduction of petroleum for light. There seems to be no way of meeting this difficulty except by constructing a new base.

The result of all these considerations seems to be that for the purpose of roughly following the general course of prices almost any index number is sufficient. But when we attempt to base upon index numbers reasoning in regard to the effect of changes in price-level or the causes of such changes, their sufficiency is more doubtful. Our "estimates" then betray their crudeness, and it becomes increasingly difficult to define what is meant by "importance."

Scientific Tests.

There are various questions of statistical technique which should be noticed here, although it must be confessed that statisticians are not altogether agreed in respect to them. In all statistics of prices, as has already been pointed out, we are obliged to use averages. For the primary prices the simple arithmetic mean is generally sufficient. When we come, however, to average index numbers indicating price-level, where the commodities are of varying importance it is certainly more correct to use the weighted arithmetic mean; although ordinarily the two results are commonly so nearly the same that the simpler method can be employed. There are two other means which possess theoretic interest in this connection. The first, is the geometric mean advocated by Jevons and the second is the median proposed by Mr. Edgeworth.

In his famous investigations in currency and prices, Jevons when he came to average the index numbers which he had calculated, employed the geometric instead of the arithmetic mean and defended it on the following grounds. He said:—'Suppose we have two commodities one of which doubles in price and the other remains stationary. According to the simple arithmetic mean the average rise in price is fifty per cent.; that is, the combined index number for the first period would be 100 and for the second would be 150. But 150, which is the mean, does not bear the same per cent. relation to 100 that 200 does to 150. For while 150 is 50 per cent. above 100, 200 is only 33⅓ per cent. above 150. The true mean in this case is 141, which is 41 per cent. above 100, just as 200 is 41 per cent. above 141. In order, therefore, to calculate the true mean index number for any year, it is necessary to multiply the particular numbers together and extract the *nth* root, *n* being the number of commodities represented. This can be done most easily by logarithms.[1]

This proceeding of Jevons was criticised by Laspeyres, who gave the following illustration. 'Suppose one ounce of gold buys one pound of cocoa, and one ounce of gold buys one pound of cloves; the price of cocoa doubles and the price of cloves falls one-half. The arithmetic index number gives 125, showing an increase of twenty-five per cent. in average prices. The geometric mean gives 100, so that according to Jevons there has been no change in price-level. What has really happened is this: before the change in prices two ounces of gold bought one pound each of cocoa and cloves. Now in order to purchase the one pound of cocoa two ounces of gold are necessary, and to purchase the one pound of cloves one-half ounce of gold is necessary, so that to purchase the same amount of commodities as before, two and one-half ounces of gold are necessary—that is, an increase of twenty-five per cent.' Jevons made no rejoinder to this except to point out that there are three means which might be used, namely, the arithmetic, the geometric, and the harmonic. The geometric lies between the other two, can be worked by

[1] Jevons, Investigations in Currency and Finance, 1884, p. 23.

logarithms, and for his particular problem, viz., a study of the rise of prices, erred on the side of safety.[1]

The only adequate reason for using the geometric mean is that it diminishes the influence of extreme variations. The great danger of index numbers is that a single article or two may rise enormously in value owing to some temporary cause, and thus distort the whole number. Edgeworth has shown that rises in price are more frequent and more extreme than falls. The geometric mean is better fitted for such a series than the arithmetic.

Sauerbeck has experimented with the geometric mean on his index number, with the following results[2]:—

	1895.	1894.	1880.
Geometric mean	60·4	60·9	87·0
Arithmetic mean	62·1	62·9	87·8
Weighted arithmetic mean	60·8	62·0	87·3

The geometric mean, as seen in this case, will give a result somewhat lower than the arithmetic.

Professor Edgeworth has proposed, in the case of a large number of prices, to take simply the middle quantity; that is, that price which is so constituted that one-half of the quotations are above and one-half below. Where the differences are not great, this "median" would correspond to the arithmetic mean. At the same time it would have the advantage, in the case of extreme prices, of diminishing the influence of the extremes.

In regard to index numbers where the commodities are weighted according to their importance, two or three systems seem to be possible. We may take the quantities in the final year at the prices then, and compare the value of the same quantities at the prices for the base year. The pro-

[1] Journal Stat. Soc., Vol. XXIX., 1865, p. 295, reprinted in Currency and Finance, 1884, p. 121. See also Edgeworth, Index Numbers, in Palgrave's Dictionary of Political Economy.

[2] Journal Stat. Soc., Vol. LIX., 1896, p. 193. For further discussion see Messedaglia, Il Calcolo dei Valori Medii. (Archiv. di Stat., 1880.)

portion between the two gives us an index number showing the change in price. This is the method pursued by Mr. Sauerbeck, and already described on page 215.

The question has been raised by Mr. Edgeworth whether it is not equally legitimate to take the quantities of the base year at their value, and compare the result with the same quantities taken at their value in the final year. The proportion of the two will also give us an index number which might differ from the above.

A third method is possible, that is to take the mean of the quantities of the two periods, and calculate their value according to the prices of the final year and of the base year. This method seems to be approved by Professors Edgeworth and Marshall. The question seems to be one of theoretic interest simply.[1]

Mr. Edgeworth has gone into theoretical considerations of the probable accuracy of a carefully chosen weighted index number, such as that proposed by the Committee of the British Association for the Advancement of Science. He shows that the probable erroneousness of such a number is greater according to the inaccuracy of the weights and the prices; the erroneousness is greater according to the inequality of the weights and prices; and the accuracy is greater according as the number of data is greater, and the number of omitted articles less. He shows, also, that the inaccuracy of the price returns affects the result more than the inaccuracy of the weights, and the same thing is true of the inequality of the prices compared with the inequality of the weights. This is shown both mathematically and experimentally. For if we have a sufficient number of articles, any system of weighting, chosen without bias, will be apt to give about the same result within certain limits.

[1] Journal Stat. Soc., Vol. LVI., 1893, p. 248. For full discussion of these and other technical points see Edgeworth, Reports of the Committee on Variations in the Value of the Monetary Standard. (British Association, Reports, 1887, 1888, 1889 and 1890).

This is the real answer to Mr. Pierson, who rejects the whole system of index numbers because the results are different, according as the prices taken as a base are equal or unequal. His argument is as follows[1]:—

Let us suppose ten commodities, all equally important; five of them are doubled in price and five of them fall to exactly one-half. Suppose these ten commodities to have been equally cheap or dear before the changes occurred; it is evident that their average price will have risen twenty-five per cent.:—

1st Period.	2nd Period.
5 × 100 = 500	5 × 200 = 1000
5 × 100 = 500	5 × 50 = 250
10)1000	10)1250
100	125

The index number in the second period is 125, and in the first 100, showing a rise of twenty-five per cent.; and this is a correct account of the alteration which has taken place. If each commodity cost originally $100, the quantities which cost $1,000 in the first period would now cost $1,250, or twenty-five per cent. more. But suppose the prices per unit are unequal. The five first commodities cost $50 a unit in the first period and double in price, and the five second commodities cost $200 per unit in the first period and fall one-half in price. Expressing the prices of the first period by 100, the index number of the second period would still be 125. What has actually occurred is shown in the following table:—

1st Period.	2nd Period.
5 × 50 = 250	5 × 100 = 500
5 × 200 = 1000	5 × 100 = 500
10)1250	10)1000
125	100

What formerly cost $1,250 now costs only $1,000; that is there has been a fall in prices. According to Mr. Pierson,

[1] British Economic Journal, Vol. VI., 1896, p. 109.

the consequence of representing unequal prices each by 100 is that we shall have different results according as the prices vary up or down. He also rejects the geometric mean which had been proposed by Jevons, and suggests the following examples:—

I.	A rises	from	50	to	100	thalers.
	B falls	,,	100	,,	50	,,
II.	A rises	,,	100	,,	200	,,
	B falls	,,	100	,,	50	,,
III.	A rises	,,	50	,,	100	,,
	B falls	,,	200	,,	100	,,

In Case I. there will be no change (150 thalers will go as far in the first period as in the second). In Case II., there will be a rise of twenty-five per cent. (that is, what at first cost 200 thalers will now cost 250 thalers). In Case III., there will be a fall of twenty per cent. (that is, what formerly cost 250 thalers will now cost only 200 thalers). The index number, using the arithmetic mean, shows a rise of twenty-five per cent. in all three cases; while using the geometric mean, that is, multiplying the two index numbers in each period and extracting the square root, it will show no change in any of the three cases.

Mr. Pierson was answered by Professor Edgeworth.[1] He contends that it is only in such artificially simplified examples that difficulty is found. Of course, by distributing our weights with the purpose of producing certain results, we can produce almost any results that we like. But in actual life and with a sufficient number of commodities, it is immensely improbable that all the high prices should work in one direction, and all the low prices in another. If the commodities were chosen without bias, according to the doctrine of probability, the different influences would tend to counteract each other. It is also shown by actual experience, that almost any system of weights, if chosen without bias, will

[1] *Ibid.*, p. 132.

give very much the same result. Both according to theory and by actual experiment, the contradictory results which Dr. Pierson shows may be possible are not at all likely to occur. The conclusion seems to be, therefore, that index numbers may be used as indicating, roughly at least, changes in price-level.

Reflective Analysis.

Effects of Changes in Prices. The most interesting question connected with prices is the effect of changes on the individual. In the case of single commodities we are accustomed to fluctuations which are of direct interest to the producer, the dealer, and the consumer. If the price of wheat goes down without corresponding decrease of cost of production, then the producer is injured. If the cost of living decreases while wages remain the same, then the labourer benefits. What happens now in case the whole price-level changes, either rising or falling? Suppose we find that prices have gone down 30 per cent. since 1867–77, what is the meaning of that to the community? It means primarily that what one hundred dollars could buy formerly, seventy dollars will buy now. Does that mean, however, tha an individual with seventy dollars is as well off now as he formerly was with one hundred dollars? That does not follow: first, on account of the imperfection of our method, and secondly, on account of psychological differences between individuals.

The imperfections of our statistics have been already mentioned. Difficulties in regard to prices and quality, while not of importance in the objective index number, may be sources of considerable error when treating of the expenditure of individuals. More important is the fact that our index number rests upon wholesale prices, while the consumer is interested in retail prices. It is probably true that the prices of manufactured articles follow the prices of raw material; but they do not necessarily follow in the same proportion. For if the price of raw material falls one-half while the cost of manufacturing remains the same, the manufactured product would undoubtedly fall in value, but not in the same proportion as the raw material. So in the same way with retail prices, although the wholesale price may fall, the middleman, or retailer, will not give the benefit of the fall to the consumer until he is compelled to do so by competition.[1]

Another difficulty is that rents of houses and wages are not comprised in any index number. It is impossible to include rents, because of the great variety of houses and the impossibility of fixing a standard; but rent, of course, is one of the most important items of expense. Wages are not entered owing to the difficulty of defining what is meant by standard wages. Wages, too, although an item of expenditure to producers, for the great mass of people are to be looked upon as a source of income rather than as an item of consumption. While it is important, therefore, to estimate the rise and fall of wages, such rise and fall is to be contrasted with the price-level of consumption goods, rather than to be confounded with it. An important exception, however, is the wages of domestic servants and the rewards of professional skill, which are items of expenditure for consumers.

The change in the quantities of goods consumed from year to year, while not of great importance in our general index number, may be indicative of considerable changes in consumption. When prices rise, the consumer commonly economises in his consumption, or seeks some substitute. When wheat is dear, rye and maize will be more used. When beef is dear, there will be increased consumption of mutton. New commodities also may become of importance

[1] See testimony of Messrs. Giffen and Sauerbeck before the Commission on Gold and Silver, 1887–88, Questions 719, 905, etc. They seem to think that direct statistics of retail prices are impracticable.

before they are recognised by the index number. The result of all these considerations is that the connection between changes in the index number and the real consumption of the community ceases to be a close one.

These technical difficulties may be partly met by greater care in choosing the commodities to be represented in the index number and by a proper system of weighting, as has already been described.

A second device is to calculate an index number weighted according to the consumption of typical families. We have already noticed in a previous chapter the attempts which have been made to analyse the expenditure of families of the working class. If now we could follow the change in prices of these different items of consumption and weight them according to the importance of each in the budget, we should have an index number representing the gain or loss to great classes in the community by changes in prices. An elaborate attempt of this sort was made by Professor Falkner in the Senate Report on Prices. He found that the distribution of expenditure of 2,561 normal families, according to the Seventh Annual Report of the Commissioner of Labour, was as follows:—

Rent	15·06	per cent.
Food	41·03	,,
Fuel	5·00	,,
Clothing	15·31	,,
Light	·90	,,
All other purchases	22·70	,,
Total	100·00	

The wholesale prices which it is proposed to use in connection with these items are grouped as follows: food, cloths and clothing, fuel and lighting, metals and implements, lumber and building material, drugs and chemicals, house-furnishing goods.

It is evidently impossible to apply one list directly to the other. Even in the case of food, so long as the particular items in the family budgets do not correspond with those in the index number, it is impossible to use them directly. It is necessary, therefore, to consider the proportionate expenditure of the families for specific articles, such as beef, fish, butter, tea, coffee, bread, and flour, and then to calculate the fall in the price of food according to the importance of these items. This is sufficiently difficult even in the case of food, because the items contained in the budgets are not all contained in the index number. The application becomes much more difficult in the consumption of clothing, which is entered in the budgets as expenditure for certain garments for husband, wife, and children, while the index numbers refer to cloths, flannels, calicoes, dress goods, leather, silks, &c. The grouping was made as follows: "for coats, &c., we have taken the group suitings; for boots and shoes, the group leather; for other items a combination of the four groups, blankets and flannels, cotton textiles, linen goods, and underwear." It is evident that this method is a very rough one for estimating the expenditure in clothing. The other items are even more difficult. Fuel is represented by an average of the various kinds of coal included in the index number. The ratio for lighting is obtained from candles; rent does not enter into the index number at all, and is assumed to have remained stationary. Finally, expenditure for miscellaneous purposes is assumed to have remained stationary, except that for furniture and utensils, which is based on the index number for house-furnishing goods. Making all these assumptions, we have the following result (Senate Report on Wholesale Prices, 1891, Part I., p. 86):—

RELATIVE PRICES OF ALL ARTICLES, 1891, MEASURED BY CONSUMPTION, (1860 = BASE = 100).

Group.	Importance.	Index.	Result.
Rent	1,506	100·0	1,506,000
Food	4,103	103·7	4,254,811
Fuel	500	98·1	490,500
Lighting	90	48·1	43,290
Clothing	1,531	75·9	1,162,029
All other purposes .	2,270	95·3	2,163,310
Total . . .	10,000	96·2	9,619,940

In this table 68·6 per cent. of the total expenditure was affected by changes in prices. "The remaining portion of the expenditure has been assumed to be equal. The relative price in 1891 by the methods pursued was 96·2. If, however, we omit from our consideration all those items on which the change of price is not measured, we find the relative cost of that portion of family expenditure directly affected by the prices of commodities to be 94·4 in 1891 as compared with 100 in 1860."

This same calculation is then carried out for each year from 1840 to 1891, and two new series of index numbers are arrived at, and contrasted with the simple average index number. The general course of prices according to this new series, is about the same as that of the simple number, but for some years the differences are very considerable. The method is so rough, that it is not of very great value as showing the real effect of changes in prices upon the working classes. It is only another illustration of the fact that almost any system of weighting, unless arranged arbitrarily, will give much the same result. In fact, the same method applied to twelve other collections of family budgets gave as index numbers for 1891 the following figures: 95·7, 96·3, 96·4, 97·7, 97·0, 95·3, 96·4, 95·2, 96·6, 90·8, 89·1, and 96·3. With two exceptions these results are very close to that of the original number, 96·1.[1]

Such elaborate attempts to measure changes in price-level do not enable us to gauge the effect of such change on the individual, owing to psychological differences. This point has been emphasised by Mr. Pierson as follows:—

"One consumes much bread and little meat, another much meat and little bread; one person smokes tobacco, another drinks wine; a third neither smokes nor drinks but makes a collection of books and etchings. In order to judge of the influence on the material condition of men exercised by variations of prices it would be necessary to divide people into numerous groups, because the relative

[1] Senate Report on Wholesale Prices, 1891, Part I., pp. 88 and 93.

importance of the commodity differs according to individual wants. And these wants vary from one period to another; some commodities also are substituted for others because they are better or cheaper. . . . No variation in the ratio of exchange between money and commodities has the same effect on the condition of the different members of the community" (British Economic Journal, Vol. V., 1895, p. 231).

Index numbers are sometimes used to indicate a change in the relative burden and advantage between debtor and creditor, brought about by a change in the level of prices. It is said that if prices go down, to repay the same money debt is more burdensome to the debtor, while to receive the same amount of money is more advantageous to the creditor. When prices have gone up, the reverse is true. Without going into the question of mitigating effects produced by variations in the rate of interest, and without discussing the justice or the expediency of the system of expressing a loan in terms of money, it may be pointed out here that index numbers cannot furnish an exact measure of the increased burden or advantage. It might happen, for instance, that the commodities upon which the debtor relied in order to procure the money with which to pay his debt had decreased in price, so that his debt was harder to pay; while those commodities which the creditor used his money to purchase had remained stationary, so that his advantage was no greater. Even in the case of the great mass of commodities falling in price, if labour had become more efficient, the debtor might be no worse off; while if labour had retained its level of wages, the creditor would be no better off in expending his money. It is impossible by any statistical device to measure these things.

Again, in considering a change of prices it must be remembered that some persons may be more injured as producers than they are benefited as consumers, and *vice versâ*. If the selling price of a manufactured commodity falls more than the price of raw products and of the labour expended in the manufacture, the business man will be injured by loss of profit although he may be partially benefited as a consumer. So, too, if the price of agricultural products falls more rapidly than rent and the wages of agricultural labour, then the tenant farmer is injured. If the cost of living rises more rapidly than the rate of wages, then the labourer is injured. Any considerable change in price-level is apt to bring about dislocation of industrial relations.

It might be possible, according to Edgeworth, to construct special index numbers for special classes. An index number of imports and exports weighted according to their importance might be of interest to the commercial classes and to those engaged in international trade. An index number of wholesale prices while not enabling us to measure well-being exactly might give us some notion of the course of trade and teach us what to expect in the future. For the class of commission merchants whose profits depend upon the value of the transactions a decrease in prices means that they must do a larger business in order to earn the same income. This very proposal to establish different index numbers for different classes reveals the difficulty of the so-called tabular standard for regulating deferred payments.

Causes of Changes in the Price-Level. We have discussed the method of determining and measuring changes in price-level. We have considered how far this method enables us to gauge the effect of changes of price-level upon different classes in the community. The first we found gave us only a rough measure, and the true technique is not always easy to define; the second is even more vague and uncertain. Our present inquiry is to assign a cause or causes for the changes in price-level when they have been established. While this is the most difficult task of all, its importance has been overrated.

Changes in prices of particular commodities are due to a variety of causes, such as a deficient or abundant harvest, anticipated interruption of supplies, like a war, improvements in production, monopolistic control of supply, speculative manipulation of demand, &c. So the whole price-level may go off in time of commercial panic or depression owing to the timidity of purchasers and investors; or the whole price-level may rise for a while owing to inflation or over speculation. We can assign the cause with greater or less certainty when it concerns the price of particular commodities only, or when the rise or fall is of temporary duration.

The important case occurs when our index number seems to show a change of price-level affecting more or less all commodities, and which extends over a number of years, persisting through and in spite of the temporary fluctuations. Such a general movement (upward) seems to have occurred during the twenty-five years from 1848 to 1873; such a general movement (downward) seems to have occurred during the twenty-five years since 1873. Our present task is to correlate such a movement with other phenomena which may be looked upon as causes. It has been found convenient for purposes of discussion to divide these causes into those primarily affecting commodities and those primarily affecting money. On account of the intricacy of the theory of the relation of money to prices it will be convenient to defer the latter inquiry to the next chapter, and to consider here those causes related directly to commodities and the methods of doing business. The quantity of money is considered to remain the same while we watch for the changes on the other side.

Causes connected with commodities which, it seems, might affect prices and might repay investigation are as follows:—

1. Relations of supply.
2. Cost of production.
3. Cost of transportation.
4. Changes in business methods.
5. Increased or decreased speculation.

The problem we have before us is to correlate facts in relation to these causes, expressed in figures, with the corresponding index numbers indicating changes in price-level. The problem is a difficult one because of the insufficiency of our statistical data; because of the difficulty of isolating a single cause where many causes are at work; and because we cannot predict that there will be an exact proportionate relation between the cause and the effect.

There are very few commodities of which we have exact statistics of supply. Where the commodity is imported our information is tolerably trustworthy as, for instance, wheat imported into Great Britain; but in regard to wheat produced at home we are dependent upon estimate. So, too, the cost of production is difficult to determine, especially where the same commodity is produced at varying cost.

The difficulty of isolating one cause is the common difficulty felt in every branch of social science. Where, for instance, supply is increased, demand may have fallen away so that the decreased price is as much due to the latter as to the former cause.

So, too, we can expect no exact proportionate relation between an increase of supply and a decrease of price. An increased supply, for instance, of 20 per cent. may be readily absorbed, while a further increase of 20 per cent. might cause an entire break in prices. General improvements in production or in transportation would affect different articles differently. When we have a cause affecting many different commodities we cannot expect that all will be affected to the same degree. In some the fall of prices will be great, in others it will be comparatively insignificant. Increased cheapness of one commodity may lead to increased expenditure on others, and thus even to a rise in price.

The striking fall in prices since 1873 has directed attention to the conditions of supply and transportation, and some economists explain the fall in this way. It must be confessed, however, that the statistical method is rather inadequate for proving this thesis. We have statistics showing the enormous increase in production during the last twenty-five years, but little attempt has been made to connect the increased supply with the decreased price. One interesting experiment of this sort was made by Mr. Luke Hansard.[1] He gives tables showing the stocks and wholesale prices of twenty-five selected articles on the 31st of December of each year for the ten years 1874 to 1883. Taking the extreme years, which are not always the extreme figures, some of the results are as follows :—

STATEMENT OF THE STOCKS AND PRICES OF CERTAIN COMMODITIES.

	United Kingdom.		Change 1874 to 1883.	
	Stocks 1874.	Stocks 1883.	Stocks per cent.	Prices per cent.
Sugar . . .	180,000 tons.	265,000 tons.	47·2 higher.	19·8 lower.
Tea . . .	87,122,000 lbs.	125,039,000 lbs.	43·5 higher.	56·8 lower.
Coffee . . .	14,000 tons.	24,500 tons.	75·0 higher.	29·9 lower.
Cocoa . . .	9,125,351 lbs.	6,680,875 lbs.	26·8 lower.	78·2 higher.
Rice . . .	102,829 tons.	131,499 tons.	27·9 higher.	6·7 lower.
Indigo (Bengal crops)	79,000 maunds.	147,000 maunds.	89·8 higher.	10·8 lower.
Silk . . .	46,133 bales.	29,388 bales.	32·9 lower.	10·3 higher.

On the basis of these returns Mr. Hansard has constructed a table of index numbers as follows :—

Year.	Stocks.	Prices.
1874	2,500	2,500
1875	2,545	2,360
1876	2,824	2,504
1877	3,351	2,248
1878	3,448	2,140
1879	3,169	2,460
1880	3,333	2,194
1881	3,361	2,232
1882	3,363	2,119
1883	3,310	2,111

[1] Commission on Depression of Trade, 1886, Third Report, Appendix C. pp. 405–412.

The result of this calculation is that taking 1874 as 100, we should have the following comparative figures:—

Population	109·3
Stocks	124·8
Prices	91·4

It cannot be contended that the data here given are sufficient to prove that the decreased prices are due simply to the fact that stocks have increased so much faster than population. But it is an interesting method showing some relation between stocks and prices.

Interesting figures of the same sort might be elicited from Mr. Palgrave's carefully prepared tables of the estimated import and home production of nineteen standard commodities already referred to. Taking, for instance, wheat, the estimated supply for Great Britain was in 1865, 79,900,000 bushels, while in 1885 it was 121,000,000 bushels. The population of the United Kingdom increased during those years from about 30,000,000 to about 36,000,000. The price of wheat, however, is affected not only by the amount imported and produced at home, but also by the amounts produced abroad, which affect the world's supply and hence market prices.

The enormous increase in production of all the more important commodities during the last thirty years is evidenced by the figures in Neumann-Spallart's Uebersichten der Weltwirthschaft. The principal figures have already been given in the chapter on Land.

Statistics of cost of production can of course only be given for single articles under specified conditions. The best evidence of decreased cost of production is that the supply continues or even increases notwithstanding the decreased prices. This becomes even more striking when we can prove, as has been done in many cases, that the wages of labour have not decreased. Much evidence of this sort was brought out before the English Commission on the Depression of Trade and that on Gold and Silver. It would be worth while to collect more exact statistics.

One particular branch of production, namely, transportation is more susceptible to statistical treatment. We have statistics of the cost of moving grain from Chicago to New York, and we have also statistics showing the sum received by certain railroads for moving one ton one mile in successive years. These figures are published annually in the Statistical Abstract of the United States and show a constant decrease in cost of transportation.[1]

Changes in business method and increase or decrease of speculative activity are scarcely susceptible of statistical treatment. It is barely possible that some light might be thrown on these questions by the statistics of direct importation of food into England, for instance, from far distant countries; by the increased traffic through direct routes like the Suez Canal; by the increased use of international cables and internal telegraph lines; by the increase of large establishments compared with small ones; by the concentration of industry in trusts and syndicates. All these things are symptomatic of economy in the methods of producing and handling products. No close correlation between these facts and a decrease in prices can of course be established, because each one is only a partial cause and its true significance can be only guessed at. The statistical method consists simply in the observation of a large number of causes which seem capable of bringing about a certain result, which result is found to have been brought about.

[1] See *post*, Chapter on Transportation and Commerce, p. 266.

CHAPTER VII.

MONEY AND CREDIT.

Economic Purpose.

The Quantity Theory. The fundamental theory of the relation of money to prices is the so-called quantity theory. This represents money as performing a useful function, namely, assisting as a medium of exchange in the transference of goods. There is a real demand and a limited supply. The demand depends upon the volume of trade, that is, the quantity of goods transferred and the number of times the same goods are transferred; upon the quantity of transactions which demand the use of money compared with the whole volume of trade; and upon the level of prices at which the business is done. The supply of money depends upon the quantity of specie in existence, or rather of that portion which is coined; upon the rapidity of circulation, that is, the number of transactions that each coin will liquidate; and upon the use of paper money, cheques, and other credit instruments as substitutes for money. These last two considerations depend largely upon the character of the trade, whether wholesale or retail, whether internal or international, whether for cash or on credit, and upon the habits of the people in the use of cheques and bank accounts.

Taking all these things into consideration, it is gravely said that the value of money depends upon demand and supply. Taking demand as fixed, then the value of money would vary inversely as the supply. The value of money is represented by its purchasing power. Its purchasing power varies inversely as the level of prices. If prices are high, the value of money is low; if prices are low, the value of money is high. Hence it follows that prices vary with the supply of money: that is when the supply of money is great, prices are high; and when the supply of money is small, prices are low. By an easy transposition of this statement of fact into the form of a proposition implying cause and effect, it is then said that low prices are *due* to a scarcity of money, and that high prices are *due* to an abundance of money.

The Modern Problem. Under the term money it will be convenient for purposes of discussion to include all specie money, both full legal tender and token coin, in circulation and in reserve. It is true, of course, that exchanges take place through credit, but in a modern monetary economy the system of credit rests also upon a metallic reserve.

There are two ways in which, under the modern system, an increase of specie is said to affect prices. In the first place, it is said that an inflow of gold into a country will increase the bank reserve; that will lower the rate of discount; that will make money easy to borrow, increase the demand for commodities, and put up prices. If the price-level remains high, an increased quantity of money will be permanently necessary to carry on cash transactions, and the increased amount of gold will be absorbed. And *vice versâ*, if gold flows out from a country, the bank reserves will be decreased, the rate of discount will be raised, demand will be crippled, the level of prices be lowered; and if this remains permanent, less money will be needed for cash transactions.[1]

A second theory of the effect of a decreasing quantity of specie money has been advanced by Professor Nicholson.[2] This theory is that even where a scarcity of money is not felt, in a rich country like England, sufficiently to decrease

[1] See Marshall, Gold and Silver Commission, 1887-88, Ques. 9686, *passim.*

[2] *Ibid.* Ques. 3980. See also Money and Monetary Problems, 1895, p. 88.

the bank reserve and raise the rate of discount, yet low prices may be brought about indirectly through international trade. In a less advanced community where transactions were still made principally through specie payments, a scarcity of money would be directly felt, and would at once affect prices. Among other prices, those of exported goods would be lowered. That would lower the prices of competing goods in the more civilised country like England. By competition the prices of other goods would also be affected, and thus the whole price-level be lowered.

Office of Statistics. Such is the present state of the theory of money in relation to prices. When we come to test this theory by statistics, we are at once met with the difficulty that so many elements enter into the process of making prices. We have no statistics of the volume of transactions, of the rapidity of transactions, of the rapidity of circulation of money, and of the relative number of transactions liquidated by the use of specie or by the use of credit. We have imperfect statistics of the level of prices (through the use of index numbers), of the quantity of specie used as money, and of the use of credit instruments. It is impossible, therefore, to use statistics directly for the solution of the problem of the relation of money to prices. About all we can do is to indicate the methods by which we approximate to a measurement of money supply, and the correlation between the movements of money supply, and the price-level measured by index numbers. For this purpose we have data under the following heads:—

(1) The annual production of the precious metals.

(2) Relative value of gold and silver.

(3) Employment of the precious metals: (*a*) coinage; (*b*) in the arts; (*c*) hoarded.

(4) The international distribution of the precious metals.

(5) Total amount of money in the world.

(6) Paper money of the world.

(7) *Per capita* supply of the circulating medium.

Statistical Data.[1]

Production of the Precious Metals. The following table is from the Report of the Director of the United States Mint on Precious Metals, 1897, (p. 364):—

	Gold. Total for period. Ounces, fine.	Gold. Total for period. Value. Dollars.	Silver. Total for period. Ounces, fine.	Silver. Total for period. Coining value. Dollars.	Percentage of production. By weight. Gold.	Percentage of production. By weight. Silver.
1493-1520	5,221,160	107,931,000	42,309,400	54,703,000	11·0	89·0
1521-1544	5,524,656	114,205,000	69,598,320	89,986,000	7·4	92·6
1545-1560	4,377,544	90,492,000	160,287,040	207,240,000	2·7	97·3
1561-1580	4,398,120	90,917,000	192,578,500	248,990,000	2·2	97·8
1581-1600	4,745,340	98,095,000	269,352,700	348,254,000	1·7	98·3
1601-1620	5,478,360	113,248,000	271,924,700	351,579,000	2·0	98·0
1621-1640	5,336,900	110,324,000	253,084,800	327,221,000	2·1	97·9
1641-1660	5,639,110	116,571,000	235,530,900	304,525,000	2·3	97·7
1661-1680	5,954,180	123,084,000	216,691,000	280,166,000	2·7	97·3
1681-1700	6,921,895	143,088,000	219,841,700	284,240,000	3·1	96·9
1701-1720	8,243,260	170,403,000	228,650,800	295,629,000	3·5	96·5
1721-1740	12,268,440	253,611,000	277,261,600	358,480,000	4·2	95·8
1741-1760	15,824,230	327,116,000	342,812,235	443,232,000	4·4	95·6
1761-1780	13,313,315	275,211,000	419,711,820	542,658,000	3·1	96·9
1781-1800	11,438,970	236,464,000	565,235,580	730,810,000	2·0	98·0
1801-1810	5,715,627	118,152,000	287,469,225	371,677,000	1·9	98·1
1811-1820	3,679,568	76,063,000	173,857,555	224,786,000	2·1	97·9
1821-1830	4,570,444	94,479,000	148,070,040	191,444,000	3·0	97·0
1831-1840	6,522,913	134,841,000	191,758,675	247,930,000	3·3	96·7
1841-1850	17,605,018	363,928,000	250,903,422	342,400,000	6·6	93·4
1851-1855	32,051,621	662,566,000	142,442,986	184,169,000	18·4	81·6
1856-1860	32,431,312	670,415,000	145,477,142	188,092,000	18·2	81·8
1861-1865	29,747,913	614,944,000	177,009,862	228,861,000	14·4	85·6
1866-1870	31,350,430	648,071,000	215,257,914	278,313,000	12·7	87·3
1871-1875	27,955,068	577,883,000	316,585,069	409,322,000	8·1	91·9
1876-1880	27,715,550	572,931,000	393,878,009	509,256,000	6·6	93·4
1881-1885	23,973,773	495,582,000	460,019,722	594,773,000	5·0	95·0
1886-1890	27,306,411	564,474,000	544,557,155	704,074,000	4·8	95·2
1891-1895	39,412,823	814,736,000	787,906,656	1,018,708,000	4·8	95·2
1896	9,804,748	202,682,300	168,178,550	217,442,900	5·5	94·5
1897	11,489,291	237,504,800	183,096,090	236,730,300	5·9	94·1
Total	446,017,990	9,220,012,100	8,351,339,167	10,797,685,200	5·0	95·0

[1] *Bibliographical Note.* No attempt will be made to give the general

This table shows the very great increase in the production, especially of silver, during the fifteenth and sixteenth centuries, the increased production of gold after 1850, the increased production of silver from 1870 to the present time, and the increasing production of gold beginning with 1890. The column of percentage of production by weight shows very great fluctuations.

Ratio of Gold to Silver. In this connection it will be well to add a table showing the relative value of gold and silver. The final Report of the Gold and Silver Commission gives the following *résumé* (p. 2):—"At the beginning of the sixteenth century the relative value of silver to gold was as 11 to 1. During that century silver depreciated slowly, and during the first half of the seventeenth century more rapidly, until in 1670 the ratio was about 15 to 1, near which point it remained until shortly after the middle of the eighteenth century. About this time there was a considerable discovery of gold in Brazil, and the ratio became about 14½ to 1. Silver then again became depreci-

literature on Money or on Bimetallism. The chief authority for statistics of the production of precious metals is the Annual Report of the United States Director of the Mint on Precious Metals. Valuable tables in regard to circulation, etc., may also be found in the Annual Finance Report of the Secretary of the Treasury of the United States. For the history of the precious metals the standard authority is Soetbeer, Materialien, etc., translated and published as Consular Report No. 87, by the Department of State of the United States. Valuable statistical tables and much information on all questions connected with money will be found in the Reports of the Royal Commissions on Gold and Silver, 1887-88, and on Agriculture, 1895-98; and of the various International Monetary Conferences. The great German authority is Professor Lexis; see his last article, Die Edelmetallgewinnung und Verwendung in den letzten zehn Jahren, (Jahrbücher für Nationalökonomie und Statistik, Band LXVI., 1896, p. 507). For imports and exports of the precious metals see the Statistical Abstract of the United Kingdom and the Statistical Abstract for the United States. For the quantity of money in circulation in England, see the Report of the Deputy Master of the Mint, 1895.

See, also, Bibliographical Note to the preceding chapter.

ated." The figures since the beginning of this century are as follows[1]:—

Years.	Ratio.	Year.	Ratio.	Year.	Ratio.
1801–10 . .	15·61	1871	15·57	1885	19·41
1811–20 . .	15·51	1872	15·63	1886	20·78
1821–30 . .	15·80	1873	15·92	1887	21·13
1831–40 . .	15·75	1874	16·17	1888	21·99
1841–50 . .	15·83	1875	16·59	1889	22·10
1851–55 . .	15·41	1876	17·88	1890	19·76
1856–60 . .	15·30	1877	17·22	1891	20·92
1861–65 . .	15·40	1878	17·94	1892	23·72
1866–70 . .	15·55	1879	18·40	1893	26·49
		1880	18·05	1894	32·56
		1881	18·16	1895	31·60
		1882	18·19	1896	30·66
		1883	18·64	1897	34·20
		1884	18·57	1898	35·03

Employment of Gold and Silver. It is commonly said that the gold and silver which are produced find employment in three ways. They are used either for money, or for industrial purposes, that is, in the arts, or else they are hoarded. Attempts have been made, through a sort of book-keeping operation, to account for the annual production by distributing it among these several uses.

Coinage. The item that seems easiest to fix is that of coinage. All coining now is by national mints, and we have exact statistics of the number of pieces turned out annually. The difficulty is that only part of the coinage is from the new gold and silver. Part of it is simple re-coinage of domestic or foreign coins, and part of it is from old metal, articles of ornament, plate, &c. The last part is not so important; for if we could estimate the re-coinage, we could say at least what is the additional amount added annually to the quantity of coined money in existence.

The Director of the United States Mint gives the follow-

[1] The ratio for each year since 1687 may be found in the Report of the Director of the Mint on Precious Metals, 1897, p. 347, and since 1833 in the Statistical Abstract of the United States. For Soetbeer's tables see Gold and Silver Commission, Final Report, 1888, Appendix, p. 160.

ing estimate of the total value of gold and silver coinage executed in the world (U. S. Finance Report, 1898, pp. 459–460):—

Year.	Gold.	Silver.
1895	$231,087,438	$126,873,642
1896	195,899,517	159,540,027
1897	437,719,345	167,760,297

The returns of the amount of re-coinages included in the above are very imperfect. For 1896 it was:—Gold $15,253,072, and silver $24,901,287. For 1897 it was:—Gold $146,622,194, and silver $14,216,656.

Gold and Silver in the Arts. It is almost impossible to determine how much gold and silver is used in the arts, and, of the quantity that is used, how much consists of new metal, how much of coin, and how much of old metal. The Director of the United States Mint has made an elaborate attempt by inquiry among dealers, in addition to the figures of the Mint, to show what is the annual consumption in the arts. He reaches figures of this sort for 1897 (Finance Report, 1898, p. 447):—

	Gold.	Silver. (Coining value).	Total.
Domestic bullion	$7,184,822	$9,200,497	$16,385,319
United States coin . . .	1,500,000	100,000	1,600,000
Foreign bullion and coin .	613,981	797,193	1,411,174
Old material	2,571,428	1,103,460	3,674,888
Total.	$11,870,231	$11,201,150	$23,071,381

Similar estimates extend back to the year 1873, but vary in the case of gold from about $10,000,000 to over $19,000,000 per annum, and in the case of silver from about $5,000,000 to $10,000,000 per annum.

The estimates of the gold used in the arts for the whole world are necessarily very imperfect. The one most generally accepted is that of Soetbeer, who made careful inquiries of manufacturers, and estimated the total net consumption of the world, deducting old material, as 90,000 kilograms of gold, equal to about £12,500,000. This estimate has been much discussed, but was acquiesced in by Sir R. Giffen in his testimony before the Royal Commission on Agriculture (Q. 18,205).[1] Mr. Soetbeer's estimate for silver was 515,000 kilograms for the whole world.[2]

The difficulty of the investigation is shown by the testimony of Sir Hector Hay, who estimates for England on the basis of information from metallurgists and refiners, that the people who prepare gold for the trades use about 1,720,000 pounds sterling a year. He adds one-third to that for gold from re-melting of jewelry, &c., making 2,200,000 pounds sterling as the amount used in the arts in Great Britain. This is evidently a very loose estimate.[3]

Gold hoarded. The third item, the amount of gold and silver hoarded, is even more difficult to ascertain than that of "used in the arts." It is customary to distinguish two kinds of hoarding, namely that of government for war purposes, and that of individuals who hoard gold or silver as a method of saving, or because they think one of the metals is going to advance in value. It is not easy to get figures even of the first kind of hoarding, and it is absolutely impossible to estimate the second. There is at the present time, for instance, a considerable amount of hoarding of gold in India; and as it is not customary for the natives to use gold coin, it is usual to attribute to hoarding the total excess of imports of gold over exports.

International Distribution of the Precious Metals. Gold and silver are produced in various countries, and thence distributed throughout the world. In this respect they are precisely like any other commodity which is imported or exported. Particular importance, however, is attached to

[1] The Director of the U. S. Mint now (1897) estimates the world's use of gold in the arts at about the same figure, viz. $59,000,000 (Finance Report, 1898, p. 455).

[2] Commission on Gold and Silver, Final Report, 1888, Appendix, p. 173.

[3] *Ibid.*, Ques. 374–381.

the movement of the precious metals, because they are used in settlement of the balance of trade. The statistics are interesting also, because they enable us to trace to a certain extent what becomes of the supply of specie money. Any unusual movement might throw some light upon the question whether or not the nations are actively striving to obtain possession of the supplies. We shall take for illustration the imports and exports of several countries showing different kinds of movements. The following table shows the exports and imports of gold for the United States, 1878–1898 (U.S. Stat. Abstract, 1898, p. 74; Finance Report, 1898, p. 662):—

Year.	Exports. Dollars.	Imports. Dollars.	Excess of Exports. Dollars.	Excess of Imports. Dollars.
1878 . .	9,204,455	13,330,215	...	4,125,760
1879 . .	4,587,614	5,624,948	...	1,037,334
1880 . .	3,639,025	80,758,396	...	77,119,371
1881 . .	2,565,132	100,031,259	...	97,466,127
1882 . .	32,587,880	34,377,054	...	1,789,174
1883 . .	11,600,888	17,734,149	...	6,133,261
1884 . .	41,081,957	22,831,317	18,250,640	...
1885 . .	8,477,892	26,691,696	...	18,213,804
1886 . .	42,952,191	20,743,349	22,208,842	...
1887 . .	9,701,187	42,910,601	...	33,209,414
1888 . .	18,376,234	43,934,317	...	25,558,083
1889 . .	59,952,285	10,284,858	49,667,427	...
1890 . .	17,274,491	12,943,342	4,331,149	...
1891 . .	86,362,654	18,232,567	68,130,087	...
1892 . .	50,195,327	49,699,454	495,873	...
1893 . .	108,680,844	21,174,381	87,506,463	...
1894 . .	76,978,061	72,449,119	4,528,942	...
1895 . .	66,131,183	35,146,734	30,984,449	...
1896 . .	112,409,947	33,525,065	78,884,882	...
1897 . .	40,361,580	85,014,780	...	44,653,200
1898 . .	15,406,391	120,391,674	...	104,985,283

From 1861, down to the resumption of specie payments there was always an excess of exports over imports of gold. During the following years there was generally an excess of imports, until 1889. During several years then, viz., in 1889 and 1891, and 1893, there was an enormous excess of exports over imports, due to commercial causes. The movement of specie in the United States can thus be explained either by the condition of our currency or by that of trade. Large quantities of gold being produced in the United States, it would seem natural that there should be an excess of exports. The movement is subject to violent fluctuations owing to the balance of trade.[1]

In Great Britain and Ireland no gold is produced, so that the balance of imports and exports must be due to trade movements. Generally there is an excess of imports over exports, but sometimes the movement is reversed. The movement for the last twenty-five years is shown in the following table (U. S. Finance Report, 1898, p. 666):—

MOVEMENT OF GOLD, GREAT BRITAIN AND IRELAND, 1872–1897.[2]

Year.	Excess of Imports over Exports. $	Excess of Exports over Imports. $
1872	...	6,226,561
1873	7,494,142	...
1874	36,203,757	...
1875	21,862,936	...
1876	33,871,944	...
1877	...	23,940,265
1878	28,726,478	...
1879	...	20,488,661
1880	...	11,552,881
1881	...	26,940,121
1882	11,449,682	...
1883	3,233,473	...
1884	...	6,172,819
1885	7,035,709	...
1886	...	1,904,990
1887	3,074,226	...
1888	4,104,625	...
1889	16,831,866	...
1890	45,070,413	...
1891	29,837,202	...
1892	28,225,700	...
1893	26,018,990	...

[1] For elaborate study of movement of gold in connection with the finances of the government and the condition of trade, see Noyes, Thirty Years of American Finance, 1898.

[2] See also Statistical Abstract for the United Kingdom, which gives countries to which and from which specie is exported and imported.

MOVEMENT OF GOLD, GREAT BRITAIN AND IRELAND, 1872–1897—*continued.*

Year.	Excess of Imports over Exports. $	Excess of Exports over Imports. $
1894	58,292,368	...
1895	72,103,120	...
1896	...	26,964,474
1897	677,509	...

Sir R. Giffen comments on the movement (see Question 18,123 of the Report of the Royal Commission on Agriculture) as follows (summarised):—In the period from 1858 to 1871 you have an excess of imports of gold into the United Kingdom of nearly £68,000,000 sterling. In the period from 1872 to 1887 you have an excess of imports of £10,195,000 sterling only. And now in the last six years the excess of the imports of gold into the United Kingdom begins to resemble what took place in 1858 and 1871, and you have an excess of imports over exports of £31,000,000. Sir Robert adduces these facts as showing a pressure upon gold during the period from 1872 to 1887, which, in his opinion, was one of the causes of low prices.

A third country of interest in this connection is India, which has a constant excess of imports over exports of silver. She has also an excess of imports of gold. This has been interrupted three times during recent years by an excess of exports. The following table shows the movement (U. S. Finance Report, 1898, p. 668):—

Year.	Gold. Excess of Imports. Dollars.	Gold. Excess of Exports. Dollars.	Silver. Excess of Imports. Dollars.	Silver. Excess of Exports. Dollars.
1888-89	13,694,009	...	44,998,963	...
1889-90	22,460,372	...	53,229,174	...
1890-91	26,698,547	...	67,147,619	...
1891-92	11,434,132	...	42,738,086	...
1892-93	...	13,323,679	60,934,726	...
1893-94	3,036,573	...	65,177,677	...
1894-95	...	23,562,284	30,381,745	...
1895-96	11,965,436	...	31,179,988	...
1896-97	10,852,646	...	27,740,012	...
1897-98	23,251,513	...	40,138,879	(1847-48)
Total 1835-98	788,620,898	41,247,189	1,896,022,357	2,404,981

The statistics of some other countries are also interesting. In the statistics for France we find evidence of the alternate use of the metals down to 1873. Since that time France has been accumulating a large supply of both gold and silver.

Italy shows the effect of a depreciated paper currency.

Austria-Hungary shows the accumulation of gold during the years 1890–93.

Germany also shows an accumulation of gold, and a considerable export of silver.

Russia shows the accumulation of gold since 1891.

It would appear from all these tables, that the countries of Europe and the United States have been accumulating large sums of gold. This fact has a double bearing. It may be interpreted as showing a general desire to accumulate gold, which increases the pressure upon gold as a money metal. Or it may be interpreted as meaning that the fright about a scarcity of gold has been exaggerated, and that the supply of specie money is really more abundant than ever.

The Total Amount of Gold and Silver in the World. Such estimates are extremely hazardous, and are protested against by eminent authorities like Sir R. Giffen and Mr. Sauerbeck. Perhaps the best statistics at present are those published by the Director of the United States Mint, as follows (Finance Report, 1898, p. 442):—

Stock of gold in the world . . .		$4,594,900,000
Stock of silver (full tender) . . .	$3,276,100,000	
Stock of silver (lim. tender) . .	701,400,000	
Total silver		3,977,500,000
Total gold and silver		$8,572,400,000

This estimate of the stock of gold and silver is a very general one. In the testimony before the Gold and Silver Commission, the figure £1,000 million sterling was commonly mentioned as the most probable sum representing the supply of gold and silver money. The stock of specie money in 1873 was estimated at $1,209,800,000 of gold and $1,057,685,000 of silver, making a total of $2,267,485,000. This estimate covers only 13 (principal) countries, while that of 1897 includes 37. The same 13 countries in 1897 showed $4,137,700,000 in gold and $1,841,100,000 in silver, making a total of $6,018,800,000.

Stock of Money of Principal Countries. The Director of the Mint assigns the following amounts to some of the principal countries (U.S. Finance Report, 1898, p. 442):—

	Stock of Gold.	Stock of Silver.		
Country.	Million. Dollars.	Full tender. Million. Dollars.	Limited tender. Million. Dollars.	Total Silver. Million. Dollars.
United States . .	925·1	561·5	76·7	638·2
United Kingdom . .	438·0	...	121·7	121·7
France	810·6	373·5	46·3	419·8
Germany	668·5	95·2	117·6	212·8
Belgium	30·0	40·0	5·0	45·0
Italy	96·5	16·0	26·5	42·5
Switzerland . . .	24·0	...	10·7	10·7
Austria-Hungary . .	227·7	48·5	97·0	145·5
Netherlands . . .	21·9	52·7	3·4	56·1
Norway	7·8	...	2·3	2·3
Sweden	8·6	...	5·7	5·7
Denmark	15·3	...	5·4	5·4
Russia	756·6	83·4	45·0	128·4
Australasia . . .	132·1	...	7·0	7·0
South American States	77·5	25·0	10·0	35·0
Japan	79·9	41·9	18·5	60·4
India	...	592·1	...	592·1
Other countries . .	274·8	1,346·3	102·6	1,448·9
Total	4,594·9	3,276·1	701·4	3,977·5

Uncovered Paper Money. This represents the paper money over and above the specie reserve that is held in banks and treasuries for its redemption. It is to be added to the stock of gold and silver as a part of the money supply of each country. The figures for two dates are as follows (Finance Report, 1897, p. 178; 1898, p. 443):—

	1894.	1898.
United States	$416,700,000	$326,100,000
United Kingdom	113,400,000	112,000,000
France	32,100,000	124,600,000
Germany	60,400,000	132,200,000
Belgium	65,400,000	79,100,000
Italy	191,800,000	169,500,000
Greece	22,400,000	30,600,000
Spain	83,700,000	137,500,000
Portugal	55,100,000	39,000,000
Austria-Hungary	204,300,000	86,200,000
Russia	539,000,000	...
Netherlands	28,600,000	45,500,000
Norway	3,800,000	3,800,000
Sweden	2,100,000	27,700,000
Denmark	5,400,000	7,000,000
South American States	550,000,000	750,600,000
India	37,000,000	117,300,000
Other countries	60,700,000	134,100,000
Total	2,469,900,000	2,322,800,000

This table shows extraordinary fluctuations. These are owing to imperfect estimates, to accumulation of specie by some countries, *e.g.*, Austria-Hungary and Russia, and to additional issues of paper money by other countries. Doubt may be felt whether such paper really increases the money supply. By giving the figures separately, they can be added or not to the specie supply.

Per Capita Supply of Money. The supply of money which any country needs will depend upon the number of people, the amount and character of the business transactions, the monetary system, and the habits of the people in respect to using credit instruments. The following table eliminates the first influence, but only serves to bring out more strongly the strength of the others (Finance Report, 1898, p. 443):—

STOCK OF MONEY. PER CAPITA.

	Gold.	Silver.	Uncovered paper.	Total.
	$	$	$	$
United States	12·42	8·56	4·38	25·36
United Kingdom	11·01	3·06	2·81	16·88
France	21·06	10·90	3·23	35·19

STOCK OF MONEY. PER CAPITA—*continued.*

	Gold.	Silver.	Uncovered paper.	Total.
	$	$	$	$
Germany	12·78	4·07	2·53	19·38
Belgium	4·62	6·92	12·17	23·71
Italy	3·08	1·36	5·41	9·85
Switzerland	8·00	3·56	4·77	16·33
Greece	0·21	0·62	12·75	13·58
Spain	2·53	2·76	7·64	12·93
Portugal	1·02	1·20	7·64	9·86
Austria-Hungary	5·02	3·20	1·90	10·12
Netherlands	4·47	11·45	9·28	25·20
Norway	3·90	1·15	1·90	6·95
Sweden	1·72	1·14	5·54	8·40
Denmark	6·65	2·35	3·04	12·04
Russia	5·86	0·99	...	6·85
South American States	2·07	0·93	20·01	23·01
India	...	1·99	0·40	2·39
Australasia	26·42	1·40	4·50	32·32

Money and Prices. Such are the principal figures relating to the supply of money. The problem now is whether we can reach any correlation between these facts and those in regard to the level of prices. The question is extremely difficult on account of the numerous influences which affect prices. We have already mentioned these, viz., the volume of business transactions, the rapidity of circulation of money, and the relations existing between the number of transactions demanding the use of gold and silver, and those which are carried on by means of credit. In regard to the number of transactions, we have no statistics whatsoever. In regard to the rapidity of circulation, we have occasionally an example such as the following:—

Sir T. Farrer has shown that the whole of the railway work of the United Kingdom, which amounts, including receipts and payments, to £140,000,000 sterling annually, and which probably employs more actual cash in proportion to its magnitude than any other large business in the country, is carried on with a supply of about £577,500 sterling of gold and notes. "Considering the additional currency work which must be done by a large proportion of this gold, it may be concluded that £500,000 sterling, sovereigns or notes representing sovereigns, are more than are required to do all the railway business of this nation outside the banks." [1]

In regard to the relative amount of transactions conducted by specie and on credit, we have isolated statistics of the character of the receipts of banks, both in the United States and in England. The statistics for this country are the results of an inquiry by the Comptroller of the Currency made at different dates. One is as far back as 1881, and shows that the receipts for a given day of the National banks were in the following proportions:—

Gold coin	1·38	per cent.
Silver coin	0·17	,, ,,
Paper currency	4·36	,, ,,
Cheques, drafts, etc. . .	94·09	,, ,,

Mr. William Fowler gave the following analysis of the receipts of a bank in Lombard Street on the 11th of November, 1886: "Coin, 0·65; bank-notes, 1·65; country notes, 0·18; cheques and bills, 97·52 per cent." The same bank reported that from 1882 to 1886 the number of cheques showed an increase of 16 per cent., the aggregate amount a decrease of 2 per cent., and the average amount per cheque a decrease of 17 per cent.[2]

These figures do not show, of course, that there is no connection between the amount of specie money and prices. It is evident, however, that when so large a proportion of transactions is carried on by means of credit instruments, any movement of the quantity of money might be temporarily disguised simply by filling up the vacancy by an

[1] Gold and Silver Commission, 1887-88. Appendix IV. p. 93.

[2] *Ibid.*, Questions, 7,801 and 7,802.

increased use of credit, or by diminishing the use of credit if there is specie enough to take its place. Temporary fluctuations in prices might also be due to extended use of credit allowing or encouraging speculation. Thus it is estimated that from twenty to thirty times the volume of business is now done in England compared with thirty or forty years ago, with an increase of only two or three times the amount of specie.

Statistics of Credit. In connection with money there should be treated also the subject of credit, because of the close relation between the two, especially in their influence on prices. Exactly what this influence is the economists have been unable to determine. It is evident, however, that purchases on credit must have the same influence on demand for commodities as purchases by money. In times of speculation prices go up, mainly because of purchases on credit; while in times of commercial crises prices go down, because of the collapse of credit. The influence of credit on prices is therefore peculiar. It is limited by confidence; but exactly when that confidence will cease, or to what extent it will be withdrawn, can never be predicted.

Credit takes on two forms, first, that of bank notes and paper money, which take the place of specie money, and secondly, that of mercantile credit, represented by instruments of exchange or simply carried on books. Of the first we have already given statistics; of the second it is extremely difficult to ascertain the actual amount at any given time or to follow the fluctuations. We have two sets of figures: (1) the amount of loans and discounts of banking institutions which make returns to the government; and (2) the amount of clearing house transactions.

Bank Statistics. For the purpose of illustrating the operations of banking institutions, we give the following summary of the condition of 3,585 National banks in the

United States, September 20th, 1898 (Finance Report, 1898, p. 191; Stat. Abstract, 1898, p. 57):—

Resources.	Millions.	Liabilities.	Millions.
Loans	$2,172·5	Capital stock . .	$621·5
Bonds for circulation	224·6	Surplus fund . . .	247·6
Other United States bonds	114·5	Undivided profits .	93·0
Stocks, bonds, etc. .	255·2	Circulation . . .	194·5
Due from banks .	525·5	Due to depositors .	2,106·6
Real estate . . .	109·9	Due to banks . .	698·3
Specie	293·9	Other liabilities . .	42·0
Legal-tender notes .	110·0		
National-bank notes	19·7		
Clearing-house exchanges . . .	110·3		
United States certificates of deposit .	16·8		
Due from United States treasurer .	13·8		
Other resources . .	36·8		
Total . . .	4,003·5	Total	4,003·5

The Comptroller of the Currency has collected returns of 5,093 other banking institutions, viz., 3,965 State banks, 934 savings banks, 246 loan and trust companies, and 758 private banks. The principal resources and liabilities of these institutions were in 1898: loans, 2,480 million dollars; bonds, 1,304 million dollars; cash, 194 million dollars; capital, 370 million dollars; surplus and undivided profits, 399 million dollars; deposits, 3,664 million dollars. The returns for loan and trust companies and private banks are not at all complete. But the total shows 4,632 million dollars of loans outstanding at one time of National, State, and private banks.[1]

Clearing House Statistics. The magnitude of business transactions and fluctuations from year to year are indicated

[1] Finance Report, 1898, p. 232.

to a certain extent by the returns of clearing houses (U. S. Stat. Abstract, 1898, p. 70):—

TRANSACTIONS OF THE NEW YORK CLEARING HOUSE, 1883–1898.

Year.	Clearings.	Balances paid in money.	Average daily Clearings.	Average daily balances paid in money.	Balances to clearings
	Dollars.	Dollars.	Dollars.	Dollars.	per cent.
1883 . .	40,293,165,000	1,568,983,000	132,543,000	5,161,000	3·9
1884 . .	34,092,037,000	1,524,930,000	111,048,000	4,967,000	4·5
1885 . .	25,250,791,000	1,295,355,000	82,789,000	4,247,000	5·1
1886 . .	33,374,682,000	1,519,565,000	109,067,000	4,965,000	4·5
1887 . .	34,872,848,000	1,569,626,000	114,337,000	5,146,000	4·5
1888 . .	30,863,686,000	1,570,198,000	101,192,000	5,148,000	5·1
1889 . .	34,796,465,000	1,757,637,000	114,839,000	5,800,000	5·0
1890 . .	37,660,686,000	1,753,040,000	123,074,000	5,728,000	4·7
1891 . .	34,053,698,000	1,584,635,000	111,651,000	5,195,000	4·6
1892 . .	36,279,905,000	1,861,500,000	118,561,000	6,083,000	5·1
1893 . .	34,421,380,000	1,696,207,000	113,978,000	5,616,000	4·9
1894 . .	24,230,145,000	1,585,241,000	79,704,000	5,214,000	6·5
1895 . .	28,264,379,000	1,896,574,000	92,670,000	6,218,000	6·7
1896 . .	29,350,894,000	1,843,289,000	96,232,000	6,043,000	6·3
1897 . .	31,337,760,000	1,908,901,000	103,424,000	6,300,000	6·0
1898 . .	39,853,413,000	2,338,529,000	131,529,000	7,717,000	5·9

The depression of trade after 1893 is very clearly visible. In considering the relation of these figures to the volume of trade, the lower price-level of recent years must be borne in mind. The total transactions of all the clearing houses in the United States in 1898 was $65,924,820,769.

The transactions of the London Clearing House were £8,097,291,000 in 1898.

Scientific Tests.

It is scarcely necessary to dwell upon the difficulties of ascertaining the annual production of the precious metals, the total stock of money in the world, the demand on gold and silver made for coinage purposes, the amount of gold used in the arts, and the imports and exports. They are the usual difficulties, where an enumeration can never be complete, and where we are obliged to put estimates in place of actual figures. For general purposes our figures may be useful enough, as for instance, when we say that the general stock of gold in the world is about $4,500,000,000, so that any annual increase must be comparatively small. So, too, it cannot make any great difference, if our estimate of the annual production of gold is a million or two pounds sterling short.

But when we come to more particular questions as to the amount of money in circulation in a country at a given time, so as to be able to trace the amount of gold necessary to carry on business, the difficulties of an exact estimate seem to be insuperable. The following points are taken from the report of a committee appointed by the British Association for the Advancement of Science for the purpose of inquiring and reporting as to the statistical data available for determining the amount of the precious metals in use as money in the principal countries, the chief forms in which the money is employed, and the amount annually used in the arts.[1] This committee reported that all the computations as applied to the United Kingdom failed, owing not to the incorrectness of the reasoning, but to the unsoundness of the data. Three methods have been tried. The first is as follows: Estimate the amount of the precious metals in circulation at some initial epoch, when there has occurred a general or partial re-coinage, or other event favourable to the formation of a precise estimate. Add thereto the coin issued from the mint in subsequent years and the coin imported, and subtract the coin withdrawn from circulation as light, the coin exported, and the coin used in the arts. This method was employed by Newmarch and breaks down, because the first datum is imperfect. The second method employed by Mr. Ottomar Haupt is similar, but more elaborate, as including not only the coin imported, but also bullion and ore. It breaks down because of the imperfections of the statistics. The third method was that of Jevons, who compared the

[1] British Association Report, 1888, p. 219.

number of coins of successive dates found in representative samples with the total number issued, and tried to calculate the number surviving. Finally, the Deputy Master of the Mint has calculated the amount of gold in circulation by five different methods based on the withdrawal of light coin.[1]

Reflective Analysis.

The statistics of the production, use, and movements of the precious metals are of great interest to the community. The monetary and credit system of every country rests ultimately upon the supply of specie. It cannot be a matter of indifference whether that supply is increasing or decreasing. And if there is a connection between the quantity of money and prices (as there must be) then every member of the community must be interested, for a change in price-level affects all incomes. In recent years, the great fall in prices, noticed in the preceding chapter, has been ascribed by numerous theorists and business men to a scarcity of gold, compared with the demand for a circulating medium. It would be unfair to go into that controversy without a much greater apparatus of facts and figures than we have had space for in this chapter. It has been our object simply to indicate the lines along which evidence of a statistical nature may be found bearing upon the discussion. From the statistical point of view the following suggestions may be made in regard to the assertion that the fall of prices since 1873, has been owing to a scarcity of money.

(1) It is not clear that there has been any scarcity of money since 1873. Lexis[2] has shown that the coinage of silver from 1876 to 1891, amounted to

[1] Deputy Master of the Mint, Report, 1895, p. 90.

[2] Quoted by Giffen, Report, Royal Com. on Agriculture, [C—7400 II.] 1894, Question 18,244. See also, Lexis, The Present Monetary Situation, Amer. Econ. Assocn. Econ. Studies, Vol. I., No. 4, 1896.

$1,560,000,000. During the same period, and since, the public treasuries and banks of the world increased their gold reserves enormously. So too, since 1890 there has been a great increase in the production of gold, but prices have still continued to fall. It seems doubtful at least to speak of an actual scarcity of specie money as the direct cause of the fall of prices.

(2) The relation between specie money and credit is so intimate that it seems impossible to trace a direct connection between the amount of specie and the level of prices. If there has been a strain on the gold supply since 1873, owing to decreasing annual output up to 1890, to increasing business, and to demonetisation of silver, the natural effect of such a strain would have been to increase the recourse to bank-notes and means of credit, to economise in the use of gold in the arts, to diminish the reserves held by bankers, and to increase the rate of discount. These would seem to be symptoms which would manifest themselves if a scarcity of gold were felt. It is impossible, however, to trace any one of these things. While it is not impossible that the increased strain on gold and apprehension of its decreased supply may have led to hoarding, and by discouraging business brought down prices, the correlation between the two things does not seem to be either very certain or very direct.

(3) These considerations show how difficult it is to correlate directly the quantity of money and the level of prices. But if we cannot do this directly, it may perhaps be done indirectly. We have as an established fact, according to the evidence of index numbers, a remarkable fall in prices.

One possible explanation of such a fall would be that the supply of money had not been equal to the demands made upon it. We are not obliged here to constitute directly a decrease in the quantity of money, or an increase in the quantity of trade, or even to show that there has been no great extension of the credit system. All of these things would be additional evidence, but they would not be essential. The line of argument is to show that there has been a fall of prices of such a character that a decrease in the supply of money is the most probable explanation of the fall. We are then confronted with the problem or problems (1) how to establish the fall of prices; (2) what sort of uniformity there must be in the fall; (3) how general must be the fall, that is, how many exceptional cases may there be.

The first question we have already considered. Index numbers are in general sufficient to show a rise or fall in prices. Only in this case our aim being to establish one general cause which is supposed to influence all commodities we ought to have as many commodities as possible. For this purpose the index numbers having a large number of commodities, would seem to be preferable to those having a small number. In addition it would seem to be necessary to have retail prices rather than wholesale, because money as a medium of exchange must affect retail transactions more than wholesale.

In regard to the second demand, it is to be observed that perfect uniformity in the rise or fall is not to be expected. Every commodity is affected by its own particular conditions of demand and supply. In some cases these may have brought about a very great fall in price; in others a less fall; and it is even conceivable, though improbable, that an increased demand may have counteracted the general tendency to fall entirely. It may be expected, perhaps, that the percentages of fall in the case of a large number of commodities, would tend to group themselves about the average percentage, according to the theory of error. Such a test was applied by Jevons to his percentages of rise in price, and was found satisfactory. It shows, of course, only the presence of a single great cause affecting all commodities, but does not show that the cause is the scarcity of money.

It follows from this that exceptions to the general rule may possibly occur, but these exceptions should be few, not very important, or else fully accounted for by particular influences.

If we examine the index numbers with these tests in mind, we shall find a certain corroboration of the general theory that one great cause has been at work since 1873 inducing a fall in prices. But the evidence that this great cause is the scarcity of money is not altogether satisfactory. This is due, first, to the nature of index numbers themselves, which deal with wholesale prices, and not with retail; and which are commonly based upon a small number of commodities rather than a large number. Still further, according to experiment, the fall in retail prices is less than in wholesale, and the fall is less when you take a large number of commodities, than when you take a small one. These things throw doubt upon the supply of money as the real cause of the fall.

In the second place, the uniformity is not very great in different articles. Mr. Sauerbeck's number for 1897 shows some articles which have fallen as much as 60 per cent., while others have fallen only 15. Testing the figures for 1897, according to the theory of errors, we find a rather wide dispersion about a mean fall of 38 per cent., showing considerable room for the introduction of varying influences.

In the third place, there are two very marked exceptions to the fall in prices, not shown by any index number. The first of these is residential rents. It has been found impossible to include them in any index number on account of the difficulty of finding a unit. There is considerable evidence, however, to show that rents have advanced during the last twenty-five years. One explanation of this is that the houses are better than they were, but it is rather remarkable that if there is a constant cause affecting prices it should not have shown itself in the rent of houses, especially as building materials are cheaper than formerly. The second very marked exception is the wages of labour. There seems to be a general agreement that the wages of labour, with some exceptions, such as agricultural labour in England, have either increased or at least held their own during the last twenty-five years. The evidence on this point is not complete, but it is sufficient to make it an important exception to the general rule.

The general conclusion would seem to be that the method of index numbers is not fitted to support the theory that the dominant cause of decrease in prices has been a scarcity of money.

CHAPTER VIII.

TRANSPORTATION AND COMMERCE.

Economic Purpose.

Economic Theory. Exchange of wealth takes place primarily between individuals living in the same place; but it may also take place between individuals living apart from each other, involving the transportation of commodities from one place to another. The machinery by which this change of place is brought about is a very productive part of the organisation of society. It cheapens all products; it enables the individual to command the commodities of distant lands; it makes labour most productive by carrying it to the place where it can best be employed; it encourages capital to invest itself in new undertakings, for the products can find an outlet. The history of civilisation shows constant advance in the efficiency of the means and methods of transportation.

Means of transportation are simply the vehicle of trade and commerce. Trade may be either internal or external. The difference is a purely artificial one, but in a statistical treatment of economic life it has considerable importance. Internal trade is commonly free and unimpeded. It represents the economic activity of the nation among its own members. It follows, generally, the lines of least resistance and marks the natural development of industrial life. Its analysis is often of great interest as showing changes in industrial development. It sometimes reflects, also, the changing conditions of political and social life, and may be made even the basis of predictions in regard to the outcome of political and social struggles.

External trade, on the other hand, is often impeded by differences in language, custom, taste, or administration. It is often more or less controlled by custom-house regulations, commercial treaties, and international complications, and may be interrupted and partially destroyed by war. It represents, however, the external policy of the nation, its relations with other nations, the extension of its influence abroad, and its position in the world. External trade is also of vital interest to internal prosperity. It may furnish the raw material necessary for the national industry, and the natural outlet for its manufactured products. Its expansion may be the measure of continued prosperity, while its restriction may act like a blight upon the whole industry of the nation. In many cases it represents the point where the nation comes into rivalry with foreigners, and "the interests of trade" is often the excuse for aggressive or even hostile movements. In modern times, it is true both that "the flag follows trade," and that "trade follows the flag." An analysis of foreign trade is always a matter of great practical interest.

The advantages of trade and commerce, whether internal or external, depend upon the principle of the division of labour. Each locality produces that which it can produce to the best advantage. This advantage need not be absolute, but only relative; the United States, for instance, may possibly produce both wheat and iron cheaper than England, but if it produces wheat at an advantage of 50 per cent., and iron at an advantage of only 20 per cent., it will be economically profitable for the United States to devote its capital and labour to the production of wheat, and to get its iron by an exchange of wheat. The terms upon which the exchange would be conducted will depend upon the relative strength of the demand of the two nations for each other's products. The cost of the American wheat to England is represented, of course, not by the labour of producing the wheat in

America, but by the labour of producing the iron which is exchanged for the wheat. The exports are supposed to pay for the imports. When they do not, the balance must be paid in some other way, either by the export of precious metals, or by selling securities, or by running into debt. The machinery by which the balance is brought about is the machinery of the Foreign Exchanges.

Office of Statistics. The phenomena of transportation, of internal and of external trade are of very great theoretic and practical interest to all students of the economic life and development of nations. The phenomena are bewildering in their multiplicity and heterogeneity. They can be grasped only by the numerical method, that is, by counting. The office of statistics is primarily descriptive. We describe the facilities for transportation by enumerating the miles of rail-road or canal, the number of ships and their size, the number of miles of telegraph wire, and the number of stations. We endeavour to measure the magnitude of the transactions by counting the number of passengers carried, or summing up the number of tons of freight, the number of messages, &c. So, too, in external commerce we sum up the imports and exports. We analyse them by values and quantities, and we endeavour to trace the direction of commerce by distributing it among different countries. All this is purely descriptive and scarcely deserves the name of statistics.

A somewhat more difficult task is to find some measure for the real efficiency of our means of transportation and some method of comparison of changes in internal and external commerce. It is still more difficult to correlate changes in commerce with other facts, such as those of taxation, bounties, encouragement of shipping, international relations, &c. It will be necessary also to consider the fluctuations of trade according to seasons and variations in foreign exchange, and attempt to explain them. The problems we have before us are chiefly those of statistical method.

Statistical Data.[1]

Means of Transportation and Communication. These are highways, bridges, rivers and canals; shipping; railroads; post-office, telegraph and telephone service.

In regard to the first class, we have no special need of applying the statistical method. Rivers are the first natural highways, and play a very important *rôle* in the earlier stages of civilisation. But as the vehicle of transportation, so to speak, is already furnished by nature, our only statistics pertain to the amount of traffic. This can be measured by the number of vessels or crafts, or by the amount of commodities transported. Such statistics are of local importance, as indicating the prosperity of the cities or countries located on the rivers, and continued from year to year are indicative of the importance, increasing or decreasing, of these facilities for commerce. Examples of this sort may be found in the statistics of river transportation in Germany.

Canals are artificial water-ways intended to serve the same purpose as rivers and and very often used to supplement river navigation, or to connect other bodies of water. With the growth of railroads, canals are diminishing in importance. In the United States not less than 4,468 miles of canals have

[1] *Bibliographical Note.* U. S. Census, 1890, Transportation, Parts I. and II. Statistics of Railways issued by Interstate Commerce Commission. Publications of the Bureau of Statistics of the Treasury Department. The principal figures will be found in the Statistical Abstract of the United States. For other countries see the Statistical Abstracts for the United Kingdom, for Foreign Countries, for India, and for the Colonies; the Statistisches Jahrbuch für das Deutsche Reich, and other similar publications; Neumann-Spallart, Uebersichten der Weltwirtschaft, and the Statesman's Yearbook. Numerous articles in the Journal of the Royal Statistical Society, especially, Sir Robert Giffen, the Excess of Imports (Vol. lxii., March, 1899); also by the same author, Use of Import and Export Statistics, in Essays in Finance, second series, 1886; Palgrave's Dictionary of Political Economy, Article—Commerce; Bastable, Theory of International Trade, 1897. A comprehensive survey of the commercial policy of all nations will be found in Handelspolitik der wichtigeren Kulturstaaten (Schriften des Vereins für Socialpolitik, 1892.)

been built, of which, however, 1,953 miles had already been abandoned in 1880. In 1889 there were reported 2,264 miles of state and corporation canals, 40·6 miles of ship canals and 1,078 miles of canalised rivers. The last two categories are increasing in importance, while the first is decreasing.[1]

Internal Shipping. The number of vessels engaged in internal commerce in the United States in 1890 was 32,059 with a gross tonnage of 8,603,489 and a commercial valuation of $220,774,250. Of these 6,205 were steamers, 8,917 were sailing vessels, and 16,937 were unrigged craft. The average gross tonnage per vessel was 295 for steamers, 202 for sailing vessels, and 294 for unrigged craft. According to locality they were distributed as-follows (U. S. Census, 1890: Transportation, Part II., p. xii):—

	All craft.	Steamers.	Sailing vessels.	Unrigged craft.
United States	32,059	6,205	8,917	16,937
Atlantic coast and Gulf of Mexico	13,466	2,933	7,108	3,425
Pacific coast	1,842	531	822	489
Great lakes	2,784	1,489	987	308
Rivers of the Mississippi valley	7,453	1,114	...	6,339
Canals and canalised rivers	6,514	138	...	6,376

This table is given simply as a sample, showing the distribution of the means of transportation in the several sections of the United States. The Atlantic coast has by far the largest number of vessels, especially of steamers and sailing vessels.

Without going into detail it may be said that these vessels carried in the year 1889, 182,848,402 tons of freight and 169,857,143 passengers; their gross earnings were $166,838,776, their expenses $130,257,970, and their net earnings $36,580,806; the number of common seamen employed was 25,848 and the "number making ordinary crews" was 114,736. These figures show the magnitude

[1] U.S. Census, 1890: Transportation, Part II., p. 472.

of the ordinary internal water commerce of the United States.

Statistics of Railroads. By far the most important means of transportation is the railroad. Starting in about 1830, the building of railroads made rapid strides, until at the present time there are over 420,000 miles in the world. Mileage and business are divided among the principal countries of the world as follows:—

	Miles of road.	Passengers (millions.)	Goods (tons) (millions.)
United Kingdom	20,910	912	325
France	24,970	337	97
Germany	27,850	521	242
Russia	23,100	55	79
Austria	18,320	199	215
Italy	8,800	51	17
Scandinavia	8,060	33	18
Belgium	2,820	97	45
Holland	2,320	24	9
Switzerland	2,270	40	10
Other States	11,160	23	11
Europe	150,580	2,292	1,068
United States	180,000	541	638
Canada	16,000	14	21
Australia	13,620	91	12
Cape Colony	2,840	8	1
India	18,780	146	33
Spanish America	28,880	24	8
Various	9,480	19	9
The World	420,180	3,135	1,790

These figures are taken from Mulhall's Industries and Wealth of Nations, 1896 (p. 389), and show roughly the importance of railroads in various parts of the world. For more particular consideration we shall take up the statistics of railroads in the United States.

Growth of Railroads. The railroads of the United States show the most wonderful growth since 1830. The record of this growth is shown in the following table (U. S. Census, 1890: Transportation, Part I., p. 6):—

	Miles of Line.	Decennial Increase in miles.	Decennial Increase Percentages.
1830 . . .	40	...	...
1840 . . .	2,755	2,715	6,823
1850 . . .	8,571	5,816	211
1860 . . .	28,920	20,349	237
1870 . . .	49,168	20,248	70
1880 . . .	87,724	38,556	78
1890 . . .	163,562	75,838	86
1897 [1] . . .	184,603	21,041 (7 years)	13 (7 years)

[1] U. S. Stat. Abstract, 1898, which gives the figures for the single years since 1830.

This table brings out the great activity in railroad building during the decennium 1850 to 1860, the slackening up caused by the Civil War, and the renewed activity during the decade 1880 to 1890. Since 1890 it has proceeded more slowly.

A similar table showing the miles of railroad in operation in England at similar periods is interesting as compared with the United States. Railroad building in England reached its highest point between 1845 and 1850. Of late years it has almost ceased, because the territory is so fully occupied. In the United States, on the other hand, we are constantly stretching out into new territory.

Railroad Equipment. The carrying capacity of railroads is partly indicated by the total number of locomotives and cars. International comparison is useless, because of the different styles of equipment. Some recent figures for the United States are as follows (U. S. Statistics of Railways, 1897):—

EQUIPMENT OF RAILROADS OF THE UNITED STATES.

	1890.	1895.	1896.	1897.
Locomotive engines . .	31,812	36,610	36,080	36,410
Cars—				
Passenger	21,664	26,419	24,788	25,654
Baggage, mail, etc. .	7,253	7,891	7,839	8,180
Freight	1,061,952	1,230,798	1,240,061	1,237,062

The Public Service of Railroads. This is shown by their traffic statistics. The statistics for two years may be seen in the following table (U. S. Statistics of Railways, 1897, p. 60):—

Item.	1897.	1896.
Passengers	489,445,198	511,772,737
Passengers carried 1 mile	12,256,939,647	13,049,007,233
Passengers carried 1 mile per mile of line	66,874	71,705
Tons carried	741,705,946	765,891,385
Tons carried 1 mile	95,139,022,225	95,328,360,278
Tons carried 1 mile per mile of line	519,079	523,832
Passenger train mileage	335,018,605	332,854,218
Average number of passengers in train	37	39
Average journey per passenger, miles	25·04	25·50
Freight train mileage	464,962,242	479,500,170
Average number of tons in train	204·62	198·81
Average haul per ton, miles	128·27	124·47

The number of passengers carried is multiplied by the distance travelled by each in order to arrive at the passengers carried 1 mile. The same thing is done for the freight traffic. These give us the most expressive figures of total business. The passengers and tons carried per 1 mile of line show how well the railroad is utilised. The average number of passengers and the average number of tons in train show the economy of railroad administration. With improvements in railroad equipment, the latter tends to increase. The comparison of these figures from year to year gives considerable insight into the character of the railroad operations of the country.

Cost of Service. The cheapness with which this service is performed is shown in the following table, giving the revenue per passenger per mile, and the revenue per ton of freight per mile. It seems that on all the railroads of the United States the revenue per passenger is about 2 cents a mile, while freight is carried at a cost of 0·8 cents per mile (U. S. Statistics of Railways, 1897, p. 82):—

	1890.	1897.
Revenue per passenger per mile, cents	2·16	2·02
Revenue per ton of freight per mile, cents	·94	·8

	1890.	1897.
Revenue per train mile, passenger trains . . .	$1·08	$0·94
Revenue per train mile, freight trains	$1·65	$1·65
Revenue per train mile, all trains	$1·44	$1·38
Average cost of running a train one mile, all trains. . . . . cents.	96	93
Percentage of operating expenses to operating income	65·80	67·06

There have been extraordinary reductions in freights during the last thirty years. In 1868, for instance, the cost of carrying one bushel of wheat by rail from Chicago to New York was 42·6 cents; in 1898 it was 11·55 cents. In 1876 the cost of sending a barrel of flour from St. Louis to New York was 79 cents; in 1898 it was 45 cents. The rate on wheat per 100 pounds was, between the same places, 39·5 cents in 1876, and 23·57 cents in 1895.[1]

Freight Traffic. The census of 1890 analysed the traffic according to commodities. The statistics apply to 542 roads, and are for the year 1889. Some of the results are as follows (U. S. Census, 1890: Transportation, Part I., p. 19):—

	Tons.
Grain	49,498,731
Flour	11,213,806
Cotton	4,917,508
Live stock	15,483,559
Dressed meats, etc.	6,186,576
Wool	495,974
Anthracite coal	73,019,850
Bituminous coal	111,346,099
Stone, sand, etc.	23,391,290
Lumber	52,807,026
Petroleum and other oils . . .	8,768,281
Sugar	2,627,715
Pig and bloom iron	15,480,913
Iron and steel rails	5,649,027
Total	380,844,355
Other tonnage	259,608,193
Total tonnage	640,452,548

[1] U. S. Stat. Abstract, 1898, p. 360.

The products of mines account for 42·4 per cent. of the total tonnage; products of agriculture, 13·5 per cent.; manufactures, 12·5 per cent.; products of forests, 10 per cent.; and products of animals, 4·2 per cent. These percentages show clearly the industries which give the bulk of the traffic to railroads.

Railroad Consolidation. The reports of the statistician of the Interstate Commerce Commission contain interesting information of the process of consolidation of railroads in the United States. In 1897, for instance, there were 1,158 separate railroad corporations operating 183,801 miles of railroad, but 103,345 miles of this were operated by 44 companies. The distribution of mileage was as follows: 56·3 per cent. was operated by 44 companies, each operating over 1,000 miles; 10·3 per cent. was operated by 24 companies, each having from 600 to 1,000 miles; 6·8 per cent. was operated by 25 companies, each having from 400 to 600 miles; 7·4 per cent. was operated by 42 companies, having each from 250 to 400 miles; and 19·2 per cent. was operated by 1,023 companies, each having a mileage of less than 250.[1]

Comparative Efficiency. Considerable doubt exists as to the best method of measuring statistically the railroads of different countries in order to draw comparisons as to their relative efficiency, and how well provided the countries are with means of transportation.

The most common method is to give the number of miles of railroad per 100 square miles of territory, or, per 10,000 inhabitants. In the United States, for instance, in 1896 there were 6·2 miles of railroad per 100 square miles of territory. The number naturally varies widely in different States, as is shown by the fact that Massachusetts has 26·4 miles; New Jersey, 29·7; Connecticut, 20·8; Ohio, 21·4; Pennsylvania, 22; Rhode Island, 20·4; while Texas has only 3·6; California, 3·2; and some of the other western States

[1] U. S. Statistics of Railways, 1897, p. 19.

even less. The comparison is inadequate for showing the railroad resources of a State.

In the same way there are for the United States 26 miles of railroad for every 10,000 inhabitants. Here the sparsely settled States show the largest figures. For instance, Montana has 192·4; Nevada, 179·5; Wyoming, 173; Arizona, 195·9 miles; while New York has only 12·1, and Rhode Island only 5·7 per 10,000 inhabitants.[1]

The comparison between European countries on this basis is equally inadequate. Belgium shows a very large number of miles of road to square miles of territory; while Sweden shows a very large number of miles of road to 10,000 of the population.

Another basis of comparison is to show the train mileage per 1,000 inhabitants. This method is illustrated by Hadley, who shows that for every 1,000 inhabitants the number of miles run by trains per annum is: in the United States, 9,700 (of which 3,700 passenger and 6,000 freight); in Great Britain, 7,504 (3,981 passenger and 3,523 freight); in Belgium, 4,499 (2,258 passenger and 2,241 freight); in France, 3,558 (2,222 passengers and 1,336 freight); and in Germany, 3,258 (1,971 passenger and 1,287 freight).[2]

Another method of measurement is the average frequency of trains. In Great Britain each mile of road is run over on an average by 40 trains, 20 each way; in Belgium by 26 trains, in France by 20, in Germany by 18, in Holland by 18, and in the United States by 13.

Still another method for measuring the railroad accommodation of different countries is that proposed by Dr. Engel.[3] It consists in calculating the so-called "Eisenbahnausstattsungsziffer," which is the geometric mean of two figures, namely, the relation of the length of road to territory, and

[1] U. S. Statistics of Railways, 1896, p. 11.

[2] Bull. de l'Institut int. de Stat., Vol. II., Part II., 1887, p. 29.

[3] Quoted in Conrad's Handwörterbuch der Staatswissenschaften, Art. Eisenbahnen (Statistik).

the relation of the length of road to population. According to this method the countries of Europe in 1888 occupied the following positions:—

1. Belgium	11·45	10. Italy	4·10
2. Great Britain and Ireland	9·21	11. Spain	3·23
3. Switzerland	8·53	12. Roumania	2·96
4. Germany	8·04	13. Portugal	2·93
5. France	7·85	14. Norway	1·99
6. Holland	7·38	15. Greece	1·82
7. Denmark	6·89	16. Servia	1·69
8. Sweden	5·20	17. Russia	1·27
9. Austria-Hungary	4·81		

Post Office, Telegraph, and Telephones. These statistics are of importance as supplementary to the statistics of transportation. About all we have, however, are the simple descriptive figures of the number of letters and packages carried, the number of messages sent, the miles of telegraph and telephone wire, and the number of stations. The statistics of all countries may be found in Neumann-Spallart, Uebersichten der Weltwirtschaft, 1885–89, (pp. 614–651). The grand totals are as follows (000's omitted):—

	Letters.	Postal cards.	Printed matter, samples, etc.	Newspapers (numbers).
Europe	4,094,250	724,377	1,731,954	1,367,234
Asia	233,444	124,474	55,800	999
Africa	22,135	443	15,345	47
America	1,351,191	379,699	644,055	977,265
Australia	102,341	1,017	12,720	63,452
Total	5,803,360	1,230,010	2,459,874	2,408,997

Owing to the different regulations in respect to carrying packages, newspapers, samples of goods, etc., it is not probable that the above figures are very accurate. They indicate, however, the magnitude of the transactions.

The telegraph system of Europe according to Neumann-Spallart covered 1,578,624 kilometers of state-owned line, and 427,386 kilometers of privately-owned line. There were 148,222,284 telegrams sent, or on an average, 40·4 telegrams for 100 inhabitants. In Great Britain and Ireland this number runs up to 140 for 100 inhabitants. These figures, however, are for 1887.

In the United States, the Western Union Telegraph Company reported for 1898 the following figures: miles of line, 189,847; miles of wire, 874,420; number of offices, 22,210; number of messages sent, 62,173,749; average toll for message, 30·1 cents. The Bell Telephone Company reported 384,230 subscribers in 1898.[1]

Ocean Shipping. The most important means of transportation is ocean shipping. In early times the coasting ship was the cheapest means of transportation, and the most effective. With the discovery of America, ocean shipping was of course the only means of transportation between the new-found continent and the old world. Railroads have reached an enormous development for inland transportation, but the extension of the world's commerce has kept shipping of equal importance with railroads. In fact, the two now supplement each other; the railroads bring the commodities to the seashore, and the ships carry them to other countries. Even in direct competition with railroads, as, for instance, on the Great Lakes or on the coast, shipping still plays an important part on account of its superior cheapness. Von Juraschek says that if we estimate the capacity of the 3·3 to 3·5 million freight wagons on railroads at from 31 to 35 million of tons, we have on the other hand steamships with a capacity of from 17 million to 18 million tons and a sailing marine with a capacity of 17 million tons, making altogether a capacity of 34 or 35 million tons; that is, about the same as the railroad wagons. The rapidity of transportation on railroads is greater than on sea, so that this equal capacity means that more goods are transported on railroads than on ships. On the other hand, the distances are much greater by sea, which renders the real business done somewhat equivalent to that done on railroads.

[1] U. S. Stat. Abstract, 1898, pp. 361–362.

It is interesting to gain an estimate of the real capacity of this great instrument of transportation, to compare its distribution among different civilized nations and in different quarters of the globe, its increase or decrease, and the changes occurring in character and kind. It is not altogether easy to make international comparisons. Counting the mere number of ships is useless, because of the differences in the registration regulations of different countries. In France, for instance, thousands of little fishing-boats are registered in the merchant marine, while in Holland and in Belgium only ships of at least 50 tons are registered; and in the French Bureau Veritas, steamships of over 100 tons are alone registered. Comparison of the mere numbers would at any rate be of little value on account of the differences in size. It is customary, therefore, to take the total tonnage as a measure of the capacity of the merchant marine of each country. Here, also, there are some differences in methods of measurement, so that the figures are not altogether comparable. It is generally advisable, also, to distinguish between the ocean marine and the inland vessels, that is, those plying upon rivers, canals and lakes. Taking account of these various difficulties, Von Juraschek gives the following estimate of the number and tonnage of ships of the different countries of the world (Neumann-Spallart, Uebersichten der Weltwirtschaft, p. 697):—

MERCHANT MARINE, 1893, OCEAN SHIPS OVER 50 TONS.

	STEAMSHIPS.		SAILING SHIPS.		BOTH TOGETHER.		
	No.	1,000 Tons.	No.	1,000 Tons.	No.	1,000Tons.	Estimated Capacity 1,000 Tons.
Great Britain and Ireland	5,931	6,183·3	7,749	2,891·1	13,680	9,074·4	21,441·0
Norway . .	542	246·1	3,559	1,420·5	4,101	1,666·6	2,158·8
Denmark . .	240	122·6	885	158·1	1,125	280·7	525·9
Sweden . .	429	145·6	1,506	325·0	1,935	470·6	761·8
Russia . .	201	108·3	1,649	213·2	1,850	321·5	538·2
Germany . .	867	783·3	1,427	686·9	2,294	1,470·2	3,036·8
Holland . .	150	177·6	447	121·4	597	299·0	654·2
Belgium . .	47	69·4	6	1·0	53	70·4	209·2
France . .	599	621·5	1,634	288·4	2,233	909·9	2,152·9

MERCHANT MARINE, 1893, OCEAN SHIPS OVER 50 TONS—*continued.*

	STEAMSHIPS.		SAILING SHIPS.		BOTH TOGETHER.		
	No.	1,000 Tons.	No.	1,000 Tons.	No.	1,000 Tons.	Estimated Capacity 1,000 Tons.
Portugal . .	51	42·6	211	44·6	262	87·2	172·4
Spain . . .	367	302·4	733	138·5	1,100	440·9	1,045·7
Italy . . .	224	223·6	1,738	529·7	1,962	753·3	1,200·5
Austria-Hungary . . .	132	118·1	241	96·7	373	214·8	451·0
Greece . . .	118	80·1	852	192·9	970	273·0	433·2
Turkey. . .	63	39·5	650	125·2	713	164·7	243·7
All Europe .	10,049	9,290·0	24,126	7,436·9	34,175	16,726·9	35,306·9
United States	2,372	825·7	4,853	1,573·7	7,225	2,399·4	4,050·8
Mexico . . .	9	2·5	52	9·1	61	11·6	16·6
Chili . . .	36	28·7	149	76·5	185	105·2	162·6
Argentine . .	60	22·2	115	29·2	175	51·4	95·8
Brazil . . .	176	81·1	282	65·2	458	146·3	308·5
Brit. Posses. in America.	300	80·9	3,416	761·9	3,716	842·8	1,004·6
Australia . .	533	181·5	751	169·5	1,284	351·0	714·0
Japan . . .	307	108·3	1,077	96·4	1,384	204·7	421·3
The World .	14,254	10,783·3	36,264	10,450·9	50,518	21,234·2	42,800·8

It is to be remarked in this table that for Asia and Africa, with the exception of Japan, only the shipping of European colonies is included. Besides these, Egypt has 23 steamships, China 32, Hawaii 17, and other countries 11, making 73 steamships with 63,300 tons capacity. China possesses besides this a large fleet of junks and other sail-boats. Taking these things into consideration, Von Juraschek reckons that the total sum of all ocean ships of the earth over 20 tons is made up of between 17,000 and 18,000 steamships, with about 11 million tons capacity, and outside of China of about 70,000 sailing vessels, with about 12 million tons capacity, that is a total tonnage capacity of between 22 and 23 million tons. It is customary to reckon that every ton in a steamship is equal to three tons in a sailing ship, on account of the greater speed. Reckoned in this way, the total capacity of the ocean marine will be between 44 and 45 million tons.

This tonnage is very unequally distributed in different parts of the world. 82·5 per cent. belongs to Europe; 13·6 per cent. to America; 1·2 per cent. to Asia; and 1·7 per cent. to Australia.

Adding to the above capacity of the ocean steamships that of the steamships on the lakes and rivers, we should have a capacity of between 11½ and 12 million tons of which 9½ million (about 80 per cent.) belong to Europe and 2 million (16 per cent.) to America.

From every point of view Europe takes the foremost place in shipping. This, of course, is owing to the fact that the European ships have a great share in the carrying trade, not only of Europe, but of the whole world. The share of Great Britain alone in the carrying capacity of the ocean marine is more than 50 per cent., and including her colonial possessions it is nearer 55 per cent., *i.e.*, more than one-half of the maritime transport is under the British Flag. The second place is taken by the United States, which possesses 9·5 per cent. of the ocean marine. Her share in international trade is unimportant; but she has an enormous coasting trade, and if the trade on the Great Lakes, rivers and canals were included, the steamship tonnage would be more than one and a half million tons, and the share of the United States in the total carrying capacity of the world would be increased to 13 or 14 per cent. The third place is taken by Germany, with 7·1 per cent., and then comes France and Norway, each with about 5 per cent.

Distinguishing between steamships and sailing ships, the dominant position of Great Britain is especially marked. She possesses 57·3 per cent. of the total steam tonnage; and with the British Possessions, 60·6 per cent. of the total steam tonnage is under the British flag. The countries next in order are the United States, 7·6 per cent., (including internal commerce from 12 to 13 per cent.); Germany 7·2 per cent.; and France 5·7 per cent. In sailing ships Great Britain possesses 27·7 per cent. and with her colonies 37·3 per cent.;

the United States possesses 14·9 per cent., Norway 13·6 per cent., Germany 6·6 per cent., and Italy 5.1 per cent. of the total sailing tonnage. This contrast shows how much more effective the shipping of Great Britain is than that of other countries.

Development of Shipping. The history of shipping since 1820 shows an enormous development in its total capacity, but shows also a steady substitution of steamships for sailing ships. In fact, since 1879, the tonnage of sailing ships has absolutely decreased, while that of steamships goes on steadily increasing. The following table gives some rough figures indicating the relative growth of steam and sail. The figures are not absolutely comparable, because it is impossible to get the statistics for the same countries at different periods. The earlier decades, 1820 to 1849, are somewhat incomplete. Beginning with 1850, almost all European countries are included, besides British Colonies and the international commerce of the United States. Since 1879 there is included, besides these, European colonies in Asia, Africa, and Australia, and Japan, but the figures like those in the preceding table include only ships of 50 tons and over. The interesting point here is to notice the decline in the relative importance of the sailing ship. As late as 1850 the sailing tonnage was 91·2 per cent. of the total. In 1879 it was only 50 per cent., and in 1890 only 27·9 per cent. of the total. In 1893 it had declined still further, to 24·4 per cent. of the total (Neumann-Spallart, Uebersichten, p. 703.) :—

GROWTH OF SHIPPING, STEAM AND SAIL. TONS.

	Steam.	Sail.	Percentage of carrying capacity. Steam.	Sail.
1820 . . .	6,200	3,165,600	0·6	99·4
1831 . . .	32,200	2,989,000	3·0	97·0
1840 . . .	97,000	4,556,200	6·0	94·0
1850 . . .	237,100	7,328,300	8·8	91·2
1860 . . .	764,600	10,712,000	17·6	82·4
1870 . . .	1,709,100	12,352,600	29·3	70·7
1879 . . .	4,436,800	13,650,000	49·4	50·6
1890 . . .	9,043,200	10,508,500	72·1	27·9

The real increase in steam tonnage is much greater than is indicated even by these proportions. The progress in the construction of ships, especially in their increased power, the invention of the screw and the triple compound engine, the facilities for loading and unloading by steam derricks—all these things combine to make the effective transportation power of steamships much greater than that of a corresponding tonnage of sailing ships, either of the present or of previous times.

While the number of ships is increasing, the size is also increasing, especially of steamships. In 1879 the average size of steamships was 457 tons; in 1886 it was 565 tons; in 1893 it was 639 tons. The size of sailing vessels has increased during that period only from 183 to 186 tons.

Shipping in the United States. The history and present condition of the merchant marine of the United States are shown in the following table (U. S. Stat. Abstract, 1898, p. 405):—

	Sailing Vessels.		Steam Vessels.		Total.	
	No.	Tons.	No.	Tons.	No.	Tons.
1869 . . .	23,941	3,041,073	3,546	1,103,568	27,487	4,144,641
1898 . . .	15,993	2,377,815	6,712	2,371,923	22,705	4,749,738

These figures show a slight growth in total tonnage, and reveal also the change from sailing to steam vessels and the increased size of ships.

Distribution of Tonnage. In 1898 the above tonnage was distributed as follows (U. S. Stat. Abstract, 1898, p. 405):—

	Tons.
Atlantic and Gulf Coasts	2,553,739
Pacific Coast	496,767
Northern Lakes	1,437,500
Western Rivers.	261,732
Total	4,749,738

The importance of the Atlantic coast is apparent; but it has decreased from 2,822,962 tons in 1883. The tonnage on Western rivers has also decreased, while that on the Northern lakes has doubled during the same period.

Employment of Merchant Marine. The tonnage was employed as follows (U. S. Stat. Abstract, 1898, p. 406) :—

	1898. Tons.	1860. Tons.
In foreign trade	726,213	2,379,396
,, coastwise trade	3,959,702	2,644,867
,, whale fisheries.	11,496	166,841
,, cod and mackerel fisheries	52,327	162,764
	4,749,738	5,353,868

The extraordinary decline in tonnage employed in foreign trade is seen in these figures. Another method of showing the same thing will be found in the next paragraph.

The Statistics of Commerce. We have been dealing hitherto with the means of transportation and communication. Their increase or decrease means, of course, an increase or decrease in trade. We can, however, reach a direct measurement of the movement of trade which is more accurate than that simply of the means of transportation. We have already done this in the case of railroads, by giving the statistics of the number of passengers and the tons of freight carried. In regard to ocean traffic we have two methods. One is by statistics of the number and tonnage of vessels cleared and entered at the seaports of any given country during the year. The second is by statistics of imports and exports. The latter includes imports and exports by land as well as by water.

In the Statistical Abstract of the United States will be found figures going back to 1869, showing the total tonnage of all vessels entered into and cleared from the seaports of the United States, from or to foreign countries. The figures for 1898 were—entered 21,700,311 tons (3,362,475 American and 18,337,836 foreign); cleared 21,891,738 tons (3,231,014 American and 18,660,724 foreign). The proportion of American to foreign tonnage steadily decreases.

These figures are then analysed in various directions, showing : (1) the tonnage of sailing and that of steam vessels ; (2) the tonnage of American and that of foreign ships ;

(3) the tonnage of foreign vessels according to particular countries; (4) the tonnage of all vessels entered and cleared at the principal and other seaports of the United States; (5) the nationality of the foreign tonnage entered and cleared at seaports of the United States to and from foreign countries.

These figures show, principally, the importance of Great Britain and of British vessels in the foreign commerce of the United States; and the importance of the port, New York, at which is entered more than one-third of the total tonnage from foreign countries.

We have one more comparison of interest, namely, the value of the foreign carrying trade of the United States in American and foreign vessels. The proportion carried in American vessels has steadily decreased since 1860. In that year, 70 per cent. of the exports and 63 per cent. of the imports were carried in American vessels. In 1898 the percentages were 5·9 and 16 respectively. Of total imports and exports the percentages were 66·5 and 9·3 for the two dates.[1]

Statistics of Imports and Exports. A more accurate way of measuring the movement of foreign commerce is by the statistics of imports and exports. These show, in the first place, the gradual growth and the enormous importance at the present time of what is called international trade. During mediæval times, foreign commerce was very much restricted by lack of means of transportation, and by the narrow policy of legislators, who were inclined to look upon the foreign merchant as an enemy, to forbid the export of money, and to prohibit the import of manufactured commodities. What little trade there was consisted of the export of a few staple articles, and the import of certain commodities which could not be produced at home. The customs accounts of England for 1354 show exports of 31,651 sacks of wool; 3,036 cwt. of wool, sheepskins and hides; 4,774

[1] U. S. Stat. Abstract, 1898, pp. 409, 420-22.

pieces of coarse cloth; and 8,061 pieces of worsted, representing a total value of 212,338 pounds sterling. The imports recorded were worsted, wax, wine, linen, mercery and grocery, the whole valued at 38,383 pounds sterling. This trade was typical of mediæval conditions.[1]

With the growth of cities, the opening of the East India trade, and the development of colonies, trade increased enormously, so that the total of exports from and imports into England amounted[2]:—

In 1770	to	£23,144,000
,, 1790	,,	34,034,000
,, 1800	,,	62,640,000
,, 1810	,,	87,741,000

The increase of manufactures, the application of steam on land and sea, the growth of population and a more liberal commercial policy developed the British foreign trade with marvellous rapidity, so that in 1890 it amounted to more than 749,000,000 pounds sterling.

In other countries the progress has also been rapid, until in 1890 the total imports and exports of the different countries of the world made a grand total of 3,600,000,000 pounds sterling, distributed as follows[3]:—

	Imports.	Exports.	Total.
	£	£	£
British Empire	685,032,747	577,755,898	1,262,787,645
Europe *	831,579,237	748,405,632	1,579,984,869
Russia and Turkey	92,507,579	92,872,479	185,380,058
Asia *	47,344,250	48,182,070	95,526,320
America *	213,517,042	233,268,360	446,785,402
Africa *	14,182,414	16,017,537	30,199,951
	1,884,163,269	1,716,501,976	3,600,664,245

* Exclusive of British Empire and Russia and Turkey.

Improved means of transportation and liberal mercantile policy have greatly changed the character of the imports and

[1] See Palgrave's Dictionary of Political Economy, Article, Commerce, I. p. 342.

[2] *Ibid.*, p. 345.

[3] *Ibid.*, p. 340.

exports. Formerly the imports were chiefly of luxuries which would pay transportation, and could not be produced at home. The chief articles of foreign commerce were wines and spirits, tobacco, tea, and colonial wares. Now the imports into European countries are composed largely of food, raw materials, and even manufactured articles. In 1890, for instance, 41 per cent. of the imports of Great Britain consisted of articles of food and drink; 30 per cent. of raw material of manufactures; 15 per cent. of manufactured goods; and 6 per cent. of metals and minerals. The exports consisted of 43 per cent. of textiles; 23 per cent. of metals and machinery; 7 per cent. of coal; 4½ per cent. of apparel; and 4½ per cent. of food and drink. These figures show how such a country as England is supplied with food and raw material by new countries, while it employs its labour in turning out manufactured goods which it exchanges for them.[1]

In a new country like the United States, the reverse is true. In 1898, the value of domestic merchandise exported consisted of 70·5 per cent. products of agriculture; 1·6 per cent. products of mining; 3·1 per cent. products of forests; 0·5 per cent. products of fisheries; and 24 per cent. exports of domestic manufactures.[2]

A single example will show how radically the trade of a country may change with the progress of civilization. In former times, each country provided its own breadstuffs and meat. Now, the countries of the New World are supplying those of the old with both. From 1852 to 1859, Great Britain produced three-fourths of the wheat it consumed. In 1889–90, it produced only 31 per cent. of what it consumed and imported the remaining 69 per cent. These imports come from the United States, Russia, and the

[1] *Ibid.*, p. 339.

[2] The details for different kinds of articles for the last ten years, giving both quantities and values, are shown in the U. S. Stat. Abstract, 1898, p. 163 ff.

Argentine Republic. The same thing is true of the meat supply. In 1898, the United States alone exported 439,255 cattle, 14,411 head of swine, and 199,690 sheep. This was in addition to over 100,000,000 dollars worth of meat products—canned, cured, or frozen, as follows:—

	lbs.	Value dollars.
Beef canned	37,109,570	$3,279,657
,, fresh	274,768,074	22,966,556
,, salted or pickled	44,314,479	2,368,467
,, other cured . .	1,589,052	150,051
Bacon	650,108,933	46,380,918
Hams	200,185,861	18,987,525
Pork, fresh	12,224,285	815,075
,, pickled . . .	88,133,078	4,906,961
Mutton	329,169	27,961
Poultry and game . .	...	85,793
Other meat products .	...	4,193,078
	1,308,762,501	104,162,042

The statistics of imports and exports may be analysed in a great variety of ways so as to give a picture of the foreign trade of any given country. This is done with great detail in the publications of the Bureau of Statistics of the Treasury Department, and the summary figures are published in the Statistical Abstract of the United States.

We have, first, the summary statistics of the total exports and imports, and of the excess of exports over imports, or of imports over exports for each year. These figures are shown in the following table (U. S. Stat. Abstract, 1898, p. 92):—

MERCHANDISE IMPORTED AND EXPORTED, AND THE ANNUAL EXCESS OF IMPORTS OR OF EXPORTS, 1860 TO 1898. SPECIE VALUES.

Year ending June 30.	Exports.	Imports.	Total exports and imports.	Excess of exports over imports.	Excess of imports over exports.
	Dollars.	Dollars.	Dollars.	Dollars.	Dollars.
1860 .	333,576,057	353,616,119	687,192,176	...	20,040,062
1861 .	219,553,833	289,310,542	508,864,375	...	69,756,709
1862 .	190,670,501	189,356,677	380,027,178	1,313,824	...
1863 .	203,964,447	243,335,815	447,300,262	...	39,371,368
1864 .	158,837,988	316,447,283	475,285,271	...	157,609,295

MERCHANDISE IMPORTED AND EXPORTED, AND THE ANNUAL EXCESS OF IMPORTS OR OF EXPORTS, 1860 TO 1898. SPECIE VALUES—*continued.*

Year ending June 30.	Exports.	Imports.	Total exports and imports.	Excess of exports over imports.	Excess of imports over exports.
	Dollars.	Dollars.	Dollars.	Dollars.	Dollars.
1865	166,029,303	238,745,580	404,774,883	...	72,716,277
1866	348,859,522	434,812,066	783,671,588	...	85,952,544
1867	294,506,141	395,761,096	690,267,237	...	101,254,955
1868	281,952,899	357,436,440	639,389,339	...	75,483,541
1869	286,117,697	417,506,379	703,624,076	...	131,388,682
1870	392,771,768	435,958,408	828,730,176	...	43,186,640
1871	442,820,178	520,223,684	963,043,862	...	77,403,506
1872	444,177,586	626,595,077	1,070,772,663	...	182,417,491
1873	522,479,922	642,136,210	1,164,616,132	...	119,656,288
1874	586,283,040	567,406,342	1,153,689,382	18,876,698	...
1875	513,442,711	533,005,436	1,046,448,147	...	19,562,725
1876	540,384,671	460,741,190	1,001,125,861	79,643,481	...
1877	602,475,220	451,323,126	1,053,798,346	151,152,094	...
1878	694,865,766	437,051,532	1,131,917,298	257,814,234	...
1879	710,439,441	445,777,775	1,156,217,216	264,661,666	...
1880	835,638,658	667,954,746	1,503,593,404	167,683,912	...
1881	902,377,346	642,664,628	1,545,041,974	259,712,718	...
1882	750,542,257	724,639,574	1,475,181,831	25,902,683	...
1883	823,839,402	723,180,914	1,547,020,316	100,658,488	...
1884	740,513,609	667,697,693	1,408,211,302	72,815,916	...
1885	742,189,755	577,527,329	1,319,717,084	164,662,426	...
1886	679,524,830	635,436,136	1,314,960,966	44,088,694	...
1887	716,183,211	692,319,768	1,408,502,979	23,863,443	...
1888	695,954,507	723,957,114	1,419,911,621	...	28,002,607
1889	742,401,375	745,131,652	1,487,533,027	...	2,730,277
1890	857,828,684	789,310,409	1,647,139,093	68,518,275	...
1891	884,480,810	844,916,196	1,729,397,006	39,564,614	...
1892	1,030,278,148	827,402,462	1,857,680,610	202,875,686	...
1893	847,665,194	866,400,922	1,714,066,116	...	18,737,728
1894	892,140,572	654,994,622	1,547,135,194	237,145,950	...
1895	807,538,165	731,969,965	1,539,508,130	75,568,200	...
1896	882,606,938	779,724,674	1,662,331,612	102,882,264	...
1897	1,050,993,556	764,730,412	1,815,723,968	286,263,144	...
1898	1,237,482,330	616,049,654	1,847,531,984	621,432,676	...

The interesting thing in this table is not only the steady growth of trade, but the alternation of excess of imports and exports. This represents, besides the exports and imports of specie (see p. 242), the borrowing of money and the repayment of the same. The principal points to be considered in the balance of trade are dealt with further on.[1]

England has a constant excess of imports running as high as £160,000,000, or 20 per cent. of the total trade. This represents England's profit on foreign trade, the return for her investments abroad, payments for freights, insurance, etc. In England also the exports are valued at the port of departure, the imports at the port of arrival. The latter include freight, insurance, etc., so that there is naturally an excess of imports over exports. The whole matter is discussed minutely by Sir Robert Giffen in an article on "The Excess of Imports" in the Journal of the Royal Statistical Society for March, 1899.

The next analysis is that of the country from which the imports come, or to which the exports are sent. For the details of this, reference is made to the Statistical Abstract of the United States. The following summary, by grand divisions, is of general interest (U. S. Stat. Abstract, 1898, p. 122):—

DIRECTION OF UNITED STATES TRADE.

	Per cent.		Per cent.
Europe—		Asia—	
Imports	49·7	Imports	15·0
Exports	79·1	Exports	3·6
North America—		Oceanica—	
Imports	14·8	Imports	4·4
Exports	11·4	Exports	1·8
South America—		Africa—	
Imports	15·0	Imports	1·2
Exports	2·8	Exports	1·4

These figures show some interesting variations. More than three-fourths of our exports are to Europe, while only 50 per cent. of our imports are from that source. In exceptional years like 1892, our exports to Europe ran up as high as 82·5 per cent., and our imports ran down as low as 47·3 per cent. In our South American trade our imports

[1] See also Noyes, Thirty Years of American Finance, 1898.

always exceed our exports. The same is true of our trade with Asia.

The next analysis is of the imports and exports, according to the particular commodities. This is carried out in great detail in the Statistical Abstract, and then summed up under five heads as articles of food, raw materials of industry, articles wholly or partly manufactured for use as materials in manufactures, manufactured articles ready for consumption, articles of voluntary use, luxuries, etc.

The course of trade may be studied more particularly by taking special commodities such as raw cotton, wheat, wheat flour, canned beef, pork, tallow, lard, butter, etc., and showing the countries to which each commodity is exported. Still further, the exports may be compared with the total production, thus showing the amount retained for domestic use. These tables are given in the Abstract.

International Comparison. The following table shows the average annual exports and imports per head of the population for four countries, 1890–94 [1]:—

	Annual Exports.			Annual net Imports.		
	£	s.	d.	£	s.	d.
United Kingdom . . .	6	2	11	9	7	3
France	3	11	4	4	8	0
Germany.	3	2	9	4	2	2
United States	2	19	0	2	11	11

Scientific Tests.

In regard to all commercial statistics, it may be said that the numbers cannot pretend to be accurate in the sense that every transaction is recorded, that every weight or measure is exact, or that every valuation rests on the true price. The statistics are collected either by transportation com-

[1] Memorandum published by the Board of Trade [c—8322], 1897, p. 11. This memorandum contains a very interesting analysis of British trade compared with that of the three other countries, showing the increasing competition from foreign countries.

panies, whose object is to fix the price of their service, or by custom house officials and inspectors, whose object is to collect a tax or duty, or in case of non-dutiable goods, simply to make a general statistical return. Business reasons, in the first case, dictate doing the work with rapidity rather than with minute exactness, and in the second case there are, in addition, temptations to underestimate quantities and values when dependence is placed upon the returns of the persons owning or importing the merchandise. In the third case, it is to be feared that the returns are often made carelessly and as a matter of form, there being no direct pecuniary interest involved.

Such returns, however, even if they are not accurate in the above sense, are generally sufficient for the purposes for which statistics are used. These purposes are comparative, that is, to study the general movement of transportation, trade, and commerce. There are, however, certain technical questions in regard to the method of collecting the statistics which are partly of practical interest as determining which is the best method, and partly of scientific interest as indicating how much confidence is to be placed in the figures themselves. These points are elaborated with some care by Von Scheel in the article Handelsstatistik in Conrad's Handwoerterbuch, and are as follows:—

The statistics must show both the quantity and the price of the different commodities. We cannot judge of the importance of an article in the trade of a country simply by its quantity. We must also have its value. Values alone, on the other hand, are not satisfactory, because owing to changes in price, the same total values may represent different quantities. Quantities and values may be obtained from the importers or exporters, or the quantities may be determined by the official inspector, and values assigned according to market prices or prices fixed upon by a board of experts. For the statistics of exports it is particularly difficult to establish values, because exports are generally free. Sometimes a small tax is levied as a statistical or registration tax. Another question is whether imports should be valued at the point of departure or at the point of entry. In the latter case they include freight and insurance. Uniformity of practice is desirable in order that we may compare the statistics of one country with those of another.

Another vexed question is as to the country of origin. If Brazilian coffee is imported into England and thence exported to Germany, shall the German statistics record it as coming from England or from Brazil? It would seem to be natural to take the country of origin, where the material was produced, but this is not always easy or practicable, because the importer may not know whence the commodity originally came. In regard to exports, it is absolutely necessary to take the country designated by the exporter, because he is entirely uncertain whether the commodity will go further or not. People seem to think that if we had the country of origin registered, we could balance the exports against the imports of different countries, and thus get a complete bookkeeper's balance, so to speak, of the commerce of the world. Considering the administrative difficulties of fixing quantities and values, it is doubtful whether this can ever be attained.

In considering a country's trade there is another difficulty also, namely, that of commodities which are in transit or which are imported, simply to be re-exported. These evidently do not belong to the country either as an import or as an export. When they are dutiable they may be held in bond, and so can be separated from the rest of the imports and exports. When they are not dutiable they mingle with the general imports and exports, and cannot be separated. The same thing is felt in respect to raw materials which are imported, and then exported as manufactured goods. Sometimes a rebate is allowed on the raw material, and thus its value can be separated from the imports.

There is one other difficulty, which has already been

mentioned. That is, that in order to sum up the imports and exports of a country, we must take values and not quantities. If now we are in a period of declining prices, we may show constantly declining values of imports and exports, although the quantity of commodities imported and exported has not fallen off, and may even have increased. The device here is to take the quantities at the prices of a preceding year. For instance, the commerce of Belgium for 1890 was valued at 1,672 million francs. Its commerce for 1880 was valued at 1,680 million francs, showing a decline in total valuation; but if we reduce both figures to the prices of the period 1866–7, we shall find that the commerce of 1880 was worth 1,652 million francs, and that of 1890 was worth 2,124 million francs, showing an increase of over 25 per cent.[1]

Reflective Analysis.

Commercial statistics may be used in two ways, first as purely descriptive, that is, as expressing in figures the general facts of the increase in the economic activity of the community; and, secondly, by correlation with facts of economic policy or legislation, in order to pass judgment upon the influence of such policy or legislation. They are very extensively used for both of these purposes, and we can give here only certain illustrations.

One of the most striking influences of the growth of railroads is seen in the concentration of population in cities. In the article already mentioned on Eisenbahnen (Statistik) the author says that, in 1867, out of 14 cities in Germany, which in 1880 had 100,000 inhabitants, all were upon railroads; out of the 102 cities (from 20 to 100,000 inhabitants), only 95; out of the 641 small cities (5,000 to 20,000 inhabitants), 340; and out of the 1,975 villages (2,000 to

[1] Denis, La Dépression économique, 1895, p. 33. Similar calculations by Sauerbeck in the Journal of the Royal Statistical Society have already been noticed in connection with index numbers.

5,000 inhabitants), 468 were upon railroads. In 1880 all of the cities above 20,000 were upon railroads, and of the small cities, of which in 1867 only 53 per cent. were upon railroads, there were now 79 per cent.; the number of villages on railroads had increased from 24 to 47 per cent. Other similar statistics follow.[1]

Much attention has been paid to the balance of exports and imports. Theoretically, exchange is simply barter, and exports should balance imports. The reasons why the statistics do not show this balancing are very numerous, and are explained by the economist as follows:—

Professor Bastable,[2] for instance, draws attention to the following points: "It is not the equivalence of imports with exports that constitutes the stable condition of trade, but the equivalence of the sum of debts due to the country, and that of debts due by it." The items making up this account are: (1) The imports and exports; (2) the loans which a country gives and receives; (3) the annual interest on capital already invested; (4) the repayment of a loan already made; (5) the earnings of native merchants living abroad, and the profits of foreigners residing in the country, so far as they are transmitted to their native country; (6) remittances of emigrants; (7) earnings of ships; (8) expenditures of governments abroad; (9) indemnities or tributes; (10) expenditures of travellers. It is not necessary to expand upon the varying effect of these various causes in making a nation a debtor or a creditor. In the first case it would enable the nation to have an excess of exports, in the second an excess of imports, without receiving or sending gold to make up the balance.

The connection of foreign exchange with the statistics of exports and imports is not very close, because the rate of discount is so strong an attractive force in drawing money into a country or keeping it there.

[1] *Cf.* Weber, The Growth of Cities, p. 201 (Columbia Univ. Studies, Vol. XI., 1899.)

[2] Theory of International Exchange, Ch. IV.

As a correlation of statistics with economic legislation may be mentioned the decline of American shipping since the Navigation Acts of 1860, and the prosperity of Great Britain since her adoption of free trade in 1846. Both of them would be subject to partisan interpretation.

Finally, we have the question of how far the statistics of exports and imports can be used as an index of national prosperity or the reverse. An example of this use is seen in the book by Denis on Commercial Crises.

Book III.

DISTRIBUTION.

Consumption and Production really exhaust the economic life of man. Consumption expresses the desires and thus directs Production which is economic effort for the purpose of satisfying those desires. Exchange (as we have just seen) is only a refined part of Production by which the community makes the most effective use of human powers armed with capital and working upon land. But while Exchange is the last word of Production it is the first step in Consumption. According to its terms (rates of exchange) the share of the product which shall come into the consuming power of each individual is determined. In other words it constitutes (to a large extent) the process of Distribution. It may perhaps be said that all wealth is not exchanged. A man may grow potatoes and eat them himself. There is here Consumption and Production, but there is no Exchange and scarcely even Distribution. Such cases in the modern community are rare. So far has the division of labour gone that almost every individual is dependent upon others for a portion of the goods he consumes and upon their demand for the valuation of the goods that he himself produces. A man may eat the potatoes he produces, but the presence of Exchange gives him the choice of consuming them or of consuming something else. The people who have something to exchange are as a rule those who have produced something. Hence Distribution may be defined as the process of assigning to each producer that share of the product which is due to him as having assisted in the work of production.

Two questions at once arise when we try to make concrete the process of distribution. One is, how much is *due* to each producer or to each contributor to production. Taking the ordinary analysis of the factors of production as land, labour, capital and organisation:—What share is due to land, to labour to capital, etc ? The answer under a theory of pure competition is that each factor will receive that share which each specifically produces ; that is, each will be rewarded according as it is necessary or useful for the work of production. The question whether this is just or ethical or best for the community involves the consideration of the principles of social organisation, and does not concern us here. We must take the economic organisation as it is, with the principles of economic freedom and private property as fundamental institutions. Competition will in the long run assign to each factor that which it has produced.[1]

The second question is whether we can determine in the modern system the share that comes to each factor—even if we admit that this share is in proportion to its contribution to the final product. The division of factors, labour, etc., is purely formal. No one individual contributes land alone, or capital alone, or labour alone ; but the productive agent is labour armed with capital and using land. Nevertheless in the modern system we have classes who contribute predominantly one factor. Thus we have land-owners, capitalists, labourers, and entrepreneurs. In wages we can study the amount that is the share of labour ; in rent, that which is the share of the land-owners, etc. This division is often obscure, but we have certain phenomena which are of great interest to many persons and to the community, and which we can observe under the statistics of wages, rent, interest, and profits. The fact of increase or decrease of any one of these items and

[1] *Cf.* J. B. Clark, in Palgrave's Dictionary of Polit. Economy, Art., Distribution.

their relative proportion are of especial interest to the community at large. The fate of the individual is here involved, and the fate of the individual determines the well-being of the community.

We have two methods of study—first, to examine wages, rent, interest, and profits, and see what we can determine about them; and second, to study the results of the present system of distribution in the possessions or incomes of individuals and their relative well-being. In the modern community we have first of all the labouring class, *i.e.*, a wage-receiving class owning no land or capital and under the direction of the entrepreneur. Their compensation is wages. On the other hand we have the land-owners, capitalists, and entrepreneurs, distinct from the wage-receiving class. Their compensation takes on the form of rent, interest or profit or a mixture of two or three of them. We can in general speak of them as the capitalist class in contrast with the wage-receiving class. We shall devote one chapter to Wages of the labouring-class; a second to Rent, Interest, and Profit as the compensation of the capitalist class; and then we shall consider certain general questions of social distribution or the fate of the individual.

CHAPTER IX.

WAGES.

Economic Purpose.

Wages as Share of the Product. Economic theory looks upon wages as the share of the product imputed to the factor labour. This share depends first of all upon the efficiency of labour. The greater that efficiency, the greater the product, and the larger the share coming to labour. The wages of each individual labourer, in like manner, depend upon his efficiency—what he is able to produce. Wages depend also upon the supply of labourers. The larger the number, the more they are driven into employments yielding small returns for a given efficiency and the smaller the reward. The marginal labourer determines the rate of wages of all men of equal efficiency in the same employment.

In actual life we find an almost infinite range of wages due to varying efficiency of individual labourers, or groups of labourers, and to varying demand for, and supply of labour in various groups.

Efficiency varies with almost every individual. It depends upon muscular strength, intelligence, education and energy. The boy does not have the same strength as the adult, the woman as the man. The apprentice does not possess the skill of the accomplished workman. Men who become tailors do not have the strength of those engaged in glass-blowing or iron smelting. In the same occupation, one man will have greater skill and dexterity, greater industry and devotion to his work than another. Temperament, education, moral habits, ambition, all are factors in determining the efficiency of labour.

Supply of labour is a very indefinite term. Labour is not a homogeneous commodity that can be used indiscriminately, first in one direction and then in another. The agricultural labourer cannot take the place of the blacksmith, nor the blacksmith that of the diamond setter. Labour is divided into groups, and these groups are to a greater or less extent non-competitive, that is, the members of one group do not compete with those of another. This division into groups is due largely to education. A man acquires skill in a certain trade and that becomes *his* trade. He is protected to a certain extent against competition from men who have not learned his trade; while on the other hand he is restrained to his own field. Supply of labour means supply of labour of a particular kind. Besides education, there may also be requirements of special strength, dexterity, youthful vigour, &c. Wages within each group are fixed by the demand and supply of labour within that group.

These groups are not unchangeable. The barriers between them are broken down in various ways. The members of one group may bring up their children to some other trade, which seems at the time to offer particular advantages. That in the long run will increase the supply, and very often increase it too much. Then machinery is constantly breaking down the advantages of acquired skill. Machinery admits the use of unskilled labour. The factory hand can be transferred from one occupation to another more easily than the old hand-labourer.[1] Labour tends to become more homogeneous. Finally migration, emigration and immigration tend to equalise the supply of labour at different places. Organisation of labour on the other hand strives to preserve the limitation of supply in particular groups, while equalising the wages of individuals in the same group.

[1] *Cf.* J. B. Clark, The Limits of Competition (Polit. Science Quarterly, Vol. II., 1887, p. 45).

Wages as Income. According to the above conception, the rate of wages would depend upon efficiency and upon demand and supply for the particular kind of labour. As both of these things vary constantly from time to time, and from place to place, it would seem to be impossible to establish any general rule showing the proportion which wages bear to the gross product, that is, the share which is its due. We must content ourselves with ascertaining what concrete wages are, that is, what members of the wage-receiving class receive per day, week, month or year. This is equivalent to saying that the statistics of wages are really statistics of income. Their object is to determine the ordinary income of that portion of the population represented by the wage-receivers, and what that income is worth in procuring a comfortable subsistence. The chief value of such an inquiry is not to elucidate a theory of distribution of the product into wages, interest, rent and profit, but to answer the question of social well-being.

Office of Statistics. The technical operations involved in such inquiries are the collection of data showing actual money wages, and what those money wages will buy in the way of necessaries and comforts of life. The investigation may resolve itself into subordinate inquiries in regard to the condition of the wage-receiving class at different places and at different times. All of these may be grouped under the following heads:—

(*a*) To determine the ordinary wages of the mass of the labouring class.

(*b*) To compare the ordinary wages of the labouring class in different countries, or in different parts of the same country.

(*c*) To compare ordinary wages in different occupations.

(*d*) To compare wages at different periods.

(*e*) To correlate money wages with cost of living in all the above cases, *i.e.*, to establish real wages.

(*f*) To correlate real wages with other economic phenomena.

Statistical Data.[1]

General Wages. The first problem is to determine the ordinary wages of the mass of the labouring class in any given country, or, at least, the wages of great classes among the labourers of that country. It is impossible to get literally

[1] *Bibliographical Note.* The chief sources of information for wage statistics in the United States are the reports of the Bureaux of Labour Statistics of the several States, the investigations of the Department of Labour at Washington, and the Tenth (1880) and Eleventh (1890) Censuses of the United States.

Of the State Labour Bureaux, by far the most important is that of Massachusetts. The Report for 1884 contained a very extensive investigation, comparing wages in Massachusetts and Great Britain for several years, ranging from 1860 to 1883. The Report for 1885 contained a condensation of the Report for 1884, and in addition an "Historical Review of Wages and Prices: 1752–1860." The Report for 1889 was devoted to "Classified Weekly Wages"; it contained classified wages for 248,200 employees. The Report for 1895 commenced the publication of 489,600 wage returns, gathered from all sources, and 166,400 price quotations. It will be several years before all of these returns are published; they are arranged by occupations, and wages are divided into five classes; high, medium high, medium, medium low, and low. The utility of this enormous undertaking may be doubted. The Report for 1897 compares wages and prices in 1872, 1881 and 1897. Other State Bureaux have collected statistics of wages, notably New Jersey in 1884, and Michigan in 1885, but none of them is comparable with the Massachusetts Report of 1884.

The Department of Labour at Washington published extensive figures of actual wages in its Sixth (1890), and Seventh (1891), Annual Reports, entitled, Cost of Production in Iron, Steel, Coal, Textiles and Glass Industries; it also investigated the cost of living of families in these industries and compared cost of living with income. (See Workmen's Budgets.) The Department of Labour also collected the figures of wages for the Aldrich Report. The Fifth (1889), Annual Report gives the wages of railroad employees.

The Tenth Census (1880) of the United States published various returns of statistics of wages; those of manufactures are contained in Volume II.; Volume XX. is devoted entirely to the statistics of wages. No effort was made to classify this enormous collection of figures, so that it has remained practically useless.

The Eleventh Census (1890) of the United States collected statistics of wages in manufacturing industries, classified as described in the text, the wages of the whole labouring population. No census could undertake to ask each individual his weekly, monthly or yearly wage, and if it did the returns would not only lack accuracy and truthfulness in all probability, but the conditions being so utterly different among different individuals, any average wage would be of little value. It is customary, therefore, to confine even the most ambitious attempts to

and published chiefly in the three volumes on Manufacturing Industries. In these returns a distinction is drawn between males, females and children, between piece workers and time workers, and between officers, firm members and clerks as contrasted with operatives, skilled and unskilled. A summary of average annual earnings per employee in different industries and in different States will be found in Part I., and detailed wage statistics for textile industries, chemicals, glass, coke, petroleum, glue, iron and steel manufactures, locomotives, clay products, shipbuilding, forest industries, etc., in Part III. The volume on Transportation Business also contains statistics of wages, but in a crude form. The Report on Mineral Industries contains statistics of wages of miners, classified as foremen and overseers, miners, labourers, and boys under sixteen years, giving also the average number of days work.

For criticism of Census Wage Statistics see Bullock, Statistics of Wages, in The Federal Census (Amer. Econ. Assocn. Publications, New Series, No. 2, 1899).

For wages since 1840 see the Report of the Senate Committee on Wholesale Prices, 1891, commonly known as the Aldrich Report. For criticism of same see Bullock, Contributions to the Study of Wage Statistics (Amer. Stat. Assocn. Publications, Vol. VI., 1899, p. 186).

For wages of railroad employees in the United States see the annual Reports of the Statistician of the Interstate Commerce Commission. For agricultural wages see the Reports of the Department of Agriculture.

For statistics of wages in Great Britain see the Publications of the Labour Department of the Board of Trade, especially the Rates of Wages paid in the United Kingdom between 1830 and 1886, [c—5172], 1887. A complete list of such publications is given in the Annual Abstract of Labour Statistics of the United Kingdom. See also the extensive investigations of A. L. Bowley in the Journal of the Royal Statistical Society for June, 1895, Dec. 1898, and March and June, 1899, and the Economic Review for 1898, and the numerous references given therein. See also Giffen, The Progress of the Working Classes (Essays in Finance, Second Series, 1890).

For other attempts to collect wage statistics and for the theoretical literature on the subject see Bullock, Contributions to the Study of Wage Statistics, cited above.

the statistics of the wages of great classes, such as those engaged in manufacturing industry, in agriculture, in transportation and the like, where the conditions are somewhat homogeneous and the terms of employment somewhat well defined. Our statistics, therefore, represent a series of attempts to determine the wages of larger or smaller classes. It is seldom that they can be compared with one another, but each must be taken for what it is worth towards enabling us to form a judgment of about what the rate of wages is. Each attempt generally involves its own peculiar difficulties, and these difficulties must be described in order to judge of the value of the particular result. It will be necessary, therefore, to introduce some of the technique of wage statistics with the statistical data.

The Average Wage. For the purpose of expressing what the ordinary wage is, and for purposes of comparison, it is necessary to have a single expression. This expression is found in the ordinary arithmetical average, or the weighted arithmetical mean. The average, even with the greatest precautions, is not altogether satisfactory, for it may not be typical of the real condition of things. It is often supplemented by classified wages or the use of percentile grades. The latter system is awkward for purposes of comparison, so that it is still necessary to use the average. This average may be obtained from a great variety of data, and by different methods.

United States Census Method. The Eleventh Census demanded of each employer the total amount of wages paid during the year, and also the average number of persons employed, distinguished into three classes, viz., officers, firm members, and clerks; operatives, skilled and unskilled; and piece-workers. Each of these classes was further subdivided into males above sixteen years of age, females above fifteen years, and children. The average number of employees, as defined by the Census, "is the number necessary to be continually employed during the time the establishment is reported as being in operation in the Census year to perform the work of a varying number employed."

By dividing the total wages paid, by the average number of employees in each class, we get the average annual earnings per employee by classes, as follows (U. S. Census, 1890: Manufactures, Part I., p 20):—

Classes.	Aggregates. Average number.	Total wages. Million dollars.	Aver. earnings. Dolls.	Males above 16 years. Average number.	Total wages. Million dollars.	Aver. earnings. Dolls.
Total	4,712,622	2,283	484	3,745,123	2,031	542
Officers, firm members and clerks	461,009	392	850	418,081	372	890
Operatives, skilled and unskilled	3,492,029	1,591	455	2,881,795	1,436	498
Pieceworkers	759,584	301	396	445,247	223	500

Classes.	Females above 15. Average number.	Total wages. Million dollars.	Aver. earnings. Dolls.	Children. Average number.	Total wages. Million dollars.	Aver. earnings. Dolls.
Total	846,614	235	278	120,885	17	138
Officers, firm members, and clerks	42,928	20	462	...	...	...
Operatives, skilled and unskilled	505,712	139	276	104,522	15	141
Pieceworkers	297,974	76	255	16,363	2	117

The average annual earnings for all employees, including officers, firm members and clerks, is $484·00; and for the employees exclusive of the officers, firm members and clerks, $444·83. This last figure is, perhaps, the nearest approach that we have to an average wage for the United States. It is not, however, a typical wage, for the reason that it includes the wages of men, women and children, of apprentices and pieceworkers. These classes are not homogeneous. Their wages do not mean the same thing. The wages of a man are commonly used to support a family; the wages of a woman to support a single person or to supplement the wages of the family; the wages of children to add to the family income a larger or smaller sum. An average made of these heterogeneous elements would vary largely according to the relative number of males, females and children employed in industry. The use of such a figure for comparative purposes is very dangerous.[1]

From the definition of the average number of employees, it seems also that we are getting statistics of the yearly income of certain positions, provided they are filled for the full working year. This may or may not correspond to the actual annual wages per employee for any particular class or occupation.

The figures that seem most worthy of confidence in the above table are the wages for operatives, skilled and unskilled, which are returned as follows: for males above sixteen years, $498·00; for females above fifteen years, $276·00; for children, $141·00.

The Eleventh Census shows the average annual earnings per employee, for all classes, and for males, females and children, in each class by specified industries.

It is impossible to give the full table, but a few specimens will show the fallacy of averaging the wages of all

[1] For example: In the cotton industry the average wage in 1880 was $243·65; in 1890 it was $301·65. This does not mean that there had been an increase of wages on the average of $58·00 or more than $1·00 per week for each employee. It is undeniable that wages have increased. But part of the apparent increase is due to the fact that the proportion of children had decreased and of men increased as follows: (U.S. Census, 1890: Manufactures, III., p. 173):—

	Percentages of all employees.	
	1880.	1890.
Men	35·4	41·3
Women	48·4	48·1
Children	16·2	10·6
	100·0	100·0

classes (U. S. Census, 1890: Manufactures, Part I., p. 23):—

	Wages. All classes.
Boots and shoes, factory product	$476
Boxes, fancy and paper	344
Clothing, men's	399
Clothing, women's, factory product	448
Cotton goods	314
Furnishing goods, men's	342
Gloves and mittens	359
Hosiery and knit goods	298
Millinery and lace goods	461
Shirts	327
Silk and silk goods	387
Tobacco, chewing and smoking, and snuff	274
Woollen goods	359
Worsted goods	364

The above industries are those employing a large proportion of females. As a consequence the average wage is low. In the following table are shown certain industries having a small proportion of females and children (*Ibid.*):—

	Wages. All classes.
Agricultural implements	$513
Brick and tile	300
Cooperage	473
Cutlery and edge tools	518
Flouring and grist-mill products	426
Foundry and machine shop products	599
Furniture, including cabinet-making, etc.	583
Leather, tanned and curried	519
Liquors, malt	816
Painting and paper hanging	670
Saddlery and harness	529

This table shows almost uniformly higher average wages than the preceding table. On page 21, the wages of the different classes of employees is correctly distinguished.

In the same volume on Manufacturing Industries (I., p. 22) is a table showing the average annual earnings per employee in the different States and territories of the United States.

The averages for "all classes" must be used with caution, for the same reason as noted above, viz., the different proportion of men, women and children among the employees. In Rhode Island the average wage is $441, and in Colorado it is $720; but a part of this difference is accounted for by the fact that in Rhode Island only 63 per cent. of the employees are males above sixteen years of age, while in Colorado 91 per cent. belong to that class.

Perhaps the safest figure for comparison is the wages of males above sixteen years of age. The following table shows some of the returns for six industries in ten different States (U. S. Census, 1890: Manufactures, I., p. 28):—

	Carpentering.	Carriages and wagons including custom work and repairing.	Clothing, men's, factory product.	Foundry and machine shop products.	Masonry, brick and stone.	Tobacco, cigars and cigarettes.
Connecticut	$682	$670	$497	$591	$685	$560
Illinois	644	543	401	554	614	516
Massachusetts	683	609	637	581	680	545
Michigan	518	446	461	526	548	490
Missouri	670	498	466	568	649	494
New Jersey	724	574	521	565	769	483
New York	727	553	596	598	654	515
Ohio	588	483	295	530	583	410
Pennsylvania	663	489	583	563	649	377
Wisconsin	539	459	374	502	470	455

It is probable that these figures are somewhat too high to be representative of actual earnings, on account of the fact already mentioned, that they are incomes of positions constantly filled rather than the earnings of individuals.

United States Census Weekly Wages. In the volume on selected industries, a weekly wage is calculated as follows: The average number of employees is multiplied by the number of weeks the establishment was run; the result is the number of weeks necessary for one employee to perform the labour. Divide the total amount paid in wages by this number and you have the true average weekly earnings.

Examples of the method are as follows (U. S. Census, 1890: Manufactures, III., pp. 134, 206, 228, 298 and 338):—

	Woollen.	Cotton.	Silk.	Chemicals.	Glass.
Officers and firm members (males)	$29·21	$34·93	$36·37	$35·28	$40·70
Clerks—					
Males above 16	19·34	18·19	19·39	21·11	22·30
Females „ 15	8·34	9·04	8·71	11·54	8·54
Operative and skilled—					
Males above 16	9·02	7·75	11·35	11·37	12·88
Females „ 15	5·94	5·53	5·73	5·69	4·95
Children	3·34	2·65	3·09	3·62	3·99
Unskilled—					
Males above 16	8·41	7·69	9·38	8·90	8·46
Females „ 15	5·31	4·37	4·70	4·74	3·58
Children	3·16	2·16	3·78	3·26	3·05

One may, perhaps, be a little sceptical about the value of this method, however ingenious it may appear. Is it probable that the employers would take very great pains to ascertain the average number of employees in each class, and the total amount paid in wages to each class? And then in order to compare yearly incomes we must multiply these weekly earnings by the number of weeks employed, which is not always the same for the different industries and the different classes of workpeople.

Wages in Great Britain. It will be impossible to enter into all the details of wage statistics in other countries. Since 1886, the Labour Department of the British Board of Trade has collected and published elaborate returns of wages in various industries, and these are to be continued. The general conclusion of the great inquiries of 1886 to 1891, was that the average rate of wages for men was 24*s.* 7*d.* per week, equal to £64 per annum if the weekly rate be multiplied by 52. Questions arise as to regularity of employment, overtime and the like, but considering that the year 1886, to which the census primarily related, was a year of depression, and that wages have been rising since, Sir Robert Giffen believes that no great mistake will be made in assuming average earnings for men in the last few years to be not far short of 24*s.* 7d. per week.

The average rate for women per week was 12*s.* 8*d.*; for lads and boys 8*s.* 11*d.*; and for girls 6*s.* 4*d.*

The average wages for men in different occupations came out as follows: railways, £60; building trades, £73; seamen, mercantile marine,* £65; seamen, royal navy, petty officers and seamen,* £65; army, non-commissioned officers and men,* £48; domestic servants, large households,* £68; employees in hospitals and infirmaries,* £61. Thus, in nearly all these trades, the average rates are about the same as the average rate in the Census of Wages Summary.[1]

The following table is interesting as giving the average earnings per annum in different occupations computed according to two different methods[2]:—

[Comparison of the average rate of wages per annum in the following trades, as obtained (1) by dividing the total wages paid in 1885 by the number employed on 1st October, 1886, and (2) by multiplying the average rate of a normal week in 1886 by 52.]

	(1)		(2)		Excess of Col. 2 over Col. 1.	
	£	s.	£	s.	£	s.
Pig iron (blast furnaces) . .	73	4	61	19	-11	5
Engineering, etc.	58	17	56	19	- 1	18
Iron and steel shipbuilding .	76	2	67	11	- 8	11
Tin plate workers	55	5	58	5	3	0
Brass work and metal wares .	54	16	57	19	3	3
Saw mills	52	16	55	14	2	18
Wood shipbuilding	57	1	53	16	- 3	5
Cooperage works	56	16	60	4	3	8
Coach and carriage building .	52	11	56	6	3	15
Boot and shoe factories . .	...		47	12	...	
Breweries	59	13	60	15	1	2
Distilleries	53	13	52	12	- 1	1
Brick and tile works . . .	45	2	48	18	3	16
Chemical manure works . .	66	2	55	18	-10	4
Railway carriage and wagon .	76	9	58	12	-17	17
Printing & engraving trades—						
A. Large works	52	13	52	11	0	2
B. Small works	42	0	43	8	1	8
C. Newspaper works . .	73	2	77	3	4	1

* Including estimated value of food and lodging where necessary.

[1] General Report on Wages of Manual Labour Classes [c—6889], 1893, p. xxxi.

[2] *Ibid.*, p. xiii.

Wages of Railroad Employees. One very distinctly defined class of employees is that of railroad men. In the pay-rolls of railroad companies we have also exact returns of the amount of wages paid. The Statistician of the Interstate Commerce Commission has calculated the average daily wages of different classes of such employees. The average is arrived at by dividing the aggregate amount paid for each kind of work by the aggregate number of days' work. This would give the compensation per day, for each kind of work, or, what may be considered as daily wages for different classes of employees. The yearly compensation of men cannot be arrived at unless one knows the number of days in the year the members of each class are likely to be employed.

The Report gives the following as daily compensation for the different classes of employees (Statistics of Railways, 1897, p. 41):—

General officers	$9·54
Other officers	5·12
General office clerks	2·18
Station agents	1·73
Other station men	1·62
Enginemen	3·65
Firemen	2·05
Conductors	3·07
Other trainmen	1·90
Machinists	2·23
Carpenters	2·01
Other shopmen	1·71
Section foremen	1·70
Other trackmen	1·16
Switchmen, flagmen and watchmen	1·72
Telegraph operators and dispatchers	1·90
Employees—account floating equipment	1·86
All other employees and labourers	1·64

In Great Britain we have the following estimates of the annual earnings of railway employees for the year 1891: England, £62 10*s.*; Scotland, £58 7*s.*; Ireland, £49 4*s.*, average for the United Kingdom, £61 10*s.*[1]

[1] General Report on Wages [c—6889], 1893, p. xviii.

The following comparison showing the average daily rates and average annual earnings of certain classes of railroad employees in Great Britain and the United States is of considerable interest (U. S. Dept. of Labour: Fifth Ann. Report, 1889, p. 145):—

GREAT BRITAIN.

Occupations.	Daily rate.	Annual earnings.
Engineers and drivers . .	$1·46	$457
Firemen	·91	285
Guards, passenger and goods	·97	304
Shunters	·85	266
Signalmen	·81	254

UNITED STATES.

Occupations.	Daily rate.	Annual earnings.
Engineers and enginemen . .	$3·22	$1,007
Firemen	1·79	562
Conductors	2·63	824
Switchmen.	1·50	471
Flagmen	1·13	354

The duties of the British guard and of the American conductor are not fairly comparable, because of the greater responsibility laid upon the latter. The table goes to show, however, the generally higher rate of wages in the United States.[1]

Wages of Domestic Servants. There is great difficulty in establishing an average rate of remuneration for domestic servants, because they are not concentrated as a rule in large numbers, and they work under varying conditions. The English Census of Wages obtained some figures from large households, where a considerable body of servants is required, and also returns from hospitals and lunatic asylums where, in addition to the expert attendance, there is also a large mass of the same kind of labour as that employed in domestic

[1] For wages of railroad employees in Europe, besides much other interesting information, see Condition of Railway Labour in Europe, by Walter E. Weyl (Bulletin of U. S. Department of Labour, No. 20, January 1899.

service. In large households the average remuneration for indoor men servants was £55 per annum, and allowing £26 a year for board and lodging, it would make this average £81 per annum. The general range would be from £60 per annum upwards, including the value of the board and lodging. In small households the average would be less. As regards indoor women servants, the average remuneration was £25 per annum with board and lodging, the great mass being paid from £10 to £30 per annum. Leaving out the classes paid £30 or more, the average would be about £20 per annum, and adding £26 for board and lodging, we should obtain an average remuneration for women servants in a good average market of about £46 per annum.[1]

A recent inquiry on the wages of indoor domestic servants gives as the average money wages £17 16*s*. in London, £15 10*s*. in the rest of England and Wales, and £17 6*s*. in the three principal Scottish towns. Wages are exclusive of presents and perquisites. Wages are higher in households keeping a large number of servants than in those keeping a smaller number. The older servants generally get more than the younger.[2]

Wages of Agricultural Labour. There is the same difficulty in obtaining wages of agricultural labour as in the case of domestic servants. The employment is scattered, the employers numerous, and the conditions different. The general result of the census of wages in Great Britain shows that agricultural wages for men only were about 13*s*. per week, ranging from an average minimum of about 9*s*. 6*d*. in Ireland to an average maximum of about 18*s*. in Scotland. There are great variations in different parts of the country. In England, Dorset, Wilts, and Berks stand lowest with an average of 10*s*., followed by a large group of agricultural counties at from 11*s*. to 12*s*. per week. "The absence of

[1] General Report on Wages [c—6889], 1893, p. xxiv.

[2] Report by Miss Collet on the Money Wages of Indoor Domestic Servants [c—9346], 1899.

any considerable industries in these counties no doubt tends to keep wages on a low level, the opposite effect being especially noticeable in the West and North Ridings of Yorkshire, Lancashire, Durham, Cumberland, and Westmoreland, where there is a demand for labour in the mines and other large works carried on in or near those counties. The influence of a large labour market is also shown in the group of counties around London." The difference between Ireland and Scotland is very remarkable, but is largely accounted for by the fact of Ireland being mainly an agricultural country, whereas Scotland in many parts is industrial.[1]

Agricultural Wages in the United States. These have been ascertained by the Department of Agriculture for a long series of years, beginning with 1866, when the monthly pay of an agricultural labourer without board was $19·07. It rose to 19·49 in 1869, and fell to $16·42 in 1879. In 1882 the rate was $18·94, and in 1885, $17·97, after which there was a rise to $19·10 in 1893, followed by a fall to $17·69 in 1895, during the financial depression. The rates for different sections of the United States for the year 1895 were as follows[2]:—

Eastern states	$29·00
Middle states	23·80
Southern states	12·71
Western states	21·82
Mountain states	30·04
Pacific states	31·68
The United States	17·69

Comparison of Wages. It will have been seen already that it is almost impossible to reach any single figure which will express the average wages or income of all labourers in a community. We are obliged to distinguish between occupations, between skilled and unskilled labour, and between labourers according to sex and age. It is difficult

[1] Report on Wages [c—6889], 1893, p. xxx.

[2] Agricultural Production and Prices, by George K. Holmes (Year Book of Dept. of Agriculture, 1897, p. 586).

therefore to make comparisons either in space or time, *i.e.*, between different countries, or between different sections of the same country, or between cities and rural districts, or at successive periods of time. Such comparisons, therefore, must be fragmentary and generally applicable only to small bodies of men.

Wages in different Countries. There is a general consensus of opinion that wages are higher in the United States than in Great Britain, and higher in the latter country than on the Continent of Europe. Without attempting to enter into a general comparison, the figures already given under railroad and agricultural wages will illustrate the method and the difficulty of such comparisons. The Massachusetts inquiry of 1884 established the following comparison of wages in manufacturing industries (Report of Mass. Bureau of Labour Statistics, 1884, p. 294):—

Average weekly wages of	Massachusetts.	Great Britain.
Men	$11·85	$8·26
Women	6·09	3·37
Young persons	5·10	2·40
Children	3·81	·79
All employees	10·31	5·86

The same caution must be repeated once more in respect to averaging the wages of men, women, and children. This is especially true when we compare two countries with one another. The final average—$10·31 for Massachusetts and $5·86 for Great Britain—is made up of such heterogeneous data that it is impossible to say how much confidence shall be placed in it as indicative of the differences of wages in the two countries.[1]

Wages in different Sections of the same Country. Whatever system of statistics we employ, we find very different

[1] For wages in France see Salaires et Durée du Travail dans l'Industrie Française. Tome IV., Résultats Généraux. Office du Travail, 1897. The principal results are published in the Bulletin of the U. S. Department of Labour, No. 21, March 1899, p. 320.

scales of wages in different sections of the same country. These differences may be traced to various causes, such as varying efficiency, *e.g.*, the wages of coloured labourers in the South; or scarcity of labour, *e.g.*, wages on the Pacific Coast.

Attempts to measure these differences by a general average wage are more or less fallacious, because of the disregard of differences in age and sex constitution of the population, and in the prevalence of skilled and unskilled trades. We have already pointed out on page 301 the fallacy in the average annual earnings of all employees for each State and territory of the United States. Even if we take only the average annual earnings for male operatives above sixteen years of age, the results are not satisfactory. For instance, the annual earnings of such employees is for New York $582, and for North Carolina $231. This enormous difference, even if the statistics be perfectly accurate, means simply that in New York we have a large number of highly skilled operatives living in cities, while in North Carolina we have large numbers of common labourers living in the country. It does not at all follow that the condition of the ordinary working man is more than twice as good in one State as in the other. Again, contrast the following figures: Earnings of males above sixteen years, in Washington, $600; in West Virginia, $375; in Wisconsin, $378; and in Wyoming, $806. What do these variations show?

If we take particular occupations and contrast the different States, as on page 302, the results are not much more satisfactory. Carpenters, for instance, are said to receive $727·00 in New York State, and only $518·00 in Michigan. If the statistics are correct, they do not point to differences in economic condition so much as to differences in trade surroundings.

Differences of locality are best brought out by specific examples of the remuneration of particular kinds of labour in different places. We quote the following from the special report on the Iron and Steel Industry in the Tenth Census:—

"The highest average daily wages of skilled labour were paid in Rhode Island, Colorado, and Wyoming Territory, $4·00; the lowest in North Carolina, $1·25. The highest average daily wages of unskilled labour were paid in Wyoming Territory, $2·00; the next highest in Colorado and California, $1·75; the lowest in North Carolina, $0·54. In North Carolina the labour employed was largely that of coloured men.[1]

The English Board of Trade gives comparisons of rates of wages in the same occupation for different sections of the United Kingdom. Wages are generally higher in Great Britain than in Ireland, and in England than in Scotland.[2]

Wages in different Occupations. Some statistics of this sort have already been given on pages 301 and 304. Where the comparison is made for an average wage, including men, women, and children, such comparison is fallacious for the reasons already insisted upon. Even where the wages are those of adult males, if in the same industry there are included skilled and unskilled employments, such comparison will be fallacious. This is clearly illustrated by the most cursory examination of the wages of adult males in different occupations, as given in the census volume on Manufactures (I., p. 23). The figures fluctuate enormously.

Comparisons in Time. The most important inquiry in statistics of wages is whether wages are increasing or decreasing. This is the fundamental question of the progress of the working classes. If we can show that wages are increasing, we have the assurance that the labouring class is at

[1] Wages in the cotton industry varied as follows (U. S. Census, 1890: Manufactures III., p. 174):—

Yearly earnings.	Men.	Women.	Children.
United States . .	$381·02	$271·80	$129·87
New England . .	390·85	286·90	158·63
Middle States . .	434·10	287·89	135·07
Southern ,, . .	274·68	185·58	93·65
Western ,, . .	410·41	236·13	124·12

[2] Report of the Labour Department of the Board of Trade, 1894–5, p. 104.

least holding its own in the changes of industrial life; and if we can show that the money wages will buy more than formerly, we can be sure that the absolute economic condition of a vast class in the community has become better.

The History of Wages. We must distinguish between long and short periods. We can jot down notices of money wages at different periods; but the value of money changes in long periods, and also the circumstances under which trade is carried on, so that the comparisons do not amount to much. Such comparisons are shown for England in Palgrave's Dictionary of Political Economy, article Wages, and for the United States in the Report of the Massachusetts Bureau of Statistics of Labour for 1885 (p. 455). The latter figures, beginning with 1800, are as follows:—

DAILY WAGES (DOLLARS). BY PERIODS OF YEARS. MASSACHUSETTS.
PERIOD ENDING WITH—

	1800.	1810.	1820.	1830.	1840.	1850.	1860.	1880.	1883.
Agricultural labourers . . .	0·48	0·78	0·78	0·80	0·87	0·95	1·01	1·31	1·37
Blacksmiths . .	...	...	0·84	1·12	1·40	1·47	1·69	2·28	1·92
Bookbinders . .	...	...	...	...	0·91	1·46	1·38	1·91	1·49
Butchers . . .	...	0·80	0·75	0·91	...	...	...	2·03	1·36
Carpenters . . .	0·74	1·09	1·13	1·07	1·40	1·37	2·03	2·42	2·41
Carriage makers .	...	...	...	...	1·34	1·59	1·85	2·40	2·27
Clock makers . .	...	...	1·13	1·29	1·29	1·29	1·96	2·30	...
Clothing makers .	...	...	1·00	1·27	0·89	1·38	1·43	1·93	1·99
Cotton mill operatives	...	...	...	0·43	0·89	0·92	1·03	1·40	1·27
Glass makers . .	...	...	...	1·13	1·62	2·44	2·96	1·79	2·01
Gold and silver workers . . .	...	...	...	...	0·97	1·28	1·69	1·53	3·21
Harness makers .	..	...	0·88	1·13	1·25	1·46	1·65	...	...
Labourers . . .	0·62	0·81	0·91	0·79	0·87	0·85	0·97	1·48	1·31
Machinists . . .	...	...	...	...	1·35	1·62	2·15	2·49	2·25
Masons	...	1·41	1·52	1·22	1·37	1·33	1·53	2·79	2·14
Metal workers .	...	...	1·05	1·23	1·54	1·42	1·35	2·16	2·00
Millwrights . .	1·09	...	1·13	1·21	1·39	1·39	1.66	2·65	2·54
Nail makers . .	...	...	1·00	1·39	0·86	1·50	...	...	1·84
Painters	...	1·15	1·34	1·25	1·32	1·47	1·85	2·32	1·97
Paper mill operatives	...	...	1·09	0·66	0·75	0·84	1·17	1·71	1·71
Printers . . , .	...	...	1·13	1·25	1·38	1·17	1·75	2·18	2·14

DAILY WAGES (DOLLARS). BY PERIODS OF YEARS. MASSACHUSETTS.
PERIOD ENDING WITH—*continued.*

	1800.	1810.	1820.	1830.	1840.	1850.	1860.	1880.	1883.
Ship and boat builders . . .	...	...	1·25	1·40	1·33	1·35	3·65	2·49	3·25
Shoemakers . .	0·73	...	...	1·06	0·87	1·12	1·70	1·76	1·87
Stone quarrymen and cutters . .	...	...	...	...	1·29	1·45	1·40	2·33	2·01
Tanners and curriers . . .	...	..	1·00	1·13	1·46	1·13	1·67	2·09	1·86
Wooden goods makers . . .	...	0·66	1·26	1·25	1·36	1·11	1·72	2·01	2·28
Woollen mill operatives . .	...	...	...	1·12	0·99	0·86	0·87	1·31	1·24

Such a comparison as this shows that the nominal wages of labour have greatly increased during long periods of time. The figures amount to but little, however, because the returns are sporadic, and we are not certain that the designations really mean the same thing from time to time. It seems of greater interest, both theoretically and practically, to take shorter periods of time, during which we are more certain of our data. There are several ways of doing this, as follows:—

United States Census Method. Wherever we get average wages for two different periods, we can of course compare the two. For instance, the average annual earnings per employee, as obtained by the United States Census in 1880, was $346·91, and in 1890 it was $444·83. Such a comparison would be just if there were any possibility of the elements entering into the two averages being the same at the two periods. It is practically impossible that this should be the case, so that the method is useless.

Giffen's Method. A second method of tracing the increase or decrease of wages is to ascertain the ordinary remuneration for the same kind of labour at the same place, at two different periods. If in the great mass of cases we find that wages are higher at the later period, we can say that on the whole there has been an increase. This is the method pursued in the table just given, and is the one adopted by Sir

Robert Giffen, in his famous essay on the Progress of the Working Classes.[1] An example of his method follows:—

Occupation.	Place.	Wages per week. About 1840 to 1850.		About 1880.		Increase. Amount.		Per cent.
		s.	*d.*	*s.*	*d.*	*s.*	*d.*	
Carpenters	Manchester	24	0	34	0	10	0	42
,,	Glasgow	14	0	26	0	12	0	85
Bricklayers	Manchester	24	0	36	0	12	0	50
,,	Glasgow	15	0	27	0	12	0	80
Masons	Manchester	24	0	29	10	5	10	24
,,	Glasgow	14	0	23	8	9	8	69
Miners	Staffordshire	2	8	4	0	1	4	50
Pattern weavers	Huddersfield	16	0	25	0	9	0	55
Wool scourers	,,	17	0	22	0	5	0	30
Mule spinners	,,	25	6	30	0	4	6	20
Weavers	,,	12	0	26	0	14	0	115
Warpers and beamers	,,	17	0	27	0	10	0	58
Winders and reelers	,,	6	0	11	0	5	0	83
Weavers (men)	Bradford	8	3	20	6	12	3	150
Reeling and warping	,,	7	9	15	6	7	9	100
Spinning (children)	,,	4	5	11	6	7	1	160

In regard to this table, Sir R. Giffen makes the following remarks:—"Thus, in all cases where I have found it possible, from the apparent similarity of the work, to make a comparison, there is an enormous apparent rise in money wages, ranging from 20 and in most cases from 50 to 100 per cent., and in one or two instances more than 100 per cent. The mean of the percentages of increases is over 70. This understates, I believe, the real extent of the change." A similar table shows an increase in seamen's wages of 40 or 50 per cent. during the thirty years from 1850 to 1880. Evidence goes to show a rise of about 60 per cent. in the wages of agricultural labour. From these figures Sir R. Giffen came to the conclusion that wages had risen nearly 100 per cent. during fifty years.

Falkner's Method. It is possible to extend this method by collecting a larger number of returns for wages, and then putting them together in the form of an index number. This was the method pursued by the statistician of the Senate

[1] Essays in Finance, Second Series, 1890, p. 372. See also a second essay on the same subject, *Ibid.*, p. 415.

Committee on Wholesale Prices, Wages, and Transportation (Aldrich Committee), and published in 1891. There are in this Report sixty-one series of wage returns, which begin as early as 1840, and as many as 543 distinct series which cover the period from 1860 to 1891. The returns are actual wages, taken from manufacturers' pay-rolls, and quotations are given for January and July of each year.

The chief object of the Aldrich Report was to determine whether wages had increased or decreased within the last fifty years. For this purpose the year 1860 was taken as the base, 100, and two series of numbers calculated, one a simple average, and the other an average weighted according to the relative number of persons engaged in each occupation. The results reduced to gold are shown by the following table (Aldrich Report, Part I., 1891, p. 14):—

Year.	Simple average.	Average according to importance.	Year.	Simple average.	Average according to importance.
1840 . .	87·7	82·5	1866	108·8	111·1
1841 . .	88·0	79·9	1867	117·1	121·8
1842 . .	87·1	84·1	1868	114·9	119·1
1843 . .	86·6	83·0	1869	119·5	123·5
1844 . .	86·5	83·2	1870	133·7	136·9
1845 . .	86·8	85·7	1871	147·8	150·3
1846 . .	89·3	89·1	1872	152·2	153·2
1847 . .	90·8	91·3	1873	148·3	147·4
1848 . .	91·4	91·6	1874	145·0	145·9
1849 . .	92·5	90·5	1875	140·8	140·4
1850 . .	92·7	90·9	1876	135·2	134·2
1851 . .	90·4	91·1	1877	136·4	135·4
1852 . .	90·8	91·8	1878	140·5	139·0
1853 . .	91·8	93·2	1879	139·9	139·4
1854 . .	95·8	95·8	1880	141·5	143·0
1855 . .	98·0	97·5	1881	146·5	150·7
1856 . .	99·2	98·0	1882	149·9	152·9
1857 . .	99·9	99·2	1883	152·7	159·2
1858 . .	98·5	97·9	1884	152·7	155·1
1859 . .	99·1	99·7	1885	150·7	155·9
1860 . .	100·0	100·0	1886	150·9	155·8
1861 . .	100·8	100·7	1887	153·7	156·6
1862 . .	100·4	101·2	1888	155·4	157·9
1863 . .	76·2	81·9	1889	156·7	162·9
1864 . .	80·8	86·2	1890	158·9	168·2
1865 . .	66·2	68·7	1891	160·7	168·6

From a consideration of this table, it becomes evident that there was a gradual advance in wages from 1840 to 1860; since that date the advance has been less regular, but more rapid. The depressing effect of the premium on gold is seen during the years 1863–66.

The increase in wages has not been the same in all industries. This is shown by the following table, which gives the increase from 1860 to 1891, by industries. The number of quotations is also given, so that it is possible to judge of the basis upon which the index number rests. Each quotation represents a series of wages (Aldrich Report, Part I., 1891, p. 12):—

RELATIVE WAGES IN 1891 COMPARED WITH 1860 (100), BY INDUSTRIES.

Industry.	Number of quotations.	Relative wages.
Agricultural implements	5	137·9
Ale, beer and porter	5	224·7
Books and newspapers	21	148·6
Building trades	39	172·5
Carriages and wagons	4	202·4
City public works	23	164·6
Cotton goods	131	165·1
Dry goods (stores)	3	183·6
Ginghams	30	152·7
Groceries (stores)	2	194·7
Illuminating gas	22	167·7
Leather	16	137·6
Lumber	5	177·9
Metals and metallic goods	130	148·6
Paper	7	182·3
Railroads	11	146·4
Sidewalks	4	187·5
Spice	5	164·2
Stone	19	165·2
White lead	3	140·6
Woollen goods	58	167·8
Total	543	160·7

This method is open to all the objections and criticisms that apply to index numbers in general. The last table shows that in many cases the number of quotations in any single industry is very small. The remuneration of clerks in dry goods stores is represented by but three quotations, and of clerks in grocery stores by only two. It might easily happen that these were not representative establishments. It does not appear, therefore, that this apparent scientific precision really carries us much further in accurately determining the real rise of wages. There is no doubt that wages have risen, but whether it is 60 per cent., or 70 per cent., or more, or less, cannot with certainty be determined.[1]

Bowley's Method. In an article in the Royal Statistical Society's Journal, for June, 1895, Mr. Bowley considers with great care changes in average wages in the United Kingdom between 1860 and 1891. For this purpose he has used all the accessible statistics. But instead of making comparison between actual wages he compares only the ratios of increase. Only figures for the same trade, in the same place, and collected apparently in the same way, are used for the computation of these ratios. Mr. Bowley contends that by this method we can arrive at a just estimate of the increase of wages, even when the figures themselves cannot be compared. This is simply a modification of the method of index numbers. The result is to show that money wages increased 40 per cent., from 1860 to 1891, and considering the increased purchasing power of money, real wages increased 92 per cent.

Wages in Massachusetts, 1872–1897. This is the latest effort to measure the course of wages. The figures were obtained directly from employers, and are supposed to represent about the same grade of labour at the different periods. The general result is to show an increase of wages in most occupations from 1881 to 1897. The quotations for the period 1872 are fewer in number, and in seven occupations

[1] For criticism of the Wage Statistics in the Aldrich Report, see Bullock Contributions to the Study of Wage Statistics (Amer. Statistical Assocn. Publications, VI., 1899, p. 187).

show a fall in wages, and in only four a rise. It must be remembered, however, that 1872 was a period of high wages. The table follows (Mass. Bureau of Labour Statistics, Report for 1897, p. 35):—

	Average Weekly Wages. Standard, Gold.			Percentage of increase (+) or decrease (−).	
				In 1897 as compared with 1872.	In 1897 as compared with 1881.
Agriculture:					
Labourers per month with board	1872. $23·09	1881. $18·0	1897. $18·50	−19·9	+ 2·8
Labourers per day without board	...	1·37	1·25	...	− 8·8
Blacksmithing	16·44	16·38	16·00	− 2·7	− 2·3
Boots and shoes	12·71	11·06	11·90	− 6·3	+ 7·5
Building trades	15·66	11·00	15·83	+ 1·1	+43·9
Cabinet making	14·21	11·51	13·02	− 8·3	+13·1
Carpetings	4·89	5·94	8·26	+68·9	+39·1
Carriages	17·31	13·43	13·51	−21·9	+ 0·6
Clothing (ready made)	9·71	10·90	9·01	− 7·2	−17·3
Cotton goods	...	7·59	7·71	...	+ 1·6
Glass	...	10·68	12·03	...	+12·6
Hosiery	...	10·22	8·97	...	−12·2
Leather	...	11·05	10·54	...	− 4·6
Machines and machinery	13·84	16·48	10·80	−21·9	−34·5
Metals and metallic goods	6·06	13·42	9·51	+56·9	−29·1
Metals and metallic goods (fine work)	...	10·07	11·59	...	+15·1
Musical instruments	...	15·81	18·06	...	+14·2
Paper	7·37	9·47	9·31	+26·3	− 1·7
Printing	...	14·95	19·59	...	+31·0
Rubber goods, elastic fabrics	...	7·56	9·96	...	+31·7
Stone	...	13·25	13·87	...	+ 4·7
Straw goods	...	10·06	11·60	...	+15·3
Woollen goods	...	8·12	8·52	...	+ 4·9

Wages and the Cost of Living. Statistics of wages are almost always simply of money wages. For the wage receiver the interesting and vital question is not in respect to money wages, but what wages will buy. This is sometimes called real wages. In order to judge whether the labouring class is well off or badly off, it is necessary to know real wages. The cost of living depends upon prices; hence the question is how to correlate wages and prices. There are several methods, all of them imperfect, but all furnishing some indication of the actual condition of things.

Let us take first the static problem: Wages in a given community, are they sufficient to give the labourer a comfortable subsistence? This will of course have to be solved for each community, and, in fact, must be solved for different classes of workmen, for, as we have seen, an average wage of different kinds of labour, skilled and unskilled, is fallacious. The method of approaching this problem has already been considered in the Chapter on Consumption, but may be recapitulated here:—

We take from our statistics of consumption the standard dietaries which are supposed to be sufficient to maintain a man at work. For a particular place and time we can estimate the cost of such dietaries and turn cost per day into cost per year. This constitutes the cost of food for an adult. From our workmen's budgets we ascertain what proportion the cost of food bears to the total expenditure of a family with a certain income. We thus calculate the annual expenditure for an adult male. We want to multiply this by that number which expresses the relation of the consumption of an ordinary family to the consumption of an adult male. Suppose this is represented by three, taking the ordinary family as composed of man, wife, and two children, any larger family having compensation for extra expenditure by reason of extra earnings of the wife or older children. We can then compare our figures of wages with those of the cost of living.[1]

It goes without saying that we do not need to have recourse to statistics to know whether a whole labouring population is living in comfort or starving from insufficient food. General observation will indicate that the labourers

[1] See Chapter on Consumption, p. 36.

of the United States are well off, and the peasants of Italy less well off. But such calculations are useful as giving us a standard by which we can judge whether wages in a particular community or in a given occupation are what they ought to be, understanding by the *ought* a subsistence sufficient to keep the labourer in health and strength. Detailed investigations of this sort show whole classes and communities with the very barest subsistence. In collecting workmen's budgets, we often find an excess of expenditures over receipts. Where the budgets are typical and trustworthy they become an indication that wages are not sufficient to meet the cost of living.

The Dynamic Problem. The question here is to correlate changes in wages with changes in prices. If wages go up and the cost of living goes up in an equal or a greater degree, the labourer may be no better off or may even be worse off than before. It is necessary to correlate the course of wages with the course of prices. This may be done more or less elaborately in a variety of ways.

For long periods of time it is sufficient to correlate wages with the prices of a few standard commodities representing the necessaries of life. Thus Thorold Rogers in his "Work and Wages in England" calculates the number of weeks' labour necessary to buy at successive periods certain fixed quantities of oatmeal and other standard articles supposed to be sufficient to provision a family for a year.[1]

A second method is simply to say that while wages (money) have been going up the cost of living has been going down.

[1] A modern example of this method is given in the Annuario statistico Italiano, 1898, p. 158. The number of hours of labour (at average wages of men in industrial establishments) required to purchase 100 kgs. of wheat was as follows :—

In 1871	183	In 1880	149
,, 1872	185	,, 1885	93
,, 1873	202 (max.)	,, 1890	92
,, 1874	199	,, 1895	83
,, 1875	146		

This is what Giffen does in "The Progress of the Working Classes." "Wheat is cheaper, everything is cheaper except meat and rent, and higher rent probably represents better house accommodation." This is the method of the English Gold and Silver Commission, 1887-88, which simply expressed the belief that wages had gone up while prices had fallen.

The Massachusetts Bureau of Labour Statistics Report for 1897 compares the retail prices of groceries and provisions for the same years as the wages given on page 318. It is difficult to average these, but weighting them on the same plan as in the Aldrich report, there was a general fall in groceries of 30 per cent. in 1897 as compared with 1872, and a fall of 6·7 per cent. as compared with 1881. Provisions show a decrease of 18·5 per cent. as compared with both 1872 and 1881. Fuel, dry goods and boots all show a fall in price. Rents of tenements are considerably lower in 1897 than in 1872. The whole report goes to show that real wages in almost all employments have increased.

The Weighted Index Number of Wages. An apparently greater precision is reached by an index number which represents the purchasing power of wages. This is simply a combination of an index number of wages and an index number of prices. The difficulty is to get an index number of prices which correctly measures the effect of changing prices on the labouring man.[1]

The general result of all these methods seems to show that wages have gone up during the last 30 years, especially when we consider the prices of commodities.

It is necessary to say, however, that the bare statistics of wages even when brought into connection with the cost of living only answers in a bald way the question whether the labouring class has improved its condition or not. There are other things of almost equal importance which must be brought in as collateral evidence. Among these are :—

(*a*) Employment and Non-employment. This is a very

[1] See Chapter VI., p. 224.

serious question. It is claimed by some that while wages are as high or higher than formerly there is greater irregularity of employment. What little information we have on this subject has already been given in the chapter on Population as Labour-Force.

(*b*) Hours of Labour. Wages are commonly given for the day or week. If they represent days of different length no comparison of bare wages is satisfactory. Hours should accompany all statistics of wages.[1]

(*c*) Intensity of Labour. Hours may be shorter and wages the same, but the labour may be made more intense. This is done ordinarily by increasing the rapidity of the revolutions of the machinery or giving the workmen more machines to tend. We have only particular facts showing the general tendency of the machine industry.[2] On the other hand the more perfect the machine the more automatic it becomes and the easier to tend. Perhaps the shorter hours and the better machinery may be held to counterbalance the increased intensity of the work.

(*d*) Conditions under which the work is carried on. This is a very important consideration but scarcely capable of statistical expression.

(*e*) Method of payment. This is of considerable importance in particular cases.

Current Changes in Rates of Wages. The Labour Department of the British Board of Trade makes an annual report on changes in wages and hours of labour. The information is gathered from employers, employers' associations, trade-unions, local authorities, and other parties concerned. A change in the rate of wages is defined as a change in the

[1] The 8-hour day seems to be making very slow progress. The Labour Department of the Board of Trade in England reported that in four years so far as could be learned the 8-hour day had been introduced into private establishments employing 10,722 workpeople, and into public establishments employing 45,421 workpeople. (Report on Changes in Wages and Hours of Labour, 1897, p. xxiv.)

[2] See Hobson, Evolution of Modern Capitalism, 1894.

weekly or hourly remuneration of a certain class of people, apart from any change in the character of the work done. It excludes changes in the wages of individuals, and changes accompanied by corresponding alterations in hours of labour or character of work done. The net effect of the changes in the amount of weekly wages is taken to be the computed difference between the wages paid for a full week's work to the workpeople affected, at the close and the beginning of the year respectively. The comparison is between the level of wages at the beginning and end of the year, internal fluctuations being neglected.

As an example of this method we give the following facts for 1898[1]:—

The total number of changes reported to the Department in 1898, in all trades except agriculture, railway service and shipping was 1,150, the increases numbering 1,100, and the decreases 50 only. The workpeople affected by increases in wages numbered 978,000 and by decreases 12,000: the total of 990,000 being the largest number affected by changes in wages in any one year since these statistics were first collected in 1893. The net aggregate rise in the wages of the 990,000 persons affected in 1898, was £78,000 per week or an average of 1*s.* 6¾*d.* per head. This is the largest recorded average increase in weekly rates of wages in a year, but if spread over the total number employed in the trades covered by the returns the weekly average rise would not be much more than 2*d.* per head. The figures for 1893–8 are brought together in the following table:—

Year.	Total number of individuals affected by changes in rates of wages.	Net result on weekly wages of *those affected by changes.* Total amount.	Average per head.	
		£	*s.*	*d.*
1893	549,977	+12,426	+0	5½
1894	670,386	−45,091	−1	4¼
1895	436,718	−28,211	−1	3½
1896	607,654	+26,592	+0	10½
1897	597,444	+31,507	+1	0¾
1898	990,000	+78,000	+1	6¾

These figures are exclusive of seamen, agricultural labourers and railway servants.

[1] Quoted from the Labour Gazette, Jan. 1899.

The report contains other interesting information. It analyses the number of workpeople by groups of trades. It shows, for instance, that, in 1898, of the 990,000 work-people affected by changes in rates of wages, 653,000 were in coal mining, and 204,000 in metal, engineering and ship-building. It analyses, also, the methods by which the changes were brought about. In 1896, for instance, in the case of 90·8 per cent. of the workpeople affected, the change was brought about without stoppage of the industry, while in the remaining 9·2 per cent. the change was preceded by strikes.

During 1896, in the case of 73,616 persons, the hours of labour were lengthened by ·24 hours per week, while in the case of 34,655 workpeople, they were shortened by 2·77 hours per week. The net result was a reduction of ·73 hours per week. The report also gives statistics of the changes in agricultural wages from the reports of County Councils as to wages in June and December. It gives changes in railway wages furnished by the Railway Trade Union. It gives changes in seamen's wages from actual contracts.

Such statistics, while they do not necessarily indicate that all labour has prospered, or the reverse, during the year, do give the general trend of the movement. They are representative statistics, and so far as they go, are based either on actual wages or upon expert opinion. They are better than general statistics from the working men themselves, and it is possible by this method to keep a continuous yearly record, while a yearly census of all wages would be impossible.

Average and Classified Wages. Average wages are as a rule very unsatisfactory. There are so many differences in skill, age, sex, hand or machine labour, that an average may be mathematically correct and yet give a false impression. So, too, the inclusion of the high wages of a foreman or superintendent would raise the whole average above what the ordinary workman gets. It has been proposed, therefore, to classify wages rather than to average them, *i.e.*, to give the number of men receiving between $5·00 and $6·00 per week, between $6·00 and $7·00, and so on. We are thus able to judge somewhat of the real income of the greater number of wage earners, which is the important question in wage statistics.

The United States Census, 1890, has proceeded upon this plan, and some of the results are published in the Statistics of Manufactures. For the sake of illustrating the method, as well as of giving wages for two important industries, the following table is given, showing the number of males above sixteen years in the iron and steel manufacture, and in the cotton manufacture, at different rates of wages (U. S. Census, 1890: Manufactures, III., pp. 390 and 208):—

Weekly rate of wages.	Iron and steel [1] manufacture.	Cotton [2] manufacture.	Percentage. Iron and steel.	Percentage. Cotton.
Under $5·00	1,643	15,164	1·0	17·1
5·00 but under $ 6·00 .	3,424	9,924	2·0	11·2
6·00 ,, ,, 7·00 .	10,198	15,491	6·0	17·5
7·00 ,, ,, 8·00 .	20,265	10,485	12·0	11·9
8·00 ,, ,, 9·00 .	25,041	9,120	14·8	10·3
9·00 ,, ,, 10·00 .	23,727	8,712	14·0	9·8
10·00 ,, ,, 12·00 .	24,516	8,409	14·5	9·5
12·00 ,, ,, 15·00 .	24,458	5,427	14·5	6·1
15·00 ,, ,, 20·00 .	17,974	3,027	10·6	3·4
20·00 ,, ,, 25·00 .	10,502	1,291	6·2	1·5
25·00 and over	7,195	1,417	4·2	1·6
Total	168,943	88,467	100·0	100·0

The advantage of such a table is that it shows the economic position of the great mass of working men in any industry. In the two industries contrasted here, it will be seen at a glance that the men in the iron and steel industry are paid much higher than the men in the cotton manu-

[1] Not including firm members, officers and clerks.
[2] Including firm members, officers and clerks.

facture. More than one-half (57·7 per cent.) of the men in the cotton industry receive less than $8·00 per week, while only 21 per cent. of the men in the iron and steel industry receive less than that sum. For the question of income such a classified wage is more interesting than an average wage.[1]

Classified Wages in Great Britain. The following table shows the proportion of men, women, lads and boys, and girls at different rates of wages, according to the great census of wages in different employments, 1886–91 (General Report on Wages [c–6889], 1893, p. xxxii.):—

	Men.	Women.	Lads and Boys.	Girls.
Half timers . . .	...	...	11·9	27·2
Under 10*s*.	0·1	26·0	49·7	62·5
10*s*. to 15*s*. . . .	2·4	50·0	32·5	8·9
15*s*. to 20*s*. . . .	21·5	18·5	5·8	1·4
20*s*. to 25*s*. . . .	33·6	5·4	0·1	...
25*s*. to 30*s*. . . .	24·2	0·1	...	...
30*s*. to 35*s*. . . .	11·6	...	...	...
35*s*. to 40*s*. . . .	4·2	...	...	...
Above 40*s*.	2·4	...	...	...
Total .	100·0	100·0	100·0	100·0
Average . .	24*s*. 9*d*.	12*s*. 11*d*.	9*s*. 2*d*.	6*s*. 5*d*.

The general effect of the above summary is that about one-third of the men earn wages at the rate of 20*s*. to 25*s*. per week, and that the proportion earning less than 20*s*. per week is only 24 per cent.

A second method is to divide the total amount paid in wages during the preceding year by the number of persons employed in each establishment on the 1st of October, 1886. The result was that the average earnings of men, women, lads and boys, and girls, indiscriminately, came out at £47 per head. The numbers classified ac-

[1] For wages in the Woollen Industry see U. S. Census, 1890: Manufactures, III. p. 146; Silk Industry, p. 230; Coke, p. 346; Refining of Petroleum, p. 361.

cording to different annual incomes were as follows (*Ibid.*, p. xxxiii.):—

	Numbers.	Proportion per cent.
Of and above £70 . . .	62,841	7·8
£60 to £70	67,320	8·2
£50 to £60	268,295	32·8
£40 to £50	67,818	8·2
Under £40	349,832	43·0
	816,106	100·0

Scientific Tests.

This survey of the various attempts to get wage statistics shows that the technical requirements are as follows:—

(1) It is best, on the whole, to confine ourselves to establishments where large bodies of men are employed at definite money wages. It is probably impossible to get the wages of all labourers in a given country. That would require a very extensive census and numerous inquiries of individuals, whose answers would be, in many cases, indefinite and uncertain. With many of these individual labourers there are peculiar circumstances governing the rate of wages which they get; in some cases, as among old domestic servants, it is fixed by custom and tradition; in some cases, it is a quasi-form of charity; in others the wages represent inadequate or partial service; while again other privileges, such as house rent, garden crops, perquisites and fees may supplement money wages. In a large establishment the wage generally represents the full return for the labour, and the labour represents the full average exertion of able-bodied individuals in that employment. Labour is more or less of uniform quality, and wages represent a definite payment for specific services rendered. Still further, it is comparatively easy to control the general run of wages in large establishments, because the rates paid must be about the same in different establishments in the same business.

(2) Wage statistics can best be obtained from employers. They alone keep the accurate figures and records from year to year. They are less likely to be influenced by personal feeling or class prejudice to make false or misleading returns. The experts of a census office can make transcripts from the pay-rolls of large establishments without betraying the secrets of any individual business man. Such returns, of course, being actual wages that have been paid, are of much greater value than any estimate of what the labourers get.

(3) As has already been said, wages must be carefully distinguished as to industries, occupations, and the sex and age of the persons employed. This has been amplified upon above, so that it is not necessary to insist upon it here.

(4) Employers must be asked to give the actual wages paid, and not mere estimates of the rate of wages.

(5) It will, probably, always be necessary that wage returns should be grouped geographically in order to be of any definite value. The conditions of life are so different for a blacksmith in a northern town from those of a negro blacksmith on a southern plantation, that to throw the two together gives a false average. The Eastern States are an advanced industrial community, the Western States are largely agricultural; the Pacific States, again, have the characteristics of the frontier community, and the Southern States bear traces of negro slavery. These sections are really economically as distinct as separate nations.

(6) It is desirable to distinguish between groups of occupations in the same way that we distinguish between age, sex and geographical position. This is, however, a more difficult matter. If we take occupations simply by name, we get almost innumerable divisions and sub-divisions. Our wage statistics become so split up, that they mean but little to us. The division between skilled and unskilled labour is so indefinite and difficult to draw, that it avails us little. The Massachusetts plan, first put into practice in 1884, and

amplified in 1895, of designating whether the wages paid are high, medium, or low, or even of intermediate grade, serves as a safeguard against laying too much stress upon extreme returns. For individual cases such direction is of considerable value. On the whole, however, such gradation depends too much upon individual judgment to be of great value.

Reflective Analysis.

In reviewing the results of our statistics of wages, two questions suggest themselves:—(1) What light do they throw upon the theory of wages? (2) What do they prove in regard to the condition and future prospects of the wage-receiving class? Both of these points have been so fully illustrated by the statistics themselves, that the briefest recapitulation here will be sufficient.

(1) All theories of wages recognise two facts, viz., that wages depend upon the efficiency and upon the supply of labour. When we say that labour in the long run gets that which it specifically produces, we are emphasising the first point; when we think of wages as expressing the value of the commodity "labour," and thus subject to the law of demand and supply, we are emphasising the second point. Statistics are not able to prove directly either of these propositions. They cannot define exactly what part of the product is represented by wages; nor can they connect wages directly with either the efficiency or the number of labourers. But our statistics may be used indirectly to illustrate the thesis of political economy. All comparisons between wages in different countries, in different occupations, among labourers of different age, sex, nationality, physical strength, intelligence and skill, demand explanation. The most obvious reason for such variations is the difference in efficiency of the labourers, or in the supply of labour. When our statistics are more perfect and correlations with facts affecting efficiency

more exact, these relations will stand out in sharp relief and constitute the strongest confirmation of theory.[1]

(2) The second point has been abundantly illustrated. All the statistics seem to show that wages have been advancing during the last thirty to fifty years. This is true of money wages, and owing to the fall in prices since 1873, still more true of real wages. This progress has been due primarily to the abundance of capital, which on the whole works to the benefit of the labouring class in two directions—by competing for labour-force and thus raising wages, and by cheapening products and thus making wages go further. This process has been aided by labour-organisation, by the sharp competition of modern industrial enterprises on a colossal scale reducing the rate of profit, by public opinion supporting all attempts to better the condition of the poorer and weaker classes, and by the new humanitarian, semi-socialistic notions of the functions of government. These topics belong, however, to the following chapters.

[1] The inquiry of the U. S. Department of Labour in regard to the wages of men, women and children, 1899, endeavoured to ascertain the prevailing opinion of employers in regard to the relative efficiency of men and women doing the same kind of work.

CHAPTER X.

RENT, INTEREST, AND PROFITS.

Economic Purpose.

THEORETICALLY the product is divided among the factors of production. If we consider the factors to be labour, land, capital, and organisation, we have wages, rent, interest, and profits as the corresponding rewards. Concretely, it is impossible to follow out this division of the product, because it is made among persons, and these persons do not correspond to the above divisions, often the same one contributing two or more of the factors, as the peasant-farmer is both landowner and labourer. Of the total annual product of a community we cannot say how much is due to labour, how much to land, how much to capital; nor can we say how much is distributed to those who contribute labour, how much to the owners of land, etc. The product is due to the national labour applied to land, with the aid of capital, and under competent direction. We can observe that the product is increased by the application of capital and by the ability of the organiser; and we remark that the owner of capital and the possessor of ability get a portion of the annual product, as well as the landowner and the labourer. The problem of political economy is to determine how much is due to each factor, and to analyse the process by which each gets that which is its due. Qualitatively, this can be done by economic theory. Quantitatively, we can approach a solution of the problem only indirectly, and more for purposes of comparison in time and space than of fixing absolute amounts.

In the statistics of wages, as we have seen, it is impossible to treat wages as the reward of a certain amount of labour, because we have no unit of labour. There is no such thing attainable as a concrete rate of wages in the sense of a proportion between the amount of labour rendered and the amount of goods received. On the other hand, the wage-receivers are a more or less distinct class, receiving a more or less specific sum of money, so that we can turn our statistics of wages into statistics of income, and get some light on the question of the economic condition of a large and important class in the community who contribute mainly labour to the process of production.

With rent, interest, and profit it is different. There is nothing like a distinct body of persons receiving anything like a known quantity of money either as rent, as interest, or as profits. We do have the class of landowners, and especially owners of agricultural land, but so far as they are also cultivators, rent is not separated from the reward of labour, capital, and even ability. We may possibly know the number of landlords and their rent-rolls. But rent in this case is not pure rent, but involves payment for interest on capital; and it is not possible to separate the two. So we can have neither a distinct rent-receiving class nor a distinct sum of rent paid for land. An average income of landlords due to land is impossible even in the limited sense in which we can speak of an average wage of a wage-receiving class due to labour. Statistically, all we can deal with is gross rent. Taking certain things for granted, viz., that the amount of capital invested in land remains about the same, we may possibly watch variations in rent from time to time.

In respect to interest, we have still less a class of capitalists and still less knowledge of the amount paid as interest. We can, however, determine the rate of interest, that is, the proportion of the annual payment to the principal borrowed; and we can watch variations in time and space.

Profit is still more difficult. As a reward of ability it

must vary with each entrepreneur. As compensation for risk, it must vary with each enterprise. There is no distinct class of profit-takers except as each man receives compensation for the risk of business and reward as quasi-rent for exceptional ability or opportunity. Profit is sometimes used as the difference between the selling price of a product and its cost. It is then conceived of as related to the cost of the goods, as in the expression "quick sales and small profits." An entrepreneur's total profit for a year would depend upon the magnitude of his transactions, commonly expressed as the number of turnovers of the capital invested in his business. A rate of profit is sometimes spoken of, but then it is the proportion of this gain for a year (say) to the amount of capital invested. This may be a convenient way of expressing it, but evidently is not consistent with our definition of profit, either as compensation for business risk or reward for ability. Statistically, there can be no general rate of profit because the elements entering into this "gain" are so various. We can, possibly, by using the above arbitrary proportion determine whether the so-called rate of profit is increasing or decreasing, but only in particular cases. Statistics labour under great difficulties in this inquiry, and we need not expect great results.

Statistical Data.[1]

Gross Rent. As already said, it is impossible by statistics to get anything except gross rent, *i.e.*, the sum actually paid

[1] *Bibliographical Note.* Statistics on the subjects of this chapter are extremely scarce and very scattered. In regard to rent, much general information will be found in the Reports of the Royal Commission on Agriculture, 1895–98. For rates of interest see the standard trade journals such as *The Economist*, *Statist*, and *Financial and Commercial Chronicle*. See also the Reports of the Royal Commission on Gold and Silver, 1887–88, for discussion as to relation between rates of discount and quantity of money. For relation between rate of interest and prices, see Irving Fisher, Appreciation and Interest (Amer. Econ. Assocn. Publications, Vol. XI., No. 4, 1896), with appendix of tables and bibliography. For question of profits: U.S. Census, 1890: Manufactures, I., p. 49 ff.; Mass. Annual Stat. of

for the use of land, whether it is due to the soil itself or to capital invested in the soil, or even to buildings and other permanent improvements. The nearest approach, perhaps, that we have to such statistics is found in the English Income Tax. There are even there three headings which contain items of rents, viz., Schedule A, rent of lands; Schedule B, farmers' profits; and under Schedule A, income from houses. Schedule B, farmers' profits, is largely estimated on the amount of rent paid, so that it can be disregarded. The returns from houses would be due very largely to the capital invested. Income from land therefore is the best index of fluctuations in agricultural rent. Gross returns at successive periods are shown in the following table (Commission on Agriculture, 1895-98, III., p. 593):—

An Account of the Total Gross Assessments on Land (including Tithes) under Schedule A, in England, Wales, and Scotland, in the Years ended 5th April, 1843, 1853, 1863, 1873, 1883, and 1894.

Year.	England.	Wales.	Scotland.	Great Britain.
	£	£	£	£
1842-43 . .	37,795,000	2,371,000	5,586,000	45,753,000
1852-53 . .	38,587,000	2,496,000	5,499,000	46,582,000
1862-63 . .	41,962,000	2,648,000	6,715,000	51,326,000
1872-73 . .	46,137,000	2,871,000	7,363,000	56,372,000
1882-83 . .	45,151,000	3,251,000	7,573,000	55,976,000
1893-94 . .	36,996,000	3,065,000	6,251,000	46,313,000

It appears from this table that the rent of agricultural land increased during the period from 1842 to 1873, but has since then decreased. For England alone the gross assessment on lands was less in 1893-94 than it was in 1842-43. For Great Britain the increase is very slight. Sir Robert Giffen has pointed out that the rental returns at the end of

Manufactures; Net Profits in Manufacturing Industries (Mass. Bureau of Labour Statistics, 21st Annual Report, 1891). The above is criticised by Hawley in Amer. Stat. Assocn. Publications, Vol. III., 1892-93, p. 38. Statistics of Railways in the United States (for dividends on stock and interest on bonds). For criticism of the methods employed by the United States and some State Censuses, see North, The Statistics of Manufactures, in the Federal Census (Amer. Econ. Assocn. Publications, New Series, No. 2, 1899). See also Steuart (*Ibid.*). Neumann-Spallart, Uebersichten der Weltwirtschaft.

the period were about the same as at the beginning, notwithstanding the large investment of capital in improvements.[1] And Mr. Pell thinks that the present rental roll no more than represents the interest on the capital that has actually been put into the land.[2]

Net Rent of Large Estates. A second method of tracing the movement in rent is by taking the estates of large landowners and tracing the gross and net return over a series of years. There are some technical difficulties, viz., the acreage may vary, larger or smaller sums may be spent on improvements, taxes may be lighter or heavier, burdens may be borne at one time by the tenant and at another time by the landlord, and temporary abatements of rent may be made to tide the tenant over hard times. These things cannot be wholly eliminated, but on large estates, where there is a system of accurate bookkeeping, allowance can be made for them. In the report of the British Commission on Agriculture there are some interesting examples of this sort.

Guy's Hospital in London owns and rents three large estates, and has the rent account ever since 1801. The Lincolnshire estate varies from 5,262 acres in 1807 to 6,315 acres in 1893. The acreage, gross rent, and rent per acre in successive years is shown in the following table (Commission on Agriculture, Vol. I., p. 423):—

Year ending Michaelmas.	Acreage.	Rent. £	s.	d.	Rent per acre. £	s.	d.
1807	5,262	5,203	6	0	0	19	9
1817	5,262	6,375	1	0	1	4	2
1827	5,262	6,396	9	0	1	4	3
1837	5,315	7,416	8	0	1	7	10
1847	5,574	9,484	17	0	1	14	0
1857	5,763	10,785	13	6	1	17	5
1867	5,967	12,423	7	2	2	1	7
1877	6,401	15,438	17	6	2	8	2
1887	6,321	10,883	15	0	1	14	4
1893	6,315	10,879	14	9	1	14	9

[1] Commission on Agriculture, 1895–98, Vol. II., p. 147.

[2] *Ibid.*, p. 150. See also Marshall, Principles of Economics (4th ed.), p. 766 note.

Of course from this table we cannot calculate the exact net income of the hospital. Improvements must be deducted, and also arrears of rent, where they are not collected, and temporary abatements of rent. It appears clearly, however, that rent per acre increased steadily down to about 1879. Since that date rents have gone down, and even more than is indicated by the table. For instance, until 1888 tithes were paid by the tenants, after which time they were at first partly, and afterwards wholly, paid by the hospital. During this period arrears were very large, and in 1883 arrears to the amount of £2,271 were remitted. In addition there were temporary abatements of rent, amounting in the last year to £1,188. The treasurer of the hospital states that in 1879 the rental of this estate was £13,189, and in 1893 it was £8,704, the tenant paying the tithes at the first period, and the landlord at the second.[1] Similar figures are given for two other estates.

In a similar way it was shown that the acreage of the estates of the Ecclesiastical Commission increased during the period 1880–92, from 212,600 to 278,000 acres, while the gross rental decreased by £2,000 sterling. Assuming rents to have been on the basis of the 1880 average, the Commission ought to have had in 1892 (including tithes and minerals) £417,000 as against £311,000.[2]

The Duchy of Cornwall Estate showed in 1878 on an acreage of 29,970 a net rent of £39,295; while in 1892 on an acreage of 38,160, it showed a net rent of £29,352. That is, with an increase of acreage of 9,000 acres, there had been a decrease of rent of £10,000. The average reduction in rent was 40 per cent.[3]

Lord Wantage testified that the net income on his estate had been reduced from £44,000 to £12,000 a year.[4]

[1] Commission on Agriculture, 1895–98, Ques. 1635.

[2] *Ibid.*, Part I., Ques. 448; table, p. 420.

[3] *Ibid.*, Ques. 5840–5846.

[4] *Ibid.*, Ques. 4553; table, p. 431.

Sir Michael Hicks-Beach testified that in the last thirty-five years he had spent the whole of the income from a certain estate on improvements. Lately rents had fallen so that the income barely maintained the land in condition. In 1876 rentals varied from 22*s.* to 14*s.* per acre; in 1893, from 10*s.* 6*d.* to 7*s.* 6*d.* On one farm taxes and tithes amounted to 5*s.* 11*d.* in the pound.[1]

Average Rent. The movement of rent may be roughly determined by taking the rental value of certain qualities of land which remain about the same from period to period.

The following table is published by Professor Nicholson (Principles of Political Economy, Vol. I., p. 422):—

RENT IN ENGLAND.

	1770.		1850.		1878.	
	s.	*d.*	*s.*	*d.*	*s.*	*d.*
Rent of cultivated land per acre . . .	13	0	27	0	30	0
Price of bread per lb.	0	1½	0	1¼	0	1½
Price of meat per lb.	0	3¼	0	5	0	9
Price of butter per lb.	0	6	1	0	1	8
Agricultural labourer's wages per week .	7	3	9	7	14	0
Rent of labourer's cottage per week . .	0	8	1	5	2	0
	Bushels.		Bushels.		Bushels.	
Produce of wheat per acre	23		26½		28	

Down to the middle of this century rent had doubled; and it continued to increase from 1850 to 1878. Price of agricultural products also increased as well as expenses in the shape of labourers' wages. The increased production of wheat per acre probably showed additional investment of capital. On the whole it is doubtful if pure rent had increased very much, and since 1878 there has probably been a fall.

The Rate of Interest. We have numerous tables showing the rate of interest on different kinds of loan. But as the rate of interest varies according to the goodness of the security, it is necessary to take some standard investment, such as Government bonds, and show how the rate varies from period to period. This is done, of course, by taking a security bearing the same rate of interest and watching

[1] *Ibid.*, Ques. 6046 ff.

the fluctuations in its price from period to period. The price of English consols has varied enormously according to political prospects and trade conditions. Three per cents. were created about 1726. In 1737 the price touched 137. During the 1745 rebellion the monthly average price dropped to 75. In 1752 the quotations reached 107, but in 1762 they dropped as low as 65, and in 1782 to 53¼. In 1791 the highest price was 97, but the war sent them down to 47¼ in 1798, and they did not recover to 97 until 1824. In 1844 and in 1852–53 they rose above par, but sank back again owing to the panic of 1846 and the Crimean War. They reached par again in 1880 and continued above par till the refunding of 1888. Refunded into 2¾ per cents. to be reduced to 2½ per cents. in 1903, they have steadily risen in value, touching the extraordinary price of 114 in 1896.[1]

The fluctuations in the rate of interest due to temporary demand and supply of loanable capital is best shown by the rates of discount. These annual rates, however, conceal in themselves wide fluctuations due to temporary changes in supply and demand, or in credit. The following table shows the rates of discount at the principal money centres of Europe during a period of twenty years (Neumann-Spallart, Uebersichten, p. lxviii.)[2]:—

RATES OF DISCOUNT.

	Amsterdam.	Berlin.	Brussels.	London.	Paris.	Vienna.	Rome.
1864 . .	5·35	5·31	5·61	7·35	6·50	5·00	7·82
1873 . .	4·84	4·85	5·06	4·80	5·15	5·22	5·00
1886 . .	2·50	3·28	2·80	3·02	3·00	4·00	4·75
1887 . .	2·50	3·41	3·10	3·30	3·00	4·12	5·50
1888 . .	2·50	3·32	3·32	3·31	3·30	4·17	5·50
1889 . .	2·50	3·68	3·53	3·61	3·13	4·19	5·17
1890 . .	2·80	4·52	3·20	4·51	3·00	4·48	6·00
1891 . .	3·12	3·78	3·00	3·30	3·00	4·40	5·78
1892 . .	2·70	3·20	2·70	2·45	2·70	4·02	5·20
1893 . .	3·80	4·08	2·83	3·07	2·50	4·24	5·18
1894 . .	2·58	3·12	3·00	2·11	2·50	4·09	5·70
1895 . .	2·50	3·15	2·60	2·00	2·20	4·30	5·00

[1] See diagram published by the *Statist*, 1899.

[2] The Commission on Gold and Silver, 1887–88, Appendix to Final

Profits. There seems to be no way of estimating profits or any rate of profit. The dividends of joint-stock companies are partly interest on the capital invested, and partly compensation for risk. They furnish no basis for a calculation of profit. The same is true of the rate of dividend on railroads, published by the Interstate Commerce Commission.

As an example of the former method we give the following table (Neumann-Spallart, Uebersichten, p. lxxxv.):—

PROPORTIONATE NUMBER OF JOINT-STOCK COMPANIES PER 100, PAYING DIVIDENDS AT VARIOUS RATES.

Dividends paid.	1871.	1877.	1886.	1890.	1891.	1893.
None	6·6	33·6	24·9	10·1	15·1	16·3
0 to 5 per cent.	12·3	27·8	29·3	12·5	18·5	23·2
5 to 10 ,, ,,	39·9	27·0	30·5	53·3	51·3	48·3
Over 10 ,, ,,	41·2	11·6	15·3	22·1	15·1	12·2

It would seem from this table that there is always a considerable number of companies that pay no dividends, and that the number paying over 10 per cent. is decreasing.

From an analysis of the railways of the United States (1897) it appears that 70·1 per cent. of the outstanding stock paid no dividend, and 16·6 per cent. of the outstanding bonds

Report, p. 207, gives fluctuations in rates of discount at various places from 1851 to 1885. The averages are as follows:—

	Bank of England.	Bank of France.	Ger. Imp. and Pruss. Bank.	Hamburg.	Vienna.
1851–1860 . .	4·12	4·16	4·39	3·40	4·44
1861–1865 . .	4·90	4·83	4·47	3·30	5·11
1866–1870 . .	3·62	3·07	4·67	3·27	4·54
1871–1875 . .	3·75	4·86	4·50	3·77	5·16
1876–1880 . .	2·87	2·65	4·17	3·24	4·34
1881–1885 . .	3·43	3·34	4·23	3·37	4·06

Elaborate tables of rates of interest on "Money" will be found in Dr. Irving Fisher's Monograph, Appreciation and Interest (Amer. Econ. Assocn. Publications, XI., p. 436, 1896).

paid no interest. The condensed table is as follows (Statistics of Railways, U.S., 1897, p. 52):—

Rate of dividend or interest.	Per cent. of total stock on which paid.	Per cent. of bonds on which paid.
Nothing paid	70·1	16·6
From 1 to 2	2·1	3·0
,, 2 ,, 3	2·5	6·3
,, 3 ,, 4	0·8	9·8
,, 4 ,, 5	6·5	25·6
,, 5 ,, 6	6·0	21·1
,, 6 ,, 7	3·6	11·0
,, 7 ,, 8	4·6	4·8
,, 8 ,, 9	2·3	1·2
,, 9 ,, 10	0·2	0·3
10 and above	1·3	0·3
	100·0	100·0

Owing to the uncertainty of the relation between nominal capital stock and real capital, it is difficult to interpret these figures as indicative of a rate of profit.

Profits in Manufactures. The ordinary conception of profits is that of an excess in the sale of a product over and above the expenses of producing it. Express this as a percentage of the capital invested and we have a rate of profit. The Census of the United States purports to give the total value of the product of manufacturing industry and also the cost of raw material, the total wages paid, and the miscellaneous expenses, such as insurance, taxes, repairs, etc. Summing up these last items as cost of production and deducting the sum from the value of the gross product, we have a figure which is sometimes supposed to represent the profit of the entrepreneur. The totals for all manufactures are as follows (U.S. Census, 1890: Manufactures, I., p. 8):—

Gross product, value of		$9,372 million
Cost of material used . .	$5,162 million	
Total wages paid . . .	2,283 ,,	
Miscellaneous expenses .	631 ,,	
Total cost		8,076 ,,
Net product over cost		$1,296 million

The total capital invested was returned as $6,525 million, or counting in hired property as $7,681 million. The profit on manufactures would seem to be nearly thirteen hundred million a year, or more than one-half of the total wages paid, and the average rate of profit on capital invested would be nearly 17 per cent.[1]

All such calculations are a delusion and a snare. The value of the gross product was said to be the estimated value at the factory. But this is very different from the actual selling value, minus shipping expenses, commissions, etc. Miscellaneous expenses were most imperfectly returned,[2] and the attempt to ascertain the annual depreciation of plant was a failure. Even if the figures were perfect (which they never will be), there always remains the element of business risk and speculation. If opportunity favours, the producer sells at a high price and makes a profit; if the market is against him he seeks to minimise his loss. Against the profit account of the successful manufacturer should be entered the losses of those who fail and lose capital as well as profit. Finally, the figures for capital are so uncertain (as shown in a previous chapter) that any rate of profit is manifestly absurd.

The fallacy of the whole calculation is best shown when we carry it out for different industries. The census has worked out the proportion which the amounts returned as cost of raw material, wages paid, and miscellaneous expenses, bear to the value of the total product. Some specimens are as follows (U.S. Census, 1890: Manufactures, I., p. 49):—

Cost of a Product valued at $100·00.

	Materials.	Wages.	Miscellaneous Expenses.	Total.
All industries	$55·08	$24·36	$6·73	$86·17
Agricultural implements	38·89	26·84	13·69	79·42
Awnings, tents, and sails	53·01	28·21	4·16	85·38
Blacksmithing and wheelwrighting	26·97	49·35	4·62	80·94

[1] See *ante* pp. 169–170.

[2] See *ante* p. 172.

COST OF A PRODUCT VALUED AT $100·00.

	Materials.	Wages.	Miscellaneous Expenses.	Total.
Iron and steel	68·63	19·65	3·93	92·21
Boots and shoes, custom work, and repairing	29·85	48·06	7·99	85·90
Boots and shoes, factory product . .	53·83	30·08	4·18	88·09
Gas, illuminating, and heating . . .	24·63	18·68	13·69	57·00
Petroleum, refining	79·90	8·22	2·43	90·55
Sugar and molasses refining	87·52	2·29	4·81	94·62
Glass	29·58	53·88	5·52	88·98

This table is misleading, because it seems to imply that after all expenses are paid there remains for every $100 of product turned out the sum of (for example) $5·38 in the sugar refining business, $43·00 in the making of gas, etc. The figures are so imperfect that even this simple implication is unwarranted. And even if the figures were perfect they would show nothing in regard to the actual rate of profit. Taking the extreme instances noticed above, viz., sugar and gas, one sees by examination of the table that the chief difference between the two industries is the cost of the raw material. But by turning over capital used for the purchase of raw material quickly enough, it might easily happen that the same capital and the same business ability would reap the same reward as in the gas industry, where the apparent expenses of production are so much less per one hundred dollars of product.

If the table is useless as showing actual profit in the sense of excess of value of the final product over cost of production, it is still more valueless for showing the relation of the reward of the entrepreneur to capital invested, trade risk, and his own energy and ability. But surely in considering whether profits are excessive or not (which is the latent thought in all attempts to measure profits), this is the essential thing. The statistical method is entirely inadequate for the solution of such a problem, and the presentation of figures (themselves notoriously imperfect) in such a way as to induce the unwary to believe that they have a solution is not only misleading but mischievous.[1]

Relative Reward of Capital and Labour. The figures given in the preceding table have sometimes been interpreted as meaning that labour in the shape of wages gets 24·36 per cent. of the total product, and the implication is that the landowner, capitalist and entrepreneur in some way get all the rest. Such interpretation is on the face of it absurd, because labour must enter into the cost of materials and miscellaneous expenses as well. No estimate of the relative reward of labour and capital is possible on the basis of these figures.

The Massachusetts Bureau of Statistics of Labour makes a more cautious use of similar figures, but with something like the same implication. From the total value of the products of manufactures, it deducts the cost of raw material or stock used. The remainder constitutes what is called the "Industry Product," that is, the value added by the industrial process to the raw material. This "industry product" goes to pay labour in the shape of wages, and what is left constitutes a "profit and minor expense fund," out of which the employer meets all the other expenses of business and

[1] It is true that the Census enters a *caveat* against the misuse of the figures in a footnote to the table as follows:—"The difference between the cost of manufacturing and the value of product at the place of production does not show the true average profit or earnings, because the cost reported does not include cost for depreciation of plant or mercantile risks." (U.S. Census, 1890: Manufactures, I., p. 49.) The same caution is repeated in the text. (*Ibid.*, p. 55.) And the incompleteness of the returns of miscellaneous expenses is mentioned: *e.g.*, "The amount expended for miscellaneous expenses for a product valued at $100 in 'Cars and general shop construction and repairs by steam railroad companies,' is given as seven cents. This small amount is due to the fact that the majority of the railroad companies reported no expenses of a miscellaneous character for their repair shops, materials and wages being the only items of expense reported as charged to this branch." (*Ibid.*, p. 54.) For the reasons mentioned in the text, these explanations seem to me entirely inadequate to justify the publication of the tables. *Cf.* The Federal Census (Amer. Econ. Assocn. Publications, New Series, No. 2 1899, pp. 280 and 313.)

gets interest and profit. The proportion in which the "industry product" is divided in different industries is as follows (Mass. Stat. Manufactures, 1897, p. 189):—

Industry.	Percentage of industry product. Devoted to profits and minor expenses.	Paid in wages.
Boots and shoes	41·9	58·1
Carpetings	34·9	65·1
Cotton goods	27·4	72·6
Leather	45·9	54·1
Machines and machinery	43·7	56·3
Metals and metallic goods	45·1	54·9
Paper	55·5	44·5
Woollen goods	40·5	59·5
Worsted goods	52·0	48·0

A footnote to this table explains that the first column does not represent profits, but covers "freights, insurance, interest on loans (credit capital), interest on stock (fixed or invested capital), rents, commissions, salaries, etc., in fact all expenses other than those for stock and wages."

A simple examination of the table shows that these items must vary enormously from industry to industry. So long as they are indeterminate, the whole comparison seems futile. For instance, in cotton goods 72·6 per cent. of the industry product is paid out in wages, and in paper only 44·5 per cent. That shows nothing in respect to the real reward of labour in the two industries, and the complementary figures reveal nothing as to the profits of the manufacturer.[1]

Profits in Agriculture. The attempt is sometimes made to estimate the amount of capital applied to agriculture, and the amount of return received on that capital. The attempt is an almost hopeless one, so far as calculating the productiveness of agriculture, or of the capital invested in agriculture. The United States Census in 1890 gave the

[1] In a more elaborate investigation made some years ago the Massachusetts Bureau of Statistics of Labour attempted to supply the missing "minor expenses," and thus arrive at net profit. The result was that

following valuation of farms (U. S. Census, 1890: Agriculture, p. 84):—

Land, fences and buildings . .	$13,279 million.
Implements and machinery .	494 ,,
Live stock on hand	2,208 ,,
Total	$15,982

These figures are supposed to represent the amount of capital invested in farming. They are, doubtless, the roughest

$100 worth of product represented the following items (Report Mass. Bureau Labour Statistics, 1890, p. 399):—

Stock used	$58·91
Salaries	1·73
Wages	22·34
Rent	0·73
Taxes.	0·56
Insurance	0·33
Freight	1·27
New equipment	0·24
Repairs	0·81
Other expenses	0·13
	87·05
Excess of selling price above cost of production	12·95
	$100·00

This excess may be fairly distributed as follows:—

Interest (5 per cent. on cash and credit capital)	$2·15
Depreciation (10 per cent. on value of machinery, implements and tools)	1·90
Allowance for selling expenses and losses by bad debts 5 per cent. on selling price)	5·00
Net profit	3·90
	12·95

This $3·90 net profit for each $100 of product is equivalent to 4·83 per cent. on amount of capital invested.

The best commentary on this table is that the attempt to include "credit capital" has since been abandoned by the Massachusetts Bureau. There is no certainty that the items of miscellaneous expenses are correctly returned, and the allowance for depreciation, selling expenses and bad debts are mere estimates. *Cf.* Hawley, Net Profits of Manufactures (Amer. Stat. Assocn. Publications, III., 1892–93, p. 38).

sort of estimate. For this capital the estimated value of all farm products for the year ending June 30th, 1890, was 2,460 million dollars. No calculation, however, can be made from these two figures as to the profitableness of farming, for the expenditures or current expenses are not given. The only item which the Census collected was the cost of fertilisers, which amounted to $38,489,598.[1]

The inquiry of 1882 in France gave the following figures for the capital invested, and the products and expenses of agriculture. The total value of landed property was placed at 91,584 million francs; the total gross production was estimated at 13,461 million francs; while the principal charges of agriculture were placed at 10,836 million francs. Subtracting this last number from the second, there is left 2,625 million francs as gross profit. There is to be deducted still further the general expenses and other charges valued at 1,470 million francs, leaving a net sum of 1,155 million francs as the profit of agriculture. The total wages and salaries paid to persons engaged in agriculture was estimated at 4,150 million francs. Adding this to the sum just found, we have agriculture yielding an annual sum of five and a quarter billion francs to the population engaged in agriculture.[2] It is unnecessary to say that all such estimates are of very little value in comparing the profits in agriculture with the profits in other forms of business, or in measuring the prosperity of the farming class. The real prosperity of the community can be measured better indirectly, by the amount of savings, by the purchases of land, by the taxes paid on inheritances, by the increase or decrease

[1] The Census of Massachusetts gives very elaborate returns of the products of agriculture and of the value of agricultural property. The former amounted to $52,880,431, and the latter to $219,957,214. The value of land alone used for agriculture was estimated at $110,271,859; of buildings, at $77,920,357; of domestic animals, at $14,854,417; and of machines, implements, etc., $8,128,031. (Census of Massachusetts, 1895, Vol. VI., p. 353.)

[2] De Foville, La France Économique, p. 104.

of mortgage indebtedness, and by the statistics of consumption of the necessaries and comforts of life, than by any direct estimate of profits on capital invested. The important consideration is that of actual income, not so much whether investments have been wisely or foolishly made.[1]

Scientific Tests.

It is difficult to add anything to what has already been said about the inadequacy of the statistical method for determining rent, interest, and profits. Ricardian rent is a differential gain due to the differences in the producing capacity of the soil. Each piece of land has its own rent, depending upon the excess of its productiveness over the productiveness of the poorest piece of land in use. An average Ricardian rent would be scientifically false, even if we could separate in actual rent that part which is due to the powers of the soil, and that which is due to investment of capital. A total rent roll would be of interest, as showing the income of a particular class in the community from one mode of investment. But even then, the impossibility of separating return from the use of land and return for the investment of capital would prevent our differentiating a Ricardian rent. Even if we knew that the landowners of England got a certain gross income from the land, it would not give us the net return from land, or even the amount which they derive from the so-called monopoly of land. We should have to deduct expenses, reward of labour, interest on capital, taxes and encumbrances. About the only statistics of rent that seem possible are the gross rents of particular pieces of land, from period to period, to enable us to determine whether the owners or occupiers of land are in a more or less favourable situation.

Statistics of interest are voluminous in record, owing to

[1] As to the amount of capital needed for good farming, much interesting testimony may be found in the Report of the Royal Commission on Agriculture, 1895–98. See Digest of Evidence, heading "Capital, Tenant's."

the enormous number of transactions from day to day in securities whose value is determined by their interest-earning power, and by the quotations of the money market. Caution about calculating the real mean rate by taking account of the amount as well as the rate, may be urged here as under the statistics of prices.

The calculation of profits seems to be altogether beyond the power of the statistical method.

Reflective Analysis.

The statistics of rent, interest, and profit give rise to the following reflections. In regard to rent, it would seem from the experience of England, that in modern times, at least, it represents very largely interest on capital invested. In fact, it may well be questioned whether the present ground rents of agricultural land represent more than a fair return for improvements made. So too, in regard to the unearned increment, it appears that there are numerous losses as well as gains, so that it is doubtful whether on the average, and in the long run, land property is any more advantageous in form than any other kind of property. The older English economists looked upon rent as a constantly increasing quantity, and it seemed to John Stuart Mill that it would be advantageous for the community to reserve for itself any increase in future rents not due to the labour or the capital of the landowner. In view of the heavy reductions in rents since 1879, the uselessness of the proceeding becomes manifest. It may well be doubted, in view of the increased cheapness of transportation, whether rents will ever attain their former height in England.

The statistics seem to show a constant decline in the rate of interest. This has been due to great accumulations of capital during the last few years, and the increased mobility of capital owing to security for property and debts. This decline, undoubtedly, comes to the good of the community, for it makes all production cheaper. It reduces the income of the leisure class and of the capitalists, who are only partly recouped by increased cheapness of living. It is evident that it is for the good of the community that the accumulation of capital should be encouraged in every possible way.

The admirable statistical investigation of Professor Irving Fisher seems to show that the rate of interest performs a very important function in mitigating the effects of appreciation or depreciation of money on creditors and debtors. When money is expected to appreciate, lenders are willing to take a less rate of interest because the money returned to them will have greater purchasing power; when money is expected to depreciate, they demand a higher rate for the contrary reason.[1]

Expressing profit either as a rate per cent. of the capital invested, or of the cost of goods produced, there is scarcely any doubt that it is also falling. Production on a large scale, enormous investments of fixed capital, and increased competition, compel the entrepreneur to put up with a smaller reward. This cannot be shown by statistics of the average rate of profit, which, as we have seen, does not exist. The thesis can be illustrated by numerous examples from the experience of entrepreneurs in special industries. The fall of prices since 1873 affords an opportunity of studying how such a fall has been met. There has been first of all a decreased cost of production, which in the long run comes to the benefit of all members of the community. But the evidence in this and the preceding chapter goes to show that of the active participants in production, the labourer has conserved or improved his position by the maintenance of, or even advance in the level of wages; the landowner has lost by falling rents; interest has fallen; and profits have

[1] Appreciation and Interest (Amer. Econ. Assocn. Publications, Vol. XI., No. 4, 1896).

been reduced to a narrower margin.[1] Of the economic and social effects of such a process it is not necessary to speak here. But it has an important bearing on the subject of a succeeding chapter, viz., Social Distribution.

[1] *Cf.* Danvers, who cites the case of a farm in Essex, where careful accounts have been kept. Since 1881 the rent has been reduced from £840 a year to £422. The tenant only makes about half the profit that he formerly made. The labourers receive higher money wages besides benefiting by the decreased cost of living. (Jour. Roy. Stat. Soc., Vol. LX., 1897, p. 259.)

CHAPTER XI.

COMPETITION AND ASSOCIATION.

Economic Purpose.

THERE is a natural law of wages, rent, interest, and profit by which the national dividend is divided among the four factors according as each has contributed to the product. This result works itself out through the action of competition. The law of substitution prevents any factor from getting more than its share. The entrepreneur looks upon the payment to each factor as one of the expenses of production. If he can reduce total expenses by shifting about the relative proportion of work assigned to each factor, he does it. If wages are high and interest low, he substitutes machinery for labour. If wages of superintendence are low and ordinary wages high, he tries to accomplish additional work by better supervision rather than by increasing the number of ordinary labourers. Progress in economic production is dependent upon the skill and quickness with which the entrepreneur discharges this function. The result of his work affects individuals by changing the demand for the particular commodity or service which they supply, and affects the whole community by reducing prices.

Competition and the law of substitution work, in the long run, by means of bringing in new supplies or by gradual diminution of old supplies. But the process requires time. Capital which has once become fixed cannot easily be withdrawn from one employment and thrown into another. It must be allowed gradually to wear out. The new capital demanded is furnished by the new savings which accumulate from year to year. This free capital is so large in the modern community, that changes in the demand are, for the most part, readily met. Labour, accustomed or trained to certain kinds of work, is bound down by such acquired skill to particular branches of industry. Ignorance and inertia combine to hinder the free transfer of labour from one employment to another. Ignorance and inertia again, together with the peculiarities of particular soils, make changes in agriculture often slow and difficult. The entrepreneur himself exercises only a specialised form of labour, and is also trammelled by acquired habits and traditional methods.

The result of this immobility is that the current reward in the case of each factor does not correspond to what would be its normal reward in the long run. On the one hand, the supply being for some reason or other greater than the demand, and the supply not being easily diminished, the current wages, interest, profit, or rent are less than the normal. This often happens to the labourer through the introduction of machinery and the competition of the machine product with the old hand-made product. The old hand-labourer, unwilling to give up his acquired skill or unable to learn the new trade, persists in producing in the face of a constantly decreasing wage. His wages are less than the reward of similar labour in other branches of industry, but he does not change. The capitalist with his capital fixed in old style machinery, will produce and sell at a price which returns much less than the current rate of interest on his investment, because it is better to get something rather than nothing. The entrepreneur and the landowner often find themselves in a similar situation.

On the other hand, when demand suddenly increases before adequate supplies can be brought in, each factor often receives a reward superior to that which it can get in the long run. Such extra gains are due either to some special demand or to the opportunity of monopolising for a time the supply of the service or commodity needed. A sudden war demand for woollen cloth would enable the existing woollen mills to get higher prices, and thus, in the first instance, increase the profits of the entrepreneur. If to meet the increased demand he employs more capital and more labour, this sudden demand will increase interest and wages; that is, the entrepreneur will be compelled to share a portion of his extra gains. These extra gains will continue until either the demand has returned to its normal level, or time enough has elapsed to bring in capital and labour and entrepreneur talent from other sources. So, in the same way, if the entrepreneur can monopolise the supply of his product, or if the labourer can monopolise the supply of his particular form of labour, each can get an extra reward.

The determination of the share of each factor of production implies thus a constant shifting and adjustment among the persons furnishing the factors. Each struggles to get his normal reward. Each struggles to avoid the exceptionally low reward occasioned by a falling demand or an over supply. Each struggles to reap as much as possible of the temporary extra reward due to exceptional demand or monopolised supply.

In this struggle the individuals representing the different factors do not occupy an equal position. The capitalist lender often has the advantage over the poor and ignorant borrower. The knowledge of this has led to the enactment of usury laws. The landowner will often indulge in rack-rents. The community then substitutes judicially determined fair rents. But the greatest struggle is between employer and employee on the question of wages. As individual against individual, the ordinary wage receiver is very much at the mercy of the capitalistic employer. The labourer is unable to find work outside of the factory, his necessities are pressing, and he is too ignorant and poor to change his occupation. If it were a matter of purely free contract, and the employer were allowed to exert his power unimpeded, the labourer would often suffer. Hence we have a whole series of devices to aid the labouring class in this struggle for wages. These devices consist first of voluntary associations by which collective bargaining is substituted for individual bargaining. This is known as the trade union, which seeks not only to drive a favourable contract with the employer of labour in regard to wages, but also to ameliorate the conditions under which the labourer does his work. Other voluntary associations, such as benefit and friendly societies, mutual insurance societies, savings banks, and co-operative stores, strive to give the labourer a more independent position by adding to his resources, and especially in helping him to tide over seasons of distress.

The community attempts to aid the labouring class by providing relief in case of extremity, such as sickness, accident, and old age, through poor relief and public works. This may even develop into a State system or State aided system of universal working men's insurance. The State also, through factory laws and sanitary regulations, attempts to better the conditions under which the labourer works and lives. The State finally, through public school education, technical schools, free libraries, and museums, attempts to secure to all members of the community a share in intellectual and moral progress.

Another device to secure to the labourer his normal reward, is to substitute arbitration and conciliation in place of strikes and lock-outs.

A third scheme is to extend association so as to enable the working man to share in the profits of entrepreneur and capitalist in addition to getting the wages of mere labour. These schemes go under the name of co-operation and profit-sharing.

Association is not confined to the labouring class. We

may have combinations of capitalists and employers. Such combinations may turn also into concentration of capital and business in the hands of trusts, syndicates, and combines. Such concentrated power may make itself felt, on the one hand, in driving down the price of the raw material or the half-finished product which the combination uses. It thus works hardship to the producer. On the other hand, it may attempt through its monopoly to raise the price of a finished product. It thus works hardship to the consumer. In the modern community, the laws of competition are very much modified by the interference of voluntary associations as depicted above. They are also modified by the action of the community endeavouring to restrain within certain limits the action of competitors. This is seen in usury laws, factory laws, &c.

Office of Statistics. The manifold workings of the law of competition and the influence of association are generally too subtle to be measured by statistics. About all we can do is to measure the numerical strength of certain obvious forms of association, such as trade unions, benefit and friendly societies, co-operative and profit-sharing enterprises. We measure statistically, also, the extent of the action of such agencies by measuring the amount of benefit distributed, the number of working men insured, the savings accumulated, the number of cases of arbitration and conciliation, the number of strikes, &c. We are sometimes able to measure, also, the results of such associated action in the success or non-success of strikes, the result on wages, and so on. The results of combined capital may sometimes be traced in prices.

Statistical Data.[1]

Trade Unions. Of all associations of working men, the trade union is the most important. It is a fighting

[1] *Bibliographical Note.* By far the best statistics on the subjects included in this chapter are to be found in the publications of the Labour

organisation for the purpose of securing to the labourer the highest possible wages, reasonable hours of work, and the best conditions under which to work. It comprises in its membership only a fraction of the labouring class, but its influence extends far beyond this membership. It is of great interest, therefore, to know the number of trade unionists, the financial resources of unions, the trades in which they are most prominently represented, the way their money is spent, and the result of their action.

The best statistics we have of trade unions are the returns made to the English Board of Trade by the trade unions of Great Britain. These are returns by the unions themselves, but they are carefully edited and compared from year to year, so that they are, probably, reasonably complete and trustworthy.

The returns for 1897 were as follows (Tenth Report by

Department of the Board of Trade, viz. :—the Annual Report by the Chief Labour Correspondent of the Board of Trade on Trade Unions, 1886—, which gives the number and membership of registered and unregistered trade unions, details of 100 principal trade unions, and statistics of federations of trade unions and trade councils; the Annual Report of the Labour Department on Strikes and Lockouts, 1888— ; First Report of Proceedings under the Conciliation (trade disputes) Act, 1896. The Board has published, also, a special report on Profit-sharing, 1894, and on Gain-sharing and certain other Systems of Bonus on Production, 1895. For these and also for statistics of conciliation and arbitration, co-operation, profit-sharing, and friendly societies, see Abstract of Labour Statistics, contained in the Annual Report of the Labour Department of the Board of Trade.

For the United States see the two great reports on Strikes and Lockouts made by the Department of Labour in 1886 and 1894. See, also, Ninth Annual Report on Building and Loan Associations, 1893. For profit-sharing see Reports of the Massachusetts Bureau of Labour Statistics. Gilman, Profit-sharing in the United States, 1889.

For France see Statistique des Grèves. For Germany, Conrad's Handwörterbuch, Articles, Gewerkvereine and Arbeitseinstellungen. For Italy, Statistica degli Scioperi.

There are numerous books and essays on all these subjects, references to the principal of which will be found in Palgrave's Dictionary of Political Economy under the several heads.

Chief Labour Correspondent of Board of Trade on Trade Unions, 1897, p. xvii.):—

NUMBER AND MEMBERSHIP OF ALL UNIONS, 1897.

Groups of Trade Unions.	No. of Trade Unions.	No. of Branches.	Members at end of 1897. Number.	Per cent. of total.
Metal, engineering, and ship-building	272	2,433	317,518	20
Mining and quarrying	64	1,543	282,432	17
Building	138	3,034	219,072	14
Textile	244	499	217,217	14
Railway, dock, and other transport	65	1,268	183,418	11
General labour	16	744	92,858	6
Clothing	48	652	75,617	5
Printing and bookbinding	54	350	52,527	3
Public employment	37	873	45,157	3
Woodworking and furnishing	115	559	38,401	2
All other unions	234	1,380	85,692	5
Total	1,287	13,335	1,609,909	100

Of the 1,609,909 members of trade unions at the end of 1897, 1,490,134 or 93 per cent. were males and 119,775 or 7 per cent. were females. The latter mainly belonged to the cotton trade, the textile group of industries including, altogether, 91 per cent. of the whole number of female trade unionists. It is estimated that about 21 per cent. of male adults and about 12 per cent. of female adults employed in factories and workshops are members of trade unions.

It appears that the mean age of all existing unions is about twenty years. The larger societies appear to be the oldest, the mean age of the one hundred principal unions being thirty-five and of the remaining 1,182 smaller unions, about nineteen years only.

The number and membership of trade unions appear to

be fluctuating. The figures for six years are as follows (*Ibid.*, p. xlviii.):—

Year.	No.	Membership.
1892	1,203	1,500,451
1893	1,250	1,478,474
1894	1,290	1,437,765
1895	1,303	1,404,898
1896	1,308	1,491,007
1897	1,287	1,609,909

The fluctuating number is due to the fact that there are small trade unions which come into existence and disappear every year. Still further, the total membership fluctuates somewhat according to the state of trade. A depression in the state of employment is generally followed by a falling off in trade union membership, and the revival of trade by a corresponding increase. The larger unions show a pretty steady increase, amounting to 17·2 per cent. in the membership of the 100 principal unions, from 1892 to 1897.

If we compare the changes in membership of the trade unions in different occupations, we shall find great fluctuations. The membership of the building trades shows an uninterrupted increase from 160,594 in 1892 to 219,072 in 1897. The trade unions in the metal, engineering, and shipbuilding trades are large and important and show a tendency to increase. The membership of the unions in the textile trades, in printing, and in woodworking and furnishing is very steady. On the other hand, the unions connected with transport show remarkable fluctuations. In 1892 the societies classified under this heading numbered 54, with 150,996 members. In 1895 the number was 60, but the membership had fallen to 119,108. Since then the number has increased. The unions of agricultural labourers and fishermen collapsed in 1894–95, the number of members falling from 36,279 in 1892 to 3,546 in 1896.

The comparative tables showing financial details are based on the accounts of one hundred selected societies from 1892 to 1897. The principal items for these one hundred principal unions are as follows (*Ibid.*, p. lvii.):—

Year.		Income.	Expenditure.	Funds at end of Year.	Membership at end of Year.
		£	£	£	
1892		1,455,885	1,418,311	1,618,790	903,981
1893		1,614,379	1,848,159	1,385,010	910,119
1894		1,629,550	1,433,867	1,580,693	924,584
1895		1,557,667	1,390,717	1,747,643	914,766
1896		1,673,571	1,233,494	2,187,720	961,026
1897		1,981,971	1,896,072	2,273,619	1,059,609
Percentage Increase of 1897	over 1896	+ 18·4	+ 53·7	+ 3·9	+ 10·3
	over 1892	+ 36·1	+ 33·7	+ 40·5	+ 17·2

The income is mainly derived from the contributions of the members, which vary a good deal in the different societies according to the benefits paid. In 44 of the 100 societies with 412,585 members the average contribution per member during 1897 was less than £1 sterling; in 35 societies with 366,902 members it was £1 and under £2; in the remaining 21 societies with 280,122 members it was £2 and upwards. The mean annual amount contributed per member during the six years, 1892–97, was 31*s.* 6½*d.*

The expenditure was distributed as follows:—

	Amount.	Per cent. of total.
Expenditure in 1892–7 on:	£	
Dispute pay	2,171,271	23½
Unemployed and other benefits	5,466,903	59½
Working expenses	1,582,446	17
	£9,220,620	100

It appears from this table that unemployed and other benefits was the chief item of expenditure. The amount spent in this and other directions fluctuates very much according to the state of employment. This is shown in the following table (*Ibid.*, p. lx.):—

Class of Expenditure.	Amount of Expenditure in					
	1892.	1893.	1894.	1895.	1896.	1897.
	£	£	£	£	£	£
Unemployed, &c. benefits . .	351,512	462,501	461,189	436,234	284,406	542,224
Dispute benefits	352,500	584,800	160,160	186,404	153,907	433,500
Sick & accident benefits . .	210,243	241,638	230,233	263,966	246,778	269,784
Superannuation benefits . .	102,432	112,588	122,434	131,861	142,518	152,207
Funeral benefits	68,589	75,343	70,104	76,443	75,858	82,156
Other benefits & grants . .	78,682	120,133	136,695	45,265	61,996	110,881
Working, &c. expenses . .	254,353	251,156	253,052	250,544	268,021	305,320
	1,418,311	1,848,159	1,433,867	1,390,717	1,233,494	1,896,072

It will be seen from this table that unemployed and dispute benefits reached a maximum in 1893. They again assumed large proportions in 1897 on account of the engineering strike. Sick and accident benefits remain pretty steady, while superannuation benefits tend to increase. The following table shows still more clearly the fluctuations in expenditure under different heads (*Ibid.*, p. lx.):—

Class of Expenditure.	Percentage of Expenditure.					
	1892.	1893.	1894.	1895.	1896.	1897.
Unemployed, &c., benefits	24·8	25·0	32·2	31·4	23·1	28·6
Dispute benefits . . .	24·9	31·6	11·2	13·4	12·5	22·9
Sick and accident benefits	14·8	13·1	16·1	19·0	20·0	14·2
Superannuation benefits	7·2	6·1	8·5	9·5	11·6	8·0
Funeral benefits	4·8	4·1	4·9	5·5	6·1	4·3
Other benefits and grants	5·6	6·5	9·5	3·2	5·0	5·9
Working, &c., expenses .	17·9	13·6	17·6	18·0	21·7	16·1
Total	100·0	100·0	100·0	100·0	100·0	100·0

The expenditure per member fluctuated from 25*s.* 8*d.* in 1896 to 40*s.* 7½*d.* in 1893. The dispute benefit reached its maximum, 12*s.* 11½*d.*, in 1893, while it decreased to 3*s.* 2½*d.* in 1896.

The statistics for other countries are not comparable with those of England, because the form of organisation is very different. In Germany the total number of trade unionists is put down as 221,030. The total expenditure was 2,036,026 marks.[1]

In France, the so-called Syndicates have a different character from the English trade unions. They are legalised unions of members of the same trade or profession. Among others there were 2,178 labour syndicates, comprising 408,025 members.[2]

In the United States there is a great variety of labour organisations, and the numbers are uncertain. Among the more important are:—

(1) The American Federation of Labour with 350,000 members, among which are the Brotherhood of Carpenters and Joiners with 51,313; the Amalgamated Association of Iron and Steel Workers with 30,000; the International Typographical Union with 29,000; the Cigar Makers International Union with 24,000; the United Mine Workers with 20,000; the Journeymen Tailors of America with 16,000; the Brotherhood of Painters and Decorators with 16,694; the Lasters Protective Union with 10,000; the Boiler Makers International Union with 10,000 members.

(2) The Knights of Labour with 205,000 members.

(3) A number of Unions which do not belong to either of the Central Unions, with 266,871 members. Among these are the International Bricklayers and Stonemakers Union with 35,000; the Brotherhood of Locomotive Engineers with 31,000; the Brotherhood of Locomotive Firemen with 25,071; the Brotherhood of Railroad Trainmen with 23,500; the Order of Railway Telegraphers with 22,506; the Granite

[1] Conrad's Handwörterbuch. Supplementband I., Art. Gewerkvereine.

[2] *Ibid.*

Cutters National Union with 20,000; the Operative Plasterers Union with 14,000; the Musicians National League with 11,000; the Order of Railroad Conductors with 10,000; the National Association of Machinists with 10,000; the Brotherhood of Railroad Carmen with 10,000.

(4) There are 14 unions of which it is not known whether they belong to the Federation or not, with 55,900 members.

(5) Other smaller unions estimated at 50,000.

These unions together make up 926,900 members, of which about 25,000 are probably numbered twice. The result seems to be that probably there are between 800,000 and 900,000 trade unionists in the United States, which is supposed to be about 10 per cent. of the wage-receiving class.

Strikes and Lockouts. The weapon of the trade union is the strike, that is the cessation of work in the hope that the employer can find no other workmen, and will thus be obliged to yield to the demands of the union or lose his profit, his business connection, and eventually, perhaps, his capital The lockout is an aggressive movement on the part of the employer to refuse work to his men except under such conditions as he sets, the penalty being that they lose their wages, that is, their means of livelihood.

It has been found difficult in many cases to distinguish between a strike and a lockout. It has generally been supposed that if the employees took the initiative it would be a strike, and if the employer took the initiative it would be a lockout. But in many cases the real provocation comes from one side, while the overt action is taken by the other. For instance, an employer announces a reduction of wages, and the employees strike against such reduction. This is a strike, but the provocation comes from the employer. So also in case where a trade union announces that it will withdraw 20 per cent. of its men unless its demands are acceded to, and the employer chooses to shut down his whole business; this is a lockout nominally, but in reality it is a strike. The truth is that the distinction between strike and lockout is not important, and at any rate cannot be used to fix the responsibility for a strike. Hence the English Labour Department has abandoned the distinction, and speaks only of "labour disputes."

The analytical study of the action of trade unions in strikes brings up the fundamental questions of distribution of wealth, of the fixing of wages, of the relations of employers and employees, of the rights of other labourers—in short, of the working of the whole modern industrial organisation To such a study statistics can contribute but little. That little, however, is of considerable importance in enabling us to get more precise notions in regard to the causes of labour disputes, the effectiveness of the trade union weapon, the strike, and the losses inflicted upon the community by this industrial warfare. We therefore collect statistics of the number of strikes, the number of businesses involved, the trades most concerned, the number of men thrown out of employment, the length of time lost, the success or failure of the strike, and the losses suffered by employers, employees, and the general public.

The Number of Strikes. It is a little difficult to determine the number of strikes. A strike may be in a single establishment or it may be the strike of a great union extending over a large number of establishments. The number of strikes is not significant unless we know also the number of men thrown out of employment. For while one strike may involve thousands of men, another may be a petty affair involving a dozen men in a small workshop. It seems best, therefore, to give not only the number of strikes, but the number of establishments, and also the number of employees thrown out of employment. The statistics for the United States are as follows (Tenth Annual Report of the

Commissioner of Labour, 1894, Strikes and Lockouts, Vol. I., p. 16):—

STRIKES, BY YEARS, JANUARY 1, 1881, TO JUNE 30, 1894.

Year.	Strikes.	Establishments.	Average establishments to a strike.	Employees thrown out of employment.
1881	471	2,928	6·2	129,521
1882	454	2,105	4·6	154,671
1883	478	2,759	5·8	149,763
1884	443	2,367	5·3	147,054
1885	645	2,284	3·5	242,705
1886	1,432	10,053	7·0	508,044
1887	1,436	6,589	4·6	379,676
1888	906	3,506	3·9	147,704
1889	1,075	3,786	3·5	249,559
1890	1,833	9,424	5·1	351,944
1891	1,717	8,116	4·7	298,939
1892	1,298	5,540	4·3	206,671
1893	1,305	4,555	3·5	265,914
1894 (6 mo.)	896	5,154	5·8	482,066
Total . . .	14,389	69,166	4·8	3,714,231

It appears from this table that during the 13½ years there were 14,389 strikes, involving 69,166 establishments, and throwing 3,714,231 employees out of work. This latter number may not represent different individuals, because two or more strikes may have occurred in the same establishment during the period. But it serves as a general index of the frequency of strikes. The variations from year to year are best measured by this figure.

During this same period lockouts occurred in 6,067 establishments, by which 366,690 employees were thrown out of employment.

In regard to sex, 91·2 per cent. of the employees thrown out of employment by strikes were males and 8 per cent. were females; in lockouts, 77·5 per cent. were males and 22·5 per cent. were females.

In regard to locality, the largest number of establishments affected by strikes was in New York, 18,786, followed by Illinois with 12,828, and Pennsylvania with 10,661. The States appear in the same order in lockouts. If we add to these three States, Massachusetts and Ohio, the five States cover 71·2 per cent. of all the establishments in which strikes occurred, and 80·9 per cent. of all the establishments in which lockouts occurred. These are, of course, the great industrial centres containing 51 per cent. of all the manufacturing establishments, and employing 56 per cent. of all the capital invested in the mechanical industries of the United States, taking the census of 1890 as the basis of computation. In the same way, during the 7½ years from January 1st, 1887, to June 30th, 1894, it is shown that 61·2 per cent. of the establishments involved in strikes were situated in 26 cities. Seven of the cities, viz., New York, Brooklyn, Chicago, Boston, Allegheny, Pittsburg and Philadelphia, reported 4,561 strikes, or 43·5 per cent. of all the strikes which occurred in the United States during the period, and 22,248 establishments, or 47·5 per cent. of the whole number of establishments involved. These figures simply show, of course, the predominance of strikes in industrial communities.

The report asserts (p. 23) that during the six years from 1881 to 1886, 82·2 per cent., and that during the 7½ years, 1887–1894, 69·6 per cent. of the strikes were ordered by labour organisations.

The object of a strike is to compel the employer to cease from business, that is, to close his establishment either temporarily or permanently. It appears that during the 13½ years, out of a total of 69,166 establishments in which strikes occurred, 41,197 or 59·6 per cent. were closed, while of the 6,067 establishments subjected to lockouts, 3,877 or 64 per cent. were closed. The average duration of stoppage or days closed in the case of strikes was 22·5 days; while in the case of lockouts, it was 32·8 days. These figures apply only to establishments entirely closed.

The duration of strikes or lockouts themselves, that is, the average length of time which elapsed before all the establishments resumed operations or were running normally, differs somewhat from the above figures. In the case of strikes, it was 25·4 days, and in the case of lockouts it was 47·6 days.

Causes of Strikes. It is very important to know what are the causes inducing employees to strike. It is somewhat difficult to analyse the different causes, because they run into each other, and often more than one cause is involved. The chief causes, however, are always those pertaining to wages and hours of work. The report for 1887 shows that the causes leading to strikes during the 6 years, 1881–1886, were:—for increase of wages, 42·3 per cent.; for reduction of hours, 19·5 per cent.; against reduction of wages, 7·8 per cent.; for increase of wages and reduction of hours, 7·6 per cent. The four causes covered 77·2 per cent. of the establishments.

The following table, showing the number and per cent. of establishments falling under each of the seventeen principal causes during the period of 7½ years, 1887–1894, brings out a complete analysis (*Ibid.*, p. 29):—

LEADING CAUSES OF STRIKES, 1887–1894.

	Establishments.	Per cent.
For increase of wages	12,041	25·69
For reduction of hours	6,199	13·23
Against reduction of wages	3,830	8·17
In sympathy with strikes elsewhere	3,620	7·73
For increase of wages and reduction of hours	3,095	6·60
Against employment of non-union men	1,688	3·60
For adoption of new scale	1,559	3·33
For recognition of union	1,314	2·80
For adoption of union scale	844	1·80
For adoption of union rules and union scale	783	1·67
For increase of wages and recognition of union	686	1·46
To compel World's Fair directors to employ none but union men in building trades	472	1·01
For reinstatement of discharged employees	467	1·00
For payment of wages overdue	383	·82
For increase of wages and reduction of hours on Saturday	378	·81
Against being compelled to board with employer, and for reduction of hours and recognition of union	366	·78
For increase of wages according to agreement	359	·77
Total of 17 leading causes	38,084	81·27
All other causes (574)	8,778	18·73
Total for the United States	46,862	100·00

This table shows how numerous are the causes which may lead to strikes, and, on the other hand, how most of them are connected with the question of wages. The number of sympathetic strikes is significant, and also the number against employment of non-union men, and for recognition of the union. These show the strength of the trade union feeling.

The Success of Strikes. It is somewhat difficult to measure whether a strike is successful or not, because, very often, it is compromised, and in other cases both sides claim the victory. For the 13½ years ending June 30th, 1894, out of a total of 69,166 establishments affected by strikes, the employees were successful in gaining their demands in 30,772, or 44·5 per cent.; they partly succeeded in 7,779, or 11·3 per cent.; while in 30,596 establishments, or 44·2 per cent., they failed. In the lockouts it appears that the employers were successful in 40·3 per cent. of the cases; in 9·6 per cent. they were partly successful; while in 47·8 per cent. they failed. The above result is not very satisfactory, because strikes are of varying importance. If we take the number of employees thrown out of employment as a better method of measurement, it appears that in the successful strikes 32 per cent. of the employees thus thrown out of employment were involved; in partly successful strikes, 12·5 per cent.; in strikes which failed, 55·5 per cent. This would seem to show that strikes, on the whole, were unsuccessful.

Losses by Strikes. The United States Report for 1894 tried to estimate the losses of employees and employers through strikes and lockouts. The loss to employees consists of the wage loss during the duration of the strike and the assistance given to strikers by other labour organisations. It cannot be pretended that these figures are exact. In some cases, the employees do not find work again until long after the strike is ended. In other cases, they make up for part of the loss by increased employment and by higher wages. The loss of employers is even more difficult to estimate. In some cases, they lose not only the profit on work which they are not able to turn out, but they lose valuable contracts, and in some cases their business is ruined or suffers a blow from which it takes years to recover. In other cases, a period of activity after the strike enables the employer to recover his losses. The money sums, therefore, given in the following table, must be regarded as the merest estimates (*Ibid.*, p. 31):—

Wage loss of employees	in strikes .	$163,807,657	
	in lock-outs .	26,685,516	
Total wage loss			$190,493,173
Assistance to employees by labour organisations . . .			13,438,704
Loss to employers			94,825,237
Total loss			$298,757,114

Labour Disputes in Great Britain. The Labour Department of the English Board of Trade publishes an annual report on the labour disputes of the preceding year. In 1897 there were 864 such disputes, affecting, directly and indirectly, 230,267 workpeople, and aggregating 10,345,523 working days. The variations from year to year in the number of people involved and the duration of the strike are shown in the following table (Report, Strikes and Lockouts, 1897, p. xiii):—

Year.	Number of workpeople affected directly and indirectly.	Aggregate duration in working days.
1893	636,386	31,205,062
1894	324,245	9,322,096
1895	263,758	5,542,562
1896	198,687	3,748,525
1897	230,267	10,345,523
1898[1]	246,540	14,564,000

[1] From "Labour Gazette."

The trades in which labour disputes chiefly occur are shown in the following table for 1897 (*Ibid.*, p. lxx):—

	No. of Disputes.	Number of work-people affected.	Aggregate duration in working days.
Building trades	193	15,047	353,348
Mining and quarrying	127	49,392	1,445,843
Metal, engineering, and ship-building	229	97,189	7,141,289
Textile trades	108	37,001	677,615
Clothing trades	56	7,016	301,082
Transport trades	48	12,523	76,497
Miscellaneous trades	95	11,734	348,459
Employees of local authorities	8	365	1,390
Total	864	230,267	10,345,523

It will be seen from this table that disputes are numerous in the building trades, but that they do not involve a very large number of employees. The large disputes are in mining and in engineering. The year 1897 was characterised by the great engineering dispute, which accounted for 6,000,000 of the working days lost, out of a grand total of something over 10,000,000.

Of the total number of workpeople affected in 1897 by disputes, 10·6 per cent. were women and 7 per cent. were young persons of either sex. Nearly all of the women were employed in the textile trades, where they constituted 55·3 per cent. of the persons affected by disputes in those trades, young persons constituting 22 per cent.

It is of interest to show what proportion of the working population belonging to certain groups of trades is directly and indirectly affected by labour disputes. As the single year is very apt to be abnormal, the following percentage is calculated on the mean of the years 1893–97. The percentages are as follows (*Ibid.*, p. xiii):—

Industry.	Per cent. of all employees.
Building trades	2·1
Mining and quarrying	22·0
Metal, engineering, and shipbuilding	4·5
Textile trades	3·6
Clothing trades	2·7
Printing trades	0·2
Woodworking trades	0·7
Glass, pottery and chemical trades	1·4
Food and tobacco trades	0·2
All of the above trades	5·6

For the year 1897 the proportion of the working population in the above trades engaged in disputes was 3·8 per cent. No disputes of any magnitude were reported during the five years affecting agricultural labourers, seamen and fishermen; and when the large numbers employed in these industries are brought into the calculation, the proportion of the total working population affected by disputes falls to about 2 per cent. in 1897, and a little over 3 per cent. in 1893–7. On the whole, the number of the industrial classes annually engaged in labour disputes is not very large.

The causes of disputes show the same predominance of the question of wages as in the figures for the United States. The percentage varies from year to year, owing very often to a single large dispute being classed under one head. The variations for the last five years are shown in the following table (*Ibid.*, p. xviii):—

Principal Cause.	1893.	1894.	1895.	1896.	1897.
Wages	89·2	72·4	54·3	58·3	46·2
Hours of labour	0·2	1·9	1·1	1·8	22·9
Employment of particular classes of persons	1·2	1·1	1·7	3·8	8·5
Working arrangements	4·0	11·7	32·0	16·7	16·6
Trade unionism	3·0	4·8	2·5	6·0	3·5
Other causes	2·4	8·1	8·4	13·4	2·3
	100·0	100·0	100·0	100·0	100·0

In the above table the large percentage under the head of wages for 1893 was owing to the bad times; in 1897 the large percentage under hours of labour was owing to the engineering dispute.

The general results of labour disputes expressed in percentages of the workpeople directly and indirectly affected by all disputes is shown in the following table:—

Results.	1894.	1895.	1896.	1897.	1898.
In favour of the workpeople	22·1	24·1	39·5	21·6	24·4
In favour of the employers	42·1	27·9	33·4	44·5	56·5
Compromised	34·2	47·1	26·9	32·7	15·8
Indefinite or unsettled	1·6	0·9	0·2	1·2	3·3
	100·0	100·0	100·0	100·0	100·0

Here, too, the percentages are affected by the termination of single large disputes like the engineering strike in 1897.

The English report gives an interesting analysis of the method of settlement of disputes. The results for 1897 were typical. Six hundred and twenty-four disputes, affecting 187,048 workpeople, or over 81 per cent. of the total number involved in all disputes, were settled by direct arrangement or negotiation between the parties or their representatives. Fourteen disputes, involving 9,756 persons, were settled by arbitration, and 27 disputes involving 9,544 persons were settled by conciliation and mediation. The rest were settled by return to work on employers' terms, by replacement of workpeople, by closing of works, or left unsettled.[1]

[1] In France in 1897 there were reported 356 strikes, affecting 2,568 establishments, participated in by 68,875 strikers, resulting in a loss of 780,944 working days, including 60,433 days lost by 5,999 persons who were not strikers. The average time lost per strike was 10½ days, the smallest average reported in five years. Having regard to the number of strikers, 28·8 per cent. of the strikes succeeded, 41·8 per cent. succeeded partly, and 29·4 per cent. failed. Of the total 68,875 persons engaged in strikes, 31 per cent. were employed in agriculture, forestry and fisheries; 24 per cent. in building trades; 12 per cent. in the textile industries; and 10 per cent. in mining. Considering the number of persons engaged in the various industries, the relative prevalence of strikes was greatest in the mining and quarrying industries, the building trades coming next. (Statistique des Grèves, 1897; Résumé given in the Bulletin of the U.S. Department of Labour, No. 19, November 1898, p. 860.)

In Austria in 1896 there were reported 294 strikes involving 1,403 establishments, 36,114 strikers, and resulting in 595,768 days lost. Of the strikers only 3,046 succeeded, 22,314 succeeded partly, and 10,754 failed. Wages and hours were the principal causes. (Arbeitseinstellungen und Aussperrungen im Gewerbebetriebe in Oesterreich während 1896; Résumé given in Bulletin of the U.S. Department of Labour, No. 17, July 1898, p. 618.)

In Italy in 1896 there were 210 strikes, involving 96,151 workpeople, and 1,152,503 days lost. In 79 cases the operatives were wholly successful, in 51 they were successful in part, and in 80 they were wholly unsuccessful. There were also 6 lockouts, involving 2,267 men and a loss of 18,243 days, There were 50 strikes in textile industries, 82 in mining, metallurgical and mechanical industries, 18 in building trades, 26 in the clothing trades, and 34 in other trades. (Annuario Statistico, 1898, p. 166.)

Employers' Associations. The trade union is a fighting association of employees in particular trades, for the purpose of collective bargaining and safeguarding the interests of the working class. The natural weapon is the strike against individual employers who do not accede to the demands of the union. As the individual workman without his trade union is at the mercy of the more powerful employer; so the single employer if standing alone, is often at the mercy of the trade union, which controls the labour force in the entire trade. The policy of the union very often takes on the form of attacking one employer after another. The men in a single establishment go out on a strike, and are supported by a contribution from the wages of the men continuing at work with the other employers. It is not surprising, therefore, that the employers in their turn should associate themselves together for mutual aid. It is not easy to ascertain how extensively employers are organised. Such association is often brought about by secret agreement, by temporary union in an emergency, by tacit agreement to resist extreme demands, or by a system of black-listing men who have been engaged in disputes with other employers.

The Labour Department of the Board of Trade publishes a grand total of 675 associations of employers in the United Kingdom, excluding associations purely for purposes of trade protection, insurance, and the diffusion of information or the advancement of technical knowledge. These associations were divided as follows among the trades:—building trades, 319; mining and quarrying, 28; metal, engineering and shipbuilding trades, 90; textile trades, 41; clothing trades, 63; miscellaneous trades, 134.[1]

Arbitration and Conciliation. The strike is a very wasteful method of settling disputes between employers and employees. It brings loss to the employee in the shape of reduced income, and to the employer in the form of reduced profits. In many cases, also, there are after-effects of

[1] Abstract of Labour Statistics, 1896-7, p. 22.

the most disastrous character, such as industrial displacement, the breaking up of homes, weakness and disease engendered by lack of proper subsistence, habits of dissipation and idleness, and even chronic pauperism on the side of the employee; permanent loss of business connection, destruction of credit, discouragement, failure and bankruptcy on the part of the employer; destruction of property, loss of life, birth of social hatred and discontent on the part of the whole community. It is, therefore, natural to ask whether such a violent and destructive method of settling disputes cannot be avoided, and more peaceful methods substituted. The obvious suggestion is to either compromise the matter by mutual concession, or refer it to a disinterested third party for decision. The first is what is known as conciliation; the second is arbitration. They correspond to diplomacy and arbitration in international relations. Conciliation is where the employers and their men, or rather representatives from each side, meet for friendly discussion of grievances or demands, and come to an arrangement to which both parties can accede. Arbitration is where the two opposing parties refer the matter in dispute to a disinterested third party and agree to abide by his decision. Theoretically the two methods are entirely distinct, but practically they often run into each other. A board established for arbitration often tries to bring about a voluntary agreement between the parties to the dispute, and thus becomes a board of conciliation; while a board of conciliation, in order to avoid deadlocks, may agree to subject matters of less importance to arbitration. The reason for this is that there are certain points of dispute which neither employer nor employee is willing to leave absolutely to arbitration. These are in respect to the rate of wages. If the arbitrator should fix a rate of wages lower than is necessary for the subsistence of the labourer, the latter cannot possibly accept it, and no outward force can compel him to work against his will. On the other hand, if the rate of wages is fixed so high that the employer is bound to lose money, he cannot submit to the decision, and no outward force can compel him to continue his business at a loss. In all such cases arbitration must give way to conciliation. There are, however, many minor matters, such as the adjustment of penalties for spoiling goods, fines for tardiness in beginning work, observance of holidays, &c., where there is a difference of opinion between employer and employee, but which it is important to settle one way or another in order to avoid friction and misunderstanding. In such cases conciliation may result in arbitration.

Conciliation and arbitration have, of course, been made use of between individual employers and employees from time immemorial. No statistical enumeration of these cases is possible. It is only when semi-official or at least public boards of arbitration and conciliation are established that their activity can be followed.

Historically the most famous system of conciliation and arbitration is the French Conseil de Prud'hommes. It is a local board consisting of representatives elected in equal numbers by masters and men, the election being conducted by the Maire and Préfet. These boards deal mostly with petty matters. They adjust about 40,000 cases a year (1892), 60 per cent. relating to wages—not as to future, but past wages,—13 per cent. to dismissals, 10 per cent. to alleged misbehaviour, 5 per cent. to apprenticeship, 13 per cent. to other matters.[1]

In England boards of conciliation were introduced as early as 1869, especially in the iron trade in the North of England, and there are now permanent boards of conciliation and arbitration in many trades.[2] The number of cases dealt with

[1] Palgrave, Dictionary of Political Economy, Art. Conseils de Prud'hommes.

[2] See L. L. Price, Industrial Peace, 1887. Also two articles by same author, in Journal of the Royal Stat. Soc., Vol. LIII., 1890, pp. 290 and 420

by permanent boards was as follows (Abstract, Labour Statistics, 1897–98, p. 61):—

	1896.	1897.
Brought before the board	1,456	1,457
Withdrawn or otherwise settled	582	602
Number settled by conciliation	613	621
Number settled by arbitration	205	182
Total number settled	818	803

Corresponding total number settled in 1895	768
Corresponding total number settled in 1894	1,146

Conciliation and arbitration may be brought in even after industrial warfare has broken out. The Board of Trade Report shows, for instance, the following figures:—

NUMBER OF STRIKES AND LOCKOUTS SETTLED BY CONCILIATION OR ARBITRATION IN EACH OF THE YEARS 1893–97.

	Settled by Conciliation.		Settled by Arbitration.		Total Number.	
	Number of disputes.	Number of persons affected (so far as reported).	Number of disputes.	Number of persons affected.	Number of disputes.	Number of persons affected.
1893	5	306,748	20	5,261	25	312,009
1894	19	5,683	23	12,642	42	18,325
1895	17	50,953	28	7,945	45	58,898
1896	25	20,439	20	10,280	45	30,719
1897	29	10,244	11	9,197	40	19,441

Co-operation. By the term co-operation is understood an association of working men for the purpose of carrying on business for themselves, thereby getting not only wages, but interest on capital and the profit which would otherwise go to the employer. Great expectations have been entertained in respect to co-operation as a solution of modern industrial problems. The employer is excluded, and hence there can no longer be disputes between employers and employees. The actual labourers will reap the full reward of their energy and enterprise, and will thus advance their material condition. They will be incited to careful, honest work, to avoiding waste of material and abuse of machinery, and thus the total and net product will be increased. The responsibilities and cares of management will have an educational effect, and give them an intelligent interest in their work.

Co-operation has not realised, altogether, these bright expectations. The difficulties seem to be the lack of sufficient capital, disinclination to pay the high salaries necessary to get the best talent for management, the danger of dissolution during periods of industrial depression, and the inability to hold one's own in the excessive and cut-throat competition of modern times.

Co-operative associations are commonly divided into two classes, namely, those for distribution and those for production. The former, commonly known as co-operative stores, are the more important. This movement has reached the greatest magnitude in the United Kingdom. The general summary for all societies is as follows (Abstract, Labour Statistics, 1897–8, p. 23):—

Number of societies in existence	1,822
,, ,, making returns	1,710
Members (in societies making returns)	1,512,128
Percentage to population of United Kingdom	3·8
Capital, share	£19,269,732
,, loan	£3,715,093
Amount of sales [1]	£59,881,039

The distribution societies making returns for the United Kingdom numbered 1,483, with a membership of 1,468,682, and sales amounting to £40,175,774.

It appears that there were only 223 societies established primarily for production, although 582 societies established primarily for distribution also engage in production. The number of persons employed in production was 29,668, and the value of goods sold by productive societies, or transferred from production to distribution department, was £9,451,572. The principal industries represented were bread making and

[1] Exclusive of value of goods (amounting to £6,202,983) produced by wholesale and retail societies and transferred to their distribution departments.

confectionery, boots and shoes, dressmaking and millinery, and tailoring, mantle and shirt-making.

The following is an analysis of the business of the Co-operative Associations for production (*Ibid.*, p. 32):—

	1896.	1897.
Number of societies making returns	192	214
Number of members in the societies making returns	32,285	35,276
Capital—		
Share	£477,417	£520,524
Loan	425,216	505,117
Reserve	63,987	73,358
Amount of sales	1,828,312	1,984,187
Profit—		
Amount including interest on shares, but not on loans	£88,753	£101,018
Percentage on share and loan capital	9·8	9·8

The profits of co-operation are divided in two ways: first, as dividends on the share capital; and secondly as dividends paid to purchasers in proportion to the amount purchased. This last form amounts, of course, to a simple reduction in price. The rate of dividends upon purchases paid to members by Workmen's Co-operative Associations for Distribution in the United Kingdom (excluding the wholesale societies) was on the average 2*s.* 7¾*d.* per pound sterling. The Report states that with few exceptions the companies pay dividends to non-members at one-half the rates paid to members.

The distribution of profit by 79 of the productive societies for the year 1897 was as follows:—

	£
To Members on capital	20,037
,, Customers on purchases	52,590
,, Workers on wages	13,150
Total	85,777

In the English system the associations themselves co-operate in forming wholesale societies for the purpose of purchasing, in some cases of producing, their own supplies. The English Wholesale Society is a federation which, at the end of 1897, included 1,046 Co-operative Associations, comprising 1,053,564 members. Its net sales amounted to £11,920,143. The Scottish Society included 290 Co-operative Associations, comprising 211,859 members, and its net sales were £4,405,854. The Irish Co-operative Agency included 31 agricultural and dairying societies; the number of members is not specified; the net sales amounted to £116,238.[1]

In addition to the above societies there are in the United Kingdom (1895) 2,373 Building Societies, with total liabilities amounting to £42,350,503.[2]

Profit-Sharing. Co-operation, especially in production, meets great difficulty in securing sufficient capital and the best talent for management in order to compete with private enterprise. To remedy these defects the scheme of profit-sharing has been proposed. This consists simply in allotting to the workman a certain share of the profits (after capital has been fairly remunerated) which will be a bonus in addition to his wages. By this scheme the advantages of single leadership and energy are retained, while the workman gains in increased pay and in intelligent interest in his work. At the same time, there is increased production due to cessation of all deliberate waste of time, to diminution in the cost of supervision, to saving effected by more careful handling of tools and machinery, and there is improvement in the quality of the production due to increased intelligence. Profit-sharing would, therefore, seem to combine the advantages of private enterprise and of co-operative production.

Profit-sharing has been tried a great many times, but very seldom with lasting or brilliant success. The Labour

[1] Abstract, Labour Statistics, 1897-8, p. 40.

[2] For co-operation in other countries, see Statistics of Co-operative Societies in Various Countries, prepared by the International Co-operative Alliance, 1898; Bemis, Co-operative Distribution (Bulletin, U.S. Department of Labour, No. 6, September, 1896, p. 610); Crüger, Der heutige Stand der Erwerbs- und Wirtschaftsgenossenschaften. (Conrad's Jahrbücher, Vol. LXV., 1895, p. 823.)

Department of the British Board of Trade has tried to trace as far as possible the profit-sharing schemes which have been started in that country. It has a record of 177 that have been started since 1865. Of these 77 have ceased to exist; in regard to 7 no particulars could be obtained; while 93 were known to be still in operation on June 30th, 1898. In these 93 enterprises there were employed, in 1898, 49,367 persons. These schemes are found in a variety of trades, especially in engineering and shipbuilding, in printing, in food and tobacco, and even in agriculture. In regard to the rate of profit, we have returns from 72 enterprises having 22,308 employees. Of these employees only 14,711 participated in the profit-sharing. The mean bonus in all cases was 7·2 per cent. on wages, or 11·4 per cent. on wages in the cases in which bonus was paid, taking into account the number of participants in each case.

From this summary it appears that profit-sharing is not very important in the United Kingdom.

An attempt is also made in the case of the 77 failures to assign a cause for the cessation. Most of these causes are very general. For instance, there were 19 due to dissatisfaction of employers with results, 13 due to losses or want of success, 14 to liquidation or dissolution, 9 to apathy of, or disputes with employees.[1]

Friendly Societies. The ordinary working man is dependent upon his wages not only for present support, but also for the future. He may at any time lose his wages and thus become helpless. Still further, sickness, accident, or infirmity may stop the source of his income absolutely and for ever. He ordinarily acquires but little property, he often has a large family, his occupation brings with it liability to accident, and the sanitary surroundings in the tenement house often inflict an unusual amount of sickness upon his

[1] Abstract of Labour Statistics, 1897–8, p. 101. See also Report on Profit-Sharing, 1894; and Gain-Sharing, 1895, both published by the Board of Trade.

wife and children. When one considers that besides the ordinary risks of human life the factory operative is exposed to all the risks of trade, to the closing of the factory on account of dull times, to the interruption of business by war, to the cessation of labour by strikes and lockouts, to the loss of his position by misunderstanding or by his own misconduct, and that any one of these contingencies may at any time destroy his income, it would seem as if his position were intolerable.

Of course, in the last resort, the community aids with poor relief, and in other cases the church and charitable societies care for the unfortunates. But besides these, which may be considered as last resorts, the working man attempts, by voluntary association, to provide for the uncertain future. The trade union, as we have already seen, often assists its members in case of non-employment, of sickness, and of death. In addition there are numerous sick clubs, benefit societies, friendly and insurance societies, which apply the principle of mutual insurance. They take on numerous forms, from the village sick club, with its weekly dues and its aid to sick members, to the great mutual insurance companies comprising hundreds of thousands of members, and administering a regular system of sickness and life insurance. This movement is very strong in England, and although it is not probable that we have complete statistics of all these enterprises, yet, through the returns of the Registrar of Friendly Societies, we can form some estimate of the number of these associations, and of the extent of their operations. The latest statistics are for 1892, giving the number of societies and branches in existence as 29,742, of which 24,598 made returns comprising 8,320,262 members, and having funds to the amount of £26,003,061. The most prominent of these societies were the Independent Order of Odd Fellows, Manchester Unity, with a membership in 1897 of 698,328, and an income of £1,294,233; and the Ancient Order of Foresters, with a membership of 656,919, and an annual income of £1,240,559. The former society had, in 1897, £8,256,489 in accumulated funds, and paid out £746,540 in benefits; the figures for the second society are £5,327,476 and £773,360.[1]

The business of these societies has not always been conducted on sound actuarial principles, and the result has been that many of them have promised greater benefits than their scale of premiums would warrant. The report of the Registrar for 1895 showed that in 1892, out of 3,292 societies, 2,479 had estimated deficiencies, and in 116 of these the deficiency exceeded £4,000. A detailed account is given of the different societies and of their efforts to put themselves on a sound financial basis.[2]

The statistics of savings banks are of interest in this same connection as indicative of the efforts of the working classes to provide for the future. In the United Kingdom there were, in 1897, 7,239,761 accounts opened in post office savings banks, and £1,527,217 in trustee savings banks. The amount due to depositors was £115,896,786 in the post office savings banks, and £48,464,797 in trustee savings banks.[3]

Scientific Tests.

All statistics of voluntary associations are imperfect. This is especially true of labour-associations. Trade unions, benefit societies, co-operative stores, are often small and local. An exact account is seldom kept of the number of members, or even of the financial transactions. Their officers are generally unpaid members, with little time to keep elaborate

[1] Abstract of Labour Statistics, 1897–98, p. 50.

[2] Annual Reports of Registrar of Friendly Societies. E. W. Brabook, The Progress of Friendly Societies, &c. (Journal Roy. Stat. Soc., Vol. LVIII, 1895, p. 286).

[3] Abstract of Labour Statistics, 1897–98, p. 199. For other countries see Wolff, Savings Banks at Home and Abroad (Journal Roy. Stat. Soc., Vol. LX, 1897, p. 278). For the German insurance of working men, see Statistics and Sociology, p. 158.

records and little skill in preparing accounts. The societies are, many of them, ephemeral, formed for a particular emergency, often dissolved and the members scattered by some ill-luck. The records are consigned to private hands, are easily lost or disappear with a change of officers or the decline of the society. The real business of the society is looked upon as a private matter of the members, secrecy is observed, and the intrusion of others resented. Official inquiries shatter upon inability to get the addresses of the active officers, upon their inability to furnish exact information, or upon their disposition to exaggerate the size and influence of their membership.

Statistics in regard to the membership and resources of trade unions, are very imperfect in most countries. The membership varies according to circumstances. In good times it often increases, because men are at work and able to pay the dues. In bad times it decreases for the opposite reason. After an unsuccessful strike, many unions or branches of unions are broken up by the exhaustion of their funds and the dispersion of their members. The real test of membership should be the payment of dues; but much leniency is often exercised towards members in arrears, and they are kept on the rolls long after they have really ceased to be active members.

The indefiniteness and fluctuating character of the number of members is shown in the case of the Knights of Labour. In 1885 its membership was reported to be 110,000. The order received a great impetus by the part it played in the strikes of 1886, and whole trade unions reorganised themselves as assemblies of the Knights of Labour. It claimed, soon after, a membership of 1,250,000, and excited considerable apprehension lest it should attain the object of its ambition, namely, a universal union of all wage-earners. Its success was ephemeral. A few unsuccessful strikes and internal dissensions reduced its membership, until in 1892, it was said to be only 200,000. The round numbers ascribed to the various labour unions in the United States betray their character of mere estimates.

In England, where the unions are more compact and better organised, the returns made every year to the Board of Trade are more trustworthy.

The same remarks may be made in respect to the statistics of friendly and benefit societies, sick clubs, and co-operative enterprises. There are numerous small associations of which it is impossible to get complete statistics. It has been found advisable to confine the detailed statistics to the larger societies. In England the financial details apply to only one hundred of the principal trade unions, which, however, include 65 per cent. of the membership of all unions making returns. But the membership, sex of members, year of formation, and address of secretary are now given for 1,330 societies. If the other details were demanded of the smaller societies it would be impossible to get reports from them. Still further particulars are given for twenty of the larger trade unions.

In the matter of friendly societies, the number of societies in existence was said to be 29,742, of which 24,598 made returns. Particulars are given of nine important affiliated orders and centralised friendly societies in regard to membership, total income, accumulated funds, total benefits, and sick and funeral benefits. These may be called representative statistics.

The statistics of profit-sharing are equally difficult to get, because such schemes are looked upon as private business.

The statistics of strikes and lockouts are particularly difficult. As already said, it is often impossible to decide whether a given dispute is really a strike or a lockout. The definitions of a strike and of a lockout adopted by the United States Department of Labour are as follows:—

A strike occurs when the employees of an establishment refuse to work unless the management complies with some demand. A lockout occurs when the management refuses to allow the employees to work unless they will work under some condition dictated by the management. It appears, therefore, that these two classes of industrial disturbances are practically alike, the main distinction being that in a strike the employees take the initiative, while in a lockout the employer first makes some demand and enforces it by refusing to allow his employees to work unless it is complied with.

If these two classes of labour disputes are practically the same, it would seem wiser to throw them all together and not attempt a distinction, resting upon the uncertain question of initiative. This is the practice in England.

The second great difficulty in statistics of strikes is how to get the information. The method pursued in the United States was as follows:[1]—

> "A thorough examination was made of the files of the leading papers in various parts of the country, of trade and commercial periodicals, and of State labour reports for the years involved in the investigation, with reference to all notices of strikes occurring during that period; all data were copied and classified, and all duplications eliminated. Furnished with these data, which in most cases located the strikes and lockouts, and in many cases supplied even the names of the firms involved, the agents of the department were assigned districts for canvassing. In addition to the information furnished them by these preliminary data they were instructed to make every possible effort, by personal inquiry and consultation with labour organisations, manufacturers, associations, &c., to secure further information as to strikes and lockouts occurring in the district assigned them, to the end that none might escape their notice. The facts were collected at the place where the strikes and lockouts occurred, both sides to the controversy being consulted, and all discrepancies reconciled with the greatest possible fairness. It is believed that the effort to get at the truth in each case has been successful, and that the facts are substantially correct."

Of course such a method is extremely rough, and only general results can be expected. Great difficulty is experienced in determining the length of a strike when the same

[1] Report on Strikes and Lockouts, 1894, Vol. I, p. 13.

strike affects different establishments, but the employees in the various establishments do not strike or return to work on the same day. The number of employees thrown out of employment must, in most cases, be a general estimate. As a consequence, the total number of days lost and the wage loss, which depend upon the above items, must, in like manner, be uncertain. The loss of the employers is the merest estimate, and has no statistical value. The analysis of causes of strikes and that of the success or failure of strikes, depends upon the judgment of the investigator. The results are not absolute statistics, but rather expert opinion.

It follows from this brief mention of the difficulties of strike statistics that they cannot pretend to any great degree of accuracy. Nor is it necessary that they should. All that can be demanded is a general measurement of the magnitude of this movement, of the number of persons in the industrial community involved, and such collateral information as to causes, results, and losses, as may aid us in our analytical discussion of the strike as a weapon of organised labour.

Reflective Analysis.

The chief question in reflecting upon the statistics of labour associations is to form a judgment as to their influence upon the remuneration of labour, and their importance as part of the modern industrial organisation. Opinion upon both of these questions will differ widely according to the position and prejudices of each observer. But the following concrete conclusions appear to be justified by the statistical data.

The trade union movement in a great industrial country like England is a very important one in its effect upon the economic and social condition of a large number of working men. This is shown by the large membership, by the very considerable accumulated funds, by the sick, funeral and out-of-work benefits, and by the fact that the larger unions seem to have reached a very considerable stability in organisation and administration. The influence of such organisations must be very considerable in the question of wages and in improving the standard of living of the working men.

The inherent difficulty of holding together in effective and permanent union, bodies of men with limited financial resources, narrow education, and changing domicile is obvious. It comes out clearly in the rapid formation and equally rapid disappearance of large numbers of small unions, and in the fluctuation in membership of the larger unions during good and bad times. This is not surprising, but gives rise to two reflections. One is that the trade union is fundamentally a difficult form of organisation, and that its greatest success must still be looked for in the skilled trades where the workmen have good wages and are more than ordinarily intelligent. Temporary victories won by organisations of unskilled labour do not change this condition of things. The growth of efficient trade unionism must in the future, as it has been in the past, be slow and painful. The second reflection is that with increasing concentration of capital, introduction of machinery and world-wide competition, the conduct of trade unions even in the skilled trades must be cautious and conservative. A well-organised trade union undoubtedly makes the employer careful about entering into disputes with his men; but, on the other hand, the narrow margin of profit compels him to watch narrowly his labour-bill, and the concentration of management gives him a feeling of power and a determination to resist what he considers to be impossible demands.

The above reflections show how distant must be the realisation of the dream of one universal organisation of labour against the capitalists. There are two methods by which such organisation has been attempted. The first is typified by the Knights of Labour in the United States. All manual labourers, skilled or unskilled, were to belong to one grand organisation which should safeguard the interests of all. Such organisation is necessarily so loose, and the elements thus brought together are so heterogeneous and undisciplined, that its power, both offensive and defensive, is very small. The collapse of the Knights of Labour shows this. The second method is to form federations of existing trade unions. That is typified by the Central Federation of Labour in the United States, with its 350,000 members. The tendency in such a federation is to recognise so much autonomy in the individual union that the central authority possesses little or no power. The central council becomes simply an arena for the ambitious struggles of rival leaders, or of attempts to commit the whole organisation to particular lines of social policy.

In England the movement towards concentration takes on the form of federations, trades councils, and trade union congresses. A federation is an association of separate trade societies or branches of societies connected with kindred trades for certain limited and specific purposes, with limited and defined powers over its constituent societies. These federations vary greatly in character and constitution. The majority of the building trades federations are purely local federations of distinct though kindred trades, linking together for certain purposes (mainly the establishment of district working rules) the local branches of the various building trades societies. There are, also, non-local federations of the same trade, such as the Federation of Sailmakers, and there may be, even, non-local federations of different trades (*e.g.* the Federation of Engineering and Shipbuilding Trades in the United Kingdom). The functions and powers of the federation vary from almost purely consultative functions to the powerful Miners' Federation, which largely directs the policy of its affiliated unions; or to bodies like the Scottish Operative Plasterers' Federal Union, which is almost to be classed among trade unions proper.

The number and membership of Federations of trade unions

in 1897 are shown in the following table (Report, Trades Unions, 1897, p. xliv.):—

Group of Trades.	Number of separate Federations.	Total Membership.[1]
Building trades	38	92,162
Mining and quarrying	12	361,182
Metal, engineering, and shipbuilding .	16	212,416
Textile trades	20	269,198
Other trades	38	157,418
Total	124	1,092,376

[1] The aggregate membership given in this table does not represent an equal number of separate individuals, since in some cases the same union belongs to more than one federation, and it often happens that local branches of unions are affiliated to local federations for certain purposes, while for other purposes the entire union belongs to some general federation.

Trades councils are purely local consultative bodies, to which their constituent societies send representatives for the purpose of discussion and advice. In 1896 returns were received from 134 trade councils, to which 652,327 members were known to be affiliated.

Trade union congresses are simple meetings of delegates, representing trade unions, for purposes of discussion. At the Congress of 1897, there were present 381 delegates, representing 149 trade unions having a membership of 1,093,191.

When we ask ourselves the question: What is the real influence of this form of association on the condition of the labouring class? the answer seems to be as follows:—The influence of trade unionism is very largely social and moral. It is a good thing for the working men to unite for purposes of mutual aid and advancement. Such association teaches habits of self-reliance and forethought. It develops talents for leadership, discipline and obedience; it interests the members in the well-being of their fellow members and, indirectly, of their whole class; it aids, directly, by the sickness, funeral, and superannuation benefits. The moral effect is felt in two ways. It teaches the working man the value of self-help and the power of organisation. It leads him, often, to reflect upon the real problem of economics, namely, the relation between capital and labour. Even the hard discipline of an unsuccessful strike is often of value, as teaching him the necessary limits to the power even of organised labour. On the other hand, trade unionism has a moral effect upon the employer through the knowledge that there is a power which will resist unreasonable action on his part.

The strike does not seem in itself to be such an important phenomenon as it is sometimes considered. Only about three per cent. of the working classes are annually involved in such labour disputes. The direct money loss from strikes is very considerable, and from the economic point of view it is doubtful if strikes pay. Less than one-half of the labour disputes are won by the employees. And even if a strike for an advance of wages is successful, it takes a very long time for the extra wages to make up for the wages lost during the period of enforced idleness. Doubtless the strike has an important moral effect on the employer. If he knows that his work-people are well organised and ready to strike, he will, doubtless, avoid controversy with them as much as possible. It is often said that the well-organised trade unions have the fewest strikes. From this point of view there is a sense in which the maxim of the labour leaders that "No strike is ever lost" is true. This is always on the supposition, however, that the union is wisely managed, and that the demands of the men are not unreasonable. Recent experience seems to show that when the employers consider the matter at issue to be of real importance, they will hold out to the bitter end with the determination, if possible, of destroying or crippling the union, so that they shall not be troubled again. The strike is a powerful weapon, but one that is apt to cut both ways unless handled with great care and skill.

The universal organisation of labour has not, as we have already seen, proceeded very far. One manifestation of the movement is the so-called "sympathetic strike." This is where men strike against their employer, not because they have a grievance against him, but to bring pressure to bear upon some other employer whose men are on a strike. Thus, when the bricklayers on a building go out on strike, they are very often followed by the carpenters, steamfitters, and others at work on the same building. Or the men on one railroad may refuse to handle freight from another road which is having a dispute with its employees. The sympathetic strike represents the solidarity of labour. Its maxim is, that the interest of one is the interest of all. Its ideal would be reached if, when one body of labourers is striking for its rights, all other labourers should cease working until the object has been attained.[1]

The sympathetic strike is of doubtful expediency. It cripples the financial aid which one union is able to give another so long as the members of the first are receiving wages. It even increases the financial burden on the strikers, who are obliged to support their friends who have struck in order to aid them. Such a strike inflicts great inconvenience and often loss upon the public, and estranges public opinion. Experience seems to show that sympathetic strikes are generally unsuccessful.

Conciliation and arbitration are the true methods of settling disputes. Experience shows that they are practicable and are applicable to the settlement of a great many disputes which would otherwise result in strikes. Statistics show, also, that there is a growing tendency to resort to them, even after strikes have once begun. The most difficult application of these methods is to the question of fixing the rate of wages. But even then a Board of Conciliation may be very effective by fixing piece-work wages, or by adopting a sliding scale, by which wages will vary according to the price of the finished product.[2]

[1] *Cf.* Hall, Sympathetic Strikes and Lockouts. (Columbia University Studies, Vol. X., 1898.)

[2] See Report of Labour Dept., Board of Trade, on Standard Piece Rates and Standard Time Rates, [c-7567], 1893.

Profit-sharing and co-operation are, in some respects, ideal solutions of the problem of the relation of labour to capital. Profit-sharing, notwithstanding its ideal advantages, seems to make but little progress. It affords too many opportunities for misunderstanding between employer and employee, and misinterpretation each of the motives of the other. Productive co-operation seems unable to compete in the sharp struggle with private enterprise. Co-operative distribution is much more successful. It seems to be admirable in every way, not only saving money for the working man, but affording him an opportunity for investment, training his intelligence, and developing his social instincts. The whole business done under the co-operative form, however, is insignificant compared with the total business of the community. While interesting in itself, co-operation does not seem to have a very great future.

The progress of friendly and benefit societies is encouraging. They have all the social and moral effects of association. They represent, in its best form, the principle of self-reliance and forethought. On the whole, the principle of self-help seems still to be prominent and to be growing in prominence, at least in England.

CHAPTER XII.

FINANCE STATISTICS.

Economic Purpose.

THE collective action of the community has a very important bearing upon the welfare of the individual. Protection of life and property are essential for any degree of civilisation. But no civilised state contents itself with bare protection of life and property, or if it seeks to explain its activity by reference to such a formula, the interpretation becomes so broad that the formula loses all its significance. The real limits of the functions of the State are not yet determined, either in theory or by the practice of civilised nations. In the United States the Government has a monoply of the post office, but not of the telegraph or railroad; in England it controls the post and telegraph, but not the railways; in Prussia it owns and administers all three. The practical limitations on the liberty of the individual vary from country to country, and are very difficult to define, because they are dependent on minute rules of administration, and even on custom, habit and tradition. Still further, public opinion in any one country is not agreed as to what should be the limits of governmental activity. As new dangers or hardships press upon the individual, intervention of the community is demanded. A striking example of this is seen in modern legislation regarding factory inspection, adulteration of food, public education, sanitary regulations, &c. In some minds new ideals have been developed, according to which the power of the State should be used for remedying the inequalities of wealth, and securing for all citizens a comfortable existence.

How far this collective action adds to the real happiness of the individual it is difficult to say. Some State expenditure, such as that for the protection of life and property, national defence, and administration of justice is absolutely necessary, and must be incurred. Some, such as for foreign war, may be demanded by public policy, and for the maintenance of the position of the nation in the world. Some, such as that for productive public works, may be justified on economic grounds by showing a balance of profit, after charging the individuals benefitted a fair price for the service rendered. But the greater portion of State services are general in their nature, and the benefit cannot be directly measured.

The negative side of all State activity is that it demands either the money or the unpaid services of the citizen, and thus involves a burden upon some one. It is on this side that we can reach a statistical measurement of the results of collective action, viz., in the burden of public taxation and public debt. We have therefore three inquiries to follow:—

(1) Public expenditure, its amount and direction.
(2) Public revenue, its amount and source.
(3) The burden of public taxation and public debt.

Statistical Data.[1]

Total Receipts and Expenditures: The United States. The classification is different in each country, and is also complicated by the separation of imperial or federal finance from

[1] *Bibliographical Note.* For the crude statistics of governmental finance see the official publications:—U.S. Finance Report; U.S. Statistical Abstract; U.S. Census, 1890: Wealth, Debt, and Taxation, two parts; Statistical Abstract for the United Kingdom; Statistical Abstract for Foreign Countries; Statistisches Jahrbuch für das Deutsche Reich; Almanach de Gotha; Bulletin de Statistique et de Legislation comparée.

For scientific treatment of questions of finance see particularly:—Seligman, Essays in Taxation, 1895; Shifting and Incidence of Taxation, 2nd local or communal finance. For the United States we have the following figures for the Federal Government (Finance Report, 1898, p. xxi.):—

RECEIPTS.[1]

From internal revenue	$170,901,000
,, customs	149,575,000
,, profits on coinage, bullion, deposits, &c.	4,756,000
,, District of Columbia	3,693,000
,, fees—consular, letters patent	2,640,000
,, tax on national banks	1,976,000
,, sales of public lands	1,243,000
,, miscellaneous	5,786,000
Total, ordinary	340,570,000
Extraordinary: From sale of Kansas Pacific R.R.	6,303,000
,, From sale of Union Pacific R.R.	58,448,000
Grand total	$405,321,000

EXPENDITURES.[1]

For civil establishment, &c.	$86,016,000
,, military establishment, &c.	91,992,000
,, naval establishment, &c.	58,824,000
,, Indian service	10,995,000
,, pensions	147,452,000
,, interest on public debt	37,585,000
,, deficiency in postal revenues	10,504,000
	$443,368,000

edition, 1899; Finance Statistics of American Commonwealths (Publications, Amer. Stat. Association, Vol. 1., 1889, p. 349); Bastable, Public Finance, 2nd edition, 1895; Adams, Public Debts, 1887, and Science of Finance, 1898; Leroy-Beaulieu, Science des Finances, 1891; Wagner, Finanzwissenschaft, and the voluminous German literature.

An excellent résumé of the principal figures will be found in Conrad's Handwörterbuch der Staatswissenschaften, Art. Finanzen; also in Palgrave's Dictionary of Political Economy. Art. Debts, Public. See also an article by Von Kaufmann, Die öffentlichen Aufgaben der grössten europäischen Länder (Conrad's Jahrbücher, Vol. 52, 1889, p. 129).

Numerous studies have been made on Local Taxation in England. The latest is by the Royal Commission on Local Taxation, 1898–99. See also Royal Commission on Agriculture, 1896 [c-7400], particularly a memorandum by Sir A. Milner on the incidence of taxation, Vol. IV., p. 582. See also, Gomme, Local Taxation in London (Jour. Royal Stat. Society, Vol. LXI., 1898, p. 442.)

[1] Excluding postal service.

On the side of receipts, this table brings out the magnitude of the indirect taxation, which is the chief source of revenue of the Federal Government. The United States has had immense tracts of public lands, but its policy has been to alienate them on easy terms, and encourage settlement, so that their sale has never been a very considerable source of revenue. In fact, taking into account the expenses of administration, it may be doubted if the public lands are any longer a source of revenue.[1]

The classification of expenditures is a very general one. The item, "Civil Establishment," includes 4½ million dollars for Congress, 11½ million dollars for the Executive, 6½ million dollars for the Judiciary, and 2½ million dollars for Foreign Intercourse. But there are still larger sums which are simply grouped under the term "Miscellaneous." The military and naval expenditures are unusually large on account of the Spanish war. But under the former head there are over 20 million dollars for improving rivers and harbours, and smaller items, such as for national parks and cemeteries, which do not properly belong there. Under "Navy" comes the expense of building new ships, which is an extraordinary expenditure. The expenditure for pensions is very large, and greatly exceeds the same item in any foreign budget. It is very difficult to reduce the expenditures to any systematic form which will show the real objects of governmental activity.

Particular Items of Revenue and Expenditure. The Federal receipts from Customs and Internal Revenue may be still further analysed as follows (Stat. Abstract, 1898, p. 27):—

CUSTOMS REVENUE.

Duties on Merchandise.

Class A.—Articles of food and live animals (including sugar and molasses $29,475,927)	$40,779,000

[1] Bastable, Public Finance, 2nd edition, 1895, p. 163. In Australia the receipts from public lands constitute a considerable share of the revenue, *e.g.* :—In Western Australia, 14·5 per cent. ; New South Wales, 21 per cent. ; Queensland, 19·6 ; South Australia, 9·1 ; Tasmania, 8·1 ; New Zealand, 8 ; Victoria, 6·7 per cent. ; average 13·8 per cent.

Duties on Merchandise.—*continued.*

Class B.—Articles in a crude condition entering into manufactures	$8,122,000
Class C.—Articles wholly or partially manufactured for use in manufactures, etc.	12,715,000
Class D.—Manufactured articles ready for consumption	42,330,000
Class E.—Articles of voluntary use, luxuries, &c.	40,151,000
Tonnage tax	844,000

INTERNAL REVENUE.

Tax collected on:	
Spirits	$87,741,000
Tobacco	36,230,000
Fermented liquors	38,885,000
Oleomargarine	1,108,000
Special taxes on manufacturers, miscellaneous, &c.	6,936,000

The analysis of Customs Revenue is interesting as showing the protective character of the United States tariff. This comes out clearly in Class D, and also accounts for much of the revenue under Class E. Under Class A, the single item "sugar and molasses" accounts for nearly 30 million dollars out of the 40 million dollars, and is also protective in its character. On the other hand, the Internal Revenue and part of Class E of Customs is taxation of luxuries.

For local expenditure in the United States it is difficult to get complete figures except for the census year. The condensed table is as follows (U.S. Census, 1890: Wealth, &c., Part II., p. 410; Abstract of Census, 1890, p. 208):—

	Receipts.	Expenditure.
State	$116,157,000	$77,106,000
Counties reported in detail	80,176,000	68,479,000
Municipalities having 4,000 inhabitants or more reported in detail	243,531,000	212,799,000
Additional, estimated for schools and for places not reported in detail	144,970,000	71,803,000
School districts or other divisions in charge of public schools	...	139,065,000
Total	584,835,000	569,252,000

The above is a merely administrative division and shows us nothing in respect to the objects of State expenditure or the sources of State revenue. The accounts are so complicated, and there are so many different administrative bodies having charge of the expenditure, that it is difficult to make any analysis. The receipts and expenditures of municipalities constitute a very large item.

The Census Report gives the receipts and expenditures of State and local governments in detail, but the information is uncertain, and is now ten years old, so that it is scarcely worth while to give it here. Out of total Receipts of 584 million dollars, ad valorem taxes on real and personal property accounted for 443 million dollars. Licenses made up 24 million dollars, and special assessments 13 million dollars. In expenditures the largest single items were 145 million dollars for educational purposes, and 72 million dollars for roads, sewers, ditches, and bridges. Large sums were entered under the head of "interest," "salaries," "new buildings," and "miscellaneous," so that it is impossible to reach a scientific classification.

In order to show the direction of finance in the United States, we reproduce the following attempt to classify the total receipts and expenditures of all governmental organs in the United States (U.S. Census, 1890: Wealth, &c., Part II., p. 409):—

RECEIPTS AND EXPENDITURES OF THE NATIONAL, STATE, AND LOCAL GOVERNMENTS COMBINED, POSTAL SERVICE AND SCHOOLS INCLUDED, ARRANGED IN ORDER OF AMOUNT, 1890.

Receipts.	Amount.
Total	$1,040,473,000
Ad valorem taxes on real and personal property	443,096,000
Customs	229,668,000
Internal revenue	142,606,000
Postal service	60,882,000
Liquor licenses	24,786,000
Income, funds and investments	14,546,000
Assessments for streets and bridges	13,196,000
Licenses other than liquor	11,144,000
Tax on railroads, separately reported	9,926,000
Profit on coinage of silver dollars	9,385,000

Receipts.—*continued.*	Amount.
Tax on corporations, except railroads, separately reported	$8,758,000
Special assessments for sewers	8,254,000
Fees, fines and penalties	7,253,000
Sale of public lands	6,358,000
Proceeds, sales of property other than public lands	3,283,000
Penal and reformatory institutions	3,154,000
Tax on banks and bankers, separately reported	3,153,000
Sinking fund for Pacific railways	1,842,000
Fees, consular and lands	1,799,000
Fees on letters patent	1,347,000
Tax, circulation of national banks	1,301,000
Customs fees, fines, penalties, and forfeitures	1,299,000
Interest on deposits	986,000
Profit on coinage other than of silver dollars	831,000
Repayment of interest by Pacific railways	705,000
Tax on seal skins	262,000
Waterworks and other enterprises, net	118,000
Miscellaneous	30,541,000

Expenditures.	Amount.
Total	$915,954,000
Pensions, charities, and gratuities	146,895,000
Educational purposes and public schools	145,583,000
Interest on debt	82,748,000
Roads, sewers, ditches, and bridges	72,262,000
Postal service	66,259,000
Public buildings and sites, construction and purchase, separately reported	38,890,000
Salaries separately reported, fees, and commissions	37,552,000
Military purposes	35,537,000
Police	23,934,000
Judiciary, including county courts, inquests, and inquiries	23,071,000
Public buildings and sites, care and maintenance, including construction, not separately reported	17,950,000
Executive departments	16,770,000
Fire	16,423,000
Naval establishments, except for new vessels	15,174,000
Penal and reformatory institutions	12,381,000
Improving harbours and rivers	11,737,000
Lighting	11,363,000
Congress and legislative	10,485,000
Constructing new war vessels	6,831,000

Expenditures.—*continued.*	Amount.
Indians	$6,708,000
Health	3,280,000
Public parks and places	2,962,000
Foreign intercourse	1,648,000
Miscellaneous	109,499,000

This is a very extraordinary showing in many respects, however imperfect the classification. On the side of Receipts one sees the importance of direct taxation in the ad valorem tax on real and personal property, besides the various taxes on corporations, railroads, banks, and the special assessments. Revenue from industrial enterprise is insignificant.

On the side of Expenditure, one is struck by the first two items, viz. pensions, charities and gratuities, and educational purposes. The administrative and even the economic purposes, such as for roads, sewers, &c., sink into a secondary place. The whole list demonstrates the fact that there is very little conscious purpose in apportioning public expenditure.

Great Britain. The Imperial budget is classified as follows (Stat. Abstract, U.K., 1897, p. 13):—

RECEIPTS, 1898.

I. Revenue derived from taxes—	
Customs	£21,798,000
Excise	28,300,000
Estate, &c., duties	11,100,000
Stamps (inclusive of fee and patent stamps)	7,650,000
Land tax	940,000
House duty	1,510,000
Property and income tax	17,250,000
Total revenue derived from taxes	88,548,000
II. Revenue derived from other sources—	
Net receipts from post office services	3,694,000
Crown lands	415,000
Suez Canal Share receipts	699,000
Total revenue derived from other sources	4,808,000
Grand Total	£93,356,000

EXPENDITURES, 1898.

I. National debt service	£25,323,000
II. Naval and military expenditure	40,094,000
III. Civil services (less extra receipts)—	
Civil and civil administration	7,586,000
Public education	10,399,000
Expenditures of a local character	3,281,000
IV. Net customs and inland services	2,745,000
V. Special services	250,000
Grand Total	£89,678,000

The English budget is very different from that of the United States. The property and income tax plays a very important part. The post office shows a profit instead of a deficit. The death duties are also an important tax on property, and the stamp taxes on business enterprises. The customs are for revenue only, as is shown by the receipts, viz.:—tobacco, £11½ million; spirits, foreign and colonial, £4¼ million; tea, £3¾ million; wines, £1¼ million. The excise is principally on liquors, viz.: spirits, £16½ million, and beer £11½ million. The details of the income tax have already been given.

The expenditures are marked by the large amount for naval and military expenditure, showing the demands for imperial defence, and for interest on the public debt, which was incurred in the wars for the maintenance and extension of the empire.

Local Finance in the United Kingdom. The analysis of local taxation and expenditure in Great Britain and Ireland is extremely complicated. The summary results are as follows (*Ibid.*, p. 46):—

RECEIPTS, 1895–96.

From rates	£53,465,000
,, tolls, dues, etc.	6,979,000
,, rents, interest, etc.	2,851,000
,, sales of property	562,000
,, government contributions	11,465,000
,, loans	13,660,000
,, miscellaneous	2,796,000
	£91,778,000

EXPENDITURES, 1895–96.

By unions and parishes for poor relief	£12,283,000
,, other parochial expenditure	2,530,000
,, school boards	11,580,000
,, town and municipal authorities for police, sanitary works, &c.	47,069,000
,, different rural authorities for police, sanitation, highways, &c.	11,162,000
,, harbour and pilotage authorities	6,328,000
,, other authorities	1,762,000
Grand Total	£92,714,000

The chief source of income consists of the rates, which are levied by a number of different authorities, and expended for a great variety of purposes. The analysis of expenditure is so connected with that of the authorities making them, that it is almost impossible to gain a clear notion of how the money is expended.

The expenditure of a great city may be illustrated by the following summary for the City of London. The expenditures are incurred by four county authorities, sixteen district authorities, seventeen union authorities, thirty-four special district authorities, and 331 parish authorities (G. L. Gomme, Royal Commission on Local Taxation, Appendix to Minutes of Evidence, Part II. [C. 8765], p. 216; Jour. Roy. Stat. Soc., Vol. LXI., 1898, p. 442):—

Maintenance of the poor in workhouses	£2,009,662
Maintenance of the poor (outdoor)	261,069
Maintenance of lunatics	422,343
Education	1,992,185
Roads, dust removal, bridges, etc.	1,536,921
Sewerage and drainage	387,685
Public health	122,264
Lighting	275,690
Police and magistracy	1,698,009
Fire brigade	153,827
Parks, gardens, and open spaces	135,678
Other ordinary services	253,546
Loans for all services	2,815,018
Establishment for all services where not separately charged	660,591
Special services	421,646
Total	£13,146,134

The first three items, charity and poor relief, are remarkably heavy, and added to the next item, education, show how much London does for the poor and for the children. Next come the economic functions, such as maintenance of roads, sewers, protection against fire, care for the public health, &c. The protection of life and property is typified by the expenditure for police and magistracy.

German and French Budgets. It is scarcely necessary to give the budgets of other countries. Each has its peculiarities, and each its own classification and distribution of expenditure, so that expert knowledge is necessary if one wishes to get beyond the larger figures.

The German imperial receipts consist principally of customs and excises, and the contributions of the States composing the Empire. In 1898 out of ordinary receipts of 1,412 million marks, 701 million came from customs and excises, and 475 million from the States. Characteristic of German finance is that the post and telegraph yield a profit of 40 million marks, and the railways a profit of 26 million.

Out of an ordinary expenditure of 1,241 million marks, the army required 511 million, and the navy 62 million; while in 1898 there was, in addition, an extraordinary expenditure of 96 million marks for the army, and 59 million marks for the navy. The imperial debt required only 73 million marks, the imperial pension fund 28 million, and the pension fund for old age and infirmity 61 million. Under the head of Treasury comes an expenditure of 446 million marks.[1]

The imperial expenditure is only a part of the total German expenditure for governmental purposes. The rest must be sought in the budgets of the particular States. In 1890 the expenditures of the States were put down at 1,986 million marks, exclusive of their contributions to the Empire, and the estimate was even then said to be incomplete.[2]

[1] Stat. Jahrbuch für das Deutsche Reich, 1898, p. 164.

[2] Conrad's Handwörterbuch, Art. Finanzen.

These figures show that the total imperial and local expenditure in Germany must be very heavy. It must be remembered, however, that much of the State and local expenditure is for productive purposes. On the other hand, we have the universal military service, which entails a heavy personal sacrifice that does not appear in the budget.

France, with receipts of 3,356 million francs, puts down 2,544 million francs to taxes (including customs 441 million, indirect taxes 624 million, direct taxes 472 million, registration tax 526 million, and stamps 179 million), and 691 million to State monoplies and industrial enterprises.

Characteristic in the expenditure of France is the enormous sum for interest on the national debt, 1,250 million francs; the ministry of war requires 650 million and the navy 303 million francs per annum. Public instruction requires 200 million francs.

International Comparison. It will be seen from the budgets given above that differents States have such various methods of classifying their expenditure, that any international comparison is almost impossible. If we take the imperial or central budgets alone, we are met by the fact that expenditures are divided in different ratio between the central and the local governments.[1] If we attempt to unite imperial and local expenditure, we find it difficult to get complete returns of the latter, *e.g.*, in the United States. Still further, in some countries many State duties are met by compulsory personal services, which in others are paid for. Especially is this true of military service. Finally what is classed under one head in one country, may be classed under another in a second country.

The following is an attempt to show the proportionate

[1] Bastable estimates the proportion of local to total expenditure as follows (Public Finance, p. 123): France (1891) 22 per cent.; Italy (1890–1) 25 per cent.; United Kingdom (1889–90) 43 per cent.; United States (1890) 61·5 per cent.

total expenditure for different purposes in six great countries (Conrad's Handwörterbuch, Art., Finanzen, p. 26):—

PERCENTAGES OF STATE EXPENDITURE UNDER DIFFERENT HEADS OF SEVERAL STATES.

Expenditure for.	Russia.	Austria.	Italy.	France.	United King.	Russia.
	Per cent.	Per cent.	Per cent.	Per cent.	Per cent.	Per cent.
General state administration	7·78	8·82	6·72	7·24	3·16	10·56
Public debt	11·00	18·00	26·62	23·74	16·94	29·54
Treasury, gross expenditures	31·46	20·98	10·21	7·15	7·17	5·65
Defence of state	12·40	12·31	15·78	17·50	19·27	25·44
Internal security	9·85	7·13	7·84	5·30	15·19	7·86
Education and science . . .	10·14	5·96	4·11	9·63	5·95	3·80
Transportation, communication	5·02	3·81	8·62	9·10	4·92	2·07
Industrial undertakings . .	1·75	3·44	0·68	1·26	1·03	0·90
Miscellaneous, including religion	10·42	19·55	19·37	21·98	26·37	14·18

It will be seen from this table how different are the necessities and the expenditures of various countries. The burden of public debt is very heavy, requiring more than one-fourth of the revenue in Italy, France and Russia. Next comes the defence of the state. The table has very little value for comparative purposes, as is seen by noticing the large percentage in Prussia and Austria under the heading Treasury, gross expenditure.[1] It is difficult to draw the line between defence of the State and internal security. Much of the military expenditure, for instance, might be put down to either.

The Burden of State Expenditure. In order to measure this roughly we can reach an approximation by studying the relation between the total expenditure and population, or national income, or national wealth. None of these figures amounts to very much, because none can determine the real

[1] The German expression is *Finanzen, Betriebskosten.* It means the gross expenses of the Treasury, including the administration of railways and other public works. In 1898-9 the gross receipts of Prussia were 2,187 million marks, and the expenses of exploitation 979 million marks (Almanach de Gotha, 1899, p. 690).

benefit derived from governmental expenditure, and none can show the real incidence of the burden.

Per Capita Expenditure. It is very easy to take the total governmental expenditure and divide it by the number of inhabitants, and thus get the *per capita* expenditure. The figures are of little use, except to show the varying expenditure from year to year.

For the United States, about the only continuous figures are the *per capita* receipts and expenditures for the Federal Government (Stat. Abstract, 1899):—

	Per capita. Receipts.	Per capita. Expenditures.		Per capita. Receipts.	Per capita. Expenditures.
1870 . . .	$10·67	$8·03	1891 . . .	$6·14	$5·55
			1892 . . .	5·43	5·28
1875 . . .	6·55	6·25	1893 . . .	5·77	5·73
1880 . . .	5·60	5·46	1894 . . .	4·36	5·39
			1895 . . .	4·49	5·11
1885 . . .	5·77	4·64	1896 . . .	4·59	4·94
			1897 . . .	4·78	5·02
1890 . . .	6·44	4·75	1898 . . .	5·45	5·96

The receipts and expenditures steadily decreased from 1870 to 1880, owing to the payment of the national debt and the rapid increase of population. Down to 1893 the *per capita* receipts were always in excess of the expenditures. Since that time the reverse has been true, showing the constant deficits, and (lately) the increased expenditure caused by war.

For local expenditure we have a few comparative figures for 1890 (U.S. Census, 1890: Wealth, &c., Part II., pp. 409, 417, 517, 557, and 581):—

Per Capita Expenditures, 1890.

National, state, and local governments combined (postal service and schools included)	$14·63
National government (postal service and premium on bonds not included)	4·76
State and local governments (including schools)	9·09
Ditto North Atlantic Division	12·89
,, South ,, ,, ...	4·81
,, North Central ,, ...	9·39
,, South ,, ,, ...	4·03
,, Western ,, ...	16·03

PER CAPITA EXPENDITURES, 1890.—*Continued.*

Expenditures of 1,319 counties reporting in detail		2·06
Expenditures in cities (55) having more than 50,000 population		12·24
,, ,,	New York, N.Y.	16·86
,, ,,	Chicago, Ill.	10·94
,, ,,	Philadelphia, Pa.	10·65
,, ,,	Brooklyn, N.Y.	9·97
,, ,,	St. Louis, Mo.	11·71
,, ,,	Boston, Mass.	25·74
,, ,,	Baltimore, Md.	11·06
,, ,,	San Francisco, Cal.	17·90
,, ,,	Cincinnati, Ohio	10·86
,, ,,	Cleveland, Ohio	11·40
Expenditures of municipalities having less than 50,000 but 4,000 or more population, and furnishing detailed report		9·54

The *per capita* expenditure of the national government is seen to be small compared with that of the State and local governments. The greater wealth of the North and West compared with the South is seen in the greater expenditure of those sections. The county expenses are not very great; but that of municipalities is very heavy considering their density of population. Of course the cities are wealthy, that is, there is a great property value and the expenditures include a great deal from which the citizen gets a direct return, *e.g.*, water, gas, &c.

Rather interesting is the expenditure of the State and local governments for public common schools in 1890 (U.S. Census, 1890: Wealth, &c., Part II., p. 417):—

PER CAPITA EXPENDITURE FOR PUBLIC COMMON SCHOOLS.

	Per capita of population.	Per capita of pupils enrolled.
The United States	$2·24	$11·03
North Atlantic Division	2·74	15·35
South ,, ,,	0·98	4·96
North Central ,,	2·81	12·56
South ,, ,,	0·94	4·39
Western ,,	3·35	19·70

A German authority gives the following estimates of the gross expenditures *per capita* state and local (about 1887) for several countries (Conrad's Handwörterbuch, Art. Finanzen):—

	Marks.		Marks.
Prussia	73·40	France	95·21
Austria	70·94	United Kingdom	87·81
Italy	64·84	Russia	33·54

Taxation and Wealth. A much more logical method of measuring the burden of national expenditure would seem to be to compare the expenditure with the national wealth or income. We have already seen the difficulties of estimating the national wealth or income. When we have such estimates we can, of course, compare the expenditure with them; but such comparisons are never very satisfactory because of the uncertainty of the estimates. Again, the expenditure may be for productive purposes, as railroads, and more than pay for itself. Finally, the real burden depends a good deal upon the incidence of taxation on property and on persons.

For certain taxes the rate would seem to measure the burden. For instance, a general property tax is levied on all property and the proportion of the tax to the value of the property gives the rate. But the assessed value is never the real value, hence the rate is a mere fiction.

In the United States we have the following figures (U.S. Census, 1890: Wealth, &c., Part II., pp. 17 and 61):—

AD VALOREM TAXATION. RATE PER $100, 1890.

	On true valuation.	On assessed valuation.
The United States	$0·73	$1·85
North Atlantic Division	0·84	1·64
South ,, ,,	0·64	1·44
North Central ,,	0·72	2·37
South ,, ,,	0·59	1·43
Western ,, ,,	0·61	1·99

The differences between the two columns are owing mainly to the differences in severity of assessment. The comparison between different sections shows that taxation is heavier in some sections than in others, or that the valuation is nearer the true valuation, or that a greater or less proportion of the revenue is raised by the general property tax. Not much can be made out of the table.

Incidence of Taxation. The vexed question in finance is in respect to the incidence of taxation. Who really pays the tax? the person on whom it is levied or some other person upon whom the original sufferer can roll off the burden? Incidence may have reference also to the economic effects of a tax. Is it paid out of income or out of capital? Is it a burden on industry or is it lightly borne? Does it discourage savings and investment or simply restrain unproductive consumption? Does the burden correspond fairly to the receipts of the tax or is it levied in such a way that the burden inflicted on the tax-payers is much greater than the benefit derived by the government? [1]

The statistical method is quite inadequate for answering most of these questions. All we can do is to get some rough approximations.

An attempt is sometimes made to show how much of the burden rests upon the working classes and how much upon the middle and upper classes. As we do not know the exact proportion of these two classes, nor their consumption, nor the exact incidence of any tax, the estimates are naturally very uncertain. A recent attempt of this sort for Great Britain is as follows (Sanger, Incidence of Taxation in the United Kingdom, *Yale Review*, Vol. 6, 1897–98, p. 352):—

	Working classes. Million £.	Other classes. Million £.	Total. Million £.
Imperial public burdens . .	34·2	53·7	87·9
Local public ,, . . .	7·3	31·5	38·8
Total public burdens .	41·5	85·2	126·7

In this calculation the working classes are reckoned as 70 per cent. and the other classes as 30 per cent. of the total

[1] For discussion of all these points see Seligman, Shifting and Incidence of Taxation, 2nd ed., 1899.

population. If we reduce the figures to a *per capita* arrangement the burden for a family of five persons would be as follows:—

PUBLIC BURDEN PER FAMILY PER ANNUM.

	Working class.			Other classes.			Whole population.		
	£	s.	d.	£	s.	d.	£	s.	d.
Imperial	6	5	0	22	17	6	11	4	7
Local	1	6	8	13	11	8	5	0	0
Total . . .	7	11	8	36	9	2	16	4	7

The elements in this calculation are avowedly uncertain. The author contends that the system is not unfair to the working classes.[1]

In regard to the incidence of taxation on different kinds of property, there is constant dispute; but each question is so bound up with the particular method of taxation and assessment that no general statement is possible. For Great Britain and Ireland we have the careful estimate of Sir A. Milner, who tried to separate the Imperial taxation as follows (Commission on Agriculture, Vol. IV., p. 582):—

INCIDENCE OF IMPERIAL TAXATION ON PROPERTY, 1894–95.

	Amount.	Per cent.
On Lands	£4,059,483	14·4
,, Other rateable property . . .	10,439,343	37·0
,, Total ,, ,, . . .	14,498,826	51·4
,, Non-rateable property . . .	13,744,353	48·6
Grand total	28,243,179	100·0

The distinction between rateable and non-rateable corresponds roughly to that between *immobilia* and *mobilia*.

Public Debt. A characteristic feature of modern public finance is the presence of great national debts. It is impossible to treat here of the history of such debts. That would involve not only the financial but very largely the political history of each country. Nor is it possible to discuss the questions of administration and public debt

[1] See Sanger, Is the English System of Taxation Fair? (*Economic Jour.* Vol. IX., March, 1899, p. 10).

policy, such as the various forms of bonds, annuities, interest-bearing and non-interest bearing securities, rate of interest, funding, redemption, repudiation, &c. That would require a treatise on finance, and even then many peculiarities could only be explained by reference to the political and financial experience of each country.[1] We shall content ourselves with the bare figures.

The total national debt of the world has been estimated as follows (U.S. Census, 1890: Wealth, &c., Part I., p. 3):—

	Mill. dollars.
National debt of foreign countries	26,633
Local ,, ,, ,,	1,690
National ,, United States	892
Local ,, ,, ,,	1,135
Total	30,350

The increase of national debt of the principal countries is shown in the following table (*Ibid.*):—

	Mill. dollars.	Increase per cent.
1848	7,627	
1860	10,399	36·3
1870	17,117	64·6
1880	27,421	60·2
1890	27,524	6·4

The *per capita* indebtedness (excluding foreign local debt) is as follows (*Ibid.*):—

	1890.	1880.
National debt of foreign countries	\$32·90	\$35·64
,, ,, United States	14·24	38·33
Local ,, ,, ,,	18·13	22·40

The above tables give a general notion of the condition of things in the world at large. Other estimates have been made[2] which vary more or less, but they all bring out the enormous indebtedness of modern nations and its great increase during this century. This increase has been

[1] See Adams, Public Debts, 1887.

[2] See Palgrave, Dictionary of Political Economy, Art., Public Debt.

brought about largely by wars and military expenditure, but at the present time there is a great tendency to increase local indebtedness for the purpose of public improvements. The proportion of the local debt in Great Britain to the national debt in 1874–5 was 12 per cent.; in 1888–9 it was 28 per cent. The local debt (£195 million) had been incurred for the following purposes:—Waterworks, £36·7 million; harbours, docks, and piers, £30·7 million; highways, street improvements, and turnpike roads, £28·7 million; sewerage and sewerage disposal, £19 million; schools, £17·7 million; gasworks, £14·7 million; poor-law purposes, £6·9 million; markets, £5·4 million; public buildings, £4·9 million; bridges and ferries, £4 million; artisans and labourers' dwellings improvement schemes, £3·8 million; lunatic asylums, £3·6 million, &c.[1]

United States Debt. The details for 1890 are shown in the following table (U.S. Census, 1890; Wealth, &c., Part I., p. 57):—

	Mill. dollars.		Per capita.	
	1890.	1880.	1890.	1880.
National . .	891·9	1,922·5	$14·24	$38·33
State . . .	229·0	297·2	3·66	5·93
County . . .	145·0	124·1	2·32	2·47
Municipal . .	724·5	684·3	11·57	13·64
School district	36·7	17·6	0·59	0·35
Total . .	2,027·2	3,045·8	32·37	60·73

It appears from this analysis that the national and state debt has decreased greatly, while the local debt has increased, but not so rapidly as population. The Census volume above referred to gives a very valuable history of the state debts.

The Burden of Debt. There are various methods of estimating the burden of public debt. The simplest is to take the *per capita* debt. For instance, the United States Census gives the following estimate of *per capita* indebtedness:—Great Britain and Ireland, $87·79; France, $116·35;

[1] *Ibid.*

Germany, \$1·72; Italy, \$76·06; Russia, \$30·79; Austria-Hungary, \$72·42. These figures are not very valuable, because the ability to bear debt depends upon wealth as much as upon population. A second reason is that the debt itself may have been incurred for productive purposes, and so not be a real burden. For instance, the Australian Colonies have a *per capita* indebtedness ranging from \$147·65 to \$333·46—much heavier than any European country, but it has been incurred in public improvements and in building railways, the profits of which serve to pay at least a part of the interest. The total interest charge on the Australasian debt in 1890–91 was £7,589,078, but £3,867,267 was covered by reproductive works.[1]

A second method of estimating the burden of national debt is by comparing the debt with the national wealth, or the interest charge with the national income. Dudley Baxter made such an estimate for four different periods in England as follows (National Debts, 1871, p. 18):—

	National income. Mill. £.	Interest on debt. Mill. £.	Per cent. of interest on debt to income.
1784	130	9·24	6·2
1815	350	32·1	9·0
1843	500	27·5	5·5
1870	860	24·3	2·8

Similar estimates have been made for other countries.[2]

A third method is to calculate what percentage of the Government's revenue is required for the debt service. The material for such an estimate is found in the different budgets at the beginning of the chapter. A striking instance of variation is found in the history of the United States. In 1880 interest on the national debt required \$95 million out of a total expenditure of \$267 million, or 36 per cent. In 1889 it had been reduced to \$41 million

[1] Palgrave, Dict. Polit. Economy, Art., Debts, Public. Bastable, Public Finance, p. 633.

[2] See Giffen, Growth of Capital, p. 140.

out of a total expenditure of $281 million, or 15 per cent. In 1898 the proportion had become even less, viz., $37 million out of $443 million, or 8·3 per cent. The total expenditures for 1898 were, however, very large.

Scientific Tests.

The difficulties of finance statistics are as follows:—

In the first place it is almost impossible to get at the total expenditure, especially of local bodies. This is shown especially in the United States. It is only once in ten years, when by special effort of the officials of the Census the numerous state and local authorities having the expenditure of money are appealed to, that we have statistics of the total receipts, expenditures, and debts of governmental bodies in the United States. For instance, 150,000 schedules of inquiries were sent out for the purpose of ascertaining the School District debt; and there were a number of local organisations for particular purposes in the United States which were known to exist and to be in debt, but from which it was impossible to get returns.[1] The local taxation returns in England and Wales were obtained from 28,233 authorities.[2]

The second difficulty is that in many countries personal service or payment in kind is made instead of money, and it is almost impossible to measure such services.

The next set of difficulties relates to classification. It is impossible to follow any scientific classification of receipts, such as that proposed by Professor Seligman, viz., gifts, public property and industry, eminent domain, fines and penalties, fees, special assessments, and taxes.[3] In official returns the conventional name of the tax or receipt is given without regard to its character. A tax may be called a fee

[1] U.S. Census, 1890: Wealth, Debt, and Taxation, Part II., p. 67.

[2] Palgrave, Dict. Polit. Econ. Art., Debts, Public.

[3] Classification of Public Revenues (Essays in Taxation, 1895, p. 265).

or a charge, while the revenue from public industry may be in reality a tax.

In like manner it is impossible to classify the expenditures or the public debt strictly in accordance with their real purpose. The official returns commonly give the expenditures according to the name of the department which makes them. The public debt is characterised according to the method of issue, *e.g.*, bonds according to the rate of interest or date of the loan. Often we have money borrowed for refunding purposes, or taxation for the purpose of paying interest on a certain loan. The original purpose of the expenditure is entirely concealed.

Little need be said in regard to the final set of difficulties viz., correlation for the purpose of measuring the real weight of taxation or public debt. When it is so difficult to trace the real purpose of the expenditure, it seems idle to speculate upon how much it is felt. For whether it is a real burden or not depends very much upon whether it has been for productive or unproductive purposes. An example has just been given above in the case of the debt of the Australian colonies. Even taking gross expenditure or gross debt, it has been shown how difficult it is to correlate it with ability to pay either on the part of the property of the whole country or on the part of individuals. International comparison on all these points is especially dangerous.

Reflective Analysis.

The science of finance deals with many important questions concerning the best methods of raising revenue, the economic effects of different taxes and expenditures, the incidence of taxation, its social expediency, and deep considerations of justice and equity. Our crude statistics do not carry us very far in solving these problems. The most superficial consideration of the figures brings out, however, one fact, viz., the great increase in governmental expenditures during the nineteenth century. One authority gives the following figures for extreme dates (Conrad's Handwörterbuch, Art., Finanzen) :—

STATE EXPENDITURES.

Prussia . . .	1849	94·1	million thalers.
	1890	478·9	,, ,,
Austria . . .	1849	163·1	million florins.
	1889	540·0	,, ,,
France . . .	1816–29 (aver.)	960	million francs.
	1890	3,046	,, ,,
Russia . . .	1859	260·2	million roubles.
	1889	895·2	,, ,,
Italy	1861	812	million lire.
	1889–90	1,857	,, ,,

One chief cause of this increased expenditure has been the military and naval preparations. Bastable declares that the military expenditures of the six great powers increased from £104 million in 1868 to £180 million in 1888.[1]

But other expenditures have increased rapidly also, especially local expenditures. The general explanation is increased administrative action, *e.g.*, sanitary and factory inspection, and secondly, the extending functions of the State, *e.g.*, taking over railways, education, workmen's insurance, &c. Some German authorities have laid this down as a general maxim or principle, that the State will continually extend its action. Wagner has added to this what he calls the dominance of the preventive principle, viz., that the State prefers to prevent evil rather than pay for the loss which would otherwise come. Other authors ascribe the increased expenditure to the "progress of democracy," that is, that the non-propertied classes have the voting of the taxes which they suppose are paid by the propertied classes. How far this is the case involves very careful consideration of the incidence of taxation and its effect on economic prosperity. How far such state expenditure is really beneficial and just, requires even closer consideration of social policy.

[1] Public Finance, 2nd ed., 1895, p. 69. See also p. 134 for figures of increased national expenditure.

CHAPTER XIII.

SOCIAL DISTRIBUTION.

Economic Purpose.

The Welfare of the Individual. The object and purpose of man's economic activity is the satisfaction of his wants. Economics is a social science inasmuch as it studies how the community, that is man living in society, may satisfy its wants. The welfare of the community is the prime question. That machinery of production, distribution and exchange which gives the community the best livelihood, the greatest progress in power over nature,—that is the best.

When we come to analyse the welfare of a community it means, of course, the welfare of the individuals composing it. That welfare is to be measured economically by command over wealth. Command over wealth may mean (1) possession of wealth, or (2) possession of income. It is necessary not to confound these two. The absolute ownership of wealth is not essential for well-being. What is wanted is income. It may even be better for the community that productive wealth should be under the control of a few. Still, it is a matter of interest to know how far wealth is actually concentrated in the hands of a few.

More important is the question of income, that is, control of the wealth ready for consumption. Here, indeed, equality is not to be expected; nor does it necessarily follow that equality in income would lead to the greatest enjoyment. But it is important to know how much incomes differ from each other, and especially what number of incomes there are which barely reach the level of subsistence. This may be called Social Distribution in distinction from that distribution of wealth which occurs among the factors of production.

In modern times much attention has been directed to the question whether the industrial organisation has a tendency to produce greater inequalities in possession and property, or less. This is the most important question in Social Distribution. It is commonly summed up in the inquiry :—Are the rich getting richer, and the poor, poorer ?

This would seem to be a question particularly fitted for the statistical method. What we want to do is to classify the members of a community according to the amount of wealth they possess or the amount of income which they enjoy. There are two possible methods of solution.

(1) The direct : (*a*) Ascertain the ownership of wealth directly, from period to period, and watch the changes ; (*b*) Ascertain incomes in the same way.

(2) The indirect : Study the condition of large classes in order to determine whether they are well-off or not, and whether their well-being is increasing or decreasing from year to year.

The direct method itself is not really direct. It is impossible to take a census by which to ascertain the exact amount of wealth which each individual possesses, or the exact income which each one enjoys. We are obliged to take returns of income or other taxes as a basis and supplement them by estimates in regard to the amount of property such incomes represent, and by estimates of the income and wealth of other classes which are not represented among the tax-payers. We can thus reach a rough classification, giving the relative number of persons enjoying different sized incomes, or possessing different amounts of wealth.

Statistical Data.[1]

Distribution of Incomes. We have already seen in a previous chapter how difficult it is to estimate the total income or wealth of a nation. It is still more difficult to

[1] *Bibliographical Note.* The statistics of distribution are beset with difficulties, and are often coloured by the economic opinions of the author. The interpretation of income-tax returns especially requires expert knowledge of the exact meaning of the tax and the way it is administered. It is not surprising, therefore, that we have many different sets of statistics and many interpretations of their meaning. Among the more eminent authorities are Soetbeer, who published numerous essays on the Prussian and Saxon Income Tax returns. See especially his article in Conrad's Jahrbücher für Nationaloekonomie und Statistik, Vol. LII., 1889, p. 414. A translation of his essay on Statistics of Income in Prussia, Saxony, and the United Kingdom, was published in the Journal of the Royal Stat. Soc., Vol. LI., 1888, p. 635. For latest comparisons of Prussian and Saxon Income returns, see W. Schulze's articles in Conrad's Jahrbücher für Nat. und Statistik, 3rd Series, Vol. XII., 1896, p. 48, and Vol. XIV., 1897, p. 417.

Sir Robert Giffen has treated the distribution of wealth in the United Kingdom in Further Notes on the Progress of the Working Classes (Essays in Finance, Second Series, p. 457), which was published originally in Journal of the Royal Stat. Soc., Vol. XLIX., 1886, p. 28. See also Mr. Goschen's Inaugural Address in the Journal of the Royal Stat. Soc., Vol. L., 1887, p. 590. An excellent summary of the various estimates may be found in Conrad's Handwörterbuch der Staatswissenschaften, Supplementband I., p. 281, Art. Einkommen.

For the United States, reference may be made especially to U. S. Census, 1890: Farm and Home Proprietorship; Real Estate Mortgages. For an estimate of the distribution of wealth, see also Holmes, Concentration of Wealth. (Political Science Quarterly, Vol. VIII., 1893, p. 589). For Probate Returns, see Mass. Bureau of Labour Statistics Report for 1894.

Spahr, in his book, "The present Distribution of Wealth in the United States," 1896, reviews the European figures as well. He may be said to represent the radical view that a very harmful concentration of both wealth and income is going on.

Works of a more general character are:—Leroy-Beaulieu, La Répartition des Richesses, 3rd ed., 1888. Charles Booth, Life and Labour of the People in London, 9 vols., 1892–97. Sir R. Giffen's Progress of the Working Classes (Essays in Finance, Second Series, p. 365), which is reprinted from the Journal of Royal Stat. Soc. for 1883, p. 593. De Foville, Art. Richesses, Dictionnaire des Finances. Neymarck, Le Morcellement des ascertain how this national income or wealth is divided among individuals. It is impossible to take a census of incomes, just as it is impossible to take a census of individual wealth. We are driven, therefore, to make estimates on the basis of certain taxes, such as the income tax, inheritance taxes, and others, where we can distinguish the individuals paying taxes according to the income or the property on which they pay. An income tax would seem to offer such opportunity, and it is probable that our estimates of the distribution of incomes are more perfect than those of the distribution of wealth. Even with an income tax there are two difficulties, viz., that persons of small income escape the tax, either through legal exemption or through the impossibility of reaching them; and secondly, that all persons have the tendency to make minimum returns, and many make fraudulent and untruthful returns. These figures are to be used, therefore, not as showing the exact truth, but mainly for purposes of comparison.

Income Tax Returns. Income taxes differ widely in their method of administration and the severity of the assessment. In Prussia, for instance, we have an income tax which is assessed even on very small incomes, and in which each individual is thrown into a class according to his total income. This is the most favourable form for the purposes of statistics, and as the administration is rigorous it is probable that the returns are approximately correct. The number of those who pay no tax must still be estimated. With these provisos the following table is given, showing the number and per cent. of persons enjoying certain sized incomes, as well as the total incomes belonging

Valeurs mobilières (Jour. de la Société de Statistique de Paris, Vol. 37, 1896, pp. 253 and 282).

For the older estimates of distribution, see Baxter, The National Income, 1868. Leone Levi, Wages and Earnings of the Working Classes, Report to Michael T. Bass, M.P., 1867; and his later Report to Sir Arthur Bass, M.P., in 1885, on the same subject.

to each class (Handwörterbuch der Staatswissenschaften, Supplementband I., p. 280):—

INCOMES. PRUSSIA, 1892–3.

Income.	No. of persons. Absolute.	No. of persons. Per cent.	Amount of income. Absolute in 1,000 marks.	Amount of income. Per cent.	Average income marks.
Under 900 marks	5,798,596	70·0	2,899,300	33·6	500
900–3,000 ,,	2,160,461	26·1	2,968,762	34·4	1,372
3,000–6,000 ,,	208,480	2·5	846,022	9·8	4,067
6,000–14,500 ,,	80,433	1·0	702,341	8·2	8,735
14,500–36,000 ,,	22,239	0·3	489,075	5·7	22,030
Over 36,000 ,,	8,165	0·1	719,135	8·3	88,022
Total . . .	8,278,374	100·0	8,624,636	100·0	1,040

This table is as complete perhaps as we can expect to have, and while the full incomes may not be returned, yet the general distribution will probably be accurate enough. The incomes under 900 marks have to be estimated, as on an average, 500 marks each. Accepting this estimate we find that 70 per cent. of the population have incomes below the income tax, and that their total income represents only one-third of the total income of the whole population. An additional one-fourth of the population enjoy one-third of the total income; while about four per cent. at the upper end of the scale enjoy the remaining one-third.

The Prussian returns for 1894–5 gave similar results. With a population of 30,387,331 there were 21,233,024 persons belonging to families with incomes of less than 900 marks. The persons who were living on taxable incomes numbered 9,147,426, represented by 2,519,008 tax payers. These latter constituted 8·3 per cent. of the entire population. It is manifest from these figures that the great mass of the people earn bare subsistence, and that it is only a fraction that can be said to be even well-to-do.

Even of those who pay taxes, over 87 per cent. pay on an income of less than 3,000 marks, *i.e.*, $750·00. How very few in comparison are the large incomes is shown by the following table, classifying the 2,519,008 physical persons who were assessed to the income tax (*Ibid.*, p. 280):—

Income.			Number.	Per cent.
Over 900	to	3,000 marks	2,197,712	87·3
,, 3,000	,,	6,000 ,,	209,538	8·3
,, 6,000	,,	9,500 ,,	55,996	2·2
,, 9,500	,,	30,500 ,,	45,551	1·8
,, 30,500	,,	100,000 ,,	8,684	0·3
,, 100,000	. . . .	,,	1,527	0·1
				100·0

In the Kingdom of Saxony the grouping was as follows (*Ibid.*, p. 282):—

Income.	Per cent. of Persons.	Per cent. of Income.
Under 800 marks	66·0	30·2
Over 800 to 3,300 marks	30·5	37·3
,, 3,300 ,, 9,600 ,,	2·7	12·7
,, 9,600 . . . . ,,	0·8	19·8
	100·0	100·0

This table shows that two-thirds of the population possess less than one-third of the income; and that 3·5 per cent. of the upper incomes receive more than the 66 per cent. at the lower end.

The British Income Tax. The British income tax is divided into categories according to the source whence the income is derived. The same individual may pay taxes in more than one of these categories, so that it is impossible to get at an accurate classification of the number of individuals enjoying different sized incomes. As far back as 1867 Mr. Dudley Baxter made an estimate of the division of incomes as follows (The National Income, 1868, p. 62):—

	Total Number of Persons.	Total Income.	Average Income.
Upper and middle classes . .	2,759,000	£489,474,000	£177
Labouring class	10,961,000	324,645,000	29 6*s.*
	13,720,000	814,119,000	

That is, 20 per cent. of the persons enjoy nearly 60 per cent. of the total income.

Or the table may be arranged as follows:—

Size of Incomes.	Number of Incomes.	Aggregate Incomes.
1,000 pounds and upwards . .	57,300	£209,481,000
1,000 to 100 pounds.	1,204,700	198,673,000
Under 100 pounds	12,458,000	405,965,000
	13,720,000	814,119,000

Less than one-half of 1 per cent. of the persons receiving incomes receive one-quarter of the nation's income; while 10 per cent. receive as much as the remaining 90 per cent.

Both of these tables depend, however, upon a correct estimate of the wages of the labouring class. The average income of the labouring class is put down at 29*l.* 6*s.*, which seems small.

Sir Robert Giffen has brought this calculation down to 1885 on the basis of the income tax returns and by using Baxter's estimate for wages with some increase. He reaches a table of this sort (Essays in Finance, Second Series, p. 461):—

Great Britain and Ireland.	Number of Persons.	Income.
Income tax incomes	1,500,000	602 million pounds.
Below income tax incomes . .	15,000,000	668 ,,
Total	16,500,000	1,270 ,,

That is, about 10 per cent. of the people receive nearly one-half of the total income.

It will be seen from this table that the distribution of incomes is more unequal in Great Britain than it is in Prussia. There are great uncertainties, however, about this classification, owing to the difficulties of the income tax and also of estimating the average income of the non-income-tax-paying classes. We turn, therefore, to some comparisons which are more satisfactory than the absolute figures.

Growth of Large and Small Incomes. Figures of relative incomes, continued from period to period, are sometimes used to throw light upon the question whether or not there are growing inequalities in the distribution of wealth. It is often asserted that the larger incomes are increasing in number faster than the smaller ones, and this is held to denote a growing inequality in wealth.

To answer this question on the basis of income tax returns is not altogether easy. The common method is to take the number of income tax payers at a certain period in each class, and then calculate the rate of increase to a subsequent period. It is necessary, of course, that the classification and the method of administration of the tax should not have changed during the period.

Dr. Soetbeer's Comparison. We have some careful estimates of the distribution of incomes on the basis of the Prussian income tax by Dr. Adolf Soetbeer, comparing the income returns for 1876 and 1888.[1] During that period the population increased by 14·2 per cent., the portion of the population enjoying taxable incomes by 35·9 per cent., and the number of individual payers by 41·9 per cent. The yield of the income tax rose from 31,054,554 marks in 1876, to 44,503,002 marks in 1888, that is, 43·3 per cent. in twelve years. In 1876 the proportion of income tax payers with their families to the whole population was 2·3 per cent., and in 1888 it was 2·8 per cent.[2] Dr. Soetbeer reaches the following table:—

Income.	1876. Per cent. of Population.	1876. Per cent. of Income.	1888. Per cent. of Population.	1888. Per cent. of Income.
Under 525 marks	25·7	16·9	29·2	17·7
From 525 to 2,000 marks	67·8	55·4	63·6	51·5
,, 2,001 to 6,000 ,,	5·6	15·5	6·0	15·9
,, 6,001 to 20,000 ,,	0·8	7·1	1·0	8·6
,, 20 to 100,000 ,,	0·1	3·6	0·14	4·5
Over 100,000 ,,	—	1·4	0·01	1·8
	100·00	100·00	100·00	100·00

According to this table the proportionate number of persons with the lowest incomes had increased, being 29·2 per

[1] Conrad's Jahrbücher für Nationaloekonomie und Statistik, Vol. LII., 1889, p. 414.
[2] *Ibid.*, p. 418.

cent. in 1888 compared with 25·7 per cent. in 1876. Their proportionate share of the whole income had increased but slightly. According to Dr. Soetbeer, the most doubtful figure is this lowest class of incomes. It is based upon an estimate of an income of 350 marks for each person engaged in industry, and of 500 marks for each household. "While this figure may be true for the earlier period, there is some evidence that income was somewhat higher at the end of the twelve years."

It is interesting to compare how much the different classes have increased in number and in income during the twelve years. We have the following figures[1]:—

Class A (under 525 m.)	from	3,311,752 persons to 4,101,550,	or 24	per cent.
	,,	1,324 mill. m. to 1,650 mill. m.	,, 11	,,
Class B (525 to 2,000 m.)	,,	4,704,757 persons to 5,259,805	,, 11·6	,,
	,,	4,354 mill. m. to 4,805 mill. m.	,, 10·1	,,
Class C (2 to 6,000 m.)	,,	384,248 persons to 458,692	,, 21·5	,,
	,,	1,219 mill. m. to 1,486 mill. m.	,, 21·9	,,
Class D (6 to 20,000 m.)	,,	58,286 persons to 83,823	,, 43	,,
	,,	559 mill. m. to 806 mill. m.	,, 44·1	,,
Class E (20 to 100,000 m.)	,,	7,501 persons to 11,029	,, 47	,,
	,,	285 mill. m. to 417 mill. m.	,, 46	,,
Class F (over 100,000 m.)	,,	532 persons to 840	,, 58	,,
	,,	113 mill. m. to 167 mill. m.	,, 47·6	,,

It would seem at first sight from this table that the higher incomes were increasing faster proportionately than the lower. Dr. Soetbeer denies that this is the case. If there is growth in national wealth, it shows itself in the smaller incomes turning into larger ones. This does not mean necessarily that there has been a concentration of wealth. As a matter of fact in the higher incomes the percentage of increase of the number of holders has been generally greater than the increase in the amount of income, so that the average income

[1] *Ibid.*, p. 419.

is less. This is shown by means of a table for the three higher classes:—

	Class D.		Class E.		Class F.	
	No. of payers.	Aver. Income marks.	No. of payers.	Aver. Income marks.	No. of payers.	Aver. Income marks.
1876 . .	58,226	9,601	7,501	38,093	532	212,681
1888 . .	83,823	9,617	11,029	37,821	840	198,731

Distribution of English Incomes. The English income tax does not lend itself to comparison of relative incomes, because the same person may pay the tax under different schedules. It has been the custom to compare the number of persons paying income tax under Schedule D, *i.e.*, on professional and trade incomes, at different periods. One such comparison is as follows (Giffen, Essays in Finance, Second Series, p. 398):—

NUMBER OF PERSONS AT DIFFERENT AMOUNTS OF INCOME UNDER SCHEDULE D (ENGLAND).

Pounds sterl.	1843.	1879–80.	1896.[1]
150 and under 200 . .	39,366	130,101	{ 68,736 117,692 }
200 ,, 300 . .	28,370	88,445	80,423
300 ,, 400 . .	13,429	39,896	32,806
400 ,, 500 . .	6,781	16,501	15,633
500 ,, 600 . .	4,780	11,317	8,190
600 ,, 700 . .	2,672	6,894	4,652
700 ,, 800 . .	1,874	4,054	4,518
800 ,, 900 . .	1,442	3,595	2,309
900 ,, 1,000 . .	894	1,396	3,543
1,000 ,, 2,000 . .	4,228	10,352	9,416
2,000 ,, 3,000 . .	1,235	3,131	2,959
3,000 ,, 4,000 . .	526	1,430	1,373
4,000 ,, 5,000 . .	339	758	854
5,000 ,, 10,000 . .	493	1,439	1,503
10,000 ,, 50,000 . .	200	785	766
50,000 and upwards . .	8	68	57
Total	106,637	320,162	355,430

[1] The last column is taken from the Report of the Commissioners of Inland Revenue [C—8548], 1897, p. 142. The first two categories are Incomes under £160 but not exempt (68,736) and Incomes of £160 and under £200. I take it that these two should be added together for purposes of comparison with the earlier years. The smaller and medium incomes seem to hold their own very well. But see the next note.

Mr. Goschen, in his annual address as President of the Royal Statistical Society,[1] tries to show that there has been a great increase of the middle incomes in England. He starts with a statement taken from the final report of the Royal Commission on Depression of Trade (p. 16). This report showed the following rate per cent. of increase of the number of persons assessed to Schedule D of the income-tax in 1884–5 over 1874–75:—

Incomes.	Rate of increase.
From £200 to £1,000	32·85 per cent.
„ 1,000 „ 2,000	12·21 „
„ 2,000 „ 3,000	6·34 „
„ 3,000 „ 4,000	3·07 „
„ 4,000 „ 5,000	7·07 „
„ 5,000 „ 10,000	5·25[1] „
Over 10,000	4·91[1] „
Total	29·84 „

[1] Decrease.

This table would seem to show that the smaller incomes of less than £2,000 a year had increased more rapidly than population, and increased more rapidly than the higher incomes.

Mr. Goschen acknowledges that qualifications are necessary. Under the heads of trades and professions in Schedule D men are arranged in certain classes according to their incomes, but those are only the incomes which they declare under that head. They may at the same time be enjoying other incomes which fall under other schedules.

Mr. Goschen shows that from 1877 to 1886 the number of persons paying tax on incomes between 150 pounds and 1,000 pounds sterling, increased 19·26 per cent., and on incomes of 1,000 pounds sterling and upward they decreased 2·4 per cent.[2]

[1] Journal of the Royal Stat. Soc. 1887, p. 589.

[2] On the other hand, the "*Economist* attributes the diminution in the number of incomes in this category to the fact that large numbers of private undertakings have been turned into limited companies, which has brought

Supplementary evidence is that assessments under Schedule E (salaries from public offices and corporate bodies) increased during ten years from 78,224 to 115,964. He thinks also that the number of shareholders in joint stock companies has lately increased, so that the income from these companies, which is also included under Schedule D, is divided among a larger number of persons. M. Neymarck makes the same assertion in respect to France.[1]

Taking all these facts into consideration, together with the decrease in the rental value of agricultural land, the statistics fail to show any marked concentration of income in the hands of a few.

Income from different Sources. The British income tax comprises five schedules, but they are largely administrative in character, and show little in respect to the real source of income. The returns of gross amount of Annual Value of certain Classes of Property and Profits assessed to the Income Tax in 1897 were as follows (U. K. Stat. Abstract, 1897, p. 37):—

	£
Schedule A :—	
Lands	54,800,902
Houses	158,669,905
Schedule B :—Occupation of land, &c.	(a) 18,496,701
Schedule C :—	
Profits arising from annuities, dividends, &c.	
Of the United Kingdom	13,641,207
Of India	3,485,654
From Indian guaranteed railways, &c.	4,580,212
Of the colonies and foreign countries	16,790,472
Schedule D :—	
Trades and professions	179,191,688
Railways in United Kingdom	37,541,260
Railways out of United Kingdom	12,833,133

(a) Estimated at one-third of the rental value of the land.

them under the heading of public companies in Schedule D." (Journal Royal Stat. Soc., Vol. LI., 1888, p. 640). Even if this is true, the effect would be counterbalanced by the facts mentioned in the text.

[1] See *post* p. 440.

Schedule D (*continued*)—	
Mines and quarries	11,709,803
Gas works	5,529,456
Water works	4,015,316
Canals (including inland navigations), &c.	3,433,931
Other public companies (including ironworks), U. K.	89,411,184
Foreign and colonial securities and other profits	18,629,496
Interest on municipal and corporation stocks and loans	5,235,680
Other interests	2,153,311
Schedule E:—	
All public offices and pensions paid out of public revenue	17,854,757
Salaries, &c., of employees of corporate bodies, &c.	38,594,508

It is impossible from this classification to trace income to its source, either as derived from capital or from labour, from land or personal property, from accumulated wealth or from trade capital. In many of the items all of these are involved. It is interesting to notice the large amount under Schedule D, which implies active exertion, and probably division among a large number of persons. The first is true again of Schedule B, and the second of Schedule E.[1]

In Prussia for incomes above 3,000 marks the tax-payer is obliged to make a return classifying the income according to its source. The percentage of income attributed to each source was as follows (Conrad's Jahrbücher, XII., 1896, p. 66):—

Source of income.	All Prussia.	Cities.	Country.
Personal property [1]	27·7	28·6	24·3
Land (ownership of) [2]	22·6	16·1	45·2
Trade and industry	29·5	33·4	16·1
Gainful occupations	20·2	21·9	14·4
	100·0	100·0	100·0

[1] Kapitalvermögen. [2] Landvermögen.

It is not clear how far these returns are to be relied upon for accuracy, but the inference would seem to be that for the higher incomes, about one-half comes from property and one-half from trade, industry, and occupations. The differences between city and country are interesting.

[1] A somewhat similar table for 1885 will be found *ante*, p. 177.

In Saxony the incomes above 1,600 marks classified according to source showed the following proportions (*Ibid*, p. 68):—

	1879. per cent.	1894. per cent.
Income from property	20·9	15·9
,, land ownership . . .	10·7	12·2
,, salaries and wages . .	34·9	42·7
,, trade and industry . .	33·5	29·2
	100·0	100·0

The comparison between the two years seems to show a marked increase in the incomes derived from salaries and wages.

Income from Capital and Labour. Sir Robert Giffen has attempted to analyse the returns of the income tax according as the income is from capital or from labour. The result of this analysis shows that while the capitalist classes from their capital derived an income of 400 million pounds sterling, the working incomes represented 800 million pounds sterling. From 1843 to 1882 the former increased 110 per cent. and the latter 145 per cent. The table follows (Essays in Finance, Second Series, p. 404):—

PROGRESS OF NATIONAL INCOME. UNITED KINGDOM.
(In millions of pounds.)

	Income in 1843.	Income in 1882.	Increase. Amount.	Increase. Per cent. of increase.
Capitalist classes from capital . . .	190	400	210	110
Working income in income-tax returns	90	180	90	100
Working income not in income-tax returns	235	620	385	160
	515	1,200	685	133

Comparisons in Space. It is almost impossible to compare incomes in different countries. Dr. Soetbeer calculates the British income *per capita* in 1887 to have been 676 marks, while that of Prussia was only 325 marks. That is to say, the average income in Prussia was only about one-half of what it was in the United Kingdom. Taking the upper and middle classes, *i.e.*, incomes over 3,000 marks in Great Britain, and over 2,000 marks in Prussia, he asserts that the average income is four times larger in Great Britain than it is in Prussia. Differences of administration and of assessment make all such comparisons extremely uncertain.

It is possible to draw comparisons between different sections of the same country. Dr. Soetbeer does this for an agricultural section like East Prussia and an industrial section like the Rhine Province, showing much greater increase in the latter than in the former. In the former during twelve years (1876 to 1888) the yield of the income tax increased 41 per cent., while in the latter it increased 77 per cent. The average income of the tax-payer increased in the former by 3·5 per cent., and in the latter by 28·3 per cent. In 1888 in the two administrative divisions of East Prussia the number of tax-payers was 1·59, and 0·93 per cent. of the population; while in the Rhine Province, in five administrative divisions, the number of tax-payers was 2·09, 2·89, 4·29, 1·15, and 2·33 per cent. of the population. In the city of Berlin it was 8·36 per cent. of the population.

Incomes in Cities and Rural Districts. The cities are richer than the country and naturally the incomes are larger. The following table for Prussia gives some interesting facts in this connection (Conrad's Handwörterbuch, Supplementband I. p. 281):—

PRUSSIA, 1893–94. NO. OF INCOME TAX PAYERS.

Income.	In the cities. No.	In the cities. Per cent. of pop.	In the country. No.	In the country. Per cent. of pop.
900–3,000 marks	1,204,589	10·09	955,872	5·27
3,000–9,500 ,,	193,831	1·62	69,775	0·38
9,500–100,000 ,,	44,862	0·38	9,270	0·05
Over 100,000 ,,	1,284	0·01	295	0·002
	1,444,566	12·10	1,035,212	5·70

Distribution of Property. For the great mass of people the absolute ownership of property is not so important as the possession of adequate incomes. The greater part of the community must live upon income derived from labour. Nevertheless, the possession of property not only yields income but also gives the owner control over the means of production. It is therefore an important question in whose hands the wealth of the community is held, and especially whether the large holdings of property tend to increase faster than the small ones.

The problem of ascertaining the ownership of property classified according to amount owned, is even more difficult than that of relative income. It is impossible to take a census of individual wealth. Our estimates therefore are based either upon taxes or upon probates. These returns are always too low, and in many cases there are frauds and evasions. No attempt has yet succeeded in showing clearly the distribution of property among classes or individuals. Attempts to distribute directly the total property of the country among the total families, arranged according to classes, have been made as follows :—

Spahr's Experiment. In 1893, Dr. Charles B. Spahr secured from the Clerks of the Probate Courts, in various parts of the State of New York, copies of their records for the three months ending December, 1892. These estates were then classified according to size. The figures for New York city were as follows (Spahr, Distribution of Wealth in the United States, p. 56):—

Estates.	No.	Realty.	Personalty.	Aggregate.
$50,000 and over . . .	53	$4,471,900	$7,965,611	$12,437,511
$50,000 to $5,000 . . .	212	1,660,833	1,867,480	3,538,313
Under $5,000	704	40,967	549,205	590,172
	969	$6,173,700	$10,382,296	$16,565,996

"During these three months twenty-five hundred men over twenty-five years of age, died." The whole number of estates left by males was barely six hundred. "In other words, only about one-fourth of the men who died left any property whatever except their clothing and household furniture." In New York City the number of families is somewhat less than the number of men twenty-five years of age and over. Mr. Spahr thinks, therefore, that about two-thirds of the families in New York city are in a strict sense of the word, propertyless.

In regard to the distribution of wealth among the propertied classes it will be seen that estates under $5,000 were nearly three times as numerous as those above $5,000; but their aggregate value was only 4 per cent of the total property, while the comparatively few estates exceeding $50,000 were nearly three times as valuable as all the remainder.

In a similar way Mr. Spahr traces the distribution of estates in five agricultural counties, containing no city or village of over four thousand people. The result is as follows (*Ibid*, p. 63):—

RECORD FOR MADISON, HERKIMER, WYOMING, CHENANGO, AND SCHOHARIE COUNTIES, OCTOBER TO DECEMBER, 1892.

	Number.	Realty.	Personalty.	Total.
$50,000 and over	3	$ 56,000	$195,000	$251,000
$50,000 to 5,000	60	334,475	288,688	623,163
Under $5,000	149	243,525	221,733	465,258
	202	$634,000	$705,421	$1,339,421

In these counties nearly three-fourths of the families owned registered property. "Even that quarter of the families which might be classed as propertyless, included a considerable number of tenant farmers who owned some of the stock and implements with which they cultivated their farms. Estates of $50,000 and over aggregated less than one-fifth of the wealth, while estates less than $5,000 aggregated more than one-third."

It is obvious that neither New York City nor the purely agricultural counties should be taken as typical of the whole nation. In fact, it seems a little hazardous to assert that any State, or any section of a State, is typical of the widely-varying conditions prevailing in the whole of the United States. Mr. Spahr, however, considers that the district lying outside of New York and Brooklyn is typical of the country at large. For this district he reaches a table of this sort (*Ibid*, p. 67):—

	Number.	Realty.	Personalty.	Total.
$50,000 and over . .	36	$2,188,540	$6,606,123	$8,794,663
$50,000 to $5,000 . .	409	2,950,325	2,233,871	5,184,196
Under $5,000 . . .	1,427	989,668	1,095,430	2,085,098
	1,872	$6,128,533	$9,935,424	$16,063,957

Some minor corrections are made affecting the distribution between realty and personalty but not disturbing the aggregate holdings of the three classes. Applying these proportions to the total number of families in the United States, and dividing the lowest class into those owning more than $500 and those owning less than that amount, and crediting the last class, each with household property worth $150, the final table stands as follows (*Ibid*, p. 69):—

THE UNITED STATES, 1890.

Estates.	Number.	Aggregate Wealth.	Average Wealth.
The wealthy classes, $50,000 and over . .	125,000	$33,000 million dollars	$264,000
The well-to-do classes, $50,000 to $5,000 . .	1,375,000	23,000 ,, ,,	16,000
The middle classes, $5,000 to $500 . . .	5,500,000	8,200 ,, ,,	1,500
The poorer classes, under $500	5,500,000	800 ,, ,,	150
	12,500,000	$65,000 ,, ,,	5,200

"The conclusion reached, therefore, is as follows: Less than one-half the families in America are propertyless; nevertheless, seven-eighths of the families hold but one-eighth of the national wealth, while one per cent. of the families hold more than the remaining ninety-nine."

This estimate by Mr. Spahr, while showing the concentration of wealth, is imperfect and inadequate on account of the bold assumptions which are made. The first assumption is that probate returns really represent the distribution of property. It is a well-recognised fact that for purposes of probate, estates are always inventoried at less than their real value. It may be said that this error would affect the large estates as well as the small ones, so that the proportion between the two would not be changed. But this is a mere assumption, and it may well be the case that small estates would escape probate more frequently than large ones. The following points are also to be taken into consideration: (1) Many men put real estate and personal property in the names of their wives or children during their own lifetime, so that this property never passes by inheritance. (2) The capital of a business enterprise is often transferred to sons, so that only part or none of the property passes by inheritance. The wives and daughters are provided for by notes or obligations assumed by the sons who take the business. (3) A man's savings are often represented by his life insurance, which is really property, but which does not pass through the Probate Court. (4) Thousands of small estates, consisting of personalty only, especially where there is a single heir or a small family, are settled without recourse to the Probate Court. (5) Among the so-called propertyless there are thousands of young men who have not yet acquired farms, or homes, or business capital, but who are on the road to success, and who later will become property owners. Mr. Spahr's whole estimate tends to accentuate the large fortunes and the inequalities in the distribution of wealth. These inequalities appear prominent because the smaller fortunes are less amenable to his method of treatment than the larger ones.

Massachusetts Probate Returns. Another investigation which suffers from the same deficiencies as that of Mr. Spahr, is the classification of estates admitted to Probate in

Massachusetts at successive periods covering three years each. The figures for the extreme periods, viz. 1829–31 and 1888–91 are shown in the table below. During sixty years the number of probates increased from 3,698 to 14,608, while the average value increased from $3,919 to $10,649. This shows an enormous growth in wealth, and there are many striking instances of the increased number of large estates. The summary for the two periods shows that, while in the earlier period estates under $5,000 were 85·6 per cent. of the total number, representing 25 per cent. of the total wealth, in the later period they represented only 69·5 per cent. of the total number, and 10·8 per cent. of the total value. This undoubtedly shows a concentration of wealth (Mass. Bureau Stat. of Labour, Report, 1894, pp. 265–6):—

PROBATES IN MASSACHUSETTS.

Summary for 1829–31.

Value.	Number.	Per cent.	Value.	Per cent.
Under $5,000 . .	3,168	85·6	$3,626,816	25·0
$5,000 to $50,000	494	13·4	5,909,429	40·7
$50,000 and over .	36	1·0	4,957,862	34·2
	3,698	100·0	$14,494,107	100·0

Summary for 1889–91.

Value.	Number.	Per cent.	Value.	Per cent.
Under $5,000 . .	10,152	69·5	$16,889,479	10·8
$5,000 to $50,000	3,947	27·0	53,489,893	34·4
$50,000 and over .	509	3·4	85,179,416	54·7
	14,608	100·0	$155,558,788	100·0

British Probate Returns. On the other hand, Sir Robert Giffen cites figures for the two years 1838 and 1882, showing that while the amount of capital paying probate duty had increased 155 per cent., the amount per estate had increased only 14 per cent. (Essays in Finance, Second Series, p. 394):—

PROGRESS OF NATIONAL CAPITAL PAYING PROBATE DUTY.

	1838. Pounds.	1882. Pounds.	Increase. Amount. Pounds.	Increase. Per cent.
Amount of capital . .	55 mlns.	140 mlns.	85 mlns.	155
,, per estate .	2,200	2,500	300	14

Number of Probates 1838 equal 25,368 ; 1882 equal 55,359.

Holmes's Estimate. On the basis of certain investigations made by the Eleventh Census in regard to home and farm proprietorship, Mr. George K. Holmes has made an estimate of the distribution of wealth among the people of the United States. He takes as his basis the percentage of farm and home families that are tenants, and the farm and home-owning families having encumbrances. He calculates that among the farm-owning families the encumbrances average $1,130, on farms whose average value is $3,190; on homes, the average debt is $1,139 on an average value of $3,354. He then allows a certain margin for additional wealth above the indebtedness and reaches a table of the following sort (Polit. Science Quarterly, Vol. VIII., 1893, p. 591):—

WEALTH DISTRIBUTION BY CLASSES (UNITED STATES, 1890).

1,440,000	farm-hiring families, worth $150 above debts of indefinite amount	$216,000,000
752,760	families owning encumbered farms worth less than $5,000, deducting encumbrance and other debts of indefinite amount, and allowing $500 for additional wealth	$1,359,741,600
1,756,440	families owning free farms worth less than $5,000, allowing $1,000 for additional wealth above debts of indefinite amount	5,309,589,600
5,159,796	home-hiring families, worth $500 above debts of indefinite amount	2,579,898,000
720,618	families owning encumbered homes worth less than $5,000 deducting encumbrance and other debts of indefinite amount, and allowing $500 for additional wealth	1,142,531,550
1,764,273	families owning free homes worth less than $5,000, allowing $2,000 for additional wealth above debts of indefinite amount	6,749,076,593
11,593,887	families worth	$17,356,837,343

If we take the whole number of families in the United States at 12,500,000 and the total wealth at $65,000 million, the conclusion is that 91 per cent. of the families of the United States own no more than about 29 per cent. of the wealth, and 9 per cent. of the families own about 71 per cent. of the wealth.

We cannot attribute any great certainty to this estimate by Mr. Holmes. It is based and built up upon a series of assumptions, not to speak of the probable imperfection of the statistics in regard to value of farms and homes and their burden of debt. The first assumption is in regard to the total amount of wealth, which Mr. Holmes takes from the volume of the Census on wealth and taxation. The method of calculating this total is extremely defective.[1] Then the whole series of estimates in respect to amount of property held by individual families above debts of unknown amount is difficult to control.

The Indirect Method. Almost all statistical analyses of the actual distribution of wealth break down, on account of the imperfection of the statistics. By careful interpretation of the general facts of economic life around us we may be able, on the other hand, to arrive at some conclusion in regard to the relative well-being of different classes in the community, and especially in regard to the tendency of the changes going on in the relative position of the rich and the poor. We have four such bodies of fact, which may be utilised in this connection. One is the optimistic argument of M. Leroy-Beaulieu that the whole trend of the modern economic process is to decrease the inequalities in conditions. The second is the great collection of facts in regard to the ownership and tenancy of farms and homes in the United States, collected by the Eleventh Census under the direction of Mr. George K. Holmes. The third is the painstaking survey by Sir R. Giffen of the advantages enjoyed by the working classes now, compared with those enjoyed by them fifty years ago. The fourth is the minute description of social conditions by Mr. Charles Booth, in his monumental work, Life and Labour of the People of London. We proceed to notice some of the facts brought out by these remarkable investigations.

Leroy-Beaulieu's Thesis.[2] The well-known French economist

[1] See *ante*, p. 176. [2] La Répartition des Richesses, 3rd ed., 1888.

maintains that "the actual present economic tendency is towards greater similarity in social conditions and to less inequality between fortunes." The method of demonstration is historical. He pictures the condition of the peasants of Europe a hundred years ago and what it is to-day. There is less difference between the rich man and the workman of to-day in command over the comforts of life than there would be between the workman of to-day and the nobleman of a few centuries ago. The general growth of well-being is shown by the increased consumption of food and luxuries such as tea, coffee, and sugar; by improvements in houses (more windows); by the cheapness and variety of clothing; by the growth of savings banks and benefit societies; by increased guarantees for the workman against sickness, unemployment and misery; by decrease of pauperism and increase of length of life. All of these things can take place on such a scale only by affecting great masses of people. The tendency of civilisation is to give to all the comforts which formerly belonged to the few, and thus to bring about a "rapprochement" in social conditions.

The second proof of the thesis is founded upon an elaborate demonstration that rent, interest, and profits tend to decline, while wages (especially real wages) tend to rise. Leroy-Beaulieu believes that the "unearned increment" has been greatly exaggerated. A large part of the nominal rent enjoyed by landowners is really investment of capital, and the net return tends to decrease with improved cultivation. If we took into account the losses in agricultural investment, the returns of the landowners would be still less. The low price of grain, the taxation of the soil, and the competition of new countries have, as a matter of fact, resulted in decreasing the share of the landowner both absolute and relative.

The rate of interest has declined owing to greater security and to enormous accumulations of savings. The result has been to render it more difficult for a leisure class to live on their incomes, more difficult to create great fortunes and to transmit them to descendants; and in fact the tendency is to a gradual dispossession of the capitalist and leisure class from the advantages of possession.

Finally the profits of the entrepreneur tend to decrease because of keener competition. The low rate of interest facilitates the borrowing of capital, and education and the spread of intelligence have broken down the monopoly which the few formerly enjoyed.

While the landowners, capitalists, and entrepreneurs find their incomes diminishing, and becoming more and more uncertain, the wages of the labouring class, both money and real, have been increasing. If these tendencies keep up (and they are necessarily involved in our present organisation) the result must be less inequality in fortunes.

Such is the thesis of M. Leroy-Beaulieu. The proof is largely deductive in its nature. Great economic forces are at work destroying the privileges of the capitalist class—landowners, capitalists, and entrepreneurs—and distributing the benefit of modern methods of production among all classes. The statistical method, showing the actual distribution of wealth, may be used to support this thesis by demonstrating that the number of large fortunes or incomes is after all comparatively small, and that the great mass of people enjoy moderate incomes, while at the bottom there is a residue of very poor or actually indigent. Leroy-Beaulieu uses the same material (largely) as Spahr, but he fixes attention on the number of persons, not upon the amount of wealth. It is not necessary to repeat the English and Prussian figures. Leroy-Beaulieu's contribution consists in the use of the French figures.

After careful consideration he comes to the conclusion that in the country about one-half of the net revenue of the soil accrues to the petty proprietors, *i.e.* those whose net revenue does not exceed 1,000 francs; that one-quarter comes to the medium proprietors, having a net revenue of between 1,000 and 3,000 francs; and that one-fourth belongs to the large proprietors, *i.e.* those who have an income of more than 3,000 francs. He confesses that these figures are not exact, but contends that they show a wide distribution of wealth.

A second set of figures is based upon the occupation tax of the city of Paris. Estimating that rent forms one sixth of the revenue, in the case of small incomes, and one-tenth in the case of large incomes, M. Leroy-Beaulieu arrives at a table of the following sort (Répartition des Richesses, p. 530):—

INCOMES OF PARISIANS.

Number of incomes.		Class of incomes.	Proportion per 1,000 of each class.
421	incomes	above 266,000 francs	0·65
1,413	,,	from 133,000 to 266,000 francs	2·35
3,049	,,	,, 70,000 ,, 133,000 ,,	5·00
9,985	,,	,, 32,000 ,, 70,000 ,,	15·00
21,453	,,	,, 12,000 ,, 32,000 ,,	31·00
6,198	,,	,, 10,000 ,, 12,000 ,,	9·00
17,202	,,	,, 7,500 ,, 10,000 ,,	25·00
21,147	,,	,, 6,000 ,, 7,500 ,,	31·00
61,083	,,	,, 4,000 ,, 6,000 ,,	89·00
74,360	,,	,, 2,400 ,, 4,000 ,,	108·00
468,641	,,	under 2,400 . . . . . ,,	684·00
684,952			1,000·00

In this table the very rich, *i.e.*, those persons possessing an income above 133,000 francs constitute only 3 per 1,000 of the Parisian population; the rich class, composed of persons with an income of from 32,000 to 133,000 francs, constitutes 20 per 1,000 of the population; the well-to-do class, with a revenue between 6,000 and 32,000 francs constitutes only 96 per 1,000; the little incomes constitute more than two-thirds of the total population.

In this connection may be mentioned the investigation of M. Alfred Neymarck in respect to the distribution of personal property in France.[1] He attempts to show that the Na-

[1] Jour. de Société de Statistique de Paris, Vol 37, 1896, pp. 253 and 286. The conclusions are found in the Jour. of the Roy. Stat. Soc., Vol. LI, 1896, p. 540.

tional Debt and the shares and obligations of banks and railroad companies are widely distributed among a large number of owners. The French Government Annuities are held by 2 million persons, each one receiving on an average 406 francs per year, representing a capital of from 13,000 francs to 14,000 francs. The capital of the Bank of France is held by 28,358 shareholders, an average of 6½ shares each of 1,000 francs. The capital of the *Crédit Foncier* of France is held by 40,339 persons, an average of 9 shares each; the debentures are even more widely diffused. The debentures and ordinary shares of the six great railway companies of France represent altogether 20 milliards of francs, which belong to more than 700,000 families. In the savings banks there are 8,600,000 books for a capital of 3,900,000,000 francs, giving an average per book of 455 francs.

The difficulty with these and similar statistics (*e.g.* number of shareholders in American railways) is, that the rich and well-to-do commonly invest in a large number of these undertakings, so that the average holding in any single enterprise has little significance. The extreme subdivision, however, especially when we remember that the large blocks are often held by savings banks and trust and investment companies, which in turn represent a large number of persons, points necessarily to a wide diffusion of this form of personal property.

Farm and Home Ownership and Indebtedness in the United States. The Eleventh Census of the United States made a very important study under the direction of Mr. George K. Holmes in regard to the ownership of farms and homes, and also in respect to real estate mortgages. The results are published in two large volumes, which contain many interesting facts in regard to the economic condition of the people of the United States. These figures do not, in our opinion, enable us to calculate exactly the distribution of wealth as has been attempted by Mr. Holmes in the study on page 436; but they enable us to form a judgment in regard to the condition of large masses of the population.

The method of collecting the facts was as follows: On the population schedule were five questions, intended to determine whether the farm or home occupied by the family was owned or hired, and, if owned, whether it was free from mortgage encumbrance or not. With those families hiring their farms or homes, or owning them free of encumbrance, nothing further was done. There remained 2,294,558 families who owned farms or homes encumbered by debt. In regard to these families, further information was obtained by mail or by special agents.

The principal results of this inquiry are shown in the following table (U. S. Census, 1890: Farm and Homes, p. 19):—

FARM AND HOME PROPRIETORSHIP IN THE UNITED STATES.

	Percentage					
	of all families				of families owning	
	owning.	hiring.	owning free.	owning encumbered.	free.	encumbered.
The United States .	47·8	52·2	34·4	13·4	72·0	28·0
North Atlantic Div.	41·1	58·9	26·5	14·6	64·4	35·6
South Atlantic ,,	39·4	60·6	35·8	3·6	90·8	9·2
North Central ,,	58·0	42·0	36·6	21·4	63·1	36·9
South Central ,,	42·1	57·9	40·1	1·9	95·3	4·7
Western ,,	54·2	45·8	43·3	10·9	79·9	20·1
FOR FARMS ALONE.						
The United States .	65·9	34·1	47·3	18·6	71·8	28·2
North Atlantic Div.	78·6	21·4	51·7	26·9	65·8	34·2
South Atlantic ,,	54·2	45·8	50·1	4·0	92·6	7·4
North Central ,,	73·5	26·5	42·2	31·2	57·5	42·5
South Central ,,	51·7	48·3	49·4	2·3	95·4	4·6
Western ,,	81·1	18·9	62·4	18·7	76·9	23·1
FOR HOMES ALONE.						
The United States .	36·9	63·1	26·7	10·2	72·3	27·7
North Atlantic Div.	33·0	67·0	21·0	12·0	63·7	36·3
South Atlantic ,,	26·9	73·1	23·6	3·3	87·8	12·2
North Central ,,	46·3	53·7	32·3	14·0	69·9	30·1
South Central ,,	29·2	70·8	27·8	1·4	95·1	4·9
Western ,,	44·1	55·9	36·1	7·9	82·0	18·0

This table at first sight appears very complicated, but there are many interesting things which will appear upon analysis. The primary distinction is that between persons occupying farms and persons occupying homes. This divides the whole community practically into the agricultural and non-agricultural classes. The second division is between those owning and those hiring farms and homes respectively. This divides the population into two classes, corresponding roughly, but not exactly, into those owning real estate and those not owning real estate. The third division is of those owning farms and homes, respectively into those owning free from encumbrance and those whose real estate is encumbered. The significance of this division will appear hereafter. In each of these subdivisions an analysis is made according to the sections of the United States, and in the report itself this analysis is carried out for the individual States. Further correlations are made, according to nationality, age, and sex, and according to the value of farms and homes, and the amount of encumbrance upon them. It will be impossible to consider all of these facts, but we may point out some of the more important.

Contrast between Farms and Homes. The families that cultivate farms number 4,767,179 or 37·6 per cent. of the entire number of families; and the families occupying homes, as distinct from farms, number 7,922,973 or 62·4 per cent. of the total. Farm families are naturally most prominent in the South; the South Central division showing 57 per cent.; the South Atlantic division, 46 per cent.; while the North Central had only 43 per cent.; the Western division 27; and the North Atlantic division 18 per cent. These figures simply reveal the relative importance of agriculture and industry in different parts of the United States.

Ownership and Tenancy. Of all the families in the United States about 48 per cent. own their homes or farms, and about 52 per cent. hire them. This is a very remarkable showing, and indicates that the great mass of people own property to a considerable extent. For besides the people who own their farms or homes, those who hire very often have considerable amounts of property, either in the shape of business capital or of furniture and chattels. Where nearly one-half of the people own real estate, it is not probable that there is a great amount of absolute poverty.

The contrast between farms and homes in regard to ownership is easily explicable. Of farm-occupying families, just about two-thirds are owners; while of home-occupying families nearly two-thirds are tenants. This means that the farmer in the United States is still owner, while in the cities men hire their homes.

The contrasts between different sections are instructive. In the South Atlantic and South Central divisions nearly one-half of the farmers are tenants. This is due to the presence of the negroes. The same influence possibly may be seen in the cities of the South, where from 70 to 73 per cent. of the occupiers of homes hire them.

The significance of tenancy of farms, as indicative of economic well-being, is not yet clear. In the United States it seems to be explicable by local circumstances. We have already spoken of it in the chapter on Land (page 145). It has been interpreted as meaning lack of financial resources compelling the farmer to hire his land rather than own it; and on the other hand it has been said to be the first step towards ownership, and to the splitting up of large estates.

Tenancy of homes is probably more indicative of lack of financial resources than tenancy of farms. It corresponds to the fact of the large number of the working classes who are obliged to live in the tenement houses of cities. This is owing to the necessity of being near their work, as well as to the generally high price of land in large cities. In Boston and Brooklyn 81 per cent. of the families live in hired homes while in New York City it is nearly 94 per cent. (In Berlin the percentage runs as high as 96·6. (There are some causes, increasing tenancy which do not necessarily indicate poverty. One is the migratory character of city populations, the influx of strangers who are not certain about remaining, and the disposition of active business men to keep their capital in business rather than to invest it in homes.

Free and Encumbered Farms and Homes. Of all the families of the United States more than one-third own a home or farm entirely free from encumbrance. For farms alone the percentage is 47; for homes alone the percentage is 27. This is certainly a remarkable showing, considering the ease with which real estate is encumbered in this country, and the temptation to raise money by mortgage for the purpose of making improvements or of extending business.

If we take the owned farms and homes alone, 72 per cent. are free, and 28 per cent. are encumbered. The percentages are about the same for farms as for homes. For different sections of the country, however, the figures are widely different—the proportion of encumbered farms running as high as 42 per cent. in the North Central division, and as low as 5 per cent. in the South Central division. The significance of encumbered farms and homes is, like that of tenancy, capable of different interpretations. On the one hand, it is thought to be a sign of distress, viz., that persons are obliged to borrow money in order to make both ends meet, and that thus an encumbrance is simply the first step to bankruptcy. On the other hand, it is notorious that many mortgages are made simply as representing part purchase money, or for the purpose of making improvements, or of raising capital for the conduct of business. Some light is thrown upon this question by the investigation into real estate mortgages. It there appears[1] that the principal portion of the mortgage debt, nearly 80 per cent., was incurred in the Northern States, *i.e.*, in the wealthiest and most prosperous part of the country. Mortgage indebtedness, too, is much greater in cities than in the country. Both investigations show that

[1] U.S. Census, 1890: Real Estate Mortgages, p. 30.

the principal object of real estate encumbrance has been purchase and improvement.

Value and Encumbrance. The figures thus far given consist simply of the enumeration of farms and homes, and whether they are owned or hired, and if owned, whether they are free or encumbered. There seems to be no reason why these statistics should not be reasonably accurate. The facts in regard to ownership or tenancy are probably within the knowledge of the person answering the questions. Those in regard to encumbrance would be somewhat more doubtful. When we come to further investigation in regard to the actual value of the farm or home and the amount of encumbrance, the figures become more doubtful, because the first is a mere estimate; and in answering the second there may be easily hesitation and suspicion. The further figures of this investigation must, therefore, be received with some caution. Of the entire number of families occupying owned and encumbered farms and homes, 20 per cent. have farms and homes worth less than $1,000, and the aggregate values of these farms and homes is 3·5 per cent. of the total value of such owned and encumbered farms and homes. The owned and encumbered farms and homes, with a value of $5,000 and over, are represented by 18·8 per cent. for number of families and 54·9 per cent. for value. The average value of all farms and homes occupied by owners and encumbered is $3,352. These figures apply to only 13 per cent. of the families of the United States, so that we are scarcely warranted in considering them as indicative of the distribution of wealth.[1]

Proprietorship according to Nativity, Sex, and Age. This is an interesting comparison, showing that as owners of farms and homes the natives of Norway, Sweden, and Denmark exceed, relatively, those of every other country. The least relative number of farm and home owners is found among the Italians. The chief influence seems to be length of residence here, and residence in city or country.

[1] U.S. Census, 1890: Farms and Homes. p. 60.

The classification by age shows that with increasing age the proportion of proprietors who are owners of real estate constantly increases. In the age period 45 to 49 years and thereafter somewhat more than one-half of the population consists of owners and heads of tenant families. The following figures are interesting (U.S. Census, 1890: Farms and Homes, p. 208):—

Age period.	Percentage of entire population.		
	Owners.	Tenants.	Remainder.
Under 25 years	0·4	1·4	98·2
25 to 29 years	7·5	19·8	72·7
30 to 34 ,,	14·2	24·3	61·5
35 to 39 ,,	19·1	26·0	54·9
40 to 44 ,,	23·3	24·6	52·1
45 to 49 ,,	27·1	24·4	48·4
50 to 54 ,,	30·3	23·1	46·6
55 to 59 ,,	35·2	20·9	43·9
60 years and over	35·6	16·3	48·1

Very naturally the number of owners and tenants combined increases with increasing age. But while the proportion of tenants reaches a maximum at the age period 35 to 39, and decreases thereafter, the proportion of owners goes on increasing to the age of 60 and over. This would seem to show that the chance of ownership increases with advancing age. Mr. Holmes's whole investigation would seem to show that property is very widely distributed among the people of the United States.

Giffen's Progress of the Working Classes. We have already looked at Sir R. Giffen's method of showing increase in money wages, demonstrating that the working class has improved its condition during the last fifty years.[1] This proof may be amplified by various collateral data as follows[2]:—

(1) The prices of most of the necessaries of life have decreased in recent years, so that real wages have advanced as well as money wages. This has already been shown with great elaboration in the chapter on Index Numbers, and is

[1] *Ante*, p. 313. [2] Essays in Finance, Second Series, p. 376 ff.

the principal thesis both of Bowley and of Falkner. Even if money wages have only maintained their level, the decrease in prices must, of course, have improved their purchasing power. The only objection that has been made to this conclusion is that there is a greater amount of un-employment in recent times, owing to the depression of industry caused by constantly sinking prices. So far as we can get statistics, however, the amount of un-employment does not seem to have increased.

(2) Sir Robert Giffen shows an enormously increased *per capita* consumption of the principal necessaries and comforts of life. Figures for this have already been given in the chapter on Consumption. The greatly increased consumption of standard articles—such as wheat, sugar, tobacco, tea, and coffee—could only have come about by the participation of great masses of people. For the wants of the rich in these directions are quickly satisfied, and even at a decreased price they would not consume a very greatly increased quantity. The low prices have come to the good of the great mass of the nation. Observation also shows that the working classes are now using many things which formerly they did not use, and improved qualities of many other articles. The peasants of Europe, who formerly lived on potatoes and black bread, and salt meat as a rare luxury, are now consuming white bread and fresh meat. The working men of England and of Scotland, who formerly dressed in the coarsest cloths and roughest shoes, now clothe themselves in comfortable woollen and cotton garments, and in many respects imitate the dress of those who are better off. Tropical fruits and commodities which formerly were the luxury of the very few, such as currants and raisins, rice and cocoa, and especially tea, take their place in the consumption of the poorer classes.

(3) The statistics show a constantly decreasing amount of pauperism in England. And pauperism has decreased absolutely, notwithstanding the increase in the population. In

1849 the number of paupers in receipt of relief in the United Kingdom was 1,676,000, while in 1881 it was only 1,014,000.

(4) The increased deposits in savings banks is also an evidence of the generally improved condition of the mass of the people. It is true that these savings bank deposits are often made by the middle classes, but notwithstanding that fact the figures seem to show not only an enormous increase in the number of depositors, but also a decreased *per capita* amount, which would indicate a spread in the habit of saving. The figures by Sir R. Giffen are as follows (Essays in Finance, Second Series, p. 391):—

	1831.	1881.
Number of depositors	429,000	4,140,000
Amount of deposits	£13,719,000	£80,334,000
Amount per depositor	£32	£19

(5) The sanitary conditions of life are more favourable than they used to be. This improvement has come to the special benefit of the labourer. It is seen in the improvement of the factory, *i.e.*, the place where he works. This has been brought about by the factory laws, compelling attention to ventilation, to cleanliness, to fencing dangerous machinery, to avoiding dangerous fumes, excessive heat and dust, and to providing fire escapes. It has been brought about also by the enlightened self-interest of manufacturers who have found it to their profit to conduct their operations under the best conditions of light, temperature, and cleanliness. Mr. Carroll D. Wright, in an elaborate monograph published in the Tenth Census,[1] comes to the conclusion that the modern working man is better off in the factory than he is in his home, and is much better off in the modern factory than he was under the old house industry system. He measured 2,140 rooms in textile factories, and found that the air-space allowed each operative in almost every case exceeded that allowed in hospitals, or that commonly said to be necessary by physicians, viz. 1,500 to 3,000 cubic feet.

[1] U.S. Census, 1880, II.. p. 552.

The former charge against the factory system, that it employed women and children, thus endangering the integrity of the family, and the health, intelligence, and strength of the rising generation, seems to be contradicted by the statistics of the employment of women and children.[1]

The sanitary condition of the labourer's dwelling leaves much still to be desired. Progress has been made in the introduction of pure water, in better systems of sewerage and cleaning streets, and in more rigorous supervision on the part of Boards of Health and municipal authorities. So far as we have statistics, they go to show that over-crowding, although still present in large cities and factory towns, is on the decrease.[2]

The result of improved sanitary conditions is shown by the decreased death rates and increased average length of life. In the period 1838 to 1854, the average duration of life in England for males was 39·9 years; in 1881–91 it was 43·7 years. Such an increase in the average duration of life could be brought about, of course, only by the participation of practically the whole community.

(6) The working class has shared in the intellectual and moral progress of the age. This is shown by the statistics of school attendance, and by the decreased illiteracy in all civilised countries.[3] We know also that opportunities for culture furnished by free libraries, museums, technical and high schools, lectures and concerts have greatly increased. At the same time the records show decreased criminality, and especially a decrease in the more serious crimes and misdemeanours.

(7) The last point made by Sir R. Giffen is the increased share of the working classes in the benefits of government. "It may be said that nearly £15,000,000 of expenditure of the Central Government for education, post-office, factory inspection, or miscellaneous purposes, is entirely new as compared with fifty years ago. Workmen get part of this

[1] See *ante*, pp. 75–86. [2] Statistics and Sociology, p. 191. [3] *Ibid.*, p. 193.

benefit. The local government expenditure is £60,000,000, as compared with £20,000,000 fifty years ago. This £20,000,000 was mainly for poor relief. Now, poor relief remains about the same, but the total is swollen by a vast expenditure for sanitary, educational, and similar purposes. Workmen pay less taxes, and get more from the government."[1]

Booth's Analysis of Social Classes in London. The very remarkable study of social classes in London by Mr. Charles Booth introduces some new methods of statistical grouping which although applicable only to a great city like London give some very interesting results. Mr. Booth undertook, on the basis of information furnished by the school inspectors, to classify the population first of the East End and afterwards of all London, according to degree of poverty or of economic resources, and then to check these results by the Census returns of number of rooms occupied and number of servants kept. The definition of classes in both of these cases is somewhat arbitrary, but the method is instructive and the coincidence of the results somewhat extraordinary.

The first method consisted in estimating the inhabitants of every street, court and block of buildings in London in proportion to the number of children, and arranging them in classes according to the known position and condition of the parents of the children.

These classes are as follows:—

A. The lowest class—occasional labourers, loafers and semi-criminals.

B. The very poor—casual labour, hand-to-hand existence, chronic want.

C and D. The poor—including alike those whose earnings are small, because of irregularity of employment, and those whose work, though regular, is ill-paid.

E and F. The regularly employed and fairly paid working class of all grades.

G and H. Lower and upper middle class and all above this level.

[1] Giffen, *op. cit.*, p. 384.

Outside of, and to be counted in addition to these classes, are the inmates of institutions, whose numbers are specially reported in every census, and finally there are a few who, having no shelter for the night, elude official enumeration and are not counted at all.

The proportions of the different classes shown for all London are as follows (Life and Labour of the People in London, Vol. II., p. 21):—

	Number.	Per cent.	Per cent.
A (lowest)	37,610 or	0·9	In poverty, 30·7
B (very poor)	316,834 or	7·5	
C and D (poor)	938,293 or	22·3	
E and F (working class, comfortable) . .	2,166,503 or	51·5	In comfort. 69·3
G and H (middle class and above) . . .	749,930 or	17·8	
	4,209,170	100	100·0
Inmates of institutions	99,830		
	4,309,000		

The second method consists in classifying the inhabitants of London according to the number of persons to a room and according to the number of servants as follows (*Ibid.* Vol. V., p. 11):—

	Number.	Per cent.	Per cent.	Per cent.
(1.) (2.) 3 or more persons per room .	492,370 or	12·0	12·0	(crowded) 31·5
(3.) 2 and under 3 „ „ „ .	781,615 „	19·0	19·5	
Common lodging-houses, etc. . .	20,087 „	0·5		
(4.) 1 and under 2 persons per room .	962,780 „	23·4	61·9	(Not crowded) 68·5
(5.) less than 1 person per room . .	153,471 „	3·7		
(6.) occupying more than 4 rooms .	981,553 „	23·9		
(a.) 4 or more persons to 1 servant .	227,832 „	5·5		
Servants	205,858 „	5·0		
Persons living in large shops, etc. .	15,321 „	0·4		
(b.) to (h.) 3 or less persons to 1 servant	248,493 „	6·0		
Inmates of hotels and boarding-houses where servants are kept .	25,726 „	0·6	6·6	
	4,115,106	100·0	100·0	100·0
Institutions (excluding inmates of hotels, lodging-houses, large shops, and their servants) . .	96,637			
	4,211,743			

"In both classifications the servants have been added to the group to which they socially belong, and in both I have excluded altogether the inmates of hospitals, workhouses and prisons, while the inmates of common lodging-houses, of large business establishments, and of hotels are in the second classification, each placed where they socially belong.

"It will be seen that the total percentages 'crowded' and 'not crowded' agree very nearly with the totals of the previous classification 'in poverty' and 'in comfort.' The similarity is even startling, and I hasten to say that no such absolute comparison as these figures might suggest can be made. Living in close quarters is no certain test of poverty, and accordingly while some districts are more crowded than they are poor, others are plainly more poor than they are crowded. It is only when we take the large average provided by the whole area of London, or in districts which represent this average, that we obtain such an agreement as is shown above."

It would be unsafe to argue from these figures as to the condition of the rest of the country or even of other large cities. In the city the extremes of poverty and wealth meet, and probably the difficulties of living for the poor assume their most exaggerated form owing to the lack of room, the stress of competition, and the isolation and separation of classes. It is certainly a very remarkable fact that not more than 8 to 12 per cent. are classed as "very poor" and that not more than 30 per cent. fall into the class of "the poor."

Scientific Tests.

The distribution of incomes or wealth offers one of the most difficult problems of statistical analysis. The direct classification of the population by a census of wealth or income is impossible. Its classification on the basis of amounts of taxable property or income is always uncertain because of the imperfection of assessment and returns. The indirect method, by taking certain indices of well-being, such as home and farm tenancy and ownership, consumption of staple commodities, number of rooms occupied, &c., is never exact, because no one of the facts corresponds to a certain degree of well-being. Probably the second method is less misleading than the first because it pretends to less exactness. When we have the returns of the number of persons paying taxes on certain amounts of income or property we seem to have a definiteness which is really an illusion. In the first place the error in the returns is undoubtedly great. How great we do not know. Nor do we know (which is even more essential) whether the margin of error is the same for the different classes of income. When we consider the great variety of sources of income or kinds of property, the ease or difficulty with which they can be concealed or fraudulently returned, and also the fallibility and social prejudices of the assessors or administrators of the tax, the presumption is that the margin of error might vary widely for different classes.

In the second place, the same income or amount of wealth does not represent the same degree of well-being; nor do multiples of incomes or amounts of wealth represent proportionate well-being. A great deal depends upon the conditions under which the income or wealth is enjoyed, such as the size of the family, the rent of houses, the prices of commodities, the social enjoyments attainable, the standard of living necessary to maintain social position or professional dignity. We need not consider here the subjective influences which determine the real enjoyment obtained from a given expenditure. They vary from individual to individual and are influenced by temperament, tradition, habit, social discontent or social ambition.

The indirect method—that is, taking certain objective conditions as indicative of well-being—although less pretentiously exact, is probably more satisfactory in the long run. This is the method of symptoms. It requires discriminating knowledge and sympathetic insight on the part of the investigator. It can best be applied to representative districts where conditions can be defined with some degree of certainty. The study of poverty and wealth is a very complicated one. It will need endless repetition. It is of perennial interest, and it is only gradually and by the aid of expert talent that we can hope to be able to form even imperfect judgments and opinions.

Reflective Analysis.

The statistics undoubtedly establish the fact, which is obvious, that there is very great inequality in the possession of wealth. The few own great sums; the many have very small sums individually, and even their aggregate does not approach in many cases the aggregate owned by the few.

The establishment of this fact does not prove that such inequality is detrimental to the community. Possibly this inequality in possession is part of the modern economic process which has resulted in the increase of wealth itself. It may be unavoidable in the modern productive process. It would be a bold step to declare that because that process results in inequality of possession, it would be better to have no wealth at all. The real problem is whether even with this inequality of possession, the whole community is not better off than under a less productive system. And the final question is: Cannot this modern system, resulting in inequality, be so controlled that it shall contribute to the welfare of the whole community?

In the modern organisation of industry, concentration of wealth for purposes of production is not only desirable but absolutely necessary. It is only by such concentration that we can manufacture on a large scale, and through the division of labour obtain that cheapness of production which gives to the mass of the community command over so many of the comforts and enjoyments of life. It is only by such concentration that the great industrial undertakings of modern times, such as railways, ocean steamship lines, great smelting works and land improvements can be carried out. Still more necessary is it to put the direction and control of such masses of capital in the hands of individuals having the ability and energy for such vast undertakings. The question for the community is what system will secure the requisite talent and means for such work.

Such concentration of productive capital may be either in the hands of individuals, or of corporations, or of the State.

In the case of corporations many persons may be interested as shareholders and bondholders. They may be directly interested, in which case such corporations really form a mode of investment for the great middle class. Or these securities may be held by savings banks, or life insurance companies who are simply the representatives of a large number of persons, many of whom belong to the lower classes. The statistics of corporate wealth, therefore, do not necessarily represent a concentration of wealth. It is, doubtless, true that these corporations are controlled very often by a few individuals, and in that respect they come under our first class.

This concentration of wealth in the hands of individuals, either privately or through corporate forms, is not altogether an evil. As we have already said, it gives us the advantage of production on a large scale. Still further, the profits of these millionaires are reinvested in the work of production. From the mere standpoint of production, it is probable that an income of $1,000,000 per annum, in the hands of one man, will result in greater investment for future production than the same income divided among one thousand men. If so divided the present enjoyment would, probably, be greater, but the marginal utility of the present enjoyment would be so much greater than the disposition to save, that probably little wealth would be accumulated. The institution of millionaires in the modern community works somewhat like the institution of slavery in former times. It is a method by which all members of the community are, to a certain extent, compelled to save and economise and lay up capital. Until human nature is such that we can safely trust all individuals to show some forethought for the future, such compulsory saving probably safeguards the welfare of the whole community in the long run.

It may still further be remarked, that even granting the concentration of wealth and income, the holders are not altogether irresponsible in the expenditure of the same. The accumulation of capital in itself tends to lower the rate of interest and narrow the margin of profits. That means that the whole community shares in the benefit of cheaper production, and that the millionaire is either obliged to save more and reinvest it, or finds his income diminished. This is an economic restraint, and fixes a limit to the concentration itself.

Other restraints are social in their nature, and are found in the functions attributed to the rich and demanded of them by public opinion, such as political service, contributions to charity and education, and participation in the public life of the whole community.

Finally, fear of legislation and of public opinion is a wholesome restraint upon the abuse of such wealth.

The alternative to such concentration of wealth in the hands of individuals lies in collectivism, or the control of the means of production by the community. Such collectivism implies the choosing of leaders, and intrusting to them extensive power over the lives and happiness of the mass of the community. The advocates of socialism have never shown that such power could be arranged so as not to constitute as great a danger to the happiness of individuals as any concentration of wealth possible under the present system.

The statistics of changes in the control of wealth or the enjoyment of incomes are chiefly useful in guiding the policy of the community, in correcting abuses, and in encouraging counterbalancing forces. The remedy for too great concentration of power lies in the formation of trade unions, benefit societies, co-operation, and other forms of association which enable the labouring class to assert its power in the struggle for a share in the national dividend. It lies also in the encouragement of factory laws, of educational and sanitary laws, by which the health, and strength, and happiness of the labouring class may be preserved. It lies in the exercise of political power, so that the instrument of government may not be used for the selfish aggrandisement of the few, but for the advantage of the many. It lies in the furtherance of public opinion and Christian sympathy for the purpose of encouraging all individuals in the community in their efforts to live an honest and decent life. Notwithstanding the concentration of wealth, it is doubtful if these great forces have ever been so active, or so powerful, as at the present time.

INDEX.

Richard Clay and Sons, Limited,
London and Bungay.

Bei Fragen zur Produktsicherheit wenden Sie sich bitte an:
If you have any questions regarding product safety,
please contact:

Walter de Gruyter GmbH
Genthiner Straße 13
10785 Berlin
productsafety@degruyterbrill.com